THE
MIDDLE AGES

THE
MIDDLE AGES

A History of International Relations

BY FRANÇOIS L. GANSHOF

Professor emeritus in the University of Ghent

Translated by Rémy Inglis Hall

Harper & Row, Publishers
New York, Evanston, San Francisco, London

Contents

v

Introduction

THE AUTHOR of these pages devoted to the history of international relations in the Middle Ages is well aware of the inadequacies of his work. Such a subject, to be treated as it deserves, would require an assemblage of knowledge that would allow for necessary controls to be made and a core of knowledge greater than that of this present volume. Many important problems have scarcely been sketched or merely indicated; it is the same with topics that do not appear: consideration could be given to the Hanses—other than the German Hanse—to insurance, to maritime law, to passports, to the laws of war, to the spread of the privileged law of certain towns, to the organization of universities, to cartography, and so on. If enumerations are to be avoided, a choice has to be made among the aspects of the subject, and a certain number of them must be sacrificed. The author accepts that equally justifiable choices different from his own could be made.

What is offered to the public is an essay. Perhaps, in certain parts, this will have merits: to oblige the reader to reflect, to revise current ideas, to experience the complexities raised by a history of international relations in the Middle Ages. Medieval European society is very different from the community of Christian peoples —the Res publica christiana, subject to two leaders, the pope and the emperor—which was so often talked about through the centuries, but which actually never existed.

This account contains two types of chapter. Nine chapters can be called "historical narrative," since their frame is chronological (1–2, 4–6, 8–11). In them the reader is obliged to follow at least the essential outlines of the development of international relations in their spiritual, political, economic, and social aspects. Three other chapters have a systematic shape: each of them, for a group of centuries, constitutes a survey of the management of international relations, principally their political but sometimes their social aspects. Because of a concern for clarity, international trade relations have often been treated together with international relations in the "narrative" chapters.

It is believed that this essay can be of service to researchers and to those embarking upon historical studies, because it is provided with a fairly extensive bibliography. The author was obliged to assemble it with a single point of view in mind: which studies best allow the reader to do personal research? This criterion explains the choice of some works that appear secondary and the omission of several important and valuable ones. With only rare exceptions the author has used all the works cited. He wishes to stress that a major part of this volume has been composed directly from the sources, and he regrets that he was not able to return to them.

It has not been thought worthwhile to illustrate this volume with sketches reproducing, and at the same time simplifying, maps that can be found in the majority of historical atlases. The four sketches that appear in this volume are intended to make certain aspects of international relations in the Middle Ages (whose translation into map form is perhaps less familiar to readers) easier to understand.

The following have added to my information or assisted me with their advice, and I am heartily grateful to them: the late Canon E. van Cauwenbergh, Professor at the University of Louvain; Professor P. Dollinger, Faculty of Letters, Strasbourg; Professor L. Genicot, University of Louvain; Professor C. Higounet, Faculty of Letters, Bordeaux; the late Professor E. Lambert, the Sorbonne; Professor T. Luykx, University of Ghent; Professor E. Perroy, the Sorbonne; the late Professor F. Quicke, University of Ghent; Professor F. Vercauteren, University of Liège; Professor C. Verlinden, University of Ghent. Finally, I wish to thank M. A. de Smet, curator at the Bibliothèque Royale, and M. G. Bonnerot, head of cartographic services at Librairie Hachette, for valuable advice willingly given in the preparation of maps.

FRANÇOIS L. GANSHOF

THE
MIDDLE AGES

1

The Breakdown of Roman Unity

℡wo facts, closely linked, dominate the history of Europe during the early Middle Ages: the collapse of the Roman Empire in the West in the fifth century and the establishment of mainly Germanic "barbarian" populations on her soil. To understand these facts and to grasp their importance require us to look a little farther back in time.

At the beginning of the last quarter of the fourth century the Roman Empire, or the Roman world (*orbis romanus*)—they are the same—still extended throughout western Europe south of the Rhine and the Danube, including Britain—nowadays England proper. It also included the Asiatic Near East, covering northern Mesopotamia but not Arabia. All of Africa that bordered the Mediterranean was part of the empire. This Roman world constituted a unity, a political unity, it goes without saying, but also an economic unity, a spiritual unity after the triumph of Christianity, and a unity of civilization based on Hellenistic culture adapted by Rome. But obviously we must delineate the picture somewhat more finely. There were vast differences between the eastern and the western parts of the empire. Greek was the language of the cultured class of the East; Latin that of the West. The religious climate was by no means the same, first of all because there were more heathens in the West than in the East, but also because Greek philosophical thought gave rise to conceptions of Christianity in the East that did not meet with the same acceptance in the West. The universally recognized authority of Roman law did not prevent the existence of local legal customs in certain regions. Social structure and economic life were not identical throughout: city living and large-scale commerce, for example, played a greater role in the East than in the West.

But, despite these reservations, unity must be stressed. There were regular linkages between the various parts of the Roman world. The Mediterranean—the heart of the empire—and the network of roads that traversed the territory guaranteed easy communications and allowed for the movement of troops, officials, churchmen, supplies, works of art, and ideas.

Beyond the frontiers stretched the "barbarian" world, mostly of Germanic stock. In the far north the northern Germanic tribes were based in Scandinavia and the Baltic islands. Eastern Germanic tribes—Ostrogoths, Visigoths, Vandals, Burgundians, and Lombards—had settled from the Don and the Carpathians as far as the Main and the Danube. Western Germanic tribes—Angles, Saxons, Jutes, Frisians, Franks, Alemans, Bavarians, Suevians, and Thuringians—occupied the area between Jutland, the Elbe, Bohemia, the Danube, the Rhine, and the North Sea. Each of these peoples, generally lacking any "national" political institutions, was made up of autonomous tribes, which were themselves based upon farflung family groupings, or *Sippen*. Several of these tribes were familiar with a monarchical system, but political power— and it was very weak—belonged less to kings than to an aristocracy of chiefs. These peoples, who raised livestock and practiced a fairly rudimentary form of agriculture, moved around as it suited them. The majority of them were heathens. Meanwhile, from the fourth century on, Christianity from the East made headway among the Goths, who brought it to other eastern Germanic peoples. They were, however, converted to the Arian form of Christianity, which Rome considered heretical. The Germanic peoples, both eastern and western, appeared to have no intellectual culture worthy of the name. Their decorative arts, in particular their work in gold, was Asiatic by origin, and it was the Sarmatians who brought both its principles and its techniques to these peoples.

Apart from the Germanic peoples, other "barbarian" nations surrounded the empire, either closely or at a distance. Iranian nomads, the Alans, roamed north of the Caucasus. The Iranians of Persia lived in an empire that extended from the Tigris-Euphrates region to Afghanistan. Persia, ruled by the Sassinian dynasty, was Rome's great enemy in the East: a political rivalry whose principal object was hegemony over Armenia, which had been Christianized in the third century; a religious rivalry, for Persia practiced a faith based upon Mazda, with its dualist character. The Persian civilization, heir to the ancient cultures of the Near East, was quite different from that of the primitive peoples of the Asiatic steppes, mounted nomads who lived as much from brigandage as from stock raising. Among these the Huns, of Turkish origin, appeared in southern Russia during the last quarter of the fourth century; another people, who were also of Turkish origin and, one hundred years later, took the name of Avars, wandered into central Asia. On the Russian plains and in Poland lived Slav populations about whom little is known. Finally there were the nomads of the deserts that lay to the south and to the west of the African provinces and in Arabia. In the north of Britain the Picts occupied most of Caledonia—present-day Scotland—while Celts, namely the Gaëls or *Scoti*, inhabited Ireland.

The Roman Empire maintained relations, either peaceful or hostile, with most of these populations. This is especially true in the case of the Germanic peoples. Thousands of them, particularly in the fourth and fifth centuries, had served the empire as soldiers, either individually or in cadres from their tribes or from their peoples which Rome had taken into her service under the title of *federati*. The situation changed when entire peoples were given permission to install themselves within the boundaries of the empire: for instance, in 380 and 382 the Ostrogoths and the Visigoths south of the Danube. The title of *federati* became misleading: despite the services they rendered to Rome against the other barbarian nations, they were at that time potential conquerors established on Roman soil. Meanwhile their situation created more frequent contacts with the Roman world and brought about a Romanization—however superficial—of certain elements among these populations. It sometimes resulted in a lessening of the contrast between the almost savage Germanic hordes and the hypercivilized society of the Lower Empire. These factors made contacts easier after the Great Invasions.

This is the appellation under which we usually group together the migrations of barbarian populations—principally Germanic —which shattered the structure of Europe between the last quarter of the fourth and the end of the fifth centuries. In some cases it is convenient to extend this period to the end of the sixth century. In this mass of events only the causes and results are of any importance. Not all the causes can be discerned. Some are known: wars between barbarian peoples, lack of space for agriculture and stock raising, the attractiveness of the Mediterranean countries, currents in the Far East which pushed the Huns westward in the fourth century and the Avars in the sixth and gradually set other peoples moving toward the interior of the Roman world. The result was the collapse of the Roman Empire in the West in the fifth century.

Germanic kingdoms set themselves up on its territory; this happened at the end of the century. The eastern Germanic peoples were the first to create kingdoms: the Visigoths in southwestern Gaul, then in Spain; the Suevians in northwestern Spain; the Burgundians in southeastern Gaul; the Ostrogoths in Italy; and the Vandals in Africa. These states were established around the Mediterranean in the most populous and heavily Romanized regions of what had been the Roman Empire. In none of these kingdoms was the Germanic element large, and the demographic ratio with the indigenous population excluded any possibility of Germanization. Besides, in the case of the Goths and the Burgundians, who had been "federated" for a long time, a considerable portion of the population had already been Romanized to a certain degree. The structure of local society hardly changed, but the economic life and culture were weakened, though they retained some of their essential traits. These Germanic Mediterranean states were weak; they were undermined by the hatred that the "Roman" Catholic had for the Arian Goth, Burgundian, and Vandal.

The creations of the western Germanic peoples were different. Those that had taken part in the Great Invasions occupied the northern provinces of the empire, whose population was usually less numerous and less Romanized. Furthermore, these conditions were favorable for a colonization that was going to continue for at least three centuries; the proximity of Germania allowed the importation of new elements, and the result was the ultimate Germanization of the whole territory, or of important segments of it. The Franks had established themselves from the Rhine as far as the Somme; the Alemans on the middle and upper Rhine, on the upper Danube, and in part of the Alpine region; the Bavarians, farther to the east on the Danube, and in the Alps. The Angles, the Jutes, and part of the Saxon people had conquered an important part of Britain that was to become England; conquest and colonization were to continue until the ninth century: the Britons would be overcome and driven into the west (especially into Wales) or forced to emigrate to Armorica, which they were to once more make Celtic, and to which they gave their name— Brittany. The majority of the Saxons remained in Germany, as did the Thuringians and the Frisians, who spread out from the lower Weser to the Rhine-Meuse-Scheldt delta.

In the fifth and sixth centuries Slav tribes occupied the lands beyond the Elbe—Bohemia, the middle Danube region evacuated by the Germanic peoples; a great number of them were to be subdued by the Avars, who installed themselves in Pannonia during the second half of the sixth century. Part of the Hun population, the Bulgarians, dominating the Slavs with whom they formed an alliance, established itself north of the lower Danube at much the same time.

If one compares the political state of Western Europe at the end of the fifth century with its state at the end of the fourth century, one is struck by the substitution, for Roman unity, of a multiplicity of diverse entities, each independent of the others and often hostile to the others.

Only the West was profoundly affected by these upsets. The former *partes orientis* of the empire were less hurt by the Invasions. In the East the Roman Empire had suffered devastating aggressions and had lost portions of territory, but it had held together in Europe as well as in Asia and Africa. The Emperor had not renounced the universality of his authority: he considered himself the sole leader of the empire, since there was no longer an emperor in the West; and he waited only for a favorable opportunity to regain what the barbarians had conquered.

In fact, efforts to restore Roman unity in the West had their beginnings in Byzantium.

The first attempt was directly connected with the Great Invasions and itself constitutes a chapter of their history. In 476, after having deposed the last emperor reigning at Ravenna, Odoacer—a Scyrrian—a Germanic commanding officer in the imperial service in Italy, exercised personal power over the peninsula; he was supported by Germanic mercenaries of various origins who garrisoned the country. The imperial authority that Odoacer recognized was in fact nonexistent. The Emperor Zeno sent to Italy Theodoric, king of the Ostrogoths, whose subjects in Moesia lacked arable land. In 493, Italy was rewon, and the reconquest extended to Dalmatia and to parts of the Alpine countries (Rhaetia and Noricum) and of the Danubian countries (Pannonia). The territorial objectives gained were still strictly limited. One could even question whether Roman unity had actually been re-established in Italy and in the territories bordering on it.

Because—although Theodoric and his advisers clearly recognized imperial authority, although Roman political institutions continued to function, and although classical art and literature really flourished—Italy and her annexed territories constituted a virtually independent realm. Besides, on more than one occasion Theodoric was to clash with Byzantium; the last three years of his reign (523–526) was a period of acute hostility, provoked by the measures that the Emperor Justin used against the Arians, of whom the King of the Ostrogoths considered himself the official protector.

Thus this first attempt at re-establishing Roman unity was checked. But another attempt was also made. This time the objective was the creation of some degree of cohesion among the various political entities that had constituted themselves in the West. The attempt sprang from Theodoric himself, and the Emperor had no part of it. Theodoric wove alliances with the kings of the Visigoths, the Burgundians, the Vandals, and the Thuringians by means of marriages arranged between these rulers and his daughters, his sister, and his niece: he himself married a sister of Clovis, the King of the Franks. One has to stress this use of marriage in the service of politics: the outcome was to be successful. The first aim could have been to prevent the Emperor from finding allies against the King of the Ostrogoths, had he wished to end the latter's domination over Italy. On the other hand, the system had the advantage of maintaining a status quo that allowed Theodoric to exercise, if not a hegemony, at least a pre-eminence in western Europe. This was, however, a short-lived state of affairs. In 506 and 507, Clovis tore the system apart when he conquered most of the Alemanic territory and almost all the Gallic part of the Visigothic realm. Theodoric, it is true, on this occasion extended his power over what remained of the Visigothic realm, annexing Provence and placing Spain and Septimania under his protection. This protectorate he extended south into Alemanic territory. All came to an end, however, following his death in 526. Theodoric's venture in turn had come to naught.

Much more important, both in itself and because of its results, was a new effort that arose in the East to re-establish Roman unity and bring it back into the lost territories of the West. The Emperor Justinian, following a policy of restoring the empire that conformed to the traditional Roman ideal that inspired his great legislative design, undertook in the period from 533 to 562 to root out the Vandals, the Ostrogoths, and the Visigoths from the territories they occupied. He succeeded in placing Africa, Italy (without its northern and northeastern marches), and some of the maritime provinces of Spain under immediate and effective imperial control. Thus the restoration of Roman unity was limited to a small number of Mediterranean countries. Nothing had been undertaken in Gaul or—and the reasons are more obvious—in Britain. Even where it had been achieved, the restoration proved itself weak and short-lived: the greater part of Italy was to be lost before the end of the century, while Africa and the Spanish territories were to go in the next century. Politically speaking, the *reconquista* under Justinian once more ended in defeat. It was the last serious effort to reconstitute Roman unity, centering on the Mediterranean, by political or military means. Moreover, the empire in the East was changing in character, becoming more and more Greek and even Asiatic. Its culture was changing; events forced the emperors to recognize that their greatest problems lay with eastern Europe or Asia: the Bulgarians, the Slavs, and the Avars on the one hand, and on the other, the Persians, and soon the Arabs, were formidable enemies; the bulk of the empire's forces had to be employed against them. In the meanwhile Justinian's reconquest had far-reaching consequences, despite the ruin that it piled up in Italy. It gave new life to the contacts and the relations between the East and Italy and Spain. The most obvious manifestation of these artistic and intellectual contacts was the flowering of "Byzantine" art in Ravenna, Rome, and elsewhere in Italy. It was also one of the most important results because of the influence this artistic outpouring was to have on the development of art and civilization in the West for some centuries. The termination of Vandal piracy enabled commercial relations to reach a certain intensity. One should not overrate either the volume or the essential character of these relations; however, they assured the more or less regular importation to the West of eastern products through Italian, Provençal, Languedocian and Spanish ports.

The end of the sixth century, the seventh century, and much of the eighth was a period when Europe not only found herself lacking unity but also saw further fragmentation. It is important, then, to review in sequence the principal political entities that made up Western Europe at that time, especially because certain of these political entities were to play a considerable role in international relations in the following centuries.

At the head stands the Frankish monarchy, from which the most important European states were to spring. This monarchy was the work of Clovis, the leader of a small Frankish realm, whose capital was Tournai. From 481 to 511 he subjected the other Frankish groupings, the last areas of Gaul where Roman authority still existed, almost all of Visigothic Gaul, and the major part of the Alemanic territory. During the sixth century his sons and grandsons added the rest of Alemania, Bavaria, Thuringia, the Burgundian realm, and Provence. Thus the Frankish monarchy comprised the whole of Gaul, except for Septimania between the Pyrenees and the Rhone. It also embraced central and southern Germania. The realm was an ethnic composite all of whose peoples submitted uniformly to the despotism of the Merovingian monarchs—such was the name of Clovis' dynasty—while they preserved in principle their own particular private law: the Gallo-Romans, Roman law; the Franks, Frankish law; the Alemanians, Alemanic law; etc. Apart from the countries on the right bank of the Rhine, only the north and the east—that is to say, the southern part of Netherland, the northern part of Belgium, a weak segment of northern France, Alsace, parts of Lorraine and the Rhineland—succumbed to Frankish or Alemanic colonization and took on a fundamentally Germanic character. The abstract notion of the State played no role: kings considered themselves proprietors of the realm's territory, and at their deaths these were divided among their sons. Nonetheless a certain awareness of the unity of the *Regnum Francorum* existed; and when civil war eliminated copartners, this unity was from time to time reconstituted. The divisions and the civil wars especially favored the aristocracy, Gallo-Roman or Germanic in origin, which progressively stripped the royalty of its effective power. They gave birth to individual entities inside the Frankish monarchy: in the east, Austrasia, which included the majority of Germanic elements; in the west, Neustria, with its immense Gallo-Roman majority; and in the southeast, Burgundy (in the main the former kingdom of the Burgundians). These regions often had their own kings. The essential factor that brought them a certain cohesion was a consciousness that developed among the regional aristocracy of being a group apart from the aristocracies of other areas of the *Regnum* whom they fought in civil wars. This was not all. Toward the end of the seventh and beginning of the eighth century these civil wars and the weakening of royal power enabled some peripheral areas to free themselves in fact from the Frankish monarchy; this was the case, in Germania, of Bavaria and Alemania, and, in Gaul, of Aquitaine, or the territory south of the Loire. These lands formed themselves into national duchies with their own dynasties. In the first two cases the key factor was the awareness of making up a distinct ethnic unity. The situation in Aquitaine appears to have been somewhat different. The population, which had been Romanized and Christianized for some centuries, had easily absorbed the Germanic elements, scarcely numerous, introduced by the invasions: it could be said that in their case the operative factor lay in a collective awareness of cultural superiority in comparison with the northern peoples.

The northern and eastern parts of Gaul, including the Rhineland, as well as parts of the territories of southern Germania, colonized by heathen Franks, Alemans, and Bavarians, had seen Christianity eliminated or reduced virtually to nought. It required four centuries of effort—from the fifth to the eighth century—to win back or to gain these lands for the Christian faith in its Catholic form. This spiritual conquest was not accomplished solely by the clergy of the region. It was the work in part of missionaries from Aquitaine and also, at the close of the sixth and the beginning of the seventh century, of Irish missionaries and, at the end of the seventh and the beginning of the eighth century, of English missionaries.

At the same time that a Frankish monarchy was being founded in western Europe and then threatening to fall apart, England was beginning to take shape: the result of the conquest and colonization of Britain by the Angles, the Saxons, and the Jutes between the fifth and the eighth centuries. Conquest and colonization had Germanized the country much more thoroughly and radically than had been the case in northeastern Gaul; but more than it had in Gaul, conquest and colonization had lowered the standard of civilization; and, also in contrast to Gaul, Christianity disappeared almost completely before the pagan cults of the invaders. Politically a series of kingdoms was created whose names sometimes recall the region where they were formed or the ethnic group to which their inhabitants belonged: Wessex, Sussex, Essex, Kent, East Anglia, Mercia, Northumbria, etc.

The most important event in English history during this period was its Christianization in the seventh century. This was the result of two currents of missionary activity: one that labored particularly in the south and was tied in with the operations of the monks sent over from Italy in 597 by Pope Gregory the Great; and the other that worked principally in the north and whose principal activity was the proselytizing by the Irish monks who became active after 634. If the Church of Ireland gave

English Christianity its missionary spirit and its taste for the literary, it is to the Roman current that the latter owed its powerful hierarchy and an intense attachment to the papacy that was not known in any continental church at this time. The unity of the Church of England, under a papal delegate, the Archbishop of Canterbury, paved the way for the political unity of England more surely than the hegemony sometimes exercised with the title of _Bretwalda_, by the chief of one of the kingdoms over the other kings. One last fact to which attention should be drawn is the development during the eighth century in the English monasteries, under the combined operation of Irish and Roman influences, of a classical literary movement, Christian in spirit. This came about the time when the foundations of culture in the Frankish monarchy reached their lowest level.

While England was coming into being, Italy was breaking up politically. Actually beginning in 568 the Lombards, the last to arrive among the eastern Germanic peoples, fled from Pannonia before the Avars and invaded the Italian peninsula. The north and important areas of central and southern Italy were wrenched from the empire, either at the end of the sixth century or in the seventh or eighth century, when the Lombard kings strove to place the whole of Italy under their control. In its first phase, following on the ruin caused by the Byzantine reconquest, the Lombard conquest was often catastrophic, especially when the invaders arrived directly from within Germania. There was a brutal lowering of the level of civilization in many of the conquered territories. After the middle of the seventh century, however, one sees a transformation. The conversion of the Lombards to Catholicism led to contacts with the local population; moreover, relations were established during the periods between wars with the parts of Italy that were still under imperial rule, and with the Byzantine East, even with the missionaries acting as intermediaries. This resulted in the Lombards accepting classical culture, which was much more deeply rooted in Italy than elsewhere; in a general raising of the level of civilization in Lombard Italy; and, in the long run, in the absorption and Romanization of the Lombards by the local population.

Imperial Italy clearly maintained her level of civilization, due, among other factors, to her contacts with the Byzantine East. The power of the exarchate—the military government at Ravenna—continued to dwindle, until the capture of the city by the Lombards (751) limited it to Venetia and Istria, to the far south with Naples and its environs, to Sicily, which was thoroughly Hellenized, and finally to Rome and its duchy, where, in fact, the prerogatives of government passed increasingly into the hands of the bishop of the Eternal City—in other words, the Pope—without challenging the Emperor's superior authority. This political activity of the Holy See developed during the seventh and eighth centuries, but it was begun by Gregory the Great (590–604). He was less successful in his attempt to re-establish a degree of unity in the West in the form of an entente among the empire, the Frankish and Visigothic monarchies, and even the Lombard kingdom, had it been possible to convert it to Catholicism. The Pope had been the moderator of this *societas;* the plan was completely defeated.

The essential factor in Italy's history, considered as a whole from the middle of the seventh century and thereafter, was the relations of every sort that she never ceased to maintain with the Byzantine East. Because of those relations, of the intellectual and artistic traditions of her culture and because of her economic system, in which foreign trade retained a more important role than elsewhere, she constituted a base capable of offering assistance to the renewal of civilization elsewhere in Europe.

Spain, with its Gallic appendage, Septimania, remained a Visigothic kingdom until the beginning of the eighth century. Its kings even succeeded in unifying the peninsula, in the sixth century by conquering the Suevian kingdom, isolated in the northwest, and in the seventh by reconquering the lands under

Byzantine jurisdiction. Here meanwhile, as in southern Gaul and Italy, the Germanic conquerors, few in number, were in the long run absorbed and Romanized, especially after the conversion of the King to Catholicism in 589, which led to the conversion of his subjects. The classical traditions seem to have remained relatively active in Spain. Although during the sixth century the monarchy showed itself to be powerful—more powerful than the Frankish monarchy, which shamed itself each time it undertook an invasion of the peninsula—in the following century it came under the power of the high clergy and the aristocracy, circles in which there were deep dissensions which reduced Spain's military and political power to virtual impotence by the beginning of the eighth century.

This state of affairs was all the more serious in that during the seventh century an event occurred that convulsed the Mediterranean world. Islam and the Arabs, for whom this had become the national religion, led by the Caliph Omar (634–644), second successor of Mahomet, had conquered Syria, Palestine, Egypt, and Cyrenaica, wresting them from the Byzantine Empire; at the same time they subjected Iraq and Persia. In the second half of the century the caliphs of the Omayyad dynasty (661–750) not only extended their empire to the east as far as Turkestan and India but also conquered Byzantine Africa—Carthage fell in 698—and Mauritania, which became the Maghreb. In 711, when their armies invaded Spain, they had little trouble conquering her, and Septimania suffered a like fate.

The world of Islam was dominated militarily and politically by the Arabs, and it used Arabic as the language of religion and of administration. Nevertheless this world was very disparate in its ethnic makeup. The same was true in religion: many conquered populations adopted Islam—in the long run, the majority of them did—and sometimes played very important roles in conquests, as did the Berbers in Africa; but others, such as the Spaniards, in a high proportion remained Christian, accepting a subordinate position in order to safeguard their faith. In every case the unity of the Mediterranean countries was hereafter thoroughly shattered. To the west, to the south, and to the east of what had been the *mare nostrum*, men lived—or, in any event, held power—whose faith and concept of life were irreducible to those of the Christian world.

A question arises if one leaves the political scene and looks at the economy: what was the condition of commercial relations in the fragmented world of the sixth, the seventh, and the early eighth centuries? Distinctions have to be made according to epochs and regions. It seems clear that Italy continued throughout to maintain commercial relations with the Byzantine East: in any event imperial Italy and, through its intermediaries, probably Lombard Italy, in peacetime, at least. No doubt is possible about the existence of commercial relations between the two Italies. Salt was certainly imported by the Venetians into Lombardy at least since the end of the seventh century. There were trade relations between Spain and the East, also between Frankish Gaul and the East. It is an incontestable fact that Oriental products—jewels, luxury cloths, spices, fine wines, papyrus, etc.—were imported into Gaul; much was shipped through the port of Marseille, as was oil imported from Africa. Much of the expediting of imported goods, even in the interior, was in the hands of Syrians, Greeks, and Jews. Moreover, this import trade was only a very secondary activity in regions where agriculture and livestock raising, chiefly in domain lands, was dominant. Trade volume, probably very small, appears to have decreased between the sixth and the eighth centuries, without entirely disappearing, at least for such articles as precious cloths and papyrus. This was without doubt a consequence of the state of semianarchy that more and more prevailed in the Frankish monarchy, of the progressive depression of the standard of living, of the changes in needs and habits, of the ever increasing shortage of gold needed for paying for foreign imports, and of the lack of an adequate supply of goods for export. Slaves captured in raids east of the Rhine were almost the only merchandise sold abroad; the slaves sold by the Anglo-Saxons were only granted passage through Gaul. The appearance of Moslem fleets in the Mediterranean put a halt to certain exports from the East or from Africa and made navigation hazardous. This was not the decisive factor in the new state of affairs. The Moslem nations had not been closed to commerce with Christian nations, and they had always traded with the Byzantine world: the commercial centers of the Venetian lagoon had sold them slaves in the seventh and eighth centuries. If Saracen piracy constituted a danger to navigation in the western Mediterranean, it had nevertheless been unable to halt it; the Byzantine fleet, based in Sicily, was prepared to protect merchant ships and convoys.

From the seventh century on, commercial relations developed between northwestern Gaul and England. An examination of objects found in certain countries of the West, especially articles of adornment, tends to support the view that in the sixth, seventh, and eighth centuries, there was an overland trade between those countries and the Byzantine world, the Avars, and the Slav peoples of central and eastern Europe.

2

The Carolingian Epoch

THE FIFTH, THE SIXTH, THE SEVENTH, and the beginning of the eighth centuries saw the breakdown of the unity of western Europe and the resulting progressive fragmentation. In contrast, the eighth century produced two groups of factors that created tendencies toward unity. These were the reorganization and the extraordinary extension of the Frankish monarchy under the new Carolingian dynasty and the development of the political power of the papacy. These two groups of factors acted and reacted upon each other.

The Pepinides (i.e., the descendents of Pepin I, mayor of the palace to the Merovingian king Dagobert I), or Carolingians—named for the surnames borne by several of them, Charles (Karl)—were from the Austrasian aristocracy; their patrimonial estates were inside Hesbaye, in the region of the Meuse and Moselle area. It was among the members of this aristocracy that they found their soundest support. Since the seventh century the heads of this family—with the title of "Mayor of the Palace" and under the nominal authority of the last Merovingian kings—had one way and another guided the Frankish monarchy. Between 719 and 741, one of them, Charles, much later called Martel, succeeded in re-establishing the unity of the monarchy by providing the central power with effective authority; by binding together Austrasia, Neustria, and Burgundy, with Austrasians preponderant; by ending the autonomy of the peripheral territories, as in Alemania, or by limiting it, as in Aquitaine and Bavaria; and by giving posts of command throughout the *Regnum Francorum* to Austrasians, who were largely Germanic in language and traditions. He conquered Frisia, the region where the Scheldt, the Meuse, and the Rhine flowed into the North Sea. In 732 at Poitiers he repulsed a dangerous invasion of the Spanish Moslems—the Saracens, as they were more often called. He protected the evangelizing activities of the English missionaries, especially those of Willibrord in Frisia and Boniface in Franconia and Thuringia. His son Pepin III, later called "the Short" (died 768), followed the same policy, extending it and consolidating the gains. He seized Septimania from the Moslems and suppressed the national duchy of Aquitaine. He backed the reforming activity of Boniface in the Frankish Church, which had fallen into the same savage confusion as the lay society. Thanks to this holy man—who was completely devoted to the Holy See, as was the whole English Church, and submitted to all its instructions, as did all the English missionaries—sound relations were established between Pepin and the Pope. In 751, when the Carolingian mayor of the palace proclaimed himself King of the Franks, thus eliminating the Merovingian dynasty, the moral support of Rome counted for a great deal in the success of Pepin's *coup d'état*. Boniface legitimized the deed by introducing a religious element into the act of accession to the throne, a rite adapted from the Old Testament and destined for extensive use. This was the unction (*consecratio*), the anointing with holy oil, to be administered by a bishop.

The new state of affairs was the result of the union of very different factors: apart from the personal worth of Charles Martel and Pepin, the energy of the Austrasian aristocracy, the missionary but yet Roman spirit of the English Church, and the now greater prestige of the papacy.

The work of the early Carolingians had brought about the internal pacification of the Frankish monarchy and had made it capable of acting effectively in foreign affairs. Inside the kingdom this led to a greater interpenetration of Germanic and Roman elements and helped to spread a uniform system of institutions. In

the West it created a state of security—at the very least relative—
in the face of the Moslem threat.

The first Carolingian king made the papacy a political power
worthy of the name. The starting point was there: we know that
during the seventh century and in the early part of the eighth,
basically because of the very limited scope of imperial authority
and the scanty means of its agents in Italy, the bishops of Rome
had progressively taken over the administration, the defense, and
the shaping of general policy in Rome as well as in its "duchy"—
that is to say, in its military government. Meanwhile the desire of
the Lombard kings to unify Italy under their authority endangered the independence acquired by the papacy and threatened to
make the Pope merely chief among the Lombard bishops. Emperor Constantine V, occupied with the war against the Arabs,
was unable to send troops to Italy; and, moreover, as an im-
placable adversary of the cult of icons, he was involved in a
religious conflict with Rome and Italy. Pope Stephen II took himself to France, to Pepin, and, in the form of a second consecration,
gave pontifical sanction to the authority the latter had usurped.
At the request of the Pope, Pepin, during his two expeditions to
Italy (755, 756), forced the Lombard king to give up his undertakings and turn over to Saint Peter—in fact, to the sovereign
pontiff—Ravenna and the territories of the exarchate he had conquered in 751 and in subsequent years. Thus, by the union of
these territories with Rome and her duchy, a papal state was
created across central Italy. This open usurpation, committed to
the detriment of the empire, was achieved without the Pope officially renouncing his subordinate status in regard to the *basileus*.
It was this inability to act effectively in the West that reduced the
rights of Byzantium to nothing.

The creation of a "pontifical state" by Pepin, to whom and to
whose sons the Pope had given a title revived from that of the
imperial exarch, *patricius romanorum*, was a fact of the greatest
importance: it was going to provide the Carolingians with new

opportunities to intervene in Italy and at Rome; it made the Pope a sovereign with all that this could bring him in terms of power, but also with all the involvements into which care of his temporal interests could drag him.

At this point Pepin's son, Charlemagne (768–814), extended the Frankish monarchy, which had been consolidated by his grandfather and father so much so that he recreated for a time a united Christian Europe. However, in contrast to the *partes occidentis* of the Roman Empire, it included Germany but excluded Spain, which had come almost entirely under Moslem control, and "Britain," which had become England. The center of this Carolingian Europe was not the Mediterranean, but the region between the Rhine and the Loire, heart of the Frankish state, and particularly the east part of this region, the land of the Carolingian family and of most of their political and military agents. The details of Charlemagne's conquests count little; what is important are the results and their effect.

To the *Regnum Francorum* he united Lombard Italy, Istria (seized from Byzantium), Saxony—all northern Germany up to the Elbe and even the lower reaches of the river—the largely Slav-populated countries of the middle Danube, until that time dominated by the Avars, and the northeastern corner of Spain, which he seized from the Saracens. The part of Frisia that had kept its independence was conquered, and Bavarian autonomy was ended. It is clear that Charlemagne's sons governed Lombard Italy and Aquitaine with the title of king, and a rather large degree of administrative autonomy was granted to Italy. Nevertheless the authority of the Frankish sovereign was effectively exercised over these two countries. In addition, a whole series of territories was placed under protection, either *de jure* or *de facto*: the Papal State; the Lombard duchy of Benevento in southern Italy; Bohemia; the eastern areas of the former Avar territories and even part of the interior of Dalmatia, populated since the first half of the seventh century by Slavs—the Croats; Celtic Brittany;

and Navarre, or the Basque country, astride the Pyrenees. Only
the protectorate over the Papal State was effective.

The union of so many diverse territories with the *Regnum
Francorum*, such as it was seen at the dawn of the eighth century,
was to bring about important consequences, certain of which
continued to have repercussions during later ages. The widespread
application of Frankish institutions in Aquitaine by numerous
Frankish personnel strengthened the bonds between the two sections of Gaul separated by the Loire, despite the persistence of
autonomistic tendencies within Aquitaine. Lombard Italy also
"received" the institutions of the Frankish monarchy, but less
effectively; and to a large extent she transformed them by adapting them to the core of Lombard institutions. Above all, Italy was
a "source": perhaps in the field of legislation, where the edicts of
the Lombard kings may have provided the Carolingians with
patterns for their capitularies; in any case this is obvious in the
field of intellectual and artistic activity and this time in papal
Italy as well as in Lombard Italy. The conquest of Saxony was a
major event: the whole of northern Germany—inhabited by warlike peoples, heathen, strangers to the essential elements of western
civilization—had been, by force but effectively, penetrated by
these elements. Not only the Frankish monarchy but also Christianity with its Latin liturgy extended as far as the Elbe. On the
other hand, one should not forget that henceforward all the continental Germanic peoples found themselves grouped under the
authority of the king of the Franks. There remained the Danubian
region, or at least its most westward part. Important here was not
only the introduction of the institutions of the Frankish monarchy and the conversion of the populations to Christianity with
its Latin liturgy, but also the beginning of a colonization that in
the long run Germanized these countries. This area made up the
eastern "march"—the advanced frontier zone—of Bavaria; it was
to become Austria.

The system of vassalic relations had been introduced into all of these territories. This had particularly developed in the Frankish monarchy during the eighth century, although its origins go back much farther in time. It was the practice of the kings to take into their service free men called "vassals," who were bound to render semipermanent service with the strictest fidelity, in exchange for the assurance of maintenance and protection from the king, their lord. Thus the kings had at their command numerous professional soldiers who were equally capable of performing other services for them. Frequently, increasingly frequently, maintenance was gained from the vassals by making over to them for life a land-holding, sometimes of considerable size, but usually small. Over such a holding the vassal exercised rights analogous to those of a usufructuary. Such a tenure was called a "benefice." The Church, the counts—the territorial representatives of royal power—and other great men also had vassals to whom they sometimes gave benefices; but they could only claim military duties from them in the service of the king. These practices had spread throughout the Carolingian monarchy and developed with it, sometimes with particular characteristics according to region. The phenomenon had very considerable consequences.

To the group of facts mentioned, just one more should be added: on December 25, 800, at Rome, Charlemagne was crowned emperor by the Pope. The importance of this event can only be grasped by means of an analysis of the ideas of "empire" and "emperor." A new concept of the imperial function, separate from its actual historical basis, had been evolving gradually in the West, partly through the influence of Pope Gregory the Great (590–604). The emperor's essential mission—naturally the Roman emperor; none other could be conceived of—was the guardianship of the Christian faith and the protection of the Church. Since the Church was universal, so therefore was the authority of the emperor. This was the idea of the scholars and educated clergy—few in number. Charlemagne's principal adviser on Church affairs, the Englishman Alcuin, was absolutely convinced that for the good of the Church, imperial authority had to be re-established in the West, where it was painfully lacking. According to Alcuin, Charlemagne was the person qualified to assume and exercise this authority: did not the complex of territories he ruled constitute the *imperium christianum*, inhabited by the *populus christianus*, the community of all Christians, subject to Rome in religious matters, and practicing the Latin liturgy (England and Spain were not taken into account)? Alcuin's grand concept was shared by others; one managed to persuade Charles himself, and advantage was taken of a political crisis at Rome to bring the Pope to crown the King of the Franks emperor.

Successive Byzantine emperors considered this a scandal and a usurpation; it was even feared—vainly—that Charles would attempt to extend his authority in the East, so much did the notion of empire imply unity. It required military and political pressure to bring the *basileus*, in 812, to recognize the Carolingian as an emperor. There were henceforth two emperors and two Roman empires, two powers with universal claims, agreeing to limit these claims, one to the east and one to the west, one to the lands of the Latin liturgy, one to the lands of the Greek. In Byzantium, however, awareness of the legitimate succession and contempt for the people of the West who, according to the Greeks, were semi-barbarians, prevented the Byzantine emperors from adhering wholeheartedly to this division of the Christian world. The recognition of the western emperor was only a concession to the misfortunes of the times.

Charlemagne had not clearly grasped the full significance of the imperial power. The situation was very different for his son and successor, Louis the Pious (814–840); he understood the abstract and universal character of this power which set him apart from the national monarchs of the Franks, the Lombards, and the English; in many respects his thinking was that of the learned clerics around him; in their minds religious considerations were decisive. Consequently, in order not to commit a mortal sin, it was of utmost importance to maintain intact the unity of the Christian *imperium* over which the Emperor exercised authority in order to defend and spread the faith and exalt the Church. From this came the *Ordinatio* of 817, which regulated the succession to the empire by excluding division and by according to younger sons the exercise of royal power only in peripheral territories, strictly subordinate to the Emperor's own authority. Thus they arrived by way of an ecclesiastical concept of empire, to the abstract notion of *res publica*, the State.

The hope of maintaining unity was not fulfilled: the empire and the Frankish monarchy, its material frame, broke apart. Many factors contributed to this result: the abstract character of the imperial idea, which made it accessible only to a small minority of cultivated people, especially clerics; the patrimonial concept of power, deeply rooted and generally accepted, and the constant tradition of successive divisions that it implied; the absence of scruples in the pursuit of their interests—that is, in the acquisition of public posts and the profits attached to them— among members of the aristocracy, who belonged to one or other of the parties; the incompetence of Louis the Pious and his sons; the radicalism of members of the clergy in the defense of their beliefs; and finally the inefficiency of public institutions. From 829 to 840, then from this year when Louis the Pious died until 843, there was a succession of intrigues, wars, and divisions. At the Treaty of Verdun (843) it was conceded that the empire would be divided among the surviving sons of the Emperor: the west, *Francia occidentalis,* which became France, went to Charles the Bald; the east, *Francia orientalis,* which became Germany, went to Louis the German; the central region, from Frisia to Italy, went to Lothair I. When the latter died in 855, his lands passed to his three sons: the north, as a whole—between the Scheldt and the upper Meuse on the one hand, and the Rhine on the other—to Lothair II, from whom these territories took the name Lotharingia or Lorraine; Italy, to Louis II; Provence to Charles. Among all these new political units there were further intrigues, wars, annexations, and divisions, complicated by uprisings and invasions. Uprisings of the various leaders of aristocratic clans and also, and more particularly, uprisings and invasions of peoples; uprisings of the Aquitanians; invasions of the Bretons in the realm of the West; Danish or Norman invasions—which will be mentioned later—in the kingdom of the West; the Saracen incursions into Italy and Provence; and Slav invasions into the kingdom of the East. At the end of the eighties, unity was reconstituted for a short time under Charles the Fat, son of Louis the German, but the divisive factors at work since the reign of Louis the Pious proved stronger: in 887 the aristocratic factions that led the various peoples subject to the totally incompetent Emperor, one by one escaped from his authority. This was the final breakdown.

In this collapse of the empire and the Frankish monarchy that had served to support it, the imperial dignity and all that was bound up with the notion of unity ceased to correspond to reality. Lothair I and his son Louis II had been emperors, although this offered them no more than a simple honorific pre-eminence. Others had been aware of the task of directing and protecting western Christendom with the aim of guaranteeing the triumph of the faith and the exaltation of the Church: the bishops of *Francia occidentalis*, especially Hincmar, Archbishop of Reims, who dominated the Church in this kingdom by the force of his character, by the extent of his knowledge, and by the firmness of his designs; then—sometimes in conflict with Hincmar—Pope Nicholas I (858–867), who succeeded in getting his authority recognized as superior to that of the Emperor Louis II and the Carolingian kings, at least to a certain extent. In fact, the situation was extremely precarious. This precariousness revealed itself on the morrow of this great Pope's death. Lacking a protector with sufficient material means, his successors became the tools or the victims of the parties into which the Italian and Roman aristocracies were divided. They were also the victims of the Saracens who harried the southern and central parts of the peninsula. One saw this in the case of a pontiff such as John VIII (872–882) who was aware of the "imperial" mission of the papacy, who reclaimed for the Holy See the prerogative of creating emperors, and who did create some—Charles the Bald and Charles the Fat—though these were powerless. John was assassinated, the victim of a palace revolution. The imperial crown, a vain plaything, was dragged through mud and blood until 924, after which men ceased to seek it. Meanwhile the imperial ideal survived: according to some, an emperor was necessary to the West to protect the Church and Christians against violence. The glorious memory of Charlemagne, by whom the empire had been established in the West, upheld the same aspirations.

The countries that, after having been made part of the empire and the Frankish monarchy, found themselves completely cut off in 887, were strongly affected, though in various degrees, by the action of common institutions and of the elements of a common civilization. This action, more keenly felt in the former territories of the *Regnum Francorum*, was experienced by other territories during the reigns of Charlemagne and Louis the Pious and, to a considerable extent, continued to make itself felt even after the political separations that began with the Treaty of Verdun in 843. Reference has already been made to the action of common institutions, including, among others, that of vassalic institutions. We should also mention the effects of elements of the spiritual civilization. In this respect the actions of Pepin, of Charlemagne, and of Louis the Pious were undertaken, in agreement with the Pope, in the same sense, but with different means: they re-established fixed forms in the hierarchy, mainly by the importance granted to metropolitan archbishops, the heads of ecclesiastical provinces; they had worked toward making a uniform Latin liturgy; they supported efforts toward a truly regular monastic life by making general the application of the rules of Saint Benedict; they had attempted to regulate the lives of the junior clergy by expanding the canonical institutions; and they favored increasing the number of parishes. This built up a common patrimony for western continental Christendom.

This was not all. The work of Charlemagne and his successors was closely linked to a grand religious design which brought about the Carolingian renaissance. It consisted of procuring for the Church a clergy that had a minimum of instruction, correct Biblical texts and liturgical books, as well as places of worship whose splendor constituted homage to God and the saints. The organization of instruction, though elementary, and the production of clerical and monastic copy workshops, which were not restricted to transcribing Biblical or liturgical texts but extended their activity to Latin literary works—Christian or classical—had far greater results: on the one hand, a modest but undeniable raising of the level of religious and secular knowledge; on the other, the conservation of and transmission to future generations of classical literature and thought in their Latin form, with all the richness they brought to the development of culture in the West. This Carolingian renaissance constituted, in its own way, one aspect of international relations of the times. For at its start Charlemagne sent for men from regions where the level of intellectual culture had maintained itself or had risen higher than in the former Frankish territories: Italy, with Peter of Pisa, Paulinus of Aquileia, and Paul the Deacon; Ireland, with Dicuil; Spain, with Theodulphus; and England, with Alcuin. Likewise, Italian, English, and Irish manuscripts—sometimes Spanish ones—were often used or copied in Carolingian *scriptoria*. They were also imitated, and often freely, in their decoration. Artistically speaking, the Carolingian renaissance was as "international" as its literature. Its architecture was particularly striking: it is enough to cite a single example, namely the ground plan, decoration, and even elevation that Carolingian architecture owes to a better knowledge of classical examples and to familiarity, acquired in Italy, with Byzantine art.

One can, in the same period, point out traces of international relations in the domain of economics. But one has to guard against errors in perspective: in the eighth and ninth centuries, as in the preceding ones, agriculture was the predominant factor in the economy of the continental West; it was very often practiced within the framework of big estates, whose form, moreover, was not always or everywhere the same. These domains, to a great extent, were self-sufficient; particularly the larger ones. Moreover, they sold part of their produce, thus sustaining a regional trade not without importance. In addition, long distance trade existed: there were certainly commercial relations between the north and the center of the Frankish monarchy on the one hand, and on the other, the Mediterranean coasts and Italy; and although navigation in the western Mediterranean was perilous because of Saracen piracy, especially after the Moslem conquest of Sicily (capture of Syracuse in 878), this navigation to or from the ports of Languedoc and Provence had not entirely disappeared. As for northern Italy, the merchants from the Venetian trade centers, of which Torcello was still the foremost, sold salt from the lagoons and eastern products they imported from Byzantium and of course from the Moslem Near East, where they exported slaves. Then there were also slaves that English, Verdun, and Jewish merchants sold in Spain. Apart from those who were English trade in transit, these slaves were mainly Slavs seized in raids beyond the Saale or the Elbe and in the Danubian or Dalmatian lands.

Traditional and in decline or, on the contrary, in the process of developing—like the Italo-Venetian traffic—these commercial ties were all oriented toward the Mediterranean. Others were oriented differently. There was certainly, at least from the beginning of the ninth century, continental commerce going east, toward the Slavs of central or eastern Europe. Whether they used the land routes, mainly issuing from Magdeburg, or whether they used the Danube, mainly departing from Regensburg, finally—and this is the most important fact—there was the development of a trade economy in the lands between the Seine and the Rhine, with new ports of great importance on the lower Rhine, at Duursstede, and on the Channel coasts, at Quentowic at the mouth of the Canche. This was an economic movement shared by the old decayed Roman towns, like Cologne or Paris, and the modest new commercial centers. Among those engaged in transportation both on the sea and along the rivers, the Frisians, sailors from the Rhine-Meuse-Scheldt delta, appear to have played an important role. This trade was directed toward England and the Scandinavian countries and, with the Danes and Swedes as intermediaries, across the Baltic and the Russian plain to the east. There has been some success in identifying certain export products: metallurgy (especially arms, often smuggled) from the Rhine-Moselle region, ceramics from the same region, wines from the north of France and from the Rhine lands; and doubtless, among other things, certain eastern products were imported, perhaps raw materials from the Slav countries. These trade relations gradually dwindled when, in the second half of the ninth century, Danes and Norwegians through pillage and conquest further affected trade in England and in Francia. When these transactions involved the use of Frankish money, silver specie was virtually the sole currency; gold had almost entirely disappeared in the continental West, and since Pepin and Charlemagne money was with very few exceptions struck only from silver. There existed only small coins, of which the heaviest was the denier (*denarius*) or penny, but in account-keeping multiples with no real base were used: the sou worth twelve deniers, the pound (*libra*) worth twenty sous (*solidus*) or shilling. This system was adopted in England in the tenth century.

We must remember that the most important fact in the history of England is the war that it had to sustain against the Danish invasions in the second half of the ninth century. From these wars England was to become a political unit. The king of Wessex, Alfred the Great (871–899), who had led the resistance, suc-

ceeded in uniting under his authority all the territories not conquered by the invader, except northern Northumbria. He had to
abandon almost all the east to the Scandinavians, who colonized
part of the land; but Alfred and, to a greater extent, his successors
were able gradually to extend their power over these regions,
known as the "Danelaw." These regions, furthermore, while
maintaining close relations with Scandinavia, supported a partly
Danish population with its strong personal characteristics. The
Scoti, Irish invaders, gradually conquered the whole of Scotland,
thus giving the latter its name and, in the tenth century, its unity.
The realization of this latter was delayed by, among other things,
the Norwegian and Danish invasions. The Norwegians founded
settlements in the islands and on the coasts of the north and held
onto them for several centuries; they achieved as much on the east
coast of Ireland, a country still divided into small rival kingdoms.

In contrast to the western Christian world where Carolingian
efforts had not succeeded in re-establishing unity, the Roman
Empire of the East, or to employ the usual term, the Byzantine
Empire, continued to form the political frame of the eastern
Christian world. Certainly, from the seventh to the ninth centuries, the greater part of Thrace and Macedonia and Dalmatia
were occupied by the Bulgarians and the Slavs, and some Mediterranean islands, among them Cyprus, Crete, and Sicily, were
conquered by the Moslems. But during these same centuries the
empire maintained itself despite everything. The Isaurian emperors, in the eighth century, and the Macedonian emperors, at the
end of the ninth and in the tenth century, succeeded within
Europe in holding off the redoubtable power wielded by the
Bulgarians who dreamed of conquering the capital itself: Constantinople. In Asia the emperors defended Asia Minor and its
eastern border against Islam, or they won it back for the empire
after it had in part been lost. At the end of the ninth century the
Emperor Basil I the Macedonian, who in these two theaters of
operations had won decisive successes and prepared for the re-

establishment of imperial hegemony over Armenia and Georgia, even rooted out the Saracens from southern Italy, which they occupied, and solidly rebuilt Byzantine authority. Naples, Amalfi, and the coastal cities of Dalmatia recognized this authority once more, while Venetia, now in fact independent, remained a precious ally.

The contrast between the Byzantine and western worlds was profound. It showed itself in all areas: that of the State, where the eastern empire had at its command regular working institutions, beside which the western political framework gave an impression of primitivism; that of culture, where Byzantium, thanks to the still lively practice of Greek literature and philosophy, maintained a level incomparably superior to that of the Latin Christian world. But it was in matters of religion that the contrast was, if not the most apparent, at least the most serious. Doubtless the authority of the Pope was not, in principle, questioned; however, the Greek Church distinguished itself clearly from the Latin Church, not only by the use of Greek as a liturgical language, but also by its impatience in regard to the interventions of Rome in matters of discipline and by the tendency of the Patriarch in Constantinople to consider himself the equal of the pontiff at Rome.

In 867 there was even a schism which, although short-lived, was provoked by the Patriarch Photios on the occasion of a clash between Rome and Byzantium on the subject of the organization of the Church in Bulgaria. Actually the Church in Greece had played a vital role in spreading Christianity among the Bulgarians and Serbs. These peoples adopted the Slavonic liturgy and the "glagolithic" alphabet—based on the Greek alphabet and created by the Greek monks Cyril and Methodius in the second half of the ninth century to allow for the translation of the holy books and the service. The religious activity of Byzantium, despite violent conflicts that placed the Bulgarians at loggerheads with the empire, brought these people to participate in the Byzantine civilization. The civilizing influence of Byzantium spread even farther during the ninth century. In the vast eastern European plain, Swedish adventurers, the Varangians or Russians, in the ninth century politically and militarily organized the first Slav states, along the great navigable routes. Going down the Dnieper, they traded with Kherson, a Byzantine center in the Crimea, and with Constantinople; reaching, via the Don and the Volga, the Khazar lands to the northeast of the Black Sea, they came in contact with merchants from Baghdad. Thus they maintained connections with the Byzantine or the Moslem east, on the one hand, and with Scandinavia and, through her, with northwestern Europe, on the other. "Russian" merchants and "Russian" mercenaries, who served in some number in the imperial army, were the first agents to bring Byzantine civilization into the territories that came to be called Russia—from the name applied to these agents—particularly in the principality of Kiev which, in the tenth century, was to impose its hegemony on the other Russian principalities.

The history of the Byzantine world in the eighth and ninth centuries is that of a world that successfully defended itself and even created a zone of influence. The history of the Moslem world at the same time is that of a world in disintegration, at least politically. Conflicts flared up through clan rivalries, different religious attitudes in the heart of Islam, and the hostility of the Berbers and of the people of Iraq and Iran toward the Arabs. One conflict led to the overthrow of the Omayyads and the accession of a new dynasty, that of the Abbassides, in 750. Thenceforth the Iraqi and Iranian elements exercised a decisive influence; and a new capital, Baghdad, was built on the Tigris after 762. But from 756 on, Moslem Spain made itself almost independent of the caliphate, under an emir, or governor, who had his seat at Cordova and belonged to the Omayyad dynasty.

For a period of time the Abbasside caliphs were able to maintain the cohesion of their empire, thanks to the development of an administration. But already in the course of the ninth century the emirs of Egypt, of Africa, of the Maghreb, and of the Khurasan in turn made themselves practically independent. The most important and lasting conquests by the Moslems in the ninth century were, moreover, the achievements of autonomous leaders or groups: the conquest of Sicily was undertaken in 827 by the emirate of Africa; the conquest of Crete, between 823 and 828, by a group of Arabs using Egypt as their base; the occupation of a site on the coast of Provence near Fréjus was achieved by a band of Saracens from Spain. Conflicts were frequent between the varied political units, caliphates, and autonomous emirates which divided the Islamic world. The powerful caliph, Haroun-al-Raschid (786–809), even appears to have been drawn to Charlemagne on account of their common hostility to the Omayyad emirs of Spain.

But there existed, nonetheless, elements of unity in this divided world. Despite theological divergencies and political struggles, the Islamic religion retained bonds: prayer, the teachings of the Koran, pilgrimages to Mecca—all these constituted a powerful cohesive force. The use of Arabic as the language of religion and of administration was another. In terms of economics, at least one part of the Moslem world was united by a web of trade relations: Egypt and Syria for one, and Iraq for another, were entrepôts of Asiatic and African trade with the Mediterranean world, trading among them and with the western Moslem world as well as with the Byzantine world or with the Russians. Islamic civilization was another unifying factor. Formed in the eighth and ninth centuries, this syncretic civilization borrowed the oldest traditions of the conquered countries. This is true in the domain of philosophy and literature. It can be seen in the field of art: the contributions of Sassanid Persia, of Byzantium, and of Egypt were considerable, but new forms in art evolved from the transformation and combining of these borrowings. As with all Moslem civilization, this art responded to the particular traits of certain regions; these regional characteristics are less clear than the features common to the whole of Moslem art.

3

*The Practice of International Relations
in the Early Middle Ages*

An ACCOUNT, even if summary, of the history of international relations would be very incomplete if a few pages were not devoted to the technical aspects of these relations. For the period that has just been treated, the sources are few and hardly explicit: nevertheless they shed some light upon important aspects of the subject.

The first problem that arises is that of the contacts among political units—among states, to use the current term—and particularly the negotiations that became indispensable in relations among these states. In certain circumstances these negotiations could have been conducted by the sovereigns themselves or at least in their presence, because often the texts have taken care to note the roles played by great men, ecclesiastical or lay, in the royal entourage. Direct negotiations were employed by the Merovingians at the time when the *Regnum Francorum* was divided: in 561, when the four sons of Clotaire I met in order to divide the kingdom among themselves; in 577, at the meeting at Pompierre between Gontran, king of Burgundy, and his nephew Childebert II, king of Austrasia; in 586, in another meeting between the same parties at Andelot; in 604, at the conference of Compiègne, between the king of Austrasia, Theodebert II, and the king of Neustria, Clotaire II; in 625, in talks at Saint-Ouen between Clotaire II and his son Dagobert I, king of Austrasia; etc. Charlemagne's sons, Pepin, king of Italy, and Louis, king of Aquitaine, were frequently summoned to their father for political discussions; but the subordination of their kingdoms to the Frankish sovereign was such that any international character of these relations could be challenged. On the other hand, after the death of Louis the Pious there were again heads of state who, with the aid of their entourages, practiced direct negotiations.

Direct negotiations were employed several times during the conflicts that set the sons of Louis the Pious at loggerheads, and their best-known conference was at Verdun in 843, when Lothair I, Louis the German, and Charles the Bald drew up the famous division of the western empire. During the following years the deliberations for the continuation of the "confraternity" among the kingdoms born of the division of the empire were undertaken within the frame of conferences that brought the three sovereigns together. Then, during the thirty or so years that followed the death of Lothair in 855, there were still many meetings of his brothers and his sons, brought on by conflicts of every sort which arose either among them or between them and some other power. It is sufficient to cite one: that of Meersen in 870, in the course of which Louis the German and Charles the Bald agreed on the division of Lotharingia. These few direct negotiations between heads of states have been cited as examples; there are several others. Perhaps special mention should be made of negotiations that certain popes conducted in person, popes who, from Gregory the Great (590–604) to Zacharias (741–752), attempted, often with some success, to press the Lombard kings—Agilulf, Liutprand, and Ratchis—to give up their undertakings against Rome, the duchy or the exarchate, or at least to show themselves less severe toward the inhabitants. The popes who left Italy to try to obtain help from foreign rulers should also be mentioned. The results of these negotiations differed greatly case by case. Those that Stephen II conducted in Francia in 754 with King Pepin ended, as we know, in an alliance that resulted in the creation of the Papal State; those that John VIII undertook in Francia in 878, especially with the king of *Francia occidentalis*, Louis the Stammerer, did not assure him of any aid.

Another method whereby heads of political units assured contacts among themselves was correspondence—the simple exchange of letters carried by couriers. It seems that this was never, at least in the West during the period considered here, a very frequent practice; but examples do exist, especially among the popes who remained committed to the intensive use of the written message that the Roman Empire had known.

As far as we know, most of the negotiations were carried on in the name of one of the parties by an embassy, in the name of the other by the chief of state himself and by members of his entourage, or even in the name of this chief of state by some important person of the court. The Byzantine empire always employed diplomacy rather than war to hold its own against the great powers that surrounded it, and to establish or maintain a kind of protectorate over certain people occupying the territories adjoining its frontiers, sometimes even the lost provinces. The highly sophisticated administration of the empire had a department—at the end of the eighth century it was that of the "logothetes of the dromos," or the ministry of posts—responsible for all that had to do with the organization and dispatch of embassies abroad. The ambassadors themselves were generally laymen of high rank at court. In the eighth and ninth centuries the *basileis* sent to the popes and to the Frankish sovereigns, especially to Pepin and Charlemagne, "silentiaries" or masters of ceremonies, "candidates," "spathairs," and even "protospathaires"—all military dignitaries; but sometimes men of the highest rank: a *primicerius*, or head of the chamberlains; a *sacellarius*, a senior officer in the treasury; even a *patricius*, a man of great importance, who held one of the highest titles of the empire. Eventually Byzantium would send to a head of state a mission made up of two or three ambassadors: in this case one of them was sometimes a eunuch, a member of the upper levels of the palace household, and sometimes a secular or regular churchman. There was no true specialization of diplomatic functions, even though certain people, because of their experience, were employed several times in succession on missions of the same type, such as the silentiary John for Italian affairs who treated with Pope Stephen II, Aistulf, king of the Lombards, and Pepin, king of the Franks. A member of the corps of interpreters was usually part of the suite of a Byzantine ambassador. It has happened that the Emperor, considering the Pope a bishop of the empire, sent him on an embassy: in 753, on the orders of Constantine V, Stephen II, together with the silentiary John, went to Aistulf, king of the Lombards, to press for the restitution of Ravenna and the exarchate to the empire. They were not successful.

The Pope himself used envoys for discussions not held at Rome on ecclesiastical or political questions, two types of business not always easily distinguishable. Like the patriarchs of Alexandria, of Antioch, and of Jerusalem, he for a long time had one or more permanent envoys with the Emperor at Constantinople; they were called "apocrisaries" and were often deacons belonging to the papal administration. Several future popes, including Gregory the Great, held this office, which ceased in the first half of the eighth century. In addition, the popes more frequently, in every period, employed *ad hoc* envoys at the imperial and royal courts and at councils. They are described in texts as *missi* or as *legati apostolicae sedis.* They were frequently selected from among the bishops or priests, or deacons, or subdeacons who made up the administrative or palatine personnel.

The heads of realms founded in the West by the Germanic peoples never had personnel in their service comparable to those of the Emperor or the Pope. To carry out the numerous missions they sent abroad, they could call upon the great lay or ecclesiastical men in service at the palace or in some part of their territories. Such was the case of the Frankish monarchy, whose ambassadors (*missi, legati*), in the Merovingian and in the Carolingian epochs, are well known to us. From this period on there was among them an important ecclesiastical element, certainly

partly on account of their culture: bishops, abbots, palace chap-
lains, and clerics belonging to the office of the chancellor. Under
Charlemagne and his successors the embassies were freqently
composed of two envoys, sometimes of three, quite like the inspec-
tion missions or groups of *missi dominici* who worked within the
frontiers; in these cases one of the envoys was most often a
layman and nearly always a count, the other one, a cleric; this
rule was generally applied in the makeup of embassies sent to
Byzantium. In contrast, the ambassadors Charlemagne sent to the
Abbasside Caliph Haroun-al-Raschid or to the Moslem potentates
in North Africa or in Spain were, it appears, always laymen: in
order to save the churchmen from possible insults from followers
of Islam. To embassies sent "outside the Christian world," someone would be added who knew the region, the customs, and the
language, like Isaac the Jew who, in 801, returned alone from a
mission to Haroun-al-Raschid at Baghdad, the ambassadors having died en route. Obviously care was taken to provide interpreters knowing Greek for the service of embassies on their way
to Constantinople, where by the ninth century Latin had become
a foreign language, as little known as Greek was in the West. It
was in Italy that one had the best chances of finding interpreters.
Certain missions, even under the Carolingians, remained entrusted
to one person, selected because of the particular trust the head of
state placed in him. Angilbert, the lay abbot of Saint-Riquier, a
close friend of Charlemagne, and official lover of one of his
daughters, was such a man and was sent in 796 to the newly
elected Pope Leo III to persuade him to lead a virtuous life and to
give him very precise instructions in the use of his power. Einhard, also a close friend of Charlemagne, was such a man and
was charged by the Emperor in 806 to bring to the Pope himself
the text of the dispositions regulating the succession to the throne
and to obtain the agreement and endorsement of Leo. The particularly close relations between the Carolingians and the Holy
See explain the fact that in certain cases the King of the Franks

and the Pope had sent joint embassies abroad. Some examples of this are known in the period of Charlemagne.

Measures were taken to assure foreign embassies, or those that the head of state was sending abroad, of the necessary means of transport and of food and lodgings during the crossing of the territory and, if necessary, during their stay in the country. In the Byzantine Empire where Roman institutions had been maintained, though completely transformed, national or foreign embassies used the imperial post for their transportation; but their victualing involved requisitions. Foreign ambassadors were lodged in the care of the imperial administration at Constantinople. In the kingdoms of the West there remained very little of the old Roman post system, except the documents called *tractoria*, which gave the right to commandeer the means of transportation, lodgings, and victualing. The population bore these burdens, which were sometimes very heavy. A considerable amount is known about the regulations governing these requisitions in the Frankish monarchy under the Merovingians and Carolingians. Of the latter, Charlemagne and Louis the Pious in particular made many efforts to ensure the satisfactory functioning of the system, while fighting the abuses that the counts and other royal agents allowed themselves in this situation. They battled also against the ill-will of those who had to provide the requisitions. It can be assumed that they were not entirely successful. In Italy, where a larger part of the Roman organization had been preserved, buildings in the principal cities belonging to the Crown had to serve for the lodgings of foreign envoys.

There is far less information concerning the documents carried by the ambassadors other than the *tractoria*. There are allusions to credentials in the sources and there still exists the text of some of these for the Frankish realm in the seventh century; we can believe that their use must have been fairly common. We know less about instructions. Reference has already been made to those given by Charlemagne to Angilbert, who was sent to Pope

Leo in 796. They were in the form of a letter from the King to the ambassador and appear to have been drawn up by Alcuin. The letter shows with great clarity the various aims of the mission. Equally well preserved are instructions of another type, intended for the ambassadors responsible for carrying a letter probably in 785 from Charlemagne to Pope Hadrian I: it even contained the terms to be used.

The ambassadors were generally responsible for carrying a letter from their masters to another head of state. Almost all the mentions of ambassadors sent or received, that have been preserved in narrative sources for the period under discussion, make note of the delivery of a similar letter. After this delivery, views on the subject treated could be exchanged between the envoys on the one side, the head of the state and his councilors on the other; and probably most often they were.

When the ambassadors were dismissed, they were generally given a letter for their master or, if the case arose, a draft for a treaty; sometimes they were accompanied or followed by ambassadors of the chief of state they had visited. The practices that have just been described were followed, for example, by Charlemagne and the Byzantine emperors during the negotiations pursued from 802 to 814 concerning recognition by Byzantium of the imperial title taken by the King of the Franks. But this was also a very general practice. Some of these imperial or royal letters, delivered by ambassadors, have come down to us, sometimes even in the original. Most of them were not intended for publication; but there is in some of them a certain degree of openness that allows us to suspect that they were intended to be made public. This is believed to be the case with the celebrated reply that the Emperor Louis II made in 871 to the Byzantine Emperor Basil I, who was contesting his right to the imperial title. His master's letter was not the only thing that the ambassador had to deliver to the sovereign to whom he had been sent. The delivery of gifts followed. Once again this was widely practiced. Gifts could have either an honorific or a symbolic character, such as the keys of the "confession" of Saint Peter sent to Charles Martel by Pope Gregory III in 739, or the keys of the Holy Sepulcher received by Charlemagne from the Patriarch of Jerusalem in 800. But the majority of them were exceedingly valuable. They could also differ in type. In 797 and 798, Alphonse II the Chaste, king of the small Christian realm of Asturias, which had won its independence in the north of Spain, through his ambassadors offered Charlemagne a tent, defensive arms, mules, and Moorish slaves, all booty taken from the Moslems in Spain. Among other sumptuous presents, Haroun-al-Raschid in 802 sent Charlemagne an elephant and in 807 a magnificent clock. When sources report that the ambassadors, their missions completed, had been honorably dismissed, it is assumed that they, too, had been given gifts for their masters and themselves. The exchange of these presents had a real importance: they signified the intention to live in peace and friendship. This notion of peace and friendship was essential. More than once, contemporary accounts assign to embassies no other purpose than to confirm the state of peace and friendship between two powers; which of course did not prevent the ambassadors from discussing more precise objectives.

The reception of embassies was always and everywhere accompanied by ceremony. At Constantinople the usages of the old Roman Empire were still more complex: a prescribed etiquette governed all the details. Though different, the etiquette was no less demanding at the court of the Caliph. Everywhere the intention was to impress the ambassadors, and through them, their master. Moreover, to impress the sovereign to whom the mission was accredited, the *basileis*, the caliphs, and other Moslem potentates had their envoys magnificently equipped and followed by a numerous retinue. There is less information about how things were done in the western realms, but identical factors must have produced analogous effects. It is known that even the last Merovingians, who had lost the realities of power, still themselves received foreign envoys so that the latter would be impressed by the majesty inherent in royalty. Einhard, Charlemagne's biographer, records that when the Emperor received a foreign ambassador, his accoutrements were noticeably more magnificent than usual. The same could certainly be said about other Carolingians.

The persons of the ambassadors were inviolate equally at Byzantium, at the court of the Caliph, and in the western kingdoms. Actually there were breaches of this rule, but they do not seem to have been very numerous. Missions abroad were certainly full of danger, particularly in periods when war or piracy made travel difficult. Account must be taken of the physical difficulties of the journey and the harshness of certain climates: for example, that of Iraq or North Africa for the Austrasians. Ambassadors sent to distant places sometimes remained abroad for years: Isaac the Jew, the only survivor of the embassy sent by Charlemagne to Baghdad in 797 did not return until 801. Sometimes envoys were detained for months in countries to which they had been sent, either because there was a delay in making up a retinue for their return journey, or because travel routes were unsure. It was thus that Charles the Bald delayed the embassy of the Emir of Cordova for a lengthy period at Senlis in 863 and 864 while waiting for conditions that would allow it to return to Spain. Ambassadors returning home made reports on their missions. These were probably verbal in many cases, except in Byzantium where it is evident that they were written.

There were times when negotiations were undertaken in conditions very different to those just described: conferences were held between the same number of envoys sent by two different parties, meeting at a frontier. This in fact was the case in 811, when Charlemagne and Hemming, king of Denmark, intended to make peace with each other. A dozen well-born Franks and a dozen well-born Danes met on the Eider in order to negotiate and conclude this peace. The success of these meetings at the frontier lasted several centuries.

Whether conducted by the heads of state themselves or by ambassadors, negotiations could be pursued and were often brought to successful conclusions. A treaty might be concluded. Among the latter a particular place deserves to be reserved for alliances or for other understandings concluded with a similar aim. The manner in which they were concluded sometimes revealed the personal traits of certain groups of people or of certain types of civilization. In this regard, one recognizes in most of the kingdoms founded by the Germanic peoples in Occidental Europe the influence of this patrimonial conception of power and the absence of the abstract notion of the state, which we have already treated. This helps us to understand why agreements so often were, so to speak, cast in molds borrowed from family life.

When at the end of the fifth century Theodoric, the king of the Ostrogoths, tried to establish in the West an entente of Germanic kingdoms, or of those founded by Germanic peoples, he was clearly practicing, as we have seen, a matrimonial policy. The same policy was followed in 567 when Sigebert, king of Austrasia, and Chilperic, king of Neustria, attempted a rapprochement with Athanagild, king of the Visigoths, by marrying his two daughters, Brunehaut and Galsvinthe. Other examples of this procedure and concept could be cited. Perhaps there was some thought of resolving the Franco-Byzantine crisis brought on by the coronation of the year 800, by arranging a marriage between Charlemagne and the Empress Irene, who then occupied the Byzantine throne. If this project actually existed, it was in no way realized since Irene was overthrown in 802. Adoption, another procedure of a "family" character, was employed for the same end, when in 577 Gontran, king of Burgundy, concluded an alliance with his nephew Childebert II, king of Austrasia. He adopted him as a son; and when, about 735, Charles Martel wished to make an ally of Liutprand, king of the Lombards, he sent him his son, the future King Pepin, so that Liutprand could adopt him.

The recourse to marriage in order to make an alliance with a sovereign or foreign people was not unknown at Byzantium: the emperors Justinian II in the seventh century and Constantine V in the eighth century married Khazar princesses. Adoption was also practiced there in connection with the chiefs of "barbarian" peoples. Among other methods of a very different type, use was made, as in the Roman tradition, of the granting of honorific titles. In 508 the Emperor Anastasius named Clovis consul, and Justinian awarded the dignity of silentiary or patrician to the potentates of the Lazes—an Iranian people settled at the edge of the Caucasus—and to Arab chieftains. The system remained constant, and at the end of the eighth century, in 787, the Lombard Duke of Benevento was created patrician on the occasion of the conclusion of an agreement directed against Charlemagne. Another method used at Byzantium to bind "barbarian" peoples was the payment of subsidies, which, despite its resources and its sound financial organization, represented a heavy charge on the empire. These payments were made largely in favor of the princes and tribes of the East, but some western peoples benefited also—especially the Franks—in the period when Byzantium was trying to reconquer or defend her positions in Italy. In 535 Justinian bought the military cooperation of the Frankish kings against the Ostrogoths, but the Franks actually fought against his own troops. In 584 the Emperor Maurice paid 50,000 gold *solidi* for the alliance of Childebert II of Austrasia against the Lombards, an alliance honored by useless expeditions in Italy. Some sovereigns of western states, financially stronger than others, tried to practice the same system: Sisenand, the fortunate claimant to the throne of the Spanish Visigothic kingdom, paid 200,000 gold *solidi* in 631 for the alliance of Dagobert I, King of the Franks.

The alliances constitute only one group among agreements that negotiations brought to a conclusion. Contemporary sources have preserved the record of an abundant series of agreements concluded in the period studied in this chapter: accords putting an end to differences, proper peace treaties, agreements on divisions, etc. We even possess the texts of some of them, either whole or in part. These agreements, as a general rule, gave way to the drawing up of writs; and these were probably provided in as many copies as there were parties, and, as necessary, in the language of each party. The provisions included in those copies were parallel, but not necessarily identical. We know that this was the case for treaties drawn up between Byzantium and the Caliph or other Moslem potentates; it was the same for agreements between Byzantium and the western empire. When in 812 the Emperor Michael III recognized through ambassadors sent to Aachen the imperial dignity of Charlemagne, he received from the Carolingian monarch the text of the treaty stating the agreement set up; other Byzantine ambassadors in 814 brought Louis the Pious a copy of the text that had been destined for his father, evidently complete with the marks of validation in use at Byzantium (doubtless a "bull," or gold seal). There is some doubt that in the West the constitutive power of written enactments—*scriptum pacti*—was recognized. The essential act of settlement was a verbal declaration, together with some gesture: in 812 at Aachen the Byzantine ambassadors pronounced in honor of Charlemagne the ritual "laud" (*landes*) which were drawn up in Greek and named him as *autocrator* and *basileus*—that is to say, emperor; these "lauds" were certainly accompanied by prostrations as the text was considered in the West as having only probative power. A similar event had occurred thirty-eight years previously, in 774, in Rome, when Charlemagne had confirmed, while considerably extending it, the donation of the territories of the exarchate his father had made to the Church of Rome; it was not the document drawn up for this occasion that constituted the constitutive act, but the depositing of this document on the "confession" of Saint Peter. True, agreements were drawn up without any written text when they concerned people who scarcely used the written word: such, for example, were the many agreements, normally broken in

a very short time, that were drawn up in the ninth century between the Frankish kings or the Anglo-Saxon kings and the
Normans, i.e., the Danish or sometimes Norwegian invaders in
England. However, we cannot generalize, for we possess the text
of a treaty, most probably dating from 886, that determined the
frontier between the independent sector of England governed by
Alfred the Great and the eastern territories under Danish domination.

Among the treaties that we know best are those drawn up
between the Carolingian sovereigns. We even know how two of
them were prepared: that of Verdun, which in 843 provided for
the division of the empire among the three surviving sons of Louis
the Pious; and that of Meersen which in 870 provided for the
division of the realm of Lothair II between his two uncles, Louis
the German and Charles the Bald. In both cases numerous com-
missioners, designated by the parties and meeting in conference,
established a list of the counties, bishoprics, abbeys, chapters, and
royal domains situated within the territories to be divided, and
attempted to prepare equivalent shares: equivalent in regard to
revenues and equivalent in regard to the amount of lucrative
offices (*honores*) and benefices that could be distributed among
the aristocracy. These shares made up the basis of divisions.
Other agreements between Carolingian sovereigns which resulted
from conferences which have already been mentioned above, were
followed by proclamations (*adnuntiatio*) made by each of the
sovereigns. They constituted for each of the realms the promulga-
tions of decisions taken jointly, and conferred an obligatory
character on them. The articles agreed upon in common and the
proclamations were signed in writing.

Often, efforts were made to provide the concluded agreements
with guarantees of execution. Two systems were particularly
used: the provision of hostages and the exchange of oaths. One
comes across very many cases; there is thus no point in providing
examples. In regard to oaths, it will be noticed that they were

sometimes given not only by the contracting parties or by their representatives, but by the important persons in their entourage. In 842, in one especially serious situation, after the conclusion at Strasbourg of the alliance between Louis the German and Charles the Bald against Lothair, not only did the two kings take the oath, but their armies also did. There is little need to recall that each of the kings took the oath in the language of the people under his brother's sway, and that the warriors took the oath in their own language, those of Louis in German dialects and those of Charles in Romance dialects. The warriors plighted themselves to abandon their leaders if the latter did not honor their oaths.

We should give special attention to a group of treaties drawn up by the Doge and the inhabitants of Venetia (Rialto, i.e., Venice, Torcello, etc.) with the people of the neighboring regions of Italy who acted under the authority or with the authorization of either the Emperor or the King of Italy. The oldest extant treaty dates from 840. It was drawn up at Pavia in the name of Lothair I. It appears to be linked up with earlier agreements that were lost, of which the first dates at least from the reign of Liutprand, i.e., the middle of the eighth century. Intended, among other things, to eliminate a series of possible conflicts and to weld good relations between neighbors, these treaties confirmed essential dispositions dealing with commerce: they guaranteed the freedom of trade and movement within the territories and waterways of the two parties; they forbade the levying of new duties on navigation and on circulation, they drew up measures against the subjugation of Italians in slavery (a very real danger on account of the slave trade practiced by the Venetians), and regulated Venetian logging in forests within the Italian territories that bordered the lagoon (an important activity for a people for whom shipbuilding was a regular activity). In 841 the agreement of 840 was completed by an imperial document guaranteeing Venetian property in the kingdom of Italy. Both these two agreements concluded as a result of negotiations were confirmed several times in the ninth and tenth centuries. No document has survived for any other western European regions that could approach this former one. This is hardly surprising. Venice, because of its regular relations with Byzantium, and, to a lesser degree, Italy proper shared in a civilization of a higher level than that of the countries north of the Alps. Nevertheless it is known that negotiations must have been undertaken by the Frankish and Anglo-Saxon sovereigns concerning the northwest trade of Francia with England. There was an important one between Charlemagne and Offa, the king of Mercia, who exercised a hegemony over the other English kingdoms, when, after a quarrel that led to the prohibiton of trade (790), commercial relations had to be re-established. The negotiator was Gervold, abbot of Saint Wandrille, who was responsible for checking the customs dues of the Frankish Channel ports.

One of the problems raised by the history of international relations for the period we are studying lies in the hierarchy of relations among political units. Thus the great powers—the Byzantine Empire, the caliphate, and the Frankish monarchy—had at certain periods exercised a more or less actual authority over states or foreign peoples. We term this a "protectorate," freely acknowledging that it is a vague term, on account of the great diversity that is to be found in the status of these peoples and states. This status could, in fact, run from effective subordination to a purely theoretical recognition of supremacy.

One of the indications of inferior status was the payment of tribute. The Frankish kings, like many others, certainly subscribed to this concept. It is enough to cite the annual tribute of five hundred cows that Clothair imposed in 556–557 on the Saxons whom he had subdued—a tribute that Dagobert I excused them from in 632–633, because they had promised to defend the eastern frontiers of the *Regnum Francorum* against the Slavic tribes of the Wends. Pepin III reimposed the tribute in 747, after having repressed an aggression by those Saxons. Other examples could be cited for the Carolingian epoch: for example, the tribute that Charlemagne required from the Lombard Duke of Benevento. In each case the tribute constituted a recognition of Frankish supremacy over territories that in fact remained independent. The Byzantine Empire had to the same extent drawn tributes from the principalities and peoples that bordered its frontiers.

Tributes were always a burden for those who paid them, and often a humiliation; but they did not necessarily imply a recognition of supremacy. Brunehaut, the queen mother of Austrasia, paid tribute to the Avars in 596 so they would evacuate Thuringia, which they had invaded. In 593 Pope Gregory the Great bought the departure of the Lombards, who were beseiging Rome, by promising that imperial Italy would pay an annual tribute of 500 pounds of gold; in 877 Pope John VIII had to pledge himself to pay the Saracens an annual tribute of 25,000 mangons; and during the ninth and tenth centuries the Venetian duchy used to pay an annual tribute to the King of Italy. Charles the Bald and his successors to the throne of *Francia occidentalis* on several occasions bought off the Normans by paying them a tribute. The Byzantine Empire frequently paid tribute to the Avars and the Caliph. In none of these cases would the subject power admit that it was dependent on the other, despite the different interpretation that could have been current within such a country.

Whatever their actual basis—conquest, agreement, partial franchisement, etc.—bonds of dependency with a political entity under protection could be created, renewed, or maintained by various legal acts. Among those most frequently used was the oath of fidelity taken by the head of the political entity under protection and sometimes by all or part of the population. The Frankish sovereigns demanded oaths from the Slavic chiefs— Moravians, Croatians, and others—in Dalmatia and in the Danubian countries. Many other examples could easily be cited. When Lothair I attempted in 824 to set up a protectorate over the Papal State and in particular over Rome with the same effectiveness previously demonstrated by Charlemagne's authority, not only did he impose an oath of fidelity on the Pope-elect before the latter could be consecrated, but he also made an oath of fidelity to the Emperor obligatory to all Romans. In certain cases more was required than a simple oath of fidelity: the heads of bands of Danes established in Frisia and in control of groups of counties were admitted by Louis the Pious, Lothair I, Charles the Bald, and Charles the Fat as vassals, and territorial authority was conceded to them in benefice. It is possible that the Frankish sovereigns acted in the same way toward certain Slavic chiefs. As far as Byzantium is concerned, the heads of populations or territories under protection had to receive the confirmation of their power or the gift of a dignity from the Emperor—letting them enter the administrative or palatine hierarchy by means of investiture with an honorific title. The latter was organized by the reception or bestowal of insignia: clothing, weapons, and crowns, etc. Similar practices seemed to have existed in the caliphate.

It is hardly possible to question that in the course of the period there was frequently great uncertainty on the subject of frontiers, and that in certain cases these assumed the character of a zone rather than that of linear delimitation. But the existence of the notion of frontiers is not to be doubted. In the Byzantine Empire this notion kept the clarity that it had in Roman public law. In the Frankish monarchy in the eighth and ninth centuries it also constituted a notion that played a role in matters of administration and policy. The Byzantine Empire drew upon personnel, subordinate to the "logothete of the dromos," which guaranteed police surveillance of the frontiers. Also there were customs officers supervising import and export duties, at least in the major ports. Customs duties on the traffic of goods also existed elsewhere, just as much in the interior of the empire as at its boundaries. The situation with the Frankish monarchy during the Carolingian epoch was similar enough; but it was, of course, infinitely less regular, and there must have been much less efficiency. An imperial ordinance, a capitulary, of 805 shows us the organization, from the lower reaches of the Elbe to the mouth of the Enns in the Danube, of the frontier zones commanded by counts under whose orders control bureaus functioned, at various obligatory crossing points. Among such were Magdeburg, Regensburg, and Lorch. This control was exercised over all trade with the north, the east, and the southeast. It is not known whether a customs service existed at these same posts; it is probable, but in every case the essential aim was of a police nature. It was specifically a question of preventing trading in arms. We do not know what all this led to. It would seem that in the Frankish monarchy no clear distinction was made between the duties collected on the passage of goods at the frontier and those collected in the interior on the same traffic or at the market. All had the same name: *teloneum*. However, a very special importance was connected to certain of these offices: those established in ports through which a major trade flowed, such as Quentowic, on the Channel, and Duurstede, at the mouth of the lower Rhine. Important also were the offices set up at the passes where the principal routes led into Italy. Thus a fiscal frontier apparently existed between the *Regnum Francorum* and this kingdom even under Charlemagne and Louis the Pious. At these posts a 10 per cent *ad valorem* tax was imposed. Agents with special powers were charged with checking the enforcement of duties at Quentowic and in the other ports opposite England. Though this function disappeared quickly enough, the taxes continued to be levied, at least when wars, troubles, and piracy were not disrupting traffic or ruining the ports.

At this point some mention must be made of foreigners. Naturally the regime to which they were subjected differed from country to country. In certain territories that had formerly belonged to the Roman Empire, a favorable attitude existed toward foreigners who resided permanently or for a long time. There were corporate groups (*schola*) who had their own leaders and insignia. The origin of these *scholae* was probably Roman. However, before the breakup of the empire, their members were not foreigners but inhabitants from other regions speaking another language, with their own customs, and sometimes of a different religion. Such was the case in western countries under imperial authority, especially in Byzantine Italy. *Scholae* of foreigners had continued to exist at Rome: it seems that in the eighth and ninth centuries *scholae* of Jews, of Greeks, of Saxons (from England), of Frisians, of Franks, and of Lombards were known.

On the other hand, the usual status of foreigners in the Frankish or the Lombard realms and in the Anglo-Saxon kingdoms carried no rights. To acquire some security, a foreigner had to obtain the protection, the *mundeburdis*, of some leading person, whose national law he adopted, and who would answer for his acts. In default of this personal protection, royal protection could be sought, and in the Frankish monarchy this was general and subsidiary, at least under the Carolingians. Some foreigners received special royal protection—*mundeburdis*. They received a document stating the bestowal of this privilege. They were under the jurisdiction of the palace tribunal. Among these foreigners were merchants. This *mundeburdis* could be effective. In contrast, the general protection afforded to strangers or to inhabitants of other regions of the same extensive state, speaking another language than that of the place where they found themselves, was without any doubt often illusory. With the Frankish monarchy under Charlemagne, cases of strangers to the kingdom or the region—at least poor strangers—being reduced to slavery cannot have been rare. Specific laws were enacted to combat these abuses.

The conditions of the Jews varied. Under the Frankish monarchy they benefited from the protection of the laws; under the Carolingians this protection, which probably left, in fact, something to be desired, was made more effective for many of the Jews when they obtained the status of "Jew protected by the King." This status was doubtless restricted to wealthy Jews. Conflicts between Jews were settled according to their own law.

Pilgrims made up a very important group of foreigners; the sovereigns and the Church concerned themselves with protecting, among others, the numerous Irish and English pilgrims (*peregrinus*) who came to Rome. Charters recommended them to authorities and to subjects; actual passports, called *tractoria*, could be given to them by the heads of state or by the ecclesiastical authorities. The Carolingian sovereigns charged everyone to offer them hospitality; they freed their luggage from duties on the traffic of goods; and in Italy they attempted to set up "hospices" (Xenodochium) where pilgrims could be sheltered. Even at Rome similar hospices also existed; the most famous in the eighth and ninth centuries was that of the Saxons (the English), which comprised, near Saint Peter's, a church and a burial ground. Pilgrimages, however, gave rise to grave abuses: a lot of monks roamed like vagabonds to escape the demands of their rule, merchants donned the garb of pilgrims to benefit from their privileges, and in the eighth century Boniface was angered to see pilgrimages of English women to guarantee an abundant recruitment for prostitution in the Frankish monarchy and in Italy.

4

The West:
From the Breakup of the Carolingian Empire
to the First Triumph of the Papacy

THE PERIOD that in 887 opens the final dismemberment of the Carolingian Empire was marked in western Europe by an extremely far-reaching political fragmentation. Eastern Francia, or Germany, extended from the Rhine, which it overstepped toward the West in its middle course, to the Elbe, the Saale and the Danube in the East. Almost all of its inhabitants spoke the Germanic dialects. Western Francia, or France, stretched from the Scheldt and from the approaches of the upper Meuse, the Saône and the Rhône, to the Mediterranean, to the south of Barcelona and to the Atlantic Ocean. The great majority of its inhabitants spoke the Romance dialects. Between them were the fragments of the former state of Lothair: Lotharingia, which was to be incorporated into Germany in 925; the kingdom of transjuranian Burgundy, between the Saône, the Aar and the Rhône, created in 888; and the kingdom of cisjuranian Burgundy, or Provence, created in 879 and reconstituted in 888. These two were to be united in 933. Lotharingia and transjuranian Burgundy were of mixed population, while Provence was exclusively Romance. In the south the Italian peninsula consisted of the kingdom of Italy, the Papal State, some independent "Lombard" principalities (Benevento, Capua, Salerno), the Byzantine territories of the extreme south, and those of Naples, Amalfi, and Venice. Beyond the Pyrenees, Christian Spain, as yet embryonic, was founded: a little kingdom of Navarre on the upper reaches of the Ebro; farther west, in the mountains of Asturias, a kingdom that came into existence in the eighth century, which spread south, and whose capital in the middle of the tenth century was León. Navarre and Asturo-León were constantly at war with the Saracens.

This was, however, only the first stage of fragmentation. In France, in Germany, in the kingdoms of Burgundy and of Italy, the territorial wielders of power, the counts, and, above all, those who commanded greater areas of land, the dukes or marquises, tended to make themselves autonomous princes thanks to the dynastic wars and the foreign invasions of the second half of the ninth century. Though the phenomenon was general, it had neither the same scope nor the same trend throughout. This movement developed most effectively in France. From the beginning of the tenth century a relatively large body of princes ruled a great part of the country and were bound to the Crown only by tenuous bonds: the Count of Flanders, the Count of Vermandois, the Duke of Aquitaine, the Duke of Burgundy, etc. The movement was to continue, giving birth to new principalities, until the third quarter of the century. The realms of Burgundy-Provence and of Italy experienced a similar development. In Germany the movement affected only part of the country, and it came to a head in the creation of several autonomous duchies with ethnic bases— Saxony, Swabia, and Bavaria—but the sovereigns succeeded before the end of the century in limiting this autonomy and in many cases keeping the counts and even the marquises under their authority. The formation of principalities and of duchies constituted a second stage of fragmentation.

A third stage was brought about in the interior of the principalities and duchies, as in the interior of territories that remained directly subject to the king: it consisted of the creation of autonomous seigneuries. Lay and ecclesiastical lords extended and developed police and lower court powers, which they exercised over the inhabitants of their domains, and succeeded in imposing these accrued powers on the inhabitants of lands not belonging to them. The strength and importance of these seigneuries varied greatly. This third stage of fragmentation was less developed in Germany than in France and, in these countries, less highly developed in certain principalities (such as Flanders and Normandy) than in others.

In the history of international relations, principalities, from the tenth century on, played as major a role as the kingdoms; the same observation could be made, but to a smaller degree, of certain seigneuries.

When grouped under terms such as "feudalism" or "feudal regime," the phenomena of the disintegration of sovereignty just discussed are sometimes connected with the spread of feudalvassalic relations and of "benefices." The great diffusion of these relations among the aristocracy of the continental countries of western Europe, at the end of the ninth century and in the tenth and eleventh centuries, is an incontestable fact; and the terms "feudalism" and "feudal system" should be reserved for these relationships, generalized and formed into a coherent system. The names "homage" and "fealty" have been given to two acts that created the bonds of vassalage: the act of the vassal placing his joined hands between those of his lord, and the oath of fealty that he swore to him. The granting of a special tenure by the lord to a vassal in order to provide him with maintenance tended to become a very widespread practice (which had exceptions); increasingly this tenure was termed "fief," though sometimes it was still called "benefice"; it became progressively hereditary.

The fief was conveyed to the vassal in a legally valid manner, in a ceremony termed "investiture," which consisted of presenting the vassal with an object symbolizing the fief. The fief could, moreover, be incorporeal, consisting of a number of rights or an annual income, etc. If the lord owed protection and support to his vassal, the latter always owed service to his lord; and this service, generally, was, above all, mounted military service. From the last years of the ninth century the practice of becoming a vassal of several lords, in order to obtain a greater number of fiefs, progressively spread. To establish a hierarchy among these lords, a "liege lord" was given pre-eminence. It was necessary to serve him before any other lord; but this remedy was scarcely effective.

Feudal-vassalic relations favored the disintegration of sovereignty by assuring a rebellious duke, marquis, or count the support of his own vassals. But these relations, above all, had some positive results: they prevented the total breakup of the states of western Europe; the fact that the territorial princes, the dukes, and many lords had been and remained vassals of the king, set some bounds to the disintegration of sovereignty; and the fact that in the duchies and principalities a number of lords had been the vassals of dukes and princes had similar consequences.

It would be difficult to understand the transformations that came about in tenth- and eleventh-century western Europe unless one took into account a very important phenomenon: the progressive elimination of the disruptive harassments brought on by the incursions of peoples from Asia or Scandinavia. At the beginning of the tenth century the Norman peril was, at least for a time, warded off in England; it was also in France in 911, at the cost of setting up a settlement for a group of Danes on the lower Seine: this settlement was to become one of the strongest territorial principalities of the kingdom, Normandy. From 895 and 896 on, Asiatic horsemen, herdsmen, and plunderers, related to the Turks—the Magyars, or Hungarians—dominated the plain of the middle Danube; they launched devastating raids toward the west, particularly into Germany and Italy. The King of Germany, Otto I, defeated them at the Lechfeld, near Augsburg, in 955, and the Hungarian people then settled down. A better organized resistance made it difficult for the Slavs to invade German territory. The Saracens were victoriously fought off in southern Italy and were expelled from Provence probably in 972; in the eleventh century Genoa and Pisa were to fight against them successfully in the western Mediterranean.

The great event in the history of international relations in the tenth century was the re-establishment of the empire in the West. Germany was the basis. Less damaged than other countries by the phenomenon of fragmentation, the German kingdom had been consolidated by the kings of the house of Saxony; the structure of the state was, in its broad outlines, that of the Carolingian state, and the Church, thanks to an adequate organization, had become a powerful instrument of government in the hands of the sovereign: one calls her rightly the imperial Church. But King Otto I (936–937), influenced by Carolingian traditions and by other, essentially German factors, turned his attention toward Italy, which was in the grip of wars between local dynasties that sustained anarchy. He intervened there and proclaimed himself king in 951.

Thus began the personal union between Germany and the kingdom of Italy that was to last for centuries. This was only the first stage. At Rome the papacy, reduced to a plaything for the aristocratic factions and deprived of its moral authority, in a moment of distress made an appeal to Otto I. The latter, again in the Carolingian tradition, was crowned in the Eternal City in 962. This new personal union, this time between Germany and the empire, was to persist: with this one reservation, however, that the imperial dignity would, until the beginning of the sixteenth century, be acquired only by a coronation conducted at Rome by the Pope. The *Römerzug*—that is, the necessary expedition to Rome and the personal duties of the emperor and his relations with the papacy—accentuated the current which was to draw the German sovereigns into the labyrinth of Italian and pontifical affairs, and to deflect in this direction a great part of German energies. Owing to the relative stability of his power in Germany, Otto I was even able to intervene in states neighboring his own, in the kingdom of Burgundy and even in France, where he arbitrated conflicts between the last Carolingian kings and the territorial princes between the Seine and the Loire, particularly the Duke of Francia.

He was even able to undertake the conquest of Slavic lands to the east of the Elbe. As he lacked a sufficient surplus of disposable population in the interior, the conquest could not be accompanied by colonization: Otto's accomplishments, like those of the evangelization that went along with it, were insubstantial. Farther south, on the other hand, the victory over the Hungarians allowed Otto to reoccupy and to extend the east march of Bavaria: Austria emerged. In the Slavic duchies that were set up in Bohemia and, much farther east, in Poland, Otto I encouraged evangelization and obliged the dukes to recognize his superior authority. These political successes were ephemeral, but the influence of the German Church in Bohemia remained a reality.

This expansive political and religious action beyond the borders, it should be noted, in part occurred before the re-establishment of the empire, and was in every case entirely foreign to it. Otto, king of the Germans, had been able to carry out this policy because he possessed the "means of power" to make it possible; and the prime factors that inspired him were the traditions of the Carolingian sovereigns, his predecessors, and of the dukes of Saxony, his ancestors. The imperial dignity was, above all, an "exaltation" of his royal power.

The conception of empire was transformed under his immediate successors. His son, Otto II (973–983), husband of the Byzantine princess Theophano, placed the imperial dignity much higher than his German royal power; he attempted, in southern Italy, to give an effective character to the rights that he believed pertained to his eminent title. There was a total setback, which brought on a disaster: the Slavs, believing Germany to be stripped of military forces, recaptured the greater part of the transelbe marches and wiped out Christianity in them. Otto III (983–1002) went much farther than his father. He returned to the purely clerical and supranational concept of empire, the reason for the existence of which was the protection of the Church and the extension of its authority throughout the world. Germany was only one of the

kingdoms subject to his universal authority: consequently he
approved quite naturally when the Pope, in the year 1000, gave a
royal crown to Stephen, duke of Hungary, and prepared the way
for the organization of a Hungarian Church exempt from the
influence of German missionaries; he himself was instrumental in
the creation of an episcopal hierarchy indigenous to Poland,
where the influence of the imperial Church could thereafter be
only feebly exercised. Installed at Rome since 999 at the side of
Pope Sylvester II (the monk Gerbert), the most learned man of his
time, Otto believed, along with Sylvester, that he should rebuild a
western Christian Roman empire, such as had existed in the
fourth century: a counterpart to the eastern Roman empire of
Byzantium. This house of cards collapsed following a Roman
uprising in 1001. Opposed to this impractical dream was the more
realistic policy of the last sovereign of the house of Saxony,
Henry II (died 1024), and of the first two sovereigns of the
Salian dynasty, Conrad II (died 1039) and Henry III (died 1056).
Certainly each of them had himself crowned emperor. But, with
exception of the last, they scarcely occupied themselves with
Roman affairs. Their essential preoccupation lay in maintaining
strong loyal authority in Germany and in Italy against the
autonomistic tendencies of the dukes, the marquises, and the
counts. They reinforced the imperial Church in this plan. They
succeeded in holding on to the marches to the east of the
Saale, whose Christianization and Germanization continued.
Poland, which was elevated to kingdom in 1025, and Bohemia
became vassals of Germany under Conrad II. It was also Conrad
II who, in 1033, succeeded in linking the royal crown of Burgundy to the crowns of Germany and Italy. This personal union
was to last also; but the authority of the German sovereigns was
even less strong in this new realm than in Italy. At Rome, since the
Renovatio of Otto III and Sylvester II had come to nothing, the
papacy, always lacking material protection, once more became
the plaything of the noble families, and its moral level sank to a

new depth. In 1046, Henry III deposed the three popes who dis-
puted among themselves; he replaced them by a German bishop:
the papacy was incorporated into the imperial Church, and the
authority of the emperor seemed to have taken an effective and
permanent character in the capital of western Christianity and in
the Church State.

How can we appraise the restoration of the empire in the West
by Otto I and the place that the restored empire took in Europe in
the tenth and eleventh centuries? The empire of Charlemagne and
of Louis the Pious included neither England nor Christian Spain,
and its structure was very different from that of the *partes
occidentis* of the empire in the fourth century. However, there
once again existed a restoration of the unity of the Christian
West. As much could no longer be said of the empire of the
Saxons and the Salians. To begin with, it lacked not only England
and Christian Spain but also France, to say nothing of Ireland
and Scotland. Also the three realms the emperors ruled—Germany, Italy, and Burgundy—were subject to them only as the
emperors were kings of each of them, not because they were
emperors. And as for the hegemony that Otto I exercised beyond
his frontiers, it was foreign to the imperial dignity, often antedat-
ing the time when he claimed it; it is explained by the power at his
disposal as sovereign of Germany, and as much could be said for
the state of affairs that existed in the reign of Conrad II. What,
then, was the positive content of the imperial dignity? On the one
hand, political authority in Rome, in the pontifical state, and over
the southern Italian principalities: an authority, moreover, that
was only intermittently effective, when the emperors or their
representatives were present with an army and had the means of
imposing it. On the other hand, there was the power that guaranteed to the Emperor in his role as protector of the Church, chosen
by God, in order to take measures for the good of the Church
and, in particular, to ensure that the seat of Saint Peter would be
occupied properly by a pontiff worthy of this holy ministry.

Herein lay an authority that was real and whose effects, because
of the universal character of the Church, could make themselves
felt outside the three realms governed by the emperor. However,
along with their power, the emperors had claims whose echoes are
found in the entirely clerical literature of the period. Without even
taking into account Otto III's dreams, it can be admitted that they
considered their authority as universal; and, moreover, such was
the tradition. This must be understood. In certain respects this
universalism amounted to an affirmation vis-à-vis Byzantium that
the western emperor was the equal of the *basileus*. It did not
imply, in the tenth and the eleventh centuries, a claim to command other kings, but it did imply a conviction that the emperor
had a pre-eminence over these kings; and this conviction was
fairly widespread, at least in Germany and even in Italy.

One fact in any case is certain: the kings of France never
admitted to any subordination in their relations with the emperor;
in the period under survey they did not even show any regard for
the imperial pre-eminence. However, France was politically virtually powerless. The greater part of the tenth century was
occupied by armed conflicts between the last Carolingians and the
"Robertinian" dukes of Francia—a war that permitted the territorial princes to extend their autonomy, while some of their
vassals succeeded in promoting themselves to the rank of princes,
such as the counts of Anjou and those of Blois. In 987, thanks to
the support of Theophano, regent for the young Otto III, worried
about the tenacious claims of the French Carolingians on Lotharingia, Hugh Capet, duke of Francia, mounted the throne. Neither
he nor his descendants and successors—the "Capetians," Robert
II (996–1031), Henry I (died 1060), Philip I (died 1108)—had
the means to play an effective role in European politics. Only
Henry I tried, by devious ways and, moreover, without success, to
seize part of Lotharingia. By contrast, it was more usual to see the
French territorial princes, sometimes more powerful than the king,
trying to extend their power beyond their frontiers. Eudes II,

count of Blois, Chartres, Tours, and Troyes, tried in opposition to Conrad II to appropriate for himself successively the kingdoms of Burgundy and of Italy, as well as Lotharingia. He lost his life there in 1037. Baldwin IV and Baldwin V, counts of Flanders, on the contrary, succeeded from 1006 to 1056 in wresting the western fringe of Lotharingia from the German sovereigns and their vassals; they agreed to hold it, moreover, as a fief of the German crown. This was to become "imperial Flanders." The most remarkable event in this respect, however, and one whose consequences were the greatest, was to be the conquest of England by a French territorial prince, the Duke of Normandy.

It is important to look back if we are to understand and grasp the importance of this event. In the middle of the tenth century, the successors of Alfred the Great had rebuilt English unity. In their reigns England was in fact a country forming a bridge between western Europe and the northern world. To western Europe, especially to France and to Germany, she was united by bonds of all kinds, principally spiritual. To cite a single example, Saint Dunstan—who in the middle of the century reorganized monastic life and then directed the Church of England as Archbishop of Canterbury and, thanks to his influence on the sovereigns, also governed the state—spent some time in Flanders and there was strongly influenced by the groups that were attempting to reform religious life. On the other hand, England's foreign trade and the regular relations that the inhabitants of the eastern regions, partly Danish, maintained with Scandinavia, linked England to the northern world. This kinship to the northern world was going to be accentuated at the end of the tenth and at the beginning of the eleventh century.

These two centuries constitute, indeed, a new phase in Scandinavian expansion. Piracy had not disappeared, but commercial navigation, distant maritime expeditions, and the creation of new settlements and conquests played a major role. The Norwegians, leaving from their own coast or from Iceland, where they had settled at the end of the ninth century, reached Greenland in the tenth and "Vinland," probably the northeastern part of the present United States, in the eleventh century. The Danes created new settlements on the southern shore of the Baltic, which allowed them to trade with the Slavic world and its hinterland. From the middle of the tenth century on, the Danish monarchy was considerably strengthened, while at the same time Christianity spread through the country. Perhaps rebel elements in this new state of affairs were encouraged to take advantage of the troubled situation that rivalries between the *ealdormen,* or the earls—the leaders of powerful governments—had created in England in the last thirty years of the century. Their first expeditions soon gave way to conquests organized by the King himself. In 1016 England was conquered and incorporated into the vast Danish empire that King Canute the Great governed from 1018 to 1035, and into which he brought Norway in 1028, while the kings of Sweden, Scotland, and Ireland recognized his pre-eminence. More deeply and certainly more manifestly Christian than the other converted Viking chiefs, Canute the Great made the pilgrimage to Rome in 1027 and attended the imperial coronation of Conrad II: he was thus the first Scandinavian king to enter the circle of Christian sovereigns on equal footing. The northern world, an economic reality that had become a political entity, was on the eve of its amalgamation with the western world.

Indeed, very shortly after the death of Canute each one of these kingdoms again seized independence; and after a period of anarchy an English king, Edward the Confessor, was restored in 1042. The earls contended with one another for the realities of power and appealed for foreign support, Danish and Norwegian certainly, but also Norman. After the death of Edward in 1066, the Duke of Normandy, William—known as "the Conqueror"—contested the rights of the new king, Harold, and invaded the country at the head of an army of knights recruited in his duchy and from the whole of western France. Quickly enough he made himself master of England. But it took him all his reign—he died in 1087—to consolidate his authority.

As an event in the history of international relations the conquest was no less important than the re-establishment of the empire in the West. This is so because a vassal of the king of France, leader of a large and strong territorial principality, became king of a neighboring state—and of a state in which, on the one hand, the circumstances of the conquest and, on the other, the monetary economy made possible by its foreign trade, would permit him to organize the country much more solidly and efficiently than the states on the Continent. There were possible, if not probable, sources of conflict and factors capable of giving the conflicts certain directions. Then although the conquest did not put an end to commercial relations between England and the northern world, it nevertheless brought England entirely into the world of western Europe. The deep reversal that the invasion caused in the ruling circles strongly contributed to this development: the English aristocracy and senior clergy were to a great extent eliminated and replaced by a large aristocracy and by a clergy who were French in language and in customs and were accompanied by numerous *suites* with the same language and the same customs. From this was born a community of language, of customs, of a conception of life, and of frequent ties of kinship between ruling circles on both sides of the English Channel. It was also the conquest that introduced feudal-vassalic relations into England; these were placed, moreover, entirely in the royal service and were to play a major role, not only in the political and social structure of the country, but also in the international relations in which the nation became slowly involved.

Norman England, as had Saxon or Danish England, was going to set up working relations with other parts of Great Britain and with Ireland. This began almost immediately with an attempt to subdue the Celtic principalities of Wales. This enterprise was to take centuries. In regard to Scotland—whose unification was pursued from the tenth century on, and which had annexed Lothian (the northern part of Northumberland) at the beginning of the eleventh century—its relations with Norman England present a rather paradoxical picture. Scotland's kings, the ruling circles, and the whole of the southern part of the country had been profoundly exposed to southern influences in language, institutions, ecclesiastical organizations, and way of life. Nevertheless, the two countries were often at war and generally in a state of latent hostility, usually over contested lands. As for the Norwegian territories of the extreme north, it was only at the end of the eleventh century that the Scottish kings subdued them; the islands only came under their authority in the thirteenth and fifteenth centuries. Ireland, which had been unified at the beginning of the eleventh century under a national king, shortly after fell back into a state bordering on anarchy; petty kings and heads of clans fought wars when they were not seeking loot in England—before the Norman conquest—or elsewhere. The Norwegian or Danish colonies of the eastern ports appeared to have kept, with a certain autonomy, a large part of the foreign trade, especially with the English ports of the west.

England was not the only country conquered and reorganized by the Norman French; however, the other Norman creation, important to note at this point, proceeded not from ducal initiative, but from that taken by simple knights who had gone to seek spoils in Italy. During the eleventh century they placed themselves in the service of those who fought over the southern part of the peninsula, and they took advantage of this to carve out seigneuries for themselves. Most of them ended by being grouped under the authority of one of their number, Robert Guiscard. From 1060 to 1076 he added to them Byzantine territories, Lombard principalities, and the duchy of Amalfi, which had up to that time recognized the superior authority of Byzantium. This assemblage made up the Norman duchy of Apulia. Roger I, brother of Robert, with his help wrested Sicily from the hands of the deeply divided Saracens. It was left to the son of Roger I, Roger II, to reunite these two dominions and to erect a kingdom in 1130 and incorporate it with the whole of southern Italy.

The foundation of the Anglo-Norman monarchy and the creation of Norman duchies and counties, and later of the Norman kingdom in southern Italy and in Sicily, cannot be understood unless one great fact of social history is taken into account: the progressive increase of the population which began in the middle of the tenth century in western Europe, and whose consequences were to be particularly felt in the eleventh century and especially in the second half of that century. This demographic phenomenon cannot be measured, but it is incontestable. In aristocratic circles it had the effect of forming a "surplus" of knights, who found it difficult to establish themselves and were disposed to seek adventure: this made possible important military enterprises followed by settlements abroad, such as the Norman expeditions to England and Italy and others that we will encounter.

The increase of population produced effects in other and more vital areas. Some of them have an importance in the history of international relations and should be noted. First of all, the extension of cultivated lands was made, at the same time, both necessary and possible by the considerable increase of the peasant population. This led to not only the cultivation of fallow and marshy lands in this or that domain or village, or the clearing of forests here and there, but also the deforestation or the drainage of entire zones—such as maritime Flanders, portions of Holland, or the episcopal principality of Utrecht in northern Lotharingia, and especially important areas of northern and eastern Germany or of the Alpine lands. These works led to enormous displacements of population: a considerable proportion of the surplus of the peasant population was, indeed, drawn toward the countries where this was happening. In many cases it was not only a question of interregional migrations: the "hosts," as one calls these agricultural elements that were attracted by offers of personal status and real privilege, moved en masse to distant foreign parts. One can cite, as an example, the Flemings who settled in the north and east of Germany. These migrations of rural populations came about especially in the twelfth and thirteenth centuries, but they began in the eleventh century and were directly connected to the demographic thrust of the tenth and eleventh centuries; it is important to note them here.

The growth of the population, while increasing the needs and allowing for a more ample production, also affected trade relations. Another factor, moreover, that had itself favored the growth of population, acted in the same way: lesser insecurity. This followed not only from the cessation of foreign invasions but also from efforts made in favor of the public peace by certain sovereigns, notably those of Germany, by the Church, and by some territorial princes such as the Duke of Normandy and the Count of Flanders in the case of France.

Most of the currents of international commerce, whose existence in the Carolingian epoch we have noted, had thinned out or even disappeared toward the end of the ninth century, but they flowed again in the tenth and developed considerably during that century and the following one; and new currents were woven into them.

North-South transcontinental commerce, which brought among others—slaves from England and from Verdun—an entrepôt for the Judeo-German slave trade in the Slavic countries—to the Mediterranean ports and from there to Moslem Spain, flourished during these last two centuries. It was an old and important current, perhaps one of those that was the least upset by the troubles provoked by the Normans and the Saracens.

Another old route had Venice as its center; for it was at Venice (Rialto rather than elsewhere) that the foreign trade of the lagoon was concentrated from the eleventh century on. Its commercial relations with the Byzantine East and with the Moslem world of the eastern Mediterranean had grown greatly. The importation of luxury products from the East, especially silks and spices, had become ever more important and had helped to develop the commercial activity of northern Italy, notably of Milan and Pavia. In the eleventh century the Italian merchants in turn transported and sold these and other products beyond the Alps. The result was a double flow toward the north: one—the most important—passed either through Provence and along the Rhône or through the Jura, but in either case thereafter through Burgundy and Champagne; the other followed the Rhine. Italian merchants must have reached the north of France and Flanders toward the end of the century. It is not known whether they were already bringing back cloth as return freight.

An important place must also be reserved for trade between East and West which, in the tenth and eleventh centuries, was handled by the ports of southern Italy: Bari, which traded with Byzantium; and, above all, Amalfi, which joined with its Byzantine business affairs those that it undertook with the whole Mediterranean Moslem world, western as much as eastern. Their imports were of the same type as those of Venice. They certainly exported wood and agricultural products, but it cannot be certain what other goods were included in their exports. Doubtless Amalfi had, like Venice and more than Venice, traded between the Moslem and Byzantine worlds and perhaps between various parts of the Moslem world. She played a role in the development of commercial activity in central Italy—the same role that Venice played in northern Italy. Much less is known of the maritime activity of Pisa and Genoa in this epoch, but it can be taken as established that their war against Saracen piracy in the western Mediterranean was accompanied by commercial operations with North Africa and even with the Orient; it was above all a promise for the future.

The commercial current that, via the plains of Russia, united the Byzantine East and the Moslem East to Scandinavia, grew in importance throughout this whole period. There was a secondary commercial movement from the Swedish wharfs (Gotland) or the Danish wharfs (Schleswig-Haithabu) which became linked with the ports of northern Germany, but especially with England and the lands between the Rhine and the Seine. In the North Sea the Danes appear to have been not the only, but the principal transporters. It can be believed that certain bulky raw materials progressively took the place of greatest importance among the imported goods, beside materials of great value but little bulk from the Orient. From the second half of the eleventh century it can be stated that the textile industry of Flanders and of northern France sometimes provided freight for the return journey. In the course of this period commercial activity was in every case considerably developed throughout the whole interior of the region between the Rhine and the Seine, as well as between this region and its neighbors—England, on the one hand, and the countries located farther south and east, on the other. It contributed to building up the intensity of continental traffic from west to east, especially toward the Slavic or Hungarian countries and the zones of German colonization in central Europe. In the tenth century, moreover, Danish commerce had opened up or developed a new access route toward these countries, utilizing the Oder from Wollin, near its estuary. In the exports of western Europe destined for the East metal products from the Meuse, the Moselle and Rhine regions (brass, iron) occupied a very favored position.

This rebirth of international commerce proceeded along with the formation and development of towns, centers of the distribution and often of the transformation of wealth. Sometimes these were former Roman cities, whose walls were still existing, and which witnessed the establishment, either within or beyond these walls, of a permanent settlement of merchants; in some cases it might happen that such settlement had existed in the eighth or ninth century, had been ruined by the invasions, and was now built up again. Of this type were Cologne and Paris. Sometimes an entirely new center was set up, or re-established when it had been destroyed at the time of the invasions: a permanent settlement of merchants near some newly built fortified place, well situated economically, such as a royal palace or a princely castle (*castrum, castellum*), as at Etampes, Goslar, Bruges, and Ghent; or an episcopal residence, as at Liège, Bremen, and Magdeburg. Certain centers, founded in the eighth century and destroyed in the second half of the ninth, were never rebuilt, such as Duurstede and Quentowic. Finally, some towns of economic importance in the preceding age spanned the finish of the ninth and the beginning of the tenth century without suffering any ravages to speak of; here we find almost continuous development. Milan and Pavia, Verdun and, to a certain extent, London, could serve as examples. If we emphasize here the urban renaissance in western Europe in the tenth and eleventh centuries, it is because in the towns commerce and industry gave birth to a new social class, the bourgeoisie, whose influence was felt in international relations, and because— the two problems are intimately linked—many of these towns will become autonomous political entities called upon to play a considerable role in these relations.

Few factors in the tenth and eleventh centuries have affected international relations as profoundly as the religious ones, both on account of the immediate consequences of their action and by their more long-range consequences. Among the facts in this context it is suitable to cite first the progress of the evangelization that had brought practically the whole heathen world of the north into the Christian community that used Latin as its liturgical language: the north of Scotland and the islands, Denmark, Sweden, and Norway. We have already mentioned the conquests made by Christianity among the Slavs and the Hungarians. On occasion the initiative for these efforts was regional: for example, the Church of Scotland; the Church of England, in Norway, Denmark, and Sweden; the imperial German Church in Denmark and Sweden, which were attached in 948 to the ecclesiastical province of Hamburg, and in the Slavic countries. The papacy limited itself to sanctioning the results obtained.

Moreover, until the middle of the eleventh century the papacy was not in a state to exercise a powerful or profound influence on Christendom. We know that, having experienced long periods of decline, the papacy had passed under German control; although the popes were at that time persons of lofty religious and moral principles, the possibilities of their acting as heads of the universal Church were limited. The subordination of the Church to lay authorities—emperor, kings, princes, and lords—was the usual phenomenon. The extent of subordination varied according to country, region, and epoch, and it would be a strong exaggeration to claim that purity in religious life and respect for ecclesiastical discipline was never to be found; nevertheless the frequency and the gravity of the abuses cannot be contested. Attempts at reform were numerous; there were some in France, especially in Flanders, and some in Lotharingia, in other parts of Germany, and in Italy. Among those reforms that were specifically monastic, the most famous centered upon the Burgundian Abbey of Cluny, founded in 910. For two centuries great abbots devoted their time to enforcing an exemplary religious life in this house, with a rigorous observation of the reformed rule of Saint Benedict. The subordination to Cluny of numerous monasteries reformed by their abbots and the penetration of Cluniac practices into other abbeys with great spiritual energy—like those in France at Saint-Benoît-sur-Loire and Saint-Bénigne at Dijon, and in Germany at Hirsau at the end of the eleventh century—spread the influence of Cluny, directly or indirectly, throughout western Europe and gave it permanency. Cluny's prestige and the role played by its monks who became bishops, even brought this influence to the secular clergy. Cluniac reform, like others, aspired to purity and the regularity of religious and especially monastic life. And there it stopped.

Nevertheless these currents of reform, while developing religious fervor, created an atmosphere favorable to the tendencies which would liberate the Church from lay authority, and which came to light in the second quarter of the eleventh century. Toward the middle of that century these tendencies reached Rome and inspired the policy of several popes. This was known as the Gregorian reform, from the name of Pope Gregory VII (1073–1085), that is to say, the Italian monk Hildebrand, in whom this current was incarnate. In fact both he and his councilors hoped to do more than just extirpate abuses and put an end to the power of laymen over the Church. The Pope claimed to possess absolute power over the latter and even the right to depose the Emperor and to release the subjects from their duty of fealty. Naturally the conflict broke out with the German king, who was also king of Italy and effectively or potentially emperor, either because of his rank or of his power. This conflict is often called the "investiture quarrel," because the immediate cause was the Pope's prohibiting the King from conferring the investiture of their functions on German bishops and certain abbots in the imperial Church; but the appellation is deceptive, because the real object of the conflict was authority over the Church in Germany, Italy, and Burgundy. If the King ceded, the imperial Church would founder, and with it the royal power. The war that was undertaken, on the one hand, by Gregory VII and his successors and, on the other, by Henry IV (1056–1106) and Henry V (died 1125), lasted from 1076 to 1122; its vicissitudes are of little importance here. Its consequences, on the other hand, are of great interest.

The Concordat of Worms, which brought an end to the conflict, was a negotiated solution. It left to the King in Germany—but in Germany alone—the possibility of exercising pressure on the election of bishops and the right to invest them with their secular powers before their consecration. However, the King—or the Emperor—was the losing party. At first because in Germany, despite the prerogatives left to him, authority over the

Church largely escaped him; and because the dukes, the marquises, and the counts had taken advantage of the conflict to free themselves more and more from royal control, and were on the road to making themselves gradually into autonomous territorial princes, as in France. And then because authority over the bishops of Italy and of the kingdom of Burgundy was almost entirely taken away from the German sovereign, the sole serious support that he had in these kingdoms was lost to him thereafter, and his power there was reduced to almost nothing.

Similar but less grave conflicts, however, developed between the reforming popes and other sovereigns of the West. In France the authority of the Pope over the Church became much more effective than in the past; however, the King and several princes at least maintained a right of approval in episcopal elections. In England, despite the efforts of two Italian reformers, who were successively archbishops of Canterbury, Lanfranc and Anselm, the papacy obtained less power than elsewhere; its authority over the Church was greater than before, but it remained much less than that of the King. As for the Norman dukes and counts of southern Italy and Sicily, they maintained a practically exclusive power over the Church and the popes, who, in need of their military support against the German sovereigns, had to resign themselves to the situation. The essential result of the war undertaken by Gregory VII was the authority the Pope acquired throughout the West. There is no question at all of his authority in matters of dogma: it was accepted before the conflict, and it remained accepted; but his disciplinary authority could now be exercised over the Church without meeting serious obstacles. In regard to secular powers, the defeat of the emperors assured him of indisputable prestige. Already nearly a quarter of a century before the Concordat of Worms, under Urban II (1088–1099), this prestige was such that the Pope, in open conflict with the Emperor and with the King of France, could go to France, there excommunicate the King, and successfully call up the knights of that country and of the whole of western Christendom to a war against Islam (1095). When the popes affirmed to the emperor, to kings, and to princes that they wielded a power superior to theirs, there was no longer a manifest contradiction between that claim and reality. Besides, the number of kings and princes who recognized themselves as vassals of the Holy See was considerable: the King of Hungary, the King of Croatia, the Norman dukes and counts and soon the King of Sicily and of southern Italy, the Count of Barcelona—theoretically still a vassal of the King of France—and the King of Aragon, leader of a new Christian kingdom in Spain, whom we will mention later. As spiritual leader of western Christianity, the Pope disposed at that time of great possibilities for action in temporal matters.

One could have a false view of the preponderant position acquired by the papacy if no account were taken of a grave defeat it suffered, and of the consequences of this defeat. In the middle of the eleventh century, in 1054—later we will see under what circumstances—a new schism was produced by the Church of Constantinople which was followed by practically the whole Church in the East. It has lasted until today. There is no doubt that the papacy did not renounce the universal character of its authority, but the possibilities of intervention in the East were extremely limited.

5

The Byzantine World and the Islamic World:
Their Contacts with the Western World from
the Beginning of the Tenth to the Beginning of
the Twelfth Century

THERE IS something artificial in separating Byzantium and even the Islamic lands from the western world in an analysis of international relations in the tenth and eleventh centuries. It becomes acceptable only through a concern for clarity. Moreover, neither Byzantium nor even the Islamic countries have been entirely neglected in the preceding chapters. It would not have been possible to clarify the characteristics of the commercial activity without giving those countries an important place. And although Byzantium continued, in the tenth and eleventh centuries to form a world of its own, it continued to comprise the two elements we have already met: a core, the empire; and a peripheral zone, the protectorates and the peoples deeply subject to the influence of Byzantine civilization.

The empire was held intact during the first thirty years of the tenth century, despite attacks against it from the Moslems of Crete and of Asia and, more important, from the Bulgars. Czar Simeon (died 927), who had imposed his protectorate on Serbia and conquered parts of Macedonia and Thrace, envisaged uniting Byzantium and his own peoples under his imperial authority; he threatened but failed in all his efforts. The penetration of Byzantine civilization into Bulgaria could continue with increased intensity. On the other hand, dissensions within the Moslem world favored the operations of the Byzantine reconquest during the last three quarters of the tenth century. The reoccupation of Crete and

Cyprus (961 and 965) gave Byzantium mastery in the northern part of the eastern Mediterranean. The eastern region of Asia Minor and the neighboring areas, northern Syria, with Antioch (969), and northern Mesopotamia were retaken; part of Armenia was annexed, while Byzantine protectorship was strengthened over other parts of that country, as well as over the Caucasian regions. Meanwhile, toward the end of the century the Bulgarian threat reappeared in Europe: the empire of Czar Samuel extended once more from the Danube to the Adriatic, to the detriment of the Byzantine Empire and of the Serbs, who had once more been placed under its protectorate. Emperor Basil II (976–1025), the last great Macedonian sovereign, ended this peril by wiping out the Bulgarian army and annexing Bulgaria to the empire while leaving it a large degree of autonomy.

These successes in Asia and in southeastern Europe were considerable. At the dawn of the second quarter of the eleventh century the Byzantine Empire extended from the outpost of the Caucasus to the Otranto Canal. The empire also held its exterior positions: in the Crimea, with the colony of Cherson; in the Slav lands of the south, where the Serbian princes and the Croatian kings recognized the superior authority of the *basileis*; and on the Dalmatian coast. In Italy the autonomous duchies and Naples and Amalfi remained loyal, and Venice, on account of its fleet, constituted a precious ally in the Adriatic. In the southern part of the peninsula Byzantine troops had helped in the expulsion of the Saracens following the battle of Garigliano in 915. Thereafter the imperial territories of "Lombardy" (the southeast) and of Calabria (the southwest) were successively defended against the Saracens of Sicily or of Africa and against the "Lombard" princes who only intermittently recognized the imperial overlord. These territories were also successfully defended against the German sovereigns. In contrast to the western empire that the latter had reconstituted, the position taken by the Macedonian *basileis* was radical: the western emperors were usurpers; their claims to southern Italy had to be fought, and with energy. The imperial title of *basileus* was not given in official correspondence to those kings of Germany who claimed to be Roman emperors. When a Byzantine princess, Theophano, was given as wife to Otto II (972), it was a concession made with reluctance. Otto had been refused a daughter of the emperor.

The greatest and the most durable success gained by Byzantium was in Russia. Despite the armed conflicts that occurred more than once between the empire and the Russians, relations of every sort were strengthened between the two; religious propaganda and Byzantine political activities ended, in 989, with the conversion to Christianity of the great Prince of Kiev, Vladimir (died 1015), who exercised hegemony over the other princes. He strongly favored the evangelization of his people by Byzantine missionaries; and his successor, Jaroslav (1018–1054), followed the same policy. An original civilization developed in Kievan Russia, where the Scandinavian element, a minority but having dynamic and organizing abilities, was gradually absorbed into the Slavic masses. Thanks to the influence of the Church, subordinate to the Patriarch of Constantinople, Byzantium profoundly affected this civilization, just as she frequently acted effectively on the policy of the princes.

The impressive results gained by Byzantine foreign policy during the century and a half in which the first "Macedonians"— many of whom were usurpers, artificially attached to the dynasty—governed the empire, could create a false impression. Certainly these remarkable persons were served by the strong administrative structure of the state, by the traditional ability of Byzantine diplomacy, and by the excellence of the navy and of the army, in which Iranians, and Scandinavians, especially the Varangians of Russia, and, after 1066, exiled Englishmen served in some number as mercenaries. However, the progressive disintegration of a free peasantry, wiped out in Asia by the monstrous developments of great seignorial domains, lay and ecclesiastical, threatened the authority of the state and in the long run endangered the recruitment of national troops and the regular gathering of taxes.

In the first quarter of the eleventh century this double peril was not yet very apparent: public finances were on the whole in a prosperous state, and the stability of the gold currency, of the bezant, the soundest means of payment in the Near East and beyond, held up remarkably, at least until approximately the middle of the eleventh century. International commercial activity was certainly considerable. The role of Byzantium can be seen as the point of departure and of arrival for the business flow whose other centers were situated in western or northern Europe; the term "Byzantium" does not here indicate only the Constantinople market—the most important of all—but also other important places, such as Thessalonica, Corinth, Cherson and, after its reconquest from Islam, Antioch. The great Byzantine markets took in the products of eastern or central Asia or of Africa, often through the intermediary role of the Moslems or of the Khazars, and the products of the Russia plains or of the west through the intermediary role of the Varangians, the Venetians, or the merchants of Amalfi, or even the Jews of Spain or southern France. They re-exported a great part of the merchandise. But among the materials sold and exported, there were also the products of industries that, in the empire, were manufactured for export, such as the textile industries—cloth, silk, wool—producing materials of such quality that they were sought for their finished fabrication, for their sumptuous colors, and for the beauty of the decorative subjects, often of Iranian origin. After the tenth century, at Constantinople itself, permanent colonies were founded by merchants belonging to those nations most interested in the businesses conducted in this city. The Varangians, or Russians, formed one; its role was vital for all trade to the north, along the Dnieper and through Novgorod on Lake Ilmen, the last great entrepôt before the Baltic. The merchants of Amalfi, it appears, were the most active Italian colony throughout this period. But the Venetians were rivals, especially after Basil II gave them considerable privileges in 992 to assure himself of the support of their fleet against the Slav pirates in the Adriatic and against the Saracens.

Byzantium in the tenth and eleventh centuries was not only the great center of the international economic network; it played the same role in the domain of art. Southern Italy and Venice, just as much as Russia, Bulgaria, or Armenia, were provinces of Byzantine art in this period. Saint Mark's of Venice bears witness to this today in the same way as Santa Sophia of Kiev. Many more examples could easily be cited. However, certain artistic influences reached far beyond those "provinces." Byzantine iconographic or decorative themes of cloth, of ivories, of illuminated manuscripts of the Macedonian period undeniably furnished themes and models to the sculptors of capitals, to the ivory workers and to the illuminators of the West. Generally speaking, the latter treated these models with a great degree of freedom.

The death of the Emperor Basil II opened a period of decline for the Byzantine Empire. Internal conflicts and the action of the forces of fragmentation, whose containment these conflicts prevented, ruined the state. At the same time an event in the religious world, already referred to, deeply divided Byzantium and the West. This was the schism of 1054. It was provoked by a conflict between the Patriarch Michael Cerularios and Pope Leo IX concerning authority over the dioceses of southern Italy and questions of liturgy and discipline; the underlying cause was the traditional incompatibility of the religious climates of Byzantium and Rome. The churches of Bulgaria, Serbia, and Russia, dependent upon Byzantium, followed the Patriarch, though it is less clearly established whether the other three eastern patriarchs—of Antioch, Jerusalem, and Alexandria—immediately followed suit. The schism was to make effective collaboration between the

West and Byzantium difficult at times when they would face common dangers.

These dangers soon emerged, and it was difficult for the empire, weakened by interior dissension, to resist them. Toward the middle of the century the Petchenegs, nomads of the Turkish race—thrust onward by other barbarians of the steppe, also Turkish, the Kumans, who were settled in the plains north of the Black Sea—established themselves south of the Danube, causing serious anxiety to Constantinople. In Italy, Robert Guiscard and his Normans succeeded in the conquest of the Byzantine provinces with the capture of Bari in 1071. Bulgaria once again rose up, with Serbia's support, and made herself independent; and the great Prince took the title of *kral*, or king. In 1076 the King of Croatia undertook to hold his crown from Pope Gregory VII. But the most dangerous threat was offered by the Seljuk Turks. Since the time of Basil II the eastern frontier of the empire had remained relatively stable. Except for some critical periods, relations between Byzantium and the caliphate—that of the Fatimites, rulers as we will see, of Syria—had been good; and apart from the rule of a lunatic, the Caliph El Hakim, in the first quarter of the eleventh century, the emperors had arranged for acceptable conditions of life for Christians who either lived in or made pilgrimages through the Holy Land. The situation changed when the Turks, who had made themselves masters of the caliphate of Baghdad—we will return to this—attacked the eastern frontiers of the empire in 1057 and after. The fighting went on for a long time. In 1071 the Byzantine army suffered total disaster at Manzikiert, in Armenia. During the preceding years and those to follow, the provinces that had been reconquered under the great Macedonian emperors were lost, Armenia and the lands of the Caucasus came under Moslem authority, and soon the greater part of Asia Minor suffered the same fate.

In 1081 Alexios Comnenos, a man of strength, seized power

through a *coup d'état*. At first he also was in a desperate situation, but he finally overcame it. Robert Guiscard intended to impose his domination over the eastern shores of the Adriatic, and perhaps his ambitions went even further; in 1081 he invaded Epirus. Thanks to the support of Venice, to which new commercial privileges throughout the empire were granted in 1082, and as a result of intrigues spun in Italy by the Byzantine diplomacy itself, Alexios, after a series of setbacks, stayed the threat; and the death of Robert Guiscard in 1085 delivered him from it. From 1086 on, the Petchenegs were particularly aggressive: there had to be an alliance in 1091 with the savage Kumans to annihilate them. The Serbs could be contained. Opposition to the Asiatic Turks had to be limited to military and diplomatic defensive measures. The weakening of the Byzantine armed forces during the preceding period made the struggle extremely difficult; it led the Emperor increasingly to seek the services of western mercenaries, among them Flemish knights; but the breakdown of both the imperial finances and the army limited the possibilities in this area.

To understand these events and those that followed, we must take into account what the Moslem world had become in the tenth century and during most of the eleventh.

The dominant theme in its history before the middle of the eleventh century was an increased political fragmentation. Very often, moreover, the latter was the consequence of religious events, such as the appearance of elements more radical and more fanatical in their attachment to Islam, or the triumph of one theological tendency over another. At the beginning of the century the appearance of a Mahdi—that is, a man sent by God—supported by Berber tribes, led to the formation of a new caliphate, that of the Fatimites (the Mahdi claimed to be descended from Fatima, daughter of Mahomet). At first it comprised Africa (909); then part of the Maghreb, Sicily, Cyrenaica (912–913);

and finally Egypt (969), where the Fatimites set up a new capital, Cairo. Shortly afterward they even overran the greater part of Syria and Palestine. In Spain loyalty to orthodox Islam—in opposing the rationalist tendencies that at this time dominated the Abbassides of Baghdad, and the Shiite fanaticism of the Fatimites —served the plans of the Ommayad Emir of Cordova when he finally broke with Baghdad and proclaimed himself caliph in 929. He maintained Cordova as his seat. In the second half of the century Moslem Spain (*El Andalus*) was strong enough to stop the Christian reconquest for some time. But the strength of the state was more apparent than real. Rivalries among local governors and hostilities among various elements of the population— Arab aristocrats, Berber peasants, Slavs (the descendants of foreign slaves), and the Mozarabs, or indigenous Christians—were powerful factors for fragmentation. Problems came to a head in the eleventh century with a political breakup: Moslem Spain divided into several independent states under "kings, leaders of groups," the *reyes de taifas*. The caliphate of Cordova disappeared: no further traces are to be found after 1031. As for the caliphate of Baghdad, torn by theological conflicts and the rivalries of military and religious leaders, and dominated by this or that dynasty of emirs, it became more or less powerless in the tenth and eleventh centuries. It was seen that, reduced to the defensive, Islam had had to withdraw to a considerable extent before the Byzantine reconquest. In the peripheral regions the emirates increased in number, making themselves in effect independent, and attempted sometimes with success to extend their domination under leaders, who were Iranians, like the Samanides of Khurasan and of Turkestan, or Turkish, but with an entourage influenced by Iranian tradition. Such were the Ghaznevids, who, in the first half of the eleventh century, added northwestern India to their territory, which comprised eastern Iran and Afghanistan.

We have referred to the role played by the eastern Islamic world in international trade relations. Egypt, Iraq, and Syria had been entrepôts for goods from central and eastern Asia, from southern Arabia, and from India and Africa. This import business was in good measure in the hands of the Jews. By sea, leaving the Mediterranean ports of which Alexandria was the most important, or overland by caravan, these goods were exported toward the Byzantine Empire, Venice or Amalfi, and the Moslem lands of the West, or Russia and Scandinavia. Products manufactured in the Islamic world and the slaves, whose trade was largely carried on by the Jews among others, also held an important place in this business. The Moslem countries of the East imported slaves, but a large part of the traffic, destined for central and eastern Asia, was limited to transit.

Although the Moslem world was politically and religiously divided into three great masses—and all three were in their turn thoroughly fragmented—we must not consider these masses or their fragments as impenetrable entities. Certainly the distance between these states was accentuated: Berber Africa, the kingdoms of Spain, because of the preoccupation of their ruling classes, were less oriented toward Baghdad and Cairo in the middle of the eleventh century than at the beginning of the tenth. But the contacts never ceased, and the closer one comes to the East, the more numerous they are: business relations, religious propaganda, a concern for learning and study, political intrigue, family affairs, not even to mention pilgrimages to Mecca, all supported regular comings and goings. There is in this a fact worthy of deep consideration. Moreover, these relations extended to the arts. Although the latter possessed their own characteristics in each of the great territorial masses into which the Islamic world was divided, borrowings and exchanges are obvious; those parts of the great mosque at Cordova built in the tenth century cannot be understood without reference to old Cairo or Kairouan.

The middle and the second half of the eleventh century are marked by the appearance of savage and fanatical peoples in the world of Islam—with the exception of Egypt—and by the decisive role that they were going to play. This applies to the Turks. Since the ninth and tenth centuries throughout the Moslem East many Turks served as mercenaries in the army and occupied senior posts in the government and in the administration. But in the second quarter of the eleventh century whole Turkish peoples called Seljuks, from the name of the dynasty to which their leaders belonged, were pushed out of central Asia by upheavals stemming from China, and invaded Iran and then Iraq. They were newly converted to Islam. The Seljuk leaders dominated the Abbasside caliphate after capturing Baghdad in 1055. At the same time they successfully attacked, as we have seen, the Byzantine Empire, fought the Fatimite caliphate, conquering Syria, and seizing Jerusalem in 1075. But although they represented a redoubtable military force, the Turks were unable to organize their conquests solidly. From the coasts of the Aegean to Palestine, sultanates and autonomous and rival emirates multiplied under the theoretical authority of the Abbasside caliph. The Byzantines took advantage of this anarchy by pitting Turkish potentates against each other; the Fatimites did the same, and in 1098 they recaptured Jerusalem.

In Africa proper the savage elements were something entirely new. When the Fatimites had left this country for Egypt, it remained theoretically subject to them; but in the first half of the eleventh century the Berber emirates, among whom it was divided, made themselves independent. Toward the middle of the century the Caliph launched against them the Hilalians, Arab tribes that had been transplanted into upper Egypt. These fanatical invaders and pillagers, followed by other nomads, ruined the mixed urban and rural civilization of Africa, bringing agriculture in the interior of the country back to a primitive state, and creating a type of permanent anarchy. The emirates maintained authority only in the coastal towns—Mahdiya, Tunis, etc. One of the most unexpected but one of the most important consequences of the Arab invasion was to direct Africa toward more maritime activity than it had had in the past: transmediterranean trade and piracy, with the capture and sale of Christian slaves.

The savages who were active in the Maghreb and in Spain were the Almoravides, nomads of the Sahara Desert, ascetic and fanatical types of warrior-monks. Toward the middle of the century they overcame the Maghreb and were careful to enforce strict observation of the Koran there. Moslem Spain, divided and weakened, fell back before the Christian reconquest: the King of Sevilla appealed to the Almoravide Emir, who crossed the sea and stopped the Christian offensive but put an end to the existence of states governed by *reyes de taifas*, with the exception of the single kingdom of Saragossa, and imposed his power on the whole of *El Andalus* as well as on the Maghreb. In theory he recognized the authority of the Caliph of Baghdad. It was, moreover, remarkable that the Almoravides, who had proposed to wipe out the religious and moral laxity that in their opinion reigned in Spain, were so quickly won over to the refinements of Andalusian civilization, which spread to the Maghreb. Here again monuments bear precious witness: the art of Cordova which gave rise to the art of the Maghreb from the end of the eleventh century and the beginning of the twelfth.

Thus about 1090 the world of Islam was divided again into four zones: that of the Turkish sultanates and emirates in the Asiatic Near East; that of the Fatimite caliphate in Egypt (and in its annexes, especially Cyrenaica); the anarchical zone of Africa, with a back country dominated by the Arabs, and Berber coastal towns oriented toward the sea; finally, in the west, Spain and the Maghreb, governed by a Saharan emir. The two extreme zones were in immediate contact with the two Christian worlds. As for the outposts of Islam—Crete and Cyprus in the eastern Mediterranean, the settlements of Provence and Italy, like that of Sicily in the western Mediterranean—all were lost.

In the Iberian peninsula the Christian states increased on account of reconquest: the kingdoms of León, Navarre, and

Aragon—the old march of Navarre—and the county of Barcelona. Castile, south of León and a "march" of this state, became a kingdom in turn in 1035, and shortly after, in 1037, this kingdom annexed León; and in 1076 Navarre was united with Aragon. The war of all these states against the "Moors" alternated between successes and reverses, explained by their own divisions and particularly by periods of strength and weakness in Moslem Spain. In 997, during the last period, when the caliphate of Cordova was strong, the Christian sanctuary of Santiago of Compostella in Galicia, a place of pilgrimage already renowned in western Europe, was sacked. In 1085, in the last period of the *reyes de taifas,* on the other hand, King Alfonso VI of Castile made himself master of Toledo and crossed the Tagus in the *reconquista.* Then, in the following year the Almoravides stopped the Christian advance for a while by inflicting a surprising defeat on the king at Sacrajas (in Arabic, Zalacca). And in 1094 a Castilian knight, a famous adventurer, Rodrigo de Bivar, called El Cid, acted on his own initiative and took possession of Valencia, where he reigned and, until his death in 1099, held out against the assaults of the Almoravides. In 1102, however, this position had to be evacuated by his widow, Ximena, as it was too isolated.

From the tenth century onwards, French knights helped the Spaniards. The first ones very naturally came from the duchy of Gascony and from the county of Toulouse, which were in close contact with the Spanish pyrenean and subpyrenean kingdoms and counties. Starting in the eleventh century, and especially from its last quarter, they came also from other parts of France, especially from Burgundy. The influence acquired by the Cluniac monks in Spain may have contributed to this new state of affairs. The scope and the frequency of the French expeditions progressed persistently until the beginning of the second quarter of the twelfth century and contributed extensively to the progress of the Christian reconquest. This latter was accompanied by the repopulation of devastated or evacuated zones. French knights, clerks, and peasants took part. This French participation in the *reconquista* and in the *poblaciones* has been one of those conquests followed by distant settlements that the increase of population made possible and in part provoked: it deserves to be placed next to the Norman undertakings in England, Italy, and Sicily.

One has mentioned Spanish "crusades." If by "crusade" we mean an expedition one of whose principal moving forces was war against the infidel, then the term can be used. But if the term is used in a technical sense, it is incorrect, for none of these expeditions was undertaken under the initiative of the Pope, none received a visible "signal" from him to distinguish the participants from other warriors, and—save perhaps the expedition of 1063–1064 against Barbastro—the participants were in no way granted privileges. The papacy encouraged the expeditions. In 1073, Gregory VII even tried vainly to organize a real crusade in Spain; the conquered lands were to be thereafter held from the Holy See. We have already discussed other manifestations of this same policy. Its success was very limited in Spain: King Alfonso VI of Castile, leader of the principal Christian state, always refused to recognize himself as subordinate to the Pope. When he happened to bear the title of emperor, it was not only to express claims to authority or hegemony over all Spain, but also to claim his independence from the papacy.

The initiative for a great warlike expedition from Christendom, undertaken to seize the Holy Places from Islam, on the other hand, came from the Holy See. The religious exaltation provoked and nourished by the tide of reform contributed to the enlargement of the concept of holy war and made this war desirable and meritorious in the eyes of many leaders: these notions were current at Rome at least from the middle of the eleventh century on. There was concern for the danger that the Turkish menace—Seljuk or Petcheneg—brought to bear on Christendom. The hope of re-creating, by providing Byzantium with military help, the unity of the Church which had been broken by the schism of

1054, was nourished. In 1074, Gregory VII had yearned for an Oriental expedition, which under his own leadership, would have obtained this result and driven the infidels from the Near East, but it never came to be. Urban II took the decisive step: in 1095, at the Council of Clermont, he called the Christians of the West to arms to deliver the Holy Places; he established the sign—a cross of red wool which was to give its name to the crusaders and to the crusade—that the participants wore, and he outlined the privileges that would benefit them.

The appeal met with a success beyond its expectations. The intense religious fervor and the prestige of the papacy, born from reformist movements and supported by the struggle between the Holy See and the emperor; the experience of the Spanish war; the thirst for adventure and the search for new settlements in knightly circles, brought about by the increase in population; and for the same reason, the great mobility of the peasant masses who lacked cultivable land—these are some of the principal factors in the enthusiastic support given to Urban II's projects.

Crusades—generally termed "popular" because they consisted, in addition to a minority of knights and adventurers, of a majority of people of peasant origin, who came from France, Germany, and elsewhere—began in 1096. The crusaders allowed themselves the worst excesses en route, notably at the expense of the Jews; and although some were stopped in Hungary, they served only to replenish the slave markets of the East like human cattle. The Crusade, properly so called, was undertaken by knights of France, Provence, England and Norman Italy: the great majority of them were French in language and manners—"Franks," as they were called in the east. Germany was represented only by knights of upper and lower Lotharingia, and most of them spoke French. Northern Italy sent hardly a soul. The divorce between the traditional conception of the emperor as the titled protector of the universal Church and brutal reality was made apparent by the fact that the Emperor did not lead the troops. He could not have done so: Henry IV, an excommunicate, was at war with the Pope. Neither the King of France nor the King of England took part in the campaign; their relations with Urban II were wretched owing to the private life of Philip I and the conflicts between William Rufus and the Pope about authority over the Church in England.

The Crusade was an expedition of princes and knights under the more or less effective command of a pontifical legate, Adhémar of Monteil, bishop of Le Puy. It lasted from 1097 to 1099 and began with a Byzantine phase. Alexios Comnenos, who had hoped to recruit mercenaries among the western knights, was scarcely satisfied to see a pontifical, Latin, turbulent, plundering, undisciplined army appear. He ordered the crusaders to reconquer the lost territories of his empire on his account, and he had a body of Byzantine troops accompany them. During the advance into Asia Minor the crusaders-obeyed, but when they arrived in the eastern part of Cilicia and on the upper Euphrates, populated by Armenian refugees, at Antioch and northern Syria, the "Franks" broke with Byzantium and launched disordered operations. The egoism of the leaders and the lack of discipline among the troops seriously compromised the war against the Turkish emirs. Nevertheless, by negotiation or by fighting, they arrived at Jerusalem in 1099. The city was taken not from the Turks but from the Fatimite Caliph, their enemy, who had, as is known, profited from their difficulties to regain the Holy City. A good quarter of a century was required to achieve, with the help of new crusades, and especially of the fleets of Genoa, Pisa, and Venice, the conquest of Palestine and of Syria. Jerusalem and its environs were placed under the authority of Godfrey of Bouillon, the duke of lower Lotharingia; they became, on his death in 1100, the center of a kingdom under his brother Baldwin I, count of Boulogne. Edessa and Tripoli constituted vassal counties. Antioch was an independent principality under Bohemund, son of Robert Guiscard; but it, too, soon became a vassal of the kingdom.

In the history of international relations the first crusade, because of its consequences, constitutes an event of considerable importance. It is necessary to indicate here at least the principal points. In the Near East the situation of the Byzantine Empire was territorially consolidated, as the west and part of the south of Asia Minor were reoccupied; but more numerous and stronger contacts with the Latins, made inevitable by the crusade and its results, were to introduce new causes of troubles into the life of the empire. Furthermore, the Greek Church was to see its influence diminish over the Christian communities of Syria and Palestine where the Roman obedience now dominated. For the time being, the Turks and the caliphate of Egypt lost their positions on the east coast of the Mediterranean. The papacy gained a success: the patriarchates of Jerusalem and Antioch were occupied by Latins and passed under its authority, with the whole of the reorganized ecclesiastical hierarchy in Palestine and Syria; but in other regards Rome experienced a setback. Not only did the Byzantine schism continue, but the frictions between Latins and Greeks lessened the chances of reconciliation. Furthermore, the state that had been created in the Holy Land was in no way a state governed by a legate; doubtless the King of Jerusalem was a vassal of the Pope, but in reality it was a scarcely effective subordination. This new step toward the unification of the Christian world under the authority of the Pope did not give the decisive results that Rome had counted upon. A kingdom surrounded by vassal principalities was born in the Holy Land and in Syria; western institutions, especially the system of feudal-vassalic relations, had been introduced, with many adaptations, into the new milieu. The kingdom and the principalities served as a political framework for a Latin population, whose importance was increased by almost constant bolstering from the West; the Latins, however, were only a dominant minority; Greek, Armenian, Syrian, and Palestinian Christians, the Jews, and even the Moslems made up the majority. The great victors were the men of the ports and the market places of Italy, Genoa, Pisa, and Venice, who created settlements in the ports of the Latin Orient for trade with Asia and considerably developed their activity; moreover, all European economic activity benefited—we will have occasion to return to this point.

The first crusade had consequences of another order, which are also of interest to the history of international relations. The crusades certainly contributed to making western Christianity more aware of its unity, at least in the circles where this was important: among the clerics and knights. On the other hand, the fact that so many knights fought in the service of a religious ideal introduced a degree of disinterest and generosity into their conception of life, and it contributed in some measure to the formation of a knightly ideal: this also we will refer to again. Finally, many knights came to their deaths in the Holy Land where they had settled: western Europe was freed for good of these violent and undisciplined elements. Thus the public peace and the strength of several states and principalities benefited from the crusade.

6

West and East:
From the End of the Eleventh Century to the
Decline of the Twelfth Century

THE SUCCESSES won by the papacy during the second half of the eleventh century and the beginning of the twelfth, caused it to act more effectively than any other power in western Europe and in the Latin East. During the twelfth century its authority over the Church was extended and strengthened. Extended, because in Germany it was at that time possible to do more than the papacy had been able to do and dare previously; and because before the middle of the century in France the last halfhearted opposition that royal power and some of the territorial princes offered to papal actions had collapsed—except in the south. In England, however, the power of William Rufus (died 1100), of Henry I (died 1135), and even of Stephen of Blois (died 1154), whose reign was, however, largely anarchical, seriously limited the efficacity of Roman intervention. If pontifical authority was strengthened, it was because of the systematic development of existing institutions and practices, which "reforming popes"— particularly Gregory VII and his successors—had actively used: among such were the exercise of appeal jurisdiction by the Pope himself and of delegated jurisdiction entrusted to an increasing number of pontifical legates. A place must be given also to the councils which the popes convoked, over which they presided, and which took decisions that consolidated the monarchical government of the Church and put into practice "reformist" concep-, tions: the first Ecumenical Council at the Lateran in 1123; the

Council of Pisa in 1135; the second Ecumenical Council at the
Lateran in 1139, attended by bishops from Italy, France, Germany, England, and Spain. This pontifical action, which was felt
throughout the whole of Latin Christendom, was going to become still more effective shortly after 1140 by the placing of a
new instrument at its disposition: the *Decretum* of the Italian
monk Gratian, at the same time a compilation of texts and a
handbook of canon law designed to eliminate the contradictions
in ecclesiastical law. It had considerable success; it was copied
and glossed throughout the whole of western Christendom; it
became the basis for the teaching of Church law and the head of a
series of canonical collections that, in the fifteenth century, made
up the Corpus Juris Canonici, the code of canon law.

Moreover, religious life experienced a renewed intensity; one
manifestation of this was the appearance of new orders or new
forms of life for the clergy. Several chapters of canons were reformed in the eleventh century to require their members to lead a
life that they believed conformed more exactly to that of the
Apostles: they lived according to various rules, the most practiced
of which was placed under the patronage of Saint Augustine; all
imposed community life and poverty on the "regular" canons.
Actually these canons were more nearly monks. The institution
appears to have gained its first successes in southern France and
was known to some extent throughout the West; but at the
beginning of the twelfth century it spread especially, and very
energetically, into northern France, including Flanders, and into
northwestern Spain and various parts of Germany. To the same
movement belongs an order of regular canons called the Praemonstratensian, stemming from the abbey of regular canons
founded at Prémontré, a place near Laon in 1120 by Saint Nor-
bert, the future Bishop of Magdeburg. In their abbeys these
regular Praemonstratensian canons observed the rule named after
Saint Augustine, supplemented by statutes particular to their
order. Their members fulfilled the parochial ministry. By their

example and their action they helped raise the spiritual level of the rural lower clergy; they also were involved in putting wastelands, heaths, and marshes under cultivation. Before the middle of the twelfth century the order had spread considerably, especially in northern France and, by way of Lotharingia, into Germany.

Beside the regular canons, true monastic orders developed. The Carthusians, who combining the eremetical tradition with the conventual life, need not be commented on here, although the order—whose center was La Grande Chartreuse, in the mountains of the Dauphiné, founded by Saint Bruno in 1084—had spread a little everywhere. The Carthusians lived in complete isolation and scarcely involved themselves in international relations. By contrast, the Cistercians—so named after the mother abbey of Cîteaux in Burgundy, founded in 1098—deserve to be mentioned on all accounts. These monks proposed to restore rigor to the Benedictine observance, and they made their observance even more rigorous than the earlier Benedictine rule. Their abbeys were established in savage and solitary places: these, however, were extremely active centers of land clearing and cultivation. The austerity and asceticism practiced in the order must have answered to widespread aspirations of the period, for the success of the Cistercians was immense: their houses, grouped in a centralized organization, multiplied in France and spread quickly to other countries, notably Germany, England, Italy, Spain, etc. The diffusion of Cistercian monasteries can be traced across Europe, because all the churches they erected, despite some differences, had the same architectural characteristics. They give the same impression of austere, unadorned majesty whether built in the romanesque style or in the gothic style: at Fontenay or at Pontigny, in Burgundy, as at Villers in Brabant; at Eberbach in the Rhineland or at Ebrach near Bamberg, as at Fossanova, on the edge of the Pontine marshes.

Another social circle, that of the lay aristocracy, also underwent certain transformations in the second half of the eleventh

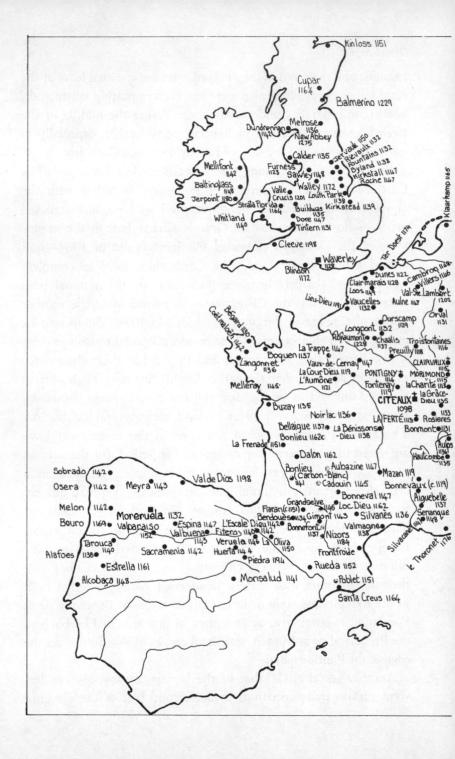

**THE DISTRIBUTION
OF THE CISTERCIAN ORDER**

✠ Head of the Order
● Head of the Branch
■ First Cistercian abbey
(England, Spain, Italy, Germany)

Varnhem 1150 Alvastra 1143

Herrevad 1144

Esrom 1154

Ruhekloster 1192 Hiddensee 1296 Buckow 1260 Oliva 1186 Pelplin 1258

Neuenkamp 1234 Eldena 1199 Koronova 1256

Schamebeck Reinfeld 1190 Dargun 1172 1209 Kolbatz 1175 Marienwalde 1294

Hade 1232 1243 Himmelspforte Himmelstädt 1286-1300

Loccum 1249 Chorin Blesen 1262 Lad 1144

1165 Marienthal 1143 Lehnin 1183 Paradies 1236

Amelunxborn Cinna 1174 Obra

Altenkamp Michelstein Dobrilugk Leubus 1175 Sulejow 1177 Koprzywnica 1185

Marienfeld 1135 1146 Grussau Heinrichau 1227 Jedrzejow 1149

Bredelar Hardhausen Walkenried 1292 Kamenz 1239 Mogila 1222

Altenberg 1135 Reifenstein 1162 Sittichenbach Buch 1192

Volkenrode 1131 Pforta Himmelwitz 1280

Heisterbach 1189 Marienstatt Georgen Altzelle 1175

1215 Eberbach 1135 thal Jeseg 1194 Sedlec 1143

Ebrach Waldsassen Nepomuk 1145

1145 Schonau 1127 Heilsbronn

Neuberg Bronnbach 1151 1152 Walderbach 1143 Hradist 1177

1131 Maulbronn 1139 Schontal Kaisersheim

Bebbenhausen 1190 1158 1134 Aldersbach 1148 Zwetl 1138 Bel-Haram-Kuti 1232

Lützel Salem 1138 Fürstenfeld 1261

1124 Heiligenkreutz 1135

Wettigen Lilienfeld 1202 Pilis 1184

1227 Ruen 1129

Hauterive 1138 Victring 1142 Szent Gotthard 1184

Acquafreda 1143 Egres 1179

Morimundo 1134 Chiaravelle 1136

Casanova Rivalta Cerredo 1136

Stafarda 1142 Scrivia (c.1169)

(c.1135) La Colomba

Tiglieto 1120-1153

Sale 1189 Castagnola 1146

S.Galgano 1181

S.Marting Casanova 1191

1150 Rabona 1209

Tre Fontane Casamari 1191

(c.1140)

Fossanova 1135 Realvalle 1277 S.Spirito della Valle

Canonica Galeso 1195 1215

1221 Acquaformosa

Sambucina 1197

1160

S.Spirito de

Palermo

1172 Roccadia 1176

Arco 1212

and the first half of the twelfth century. These occurred in the greater part of western Europe, this time with different characteristics according to the country or the region. They cannot be passed over in silence here, because they profoundly affected a circle whose activity in international relations was decisive throughout the Middle Ages, and they themselves constitute, in certain respects, an essential element in these relations.

The lay aristocracy in the West was, as we know, the knighthood, the group whose social role was to fight, and to fight on horseback; most of its members lived on the revenues of their landed patrimony, be it great, middling, or even extremely modest. For various reasons this social milieu assumed the character of an international brotherhood of all knights, with rites of admission, rules of conduct, and a common ideal: an ideal in which honor, courtesy toward women, the protection of the Church and of the weak, and the performance of feats of valor dominated this brotherhood of knights even beyond frontiers. Vassal loyalty, the influence of ideas of justice and charity preached by the Church, and to a certain extent the influence of women belonging to the aristocratic milieu—especially in the south of France—were factors of major importance. This transformation was already well advanced toward the end of the eleventh century. But, without doubt, it must be recognized that the first crusade played a decisive part in its total realization. Considered as the brotherhood led by the ideal we have analyzed, the community of the knights, as well as their ideal, is generally termed chivalry. It was in France and in the kingdom of Burgundy-Provence that the transformation was at first and most completely realized; it almost immediately gained strength in those countries that had a French-speaking aristocracy—England, southern Italy, and Lotharingia. It penetrated into Scotland, Spain, Italy, Germany and, across this land, into central and northern Europe. One of the factors contributing to this diffusion was the birth in eleventh-century France of an epic literature and later of Arthurian romances in the colloquial tongue, inspired by chivalrous ideals. Among the epic poems, the most celebrated is the *Chanson de Roland*. These poems, translated and imitated, contributed to the spread of the French conception of knighthood through Germany and Italy. Without wishing to minimize the contribution of knighthood to the humanization and civilizing of mores, it is important not to add illusion to reality: the knightly rules and ideals were a most imperfect bridle on the savagery of these mores.

The phenomenon we have just described was a social one. The phenomenon we shall discuss now is a legal one. In the various countries of western Europe, there appears at the latest in the eleventh century, a legal class of noblemen enjoying a privileged legal status. As a rule, this status became hereditary in the twelfth century. In most countries the nobility included the greatest number of the knights, although this was not necessarily everywhere the case since the beginning of its existence. The origins of that legal class have varied from country to country. In several regions, a part of the knights remained outside the nobility, as in England; in Germany, the numerous and important group of *ministeriales* or unfree knights, were only relatively late considered as free and admitted into the nobility.

Only certain aspects of the transformations produced in agriculture and livestock raising between the eleventh and the thirteenth centuries are of interest to a history of international relations. We need not mention here important facts such as the increase of domains along with a decrease in their size, and the breakup of desmenes subject to direct exploitation, the far-reaching changes in types of tenure, and the appearance and the diffusion of fixed-term leases for a share of the harvest or for a fixed rent.

On the other hand, we must say a few words about the effect that certain new phenomena in the exploitation of the soil had on international commerce, and about the influence that international commerce or the industry working for it had on agriculture and livestock raising. The extensive lands won from the sea in Flanders in the tenth, the eleventh and even the twelfth century were mainly used for sheep raising; their wool was used by the Flemish cloth industry whose products, as we know, were exported. In the twelfth century a number of these "sheep runs" were converted into pasture for cattle raising, or even into fields. This change in the agricultural economy of Flanders was one of the factors that led to a sharply increased importation of English wool. This increase of demand caused a considerable expansion of sheep raising in England, especially in the isolated regions where the new orders, the Cistercians and the Praemonstratensians, had established their houses. They became great producers of wool. A similar phenomenon, also linked with the development of the cloth industry in Flanders, Brabant, and Italy (Lombardy and Tuscany), was the cultivation of dye plants. The production of woad and pastel (blue dye) around Amiens and Pavia and the exportation of the products of these places to Tuscany and the Low Countries grew in the twelfth century, because the cloth industry, expanding considerably, required them in ever increasing quantities. A third phenomenon of the same order was apparent only in commerce and agriculture. The union of Aquitaine and England under one ruler, which came about in the middle of the twelfth century—and we will return to this—worked for better commercial relations between the two countries. At that time viniculture was developing fast in Bordelais, as a result of putting marshy or heathy areas into cultivation; and the merchants of Bordeaux began to export their wines to England and to Flanders, as doubtless also did those of the Isle of Oleron and those of La Rochelle with the wines of Aunis, and as did the Bayonne carriers for all the wines of the southwest. In turn, the success of these southwestern wines in England and in the Low Countries after the second half of the century contributed strongly to grape production in southwestern France. The cases discussed here of progress and reaction to it among agricultural transformations, the development of international trade, and the development of industries, working for the export market are very characteristic; but without too much difficulty other examples could be found.

Actually the twelfth century saw considerable developments in international trade, the growth of which has been followed from the Carolingian period, but especially since the tenth century. This development can be traced not only through a much greater volume of transactions, but also through changes in the structure of the trade.

Some currents disappeared, such as the north-south transcontinental slave trade. The practice of this trade in England ceased shortly after the conquest. The Slav slave trade undertaken in Germany with its inflow via Verdun also died out in the course of the eleventh century, and Moslem Spain had replaced its Slav slaves with black ones imported principally across the Sahara from the Niger region. On the other hand, transcontinental trade between Italy and countries north of the Alps had in every way intensified, and at least by the second half of the twelfth century the trading of goods acquired a very regular character. The development of a great export industry in Flanders, in the north of France, and somewhat later in Brabant—cloth manufacture producing quality wares—furnished one of the main materials of this trade. Throughout the whole century Flemish and French merchants transported their merchandise to Italy themselves, especially to Genoa, and there sold it. We can presume that Lombard merchants, who came to Flanders to sell Oriental or Mediterranean products—spices, silks, leather, etc.—brought back cloth as return freight. But from the middle of the century many merchants did not make the whole trip; instead they met at the trade fairs of Champagne (Troyes, Provins, Lagny, Bar-sur-Aube), which began to centralize an important part of the trade between northwestern Europe and the Mediterranean countries. Their role was to become increasingly important in the following century.

A concentration of great international trades was, in fact, created in Italy for the profit of a few northern maritime cities— Genoa and Pisa, on the one hand, and Venice, on the other—setting aside Sicily, to which we will refer later. Amalfi was deprived of its privileged position in the Byzantine Empire and even in the Moslem countries, following its annexation by Robert Guiscard. It went into a speedy decline, and after being sacked by the Genoese in 1135, lost all importance. The crusades—both the first and those of the twelfth century—allowed Genoa, Pisa, and Venice to create permanent settlements throughout the Latin Near East and, as a result, to guide a great part of the commerce from Asia to Europe directly through their own hands. Since 1082 Venice had enjoyed a privileged status in the Byzantine world: specifically an exemption from customs duties and from taxes on purchases and sales. This situation was threatened several times during the century by conflicts between Venice and the Byzantine authorities, who in 1171 had arrested all the Venetians within the empire and confiscated their goods. There were even wars (1124–1126; 1171–1176). Venice always ended by maintaining her position. Genoa and Pisa gradually succeeded in gaining a place in the empire alongside their former ally. Fierce hatreds stemmed from the rivalry between these three cities. Even in the Moslem ports, especially at Alexandria, and—where Genoa and Pisa are concerned—in Africa as well, in the Maghreb, and in Moslem Spain, the Italians developed or built up important sources of business; the Genoese and the Pisans even played the role of intermediaries between the various parts of the Islamic world. They dominated the Mediterranean and reduced other ports—such as those of Narbonne, Montpellier, Saint-Gilles, and Arles—to an activity that was entirely secondary compared with their own. Barcelona and Marseille, with whom the Genoese and the Pisans maintained relations, lagged behind. This Mediterranean trade, moreover, was linked with the north-south trade across Europe. Indeed, the Genoese and the Pisans exported to the Orient and to Barbary— Africa and the Maghreb—not only Italian products, but also products from north of the Alps, including cloth from Flanders, northern France, and Brabant. They also imported products for northern Europe from the Orient and from Barbary. Venice appears to have maintained her traditional exports, specifically slaves, for the Moslem countries and had developed her importation of eastern products for resale principally in Italy, Germany, and the Slav countries of central Europe. It seems that from the twelfth century on, the Italian merchant cities bought, in the ports of northern Africa, gold from the transsaharan countries, and that this latter was used to liquidate the debit balances that often arose from trade with the Orient.

We have already referred to a new current that appeared in international trade in the second half of the twelfth century. This was the Atlantic trade: the export of wines from southwestern France to England and to Bruges, in Flanders, which was carried on by the people of the southwest themselves but soon also by the Flemings, was the oldest and the principal element in this trade. By the end of the century the volume of business must have been considerable. Perhaps salt from the Bay of Bourgneuf, the south of Brittany, also began to be exported to Bruges in this period.

There were many new aspects to the east-west commercial flow and to the routes that joined it. Trade from the Byzantine or Moslem Orient, through Russia toward the Baltic, fell off completely. There are many reasons for this decline: the rerouting of an important part of trade from Asia toward the ports of the Latin East; the fact that the Italian colonies drained the Byzantine markets toward the West; the difficulties created for trade in southern Russia, at first by the Petchenegs and then by the Kumans. Northern Russia, together with Novgorod, was to continue to play an important role, but in a very different context.

There was a great development of the west-east commercial flow during the twelfth century. In this the cloth industry of Flanders, northern France, and Brabant also played a role of capital importance: on the one hand, through the importation of English wool and, on the other, through the exportation of cloth back to England and to the East. Two different routes gave access to the East: the Scheldt-Meuse-Rhine delta, and then along the Rhine; or the land route that grew up between Bruges and Cologne and favored the development of the Brabant towns. It was the Rhine trade, starting from Cologne, that conveyed to the east and the southeast the cloths and other products that reached this place: for example, those of the brass industry from the region of the Meuse and those of the Rhine-Westphalian metallurgical industry. The routes followed were either the land routes to Hamburg and to Magdeburg and the crossings of the Elbe, or the upper Rhine, the Main, and more distantly, the Danube; more distantly here means in Hungary and the Slav countries of central Europe. Besides the Flanders-Cologne routes and their extensions, there was navigation in the North Sea between London and Bruges, on the one hand, and between Bremen and Hamburg, on the other. This navigation passed from the hands of the Danes to a great extent into those of the northern Germans during the twelfth century; but the Flemings and the English participated in it. Here also the export of Flemish cloth played a major role. The chief factor that gave this commercial route its entire importance in the second half of the twelfth century, was the German colonization beyond the Elbe and the beginning of a movement that led immigrants from lower Saxony, Westphalia, and the Rhineland to found a series of German towns along the shores of the Baltic. The first and the most important of these was Lübeck (founded in 1143 and, after being destroyed, again in 1158) ; and before the end of the century a German settlement had been founded at Visby, on the Swedish island of Gotland. Increasingly, Lübeck and Visby, and later still other towns, began to establish entrepôts for raw goods from the Slav lands of the Baltic; in a large measure, they took the place of the Danish port of Schleswig and of other Danish or Swedish commercial centers. Relations were established with Novgorod, which collected these same kind of goods from the Russian plain. These were pitch, potassium, wax, and furs, etc. The Flemings, from the second half of the century, probably took these goods as return freight in German North Sea ports; meanwhile it is probable that the North Germans themselves transported these goods to Bruges, where they perhaps were already buying wines and salt from southwestern France. This North Sea trade, with its Baltic extensions, was, however, only just beginning to develop at the end of the twelfth century.

Up to this point we have dealt only with the principal commercial currents, without concealing the existence of others that were also important. The extensions into the Baltic of the new trade flow, which we have just mentioned, was closely related to German colonization across the Elbe. Now conquest actually went hand in hand with the settlement of colonists in the occupied lands—knights and peasants—coming from western Germany and the Low Countries (Flanders and Lotharingia) : a consequence once again of the increase of population in the western countries and the lack of cultivable land despite clearance. This movement was supported by the Emperor Lothair (1125–1138), who was the successor of Henry V, and by two territorial princes: Albert the Bear, marquis of the northern march of Saxony, who was to make himself master around 1150 of what was to become the marquisate of Brandenburg (the Havel region) ; and Henry the Lion, duke of Saxony, who conquered the northeastern parts of the transelbe lands toward the Oder. The influx of German or Netherland peoples continued the germanization of the conquered Slav lands. At the same time the conversion of the Slav population to Christianity, already undertaken by missionaries, was pursued. This was principally the work of the

Praemonstratensian or Cistercian abbeys, "daughters" of those fixed in western Germany. Regular canons and monks both played a major role in enhancing the productive capacity of the country. The submission of the neighboring regions of the Baltic to the King of Denmark following the removal of Henry the Lion, who was condemned for felonious offenses toward the Emperor in 1180, lasted only until the end of the first quarter of the thirteenth century—and neither halted the germanization of these lands nor, of course, their conversion to Christianity.

While the Christian world was expanding into northeastern Europe, the positions that it had reoccupied in the Near East were being threatened. Because of their internal divisions, the Latin settlements in the Holy Lands and in Syria were too weak to resist well-led attacks from the Turks or from the Fatimites. The foundation of the military religious orders, composed of knight-monks—the Knights Templars and the old charitable brotherhood of the Hospitalers of St. John, whose character had changed —placed a small permanent army at the disposal of the King of Jerusalem: this was insufficient to counterbalance the political or military incompetence and the lack of discipline that prevailed among too many of the "Frankish" knights and, above all, among too many of the leaders of autonomous principalities. Furthermore, the hostility, sometimes overt and always latent, of the Byzantine Empire, which claimed to re-establish its authority over Syria and especially over Antioch, was to make a "counter crusade" easier. This latter was undertaken by the Turkish atabeg of Mosul, Imâd ad Dîn Zenguî, who was in fact an independent governor. This would have come to a head after 1137 had it not been defeated by the Emperor John Comnenos. When relations between Byzantium and the "Franks" once more worsened, Zenguî again took up the offensive; Edessa and the greater part of the county were conquered in 1144.

This disaster profoundly affected western Christendom; it feared the worst. The Pope appealed to Christendom to rescue the

Holy Land. But it was another person who brought this about: a powerful personality, owing less to his intelligence than to the firmness of his convictions, the ardor of his passions, and his strength of will: Saint Bernard, of the Cistercian order, Abbot of Clairvaux. His policy during the second quarter of the twelfth century had a profound effect on the life of the Church and of western Europe; the supremacy of the Church, at least as spiritual power, the literal and rigorous observation of the rules prescribed by her, were to have no defender more eager than he. He brought to the Holy Land no less a person than the King of Germany, Conrad III of the Swabian house of Hohenstaufen, and the King of France, Louis VII. Once more the incompetence of the leaders and the lack of discipline among the troops, both among the crusaders and in the kingdom of Jerusalem and among the vassal principalities, brought all to ruin. The second crusade, which was undertaken in 1147, failed lamentably and even increased the dangers threatening the Christian states of the East. In the West it was thought important to avenge this failure by attacking the Byzantine emperor, who was accused of treason: Roger II of Sicily inspired a crusade against Byzantium, which was supported by Saint Bernard, but which broke down before the opposition of Conrad III.

The Greek-speaking Christian world—that is to say, the Byzantine Empire—represented at this time, moreover, as we have mentioned, in passing, a considerable force. The sons and the grandsons of Alexios Comnenos, John (1118–1143) and Manuel (died 1180)—due among other things to the reorganization of their military forces, to the resources of their diplomacy, and to the strict dependence in which they had held the aristocracy— had succeeded in maintaining, or even in extending, the territories subject to the imperial power. Important areas of Asia Minor were reconquered from the Turks; the Armenian principality of Cilicia ("Little Armenia") was reduced to obedience; the principality of Antioch, the northernmost of the Latin states in the Near-East, was forced to become once more a vassal of the empire; and the King of Jerusalem, Amaury I (1162–1174), recognized Manuel Comnenos as his overlord. Byzantine protection could be seen to constitute at certain times the most effective defense of the Christian states of the Levant. In Europe also Manuel Comnenos, following in his father's footsteps, strengthened the Byzantine position. He imposed his suzerainty over the prince of the revolting Serbs, and he seized Dalmatia from Hungary in order to establish it as a Byzantine duchy. If he was not able to root out from this realm Croatia, which had been reunited at the beginning of the century (1102), in Hungary he nevertheless held German influence in check and even, after 1173, succeeded in submitting its king to his authority.

Manuel Comnenos was very attracted by the West; he was deeply sensitive to the civilization represented by western chivalry, although he despised all western sovereigns from the heights of his own legitimacy. He obviously had as a program the re-establishment of his imperial authority in Italy. The first obstacle he met was the Norman kingdom of Sicily. The power of this state had done nothing but increase. Roger II, on the occasion of a Roman schism brought on by a double election (1130), recognized the unfortunate Anacletus over Innocent II, who had had the good fortune to be supported by Saint Bernard and was thus to triumph. He had obtained from "his" pope a royal crown and recognition of the authority of his crown over Apulia, which was a papal fief. He had forced Innocent II, after the death of Anacletus in 1139, to recognize—though unwillingly—what he had acquired. The King of Sicily's financial, military, and naval power enabled him to fight the Moslem states of northern Africa and to found settlements on their shores, which were designed to transfer to Palermo part of the transmediterranean trade. As for Byzantium, Roger once more took up Robert Guiscard's plans, occupied Corfu, attacked the empire on the Aegean Sea, sacked the industrial towns of Thebes and Corinth, and deported the workers and their silk businesses to Palermo (1147). This was the beginning of a war in which Manuel, for a period of time, was supported by the Venetian navy and had at least the diplomatic support of Conrad III. Beginning with the recapture of Corfu in 1149, the Byzantine emperor made a major effort to reconquer Sicily and southern Italy. He failed completely, however; and in 1158 peace was concluded. The Norman kingdom of Sicily continued to dominate the central Mediterranean.

Nevertheless, Manuel by no means abandoned his western ambitions. In 1152 Frederick Barbarossa succeeded his uncle, Conrad III, and immediately before his Roman coronation in 1155 placed, as we will see, the emphasis of his policies on the imperial power of the German sovereigns. There was total opposition between him and Manuel. Not only did the *basileus* make an anti-Frederick citadel of Ancona, which he had occupied during the Sicilian conflict, but he provided subsidies to the Lombard towns that were at war against Barbarossa, and perhaps he would have supported the German adversaries of an emperor whom he openly treated as a usurper, and who in reply termed him "king of the Greeks." Manuel negotiated, though without success, an alliance with Pope Alexander III and King Louis VII of France against Frederick. In 1166 he even proposed to the Pope to put an end to the Greek schism, on condition that he was himself crowned emperor by the Pope or by one of his legates. One could go no farther. But here also Manuel failed: the Byzantine clergy opposed his plans; and on the other hand, Alexander III failed him. Mistrust of Byzantium remained great, and the danger of seeing the apostolic throne subject to the tyrannical authority of the *basileus* appeared by no means imaginary. The whole "Justinian" policy, as one might call it, of Manuel Comnenos in the West came to nothing, save to sap the strength of the eastern empire.

Much the same could be said about the imperial policies of Frederick Barbarossa and about their consequences for Germany.

We must review a little in order to understand this. We have seen how much the investiture struggle had reduced and weakened the imperial and royal power of the German sovereigns. The facts that in 1125, after the death of Henry V, the princes elected King Lothair, of the house of the dukes of Saxony, and then in 1138, Conrad of the house of Hohenstaufen in Swabia, showed their intention of avoiding hereditary succession. Altogether, these kings—of whom only Lothair had himself crowned emperor— were too weak to show themselves independent of the popes, and it was during the second quarter of the century that a pontifical doctrine concerning the empire took shape. It was a new and decisive extension to the system of feudal dependence in relations with the Holy See, as it had been applied by Gregory VII and Urban II to many states. Innocent II and Hadrian IV (1154–1159) attempted to have it declared that imperial power was held in fief from the Pope. By one of those contradictions that seem scarcely apparent to the people of the high Middle Ages, this doctrine was developed at a time when pontifical authority, at Rome itself, was held in check. As she no longer had the support of a secular authority possessing the material means to maintain order in Church territories, she was unable to prevent a communal revolution at Rome in 1143. Arnold of Brescia, a mystical demagogue, exercised from 1145 onward great authority under the cover of a republican constitution that had supposedly been restored, with a senate as its principal organ. This regime was to last ten years or so, and the Romans claimed that it was to them and not to the pope or to anyone, no matter who, that the right of conferring the imperial dignity belonged.

In 1152 Frederick Barbarossa, the nephew of Conrad III, was elected king. His intention was to re-establish in Germany, Burgundy, and Italy the authority that the sovereigns of the eleventh century had exercised. He succeeded in the first of these countries. Systematically using the prerogatives granted to him by the Concordat of Worms he succeeded in bringing the imperial

Church under his power to a large extent, and he undertook to set up a type of "crown domain" by bringing together an important group of counties and seigneuries. The King of Denmark, a vassal of the German crown since the reign of Lothair (1134), continued this subordinate relation to Frederick, though it was purely theoretical. In the kingdom of Burgundy-Provence, Barbarossa attempted to give some reality to royal authority by his marriage with Beatrice, who came from the family of the counts of Burgundy (the future Franche-Comté).

In Italy the situation was more difficult than elsewhere. It was a question of dealing not only with princes and bishops but also with urban republics. The cities of Lombardy, Liguria, Tuscany and Emilia, subsisting from commerce and industry, were governed by "consuls" and other elected magistrates belonging to the nobility of the region or to the patriciate of merchant origin; both groups had been enriched by business. They made their policies for themselves, attempted to dominate the surrounding areas, and, to serve their own interests, fought each other savagely. Milan, the economic capital of Lombardy, where the routes of the Alpine passes met, was distinguished by its violent reactions.

In 1155 Frederick helped the Pope to fight the Roman commune and delivered Arnold of Brescia to him. Arnold was executed. Then Barbarossa had himself crowned emperor at Rome, but he was convinced that he had acquired the imperial dignity independently of this coronation, at the same time as he had acquired the German kingship. After a period when the imperial dignity had suffered an eclipse, heavy stress was once more placed upon it. Frederick considered this imperial dignity as an absolute authority, and of course as a universal authority, equal to that of the *basileus* and even, as we have seen, superior to the latter. His universality nevertheless was expressed, not by aspirations to exercise some sort of power over the kings of France, England, etc., but by the vindication of a pre-eminence (*auctoritas*) over those whom an imperial functionary termed "Kinglets" (*reguli*).

In any event, in the eyes of Frederick and his councilors, the imperial dignity implied not only the protection of the universal Church but, as a consequence, the right to intervene in questions pertaining to the papacy. Following the death of Hadrian IV in 1159 and the schism provoked by a double election, the Emperor tried through every means, though without success, to impose Victor IV rather than Alexander III as pope and, after the death of Victor IV, two antipopes in succession, Pascal III and Calixtus III.

At the center of Barbarossa's immediate concerns was his Italian policy: to re-establish peace under his effective authority in this realm, through having the towns and territories governed by imperial functionaries. Perhaps he had secret ideas of drawing upon the financial resources of a country whose money economy, supported by international trade, was vastly more developed than in Germany. He used, in support of his policy, legal weapons furnished by the renaissance of Roman law: the discovery of the texts of the Digesta at the end of the eleventh century had led to an extraordinary development of the study of law in Italy, at Bologna, and elsewhere. There were, moreover, dispositions of Roman public law which, as they aptly served a monarchist policy, played the foremost role in political life. And private Roman law, especially law of contracts, entered increasingly into the law of many European countries—it failed in England in the thirteenth century—and was finally "received" as common law in Germany in the fifteenth century.

The war that Frederick Barbarossa pursued for twenty years in Italy broke down before the opposition of all those whose interests were compromised, or whose ambitions were countered: the Lombard towns, of course; the popes, threatened with subordination to the Emperor when they considered themselves his superior; the kings of Sicily, with whom the papacy had been reconciled when confronted by a danger that, for them as much as for the papacy, represented an effective imperial authority in Italy; and finally, as we know, the Byzantine Emperor. And lastly—and this is a very important fact—non-German western Christian opinion. The French and the English clergy came out in support of Alexander III against the pope whom the Emperor supported, and their kings followed suit. This attitude was in part determined and maintained *because* the Emperor supported the adversary of Alexander III; there was indignation against German claims to rule the Church and thus indirectly to rule the Christian world. The French, the English, the Spaniards, the Scandinavians, the Hungarians rightly considered the Emperor as being essentially a German sovereign.

Frederick Barbarossa's grandiose efforts to make the empire a reality once more led to nothing positive; the principal effect was to precipitate the political breakup of Germany. The Emperor had to make concessions extending the autonomy of lay princes in order to obtain and keep their support. The most famous and the most important, on account of its later consequences in the plan of international relations, was the elevation of Austria into a duchy, with privileges strictly limiting the power of the Crown (1156). It had been up to this time simply the eastern "march" of Bavaria. In 1180—in order to win the support of the princes against the Duke of Saxony and Bavaria, Henry the Lion, head of the house of Guelph, and a rebel—it had also been necessary to consent in the main to the substitution of the system of feudal-vassalic relations—in essence contractual—to that which was still composed of essentially monarchical elements in the political structure of Germany; and it was even necessary to follow a policy that ruined the effort to create a "crown domain." The reign of Barbarossa was an important step in the transformation of Germany into a conglomerate of sovereign states. The relations of the Slavic vassal states with Germany were scarcely altered. In Poland, where royalty had died out at the end of the eleventh century, a vassal status still existed; the Grand Duke, living in Cracow, exercised very weak authority over the dukes and his relatives who governed various parts of the state, and he himself paid homage to the German sovereign while remaining in fact almost independent. The Duke of Bohemia, raised in 1158 to royal status by Barbarossa, was also attached by the bonds of vassality to the German crown; his subordination was more of a reality than that of the Polish Grand Duke.

Even though Henry II, King of England, at the beginning of his reign in 1157—a time when he was chiefly concerned with gaining eventual support against the King of France by understandings with Germany—recognized the preeminence, or imperial *auctoritas*, for a short period, at no time did the twelfth-century Capetians allow themselves to make any similar gesture. They even took the greatest care to avoid anything that could let anyone think they admitted to any such pre-eminence. Nevertheless, the French realm under Philip I (died 1108), under Louis VI the Fat (died 1137), and even under Louis VII (died 1180) was politically very weak. Without the support of the bishops and abbots of northern France, who commanded the resources of important seigneuries, and above all, without the support of several powerful territorial princes—the Count of Flanders, traditionally loyal to the Crown, and the Count of Anjou, who was occasionally loyal—the French kings would have had difficulty in resisting Anglo-Norman expansion. The conflicts between the Capetians, on the one hand, and William Rufus (1087–1100) and Henry I (1100–1135)—both sons of William the Conqueror —on the other, broke out in 1097 with an English attempt to conquer the French Vexin. It would be worthless to analyze this interminable series.

It is more important from our point of view to note Louis VI's efforts—and they were successful—to make royal authority effective in the "crown domain" to the north and south of Paris, and to expand this latter, be it only modestly. The increase in authority and prestige, which resulted from this for the Crown, became apparent in 1124. In that year, the Emperor Henry V, allied with

Henry I, king of England, invaded France. Almost all the territorial princes of northern France were present in the royal army or sent their contingents to it. Even the counts of Chartres-Blois and of Troyes did so, although they were sworn enemies of the Capetians, and until that very moment had been at war with the King as allies of the King of England. This last fact is particularly significant. It allows us to believe in the existence of sentiments hostile to the Germans. There were, moreover, other indications of this state of mind; perhaps the claims of the German sovereign, in as much as he was emperor, to rule the affairs of the universal Church, contributed to the development of this hostility, especially in a country where "reformist" ideas had penetrated widely and deeply. The consolidation and extension of royal power made some real though modest progress under Louis VII.

Yet, one could have believed that this progress should be more important. The King's marriage to the Duchess Eleanor of Aquitaine seemed to pave the way for the union of this great southwestern principality with the "crown domain." But nothing came of it; the separation of husband and wife in 1152 altered the course of affairs considerably. On the other hand, the problems that Italian affairs caused the Emperor, King of Burgundy-Provence, did not allow him to prevent Louis VII from becoming the liege lord of the Count of Forez and from uniting this imperial territory on the right bank of the Rhône with France.

Some very important parts of twelfth-century France were gathered under a single authority, but this was the authority of the King of England, Henry II. Under William Rufus and especially under Henry I the structure of the English kingdom had been consolidated, partly through the Crown's systematic use of feudal-vassalic relations, and partly through the development of administrative institutions served by a core of paid officials. As much could be said of Normandy. The reign of Stephen of Blois (1135–1154) was a period of anarchy, and it took his successor, Henry II (1154–1189), several years to rebuild firm power in

England. Throughout his reign he applied himself to perfecting judicial, financial, and administrative institutions. These intelligent and continued efforts brought to the English monarchy the means for military and political action—thanks to the employment of hired troops, among which were numerous foreign mercenaries. At this time the country gained an internal security rarely achieved in western Europe. Henry II, through his mother Matilda, was the grandson of Henry I, and he held his rights in England and Normandy through her. From Geoffrey Plantagenet, his father, he held the county of Anjou, with its annexes of Maine and Touraine. Through his marriage with Eleanor, the divorced wife of Louis VII, he acquired the duchy of Aquitaine; furthermore he succeeded in imposing his suzerainty over the county of Toulouse and over the duchy of Brittany, which, moreover, was governed by one of his sons. In Great Britain he had his suzerainty recognized by the King of Scotland, a country where English influence had increased in the reigns of Henry I and of Stephen of Blois, owing to the immigration of many members of the Anglo-Norman aristocracy. The system of feudal-vassalic relations and several English institutions had been introduced there. Wales remained less penetrable; however, Henry II imposed his supremacy over the Welsh princes. He also imposed his supremacy over the kinglets and local chiefs of Ireland, including the English lords who had settled there. The term "Anglo-Angevin empire" lends itself to confusion, since Henry II never bore an imperial title. But the image that it evokes is correct: a vast collection of lands comprising a considerable core of immediate territories and a fringe of realms or of principalities subject to the feudal authority or to the supremacy of Henry II. He was, directly or indirectly, overlord of more than half of France; a man, French in manners and speech, who, moreover, spoke no English. In the mass that was the French portion of the "Anglo-Angevin empire" there was no simple juxtaposition of duchies or counties. In the French territories he personally held, Henry II introduced administrative practices similar to those that he used in England. There is no need to become involved in detail with the wars that Henry II had to undertake: the revolts of his sons, rebellions in his states, and wars with the King of France, whose vassal he was, for so many of his duchies and counties. It is only important that he remained the victor.

Until the death of Louis VII nothing disrupted the "Anglo-Angevin empire." Nothing save for a struggle of an ecclesiastical nature. In 1164, with the support of the Pope, Thomas Becket, the archbishop of Canterbury, opposed measures taken by the King to further the Church of England's subordination to his authority. After many mishaps, Thomas was assassinated in 1170. The King was considered responsible. The indignation that seized a great part of Christian opinion both in England and on the Continent was so strong, and the worldwide authority acquired by the Church showed itself to be once more so great that Thomas Becket, a courageous and cunning political prelate, was immediately considered a saint and martyr, and in 1173 was canonized by Alexander III, while Henry II was forced in 1172 to humiliate himself and to compromise with the Church. In 1173, when pressured by the revolt of his sons, he even declared England to be held as a fief from the Holy See, in the fallacious hope that Pope Alexander III would send him help. This declaration, however, had no immediate effects.

The twelfth century saw the Christian states in Spain continue to thrust toward the south. Until around 1130 Spain benefited from the aid of French knights, who more than once received the privileges of "crusaders" from the Holy See for their expeditions against the Moors. After 1130 this tide dried up. At this time Castile did not extend much beyond the Tagus; on the other hand, Aragon, following the capture of Saragossa in 1118, became the mistress of the middle reaches of the Ebro. In the west, south of Galicia, Portugal came into being: a county set up in 1097 by Alfonso VI of Castile for a bastard daughter, who had married Henry, a French knight of the house of Burgundy. During the period that followed, the *reconquista* continued but with less impetus. The political transformations among the Christian states sometimes but not always favored it. The separation of Navarre from Aragon in 1134 was not favorable to the *reconquista*, because it accentuated the Pyreneean character of the restored kingdom. On the other hand, the union of the kingdom of Aragon with the county of Barcelona in 1137—which was completely independent, in fact, of France, but whose counts had won considerable areas of western Langedoc to their authority— aided Christian conquests in the east of the peninsula: the capture of Tortosa at the mouth of the Ebro in 1148, with the help of a Genoese fleet; then the advance toward the south in the direction of Valencia. Castile, despite its claims to hegemony—King Alfonso VII took the imperial title and diadem in 1135—and despite remarkable warlike exploits, progressed but little: internal dissensions and conflicts with other Spanish states limited possibilities for action; moreover, the separation of León from Castile in 1157 was also a cause of military and political weakness for Christian Spain. But we must point out that the repopulation of reconquered regions continued throughout the century.

The outstanding factor that upheld the power of Islam over the greater part of the Iberian penninsula during the thirteenth century was once again the appearance of a savage force in the Moslem world. Naturally this force stemmed from a religious event. A Mahdi created a large hearing among the Berbers by preaching a new orthodoxy together with a rigorous austerity and by accusing the Almoravides of anthropomorphism. There were passionate attacks upon the Christians. The Mahdi's partisans, called "Almohades," conquered the Maghreb; and after the death of the Mahdi (1127–1129) his successor proclaimed himself caliph. The conquest of the south of Spain and of the Almoravides or of the local chiefs who had succeeded them, followed from 1146. The Almohades checked the Christian advance toward the center of the peninsula. The reconquest slowed down, despite the help given at first by the Templars and the Hospitalers and later by the Spanish military orders that were founded on the example of the former in the second half of the century—among them, Calatrava, Santiago, Alcantara. Meanwhile, in the west, Portugal continued to progress: in 1147, with the arrival of a fleet manned by Germans, English, Flemings, and Brabanters, en route for the second crusade, Lisbon and the Tagus estuary were conquered, and the war continued. The Count of Portugal proclaimed himself king in 1139, and forty years later he threw off all vassal subordination to Castile. Portuguese energy contributed much to neutralize the attempts at reconquest of the Almohades in the second half of the century.

The latter, on the other hand, did not limit their activities to Spain. With the Maghreb as a base, they attacked Africa proper —*Ifrikia*—from 1152 on and they extended their domination to the confines of Cyrenaica. This fact had its repercussions in Europe, for they sacked the coastal towns and the Norman settlements set up by Roger II. Only economic necessity made them grant concessions despite their fanaticism. In the second half of the century the Genoese and then the Pisans succeeded in re-establishing commercial relations with the ports where the caravan routes started that linked the Mediterranean to the trans-Saharan lands. There they bought gold, alum, and wax. Before the end of the century Sicily also once more set up contacts with the African coast.

If a study of international relations in the twelfth century were limited to subjects of a political, economic, or social category, there would be something essential lacking. We have already mentioned religious subjects, and a concern for clarity requires that some other ones should be dealt with in a later chapter. But it is important to say a few words about certain very important artistic and intellectual phenomena that belong to a history of international relations. Chronologically these occur not only within the twelfth century but in part in the eleventh and even in the tenth.

One must stress the influence that certain schools, their teachers, and their pupils exercised in the intellectual domain. There is no need to cite all. Without any question, from the end of the tenth century and especially in the eleventh, the most famous was the cathedral school of Chartres—and it was to remain important during the twelfth century. There within the traditional framework of the *trivium*—the three oral sciences: grammar, rhetoric, and dialectics—and of the *quadrivium*—the four sciences of number: arithmetic, geometry, astronomy, and music—a more exact knowledge of mathematics, classical authors, and platonic philosophy was sought. Among its students in the eleventh century Olbert was to teach at the Abbey of Gembloux in Lotharingia; and through the methods learned at Chartres, he helped the famous German canonist Burchard of Worms put together his collection of ecclesiastical law, the *Decretum*.

Sometimes influences combined. Another student of the school of Chartres, the Italian Lafranc—the future Archbishop of Canterbury under William the Conqueror and William Rufus— had at first studied law, doubtless in Pavia, the town of his birth. After 1042 he also taught at the Abbey of Le Bec. His own conception of dialectic, his knowledge of authors acquired at Chartres, and his legal education acquired at Pavia allowed him to form the mind of the greatest jurist who was to live north of the Alps in the first half of the twelfth century, the canonist Yves, bishop of Chartres.

Paris was another center. Here schools, subject to the authority of the bishop, grew in number on the Sainte-Geneviève hill. The great master who drew disciples here in the first half of the twelfth century was the Breton Peter Abelard (died 1142), particularly famous for a love life that was tragically interrupted.

As a dialectician who had been strongly influenced by the current knowledge of Aristotle in France, he applied dialectics to the exposition of dogma, seeking to establish concordances between opposed propositions. Saint Bernard, a man lacking intellectual strength, certainly judged Abelard's views to be dangerous to the faith and had them condemned at the Council of Sens (1140). However, they were surprisingly fecund, and in the most varied of places. Two Italians became their propagators, though they differed from each other in every way. One was a student of Abelard's, Arnold of Brescia, leader of the republican and antiquitarian Roman commune. The other was Cardinal Roland Bandinelli, the future Alexander III, a canonist and theologian who cautiously but quite obviously used Abelard's methods in his *Sententiae* to comment upon revealed truths.

If Otto, bishop of Freising, the uncle and the biographer of Frederick Barbarossa, was able to design his own historical works with a rigorousness and a very rare philosophical sense for his time, an explanation should be sought in the instruction of the Parisian schools that he had formerly frequented. The intellectual movement that developed in Norway in the second half of the twelfth and at the beginning of the thirteenth century was directly influenced by the instruction given by the canons of the Parisian Abbey of Saint-Victor. We have cited only these examples, in order to illustrate an important aspect of international relations.

As for art: we referred to it earlier; and here we shall be content with a few facts dealing with religious architecture, the greatest of the arts in the tenth, eleventh, and twelfth centuries, an art to which other western arts were only complementary. First we shall consider what concerns the romanesque style that flourished throughout the West at this time. It was in many respects regional art with its own characteristics; but, as has been known for a long time, the romanesque "schools" should not be thought of as fixed with clearly defined boundaries. In every case, actions and reactions were numerous. German churches, very close to the

Carolingian traditions, had many traits in common with the Lombard churches: the influence of clerics who traveled a great deal between these two countries, or an imprint left by architects coming from northern Italy, could be the explanation. A whole group of churches in the west of France have pendentives supporting a cupola. Serious archeologists accept that Byzantine cupolas are not at all foreign to this type of vaulting. It is not excessive to claim that contacts with the art of Moslem Spain can be seen in the decorative elements in the cathedral of Le Puy and in the shape of certain of its arches. The uniform plan of important churches that rose up along the pilgrimage routes— from Saint Martin of Tours to Santiago of Compostella, by way of Sainte-Foy of Conques and Saint-Sernin of Toulouse—is a fact of equal importance to be cited here. As for the romanesque churches of Normandy, they served as models for English cathedrals of the twelfth century. This truly does not need any other comment.

Since the end of the eleventh century people had sought in various places for means of the development of vaults that would give roofs a greater solidity and allow for higher walls and better illumination of naves and choir. These experiments produced several systems that have been termed ribbed vaults or "crossed ogives." From the second quarter of the twelfth century on, one of them was going to allow for the construction in royal France of great churches commonly and rather oddly called "Gothic." The oldest of these is the Abbey of Saint-Denis, whose choir was consecrated in 1144. Perhaps one of the most relevant facts of a history of international relations can be found in the origins of this new "French" style, as it could be more exactly described.

Certain vaults from Moslem Spain were able to influence the so-called crossed ogives of southern France, but they are very different from those that gave rise to "Gothic" architecture. We are already closer to these latter with the ribbed vaults that were to appear at Durham in the north of England toward the end of the eleventh century, and that will be found again not only in great English but also in great Norman churches, all of them Romanesque, of the following century. It would be wise to stop here. A fully developed Gothic art from the end of the twelfth and of the thirteenth centuries will furnish important elements in the history of international relations.

7

The Practice of International Relations in the Tenth, Eleventh, and Twelfth Centuries

FOR THE tenth, the eleventh, and especially the twelfth century the greater wealth of documentation allows a more generous survey of the organization of international relations than that of which the early Middle Ages had formed the chronological frame. The changes that had occurred in the state of the western world, in the Byzantine and Moslem worlds during this new period, and the individual character of the available sources will certainly act upon the structure of the present chapter. It will not exactly conform to that of the chapter given to the sixth, seventh, eighth, and ninth centuries.

Nevertheless we will start once more with the problem of relations between political units and in particular with the problem of the negotiations that these relations made necessary. The term "state" will be used to designate these political units, sometimes even with reference only to duchies and to important territorial principalities making up part of the realm of Germany, France, Burgundy-Provence, or Arles, as this last realm was beginning to be called at the end of the twelfth century. In Norman England there were no principalities: only the English kingdom will appear. The important place reserved here for negotiations is justified by the frequency and the importance of the questions that were their object. It is even important to insist on the fact that a political unit of the first magnitude, the Byzantine Empire, resorted more to negotiations than to war to gain its objectives, and usually with greater success. It appears that, besides other considerations, an ethical and religious viewpoint played a role in the superiority recognized by the Byzantine world of diplomatic means as compared to military measures.

Negotiations conducted directly between heads of state seem to have been more numerous than in the preceding period, at least in the West. Obviously this was a consequence of the personal character of imperial power, royal or princely, that was now even more accentuated than had been the power of the Carolingians. These direct negotiations could have been conducted by correspondence, but more frequently they took place in the course of meetings. The many meetings of German and French sovereigns in the tenth, eleventh, and twelfth centuries and those of the French and English sovereigns in the twelfth century provide excellent examples. The meetings of sovereigns were, moreover, often prepared by envoys or by intermediaries, whom we will discuss later; they could also be real conferences to which each side sent its delegates, such as the conference of Chioggia, in 1177, where Frederick Barbarossa, Pope Alexander III, the Lombard cities, and the King of Sicily were represented. Here a peace was concluded between the Pope and the Emperor, and a truce was set up between the latter and the Lombards and the Sicilian king. The meetings were able to settle on the goals of making common dispositions, regulating difficulties, preventing conflicts, or even reestablishing peace. It happened that they took place on "neutral" territory. The best-known case is that of the meeting at Venice, where Frederick Barbarossa and Alexander III made peace in 1177. Often conferences took place "in the marches"—at the frontier or at least in its vicinity—as a security measure or in order to guard the prestige of each party. In this category were the meetings between the German kings or emperors and the kings of France on the Meuse in 1006 and in 1033; at Ivois, on the Chiers, in 1023, 1043, 1048, and 1056; the unsuccessful meeting between Frederick Barbarossa and Louis VII for ending the papal schism, held in 1162 at Saint-Jean-de-Losne, in France (in the duchy of Burgundy), but within the immediate neighborhood of the kingdom of Arles (county of Burgundy); and the meeting between Frederick and Philip Augustus between Ivois and Mouzon, on the Meuse, in 1187. Such also were the interviews at Neaufles-sur-l'Epte and at L'Ormeteau-Ferré, near Gisors, on the Norman frontier, between Louis VI and Henry I in 1109 and 1113; and that at Gisors between Louis VII and Henry II in 1165. Also there were the abortive interviews that ought to have brought the same kings together on the Norman frontier between Pacy and Mantes in 1168, and in the same year at La Ferté-Bernard, on the Huisne, on the frontier of Maine; or even those that brought these kings together at the frontier of Normandy between Gisors and Trie in 1173, at Gisors in 1174, and at Ivry in 1177. The practice continued under the reign of Philip Augustus, beginning in 1180. A pilgrimage provided the pretext for a king or a prince to meet another in his own country and to deliberate with him. This was, for example, the case with Philip of Alsace, count of Flanders, in 1177 and with Louis VII in 1179, when they went to the tomb of Saint Thomas Becket at Canterbury and there met with Henry II.

Similar meetings also took place in the East. At all times the *basileus* awareness of his own superiority prevented him from meeting heads of state except in his capital, and preferably in his palace except when he himself was in the field or bound by some other case of *force majeure*. When in 924 the Emperor Romanos Lecapenos had met with Czar Simeon of Bulgaria before the walls of the capital, it was to induce the Bulgarians to raise the siege of the city. But it was in the palace at Constantinople that Alexios Comnenos concluded agreements with the leaders of the first crusade in 1096 and 1097, and that at the time of the second crusade in 1147 Manuel Comnenos received Conrad III and Louis VII. There also he had important meetings with the Turkish Sultan of Iconium, in Asia Minor, Kilidj Arslan II (1162), with Bohemund III, prince of Antioch (1165), and with Amaury I, king of Jerusalem (1171)—to cite a few very important facts in the history of the Christian and Moslem Near East. This difference of attitude reveals the profoundly different conceptions that the western sovereigns and the heirs of Theodosius and Constantine had of their power.

Despite the importance of meetings between chiefs of state, the majority of negotiations in the period treated in this chapter for which we have evidence, were conducted by envoys representing one of the parties. These envoys generally tried to deal with the head of state of the other party or of one of the other parties. This was not always easy, especially in courts where etiquette isolated the sovereign, as in Byzantium or among the Moslem caliphs or emirs. The monk, John of Gorze, from Lorraine, sent by Otto I and received by the Caliph of Cordova in 956, spoke of him as a solitary king, seemingly a divinity, to whom no one, or almost no one, had access. Moreover, even in the West where the sovereigns were more accessible, negotiations were often conducted in part or entirely with the chief councilors of the head of state.

We still do not come across the use of specialists in these negotiations and, curiously enough, less at Byzantium than anywhere else—with the sole reservation that certain people, owing to their experience or to the favor the prince's bore them, were employed more frequently than others on certain missions. Most often these were embassies made up of at least two and more frequently three or four envoys who were sent to a foreign sovereign; and in very solemn circumstances these embassies were even more numerous. Among the envoys—more frequently called *nuntius, legatus,* or *mandatarius* in the documents—there were both clerics and laymen. When it was a question of negotiations with the Pope, or with the Byzantine emperor or a king, or even with the Slav princes of the East, such as the Duke of Poland, the German kings and emperors frequently called upon the services of archbishops, bishops, abbots, and counts, usually German but sometimes Italian. Sometimes a duke was part of the embassy. The real leader of the latter, he who effectively directed negotiations, was not always able or even allowed to appear among the plenipotentiaries; this seems to have been the case when on the occasion of the conference of Châlons (1107) with Pope Pascal II, the German chancellor Adalbert remained in the background and let the Archbishop of Trier appear to be playing the principal role. In other cases, less notable persons were called upon, but always clerics or nobles, Germans or sometimes Italians. The customs were not much different in other monarchies: however, if the Capetians utilized the services of the high secular or regular clergy, their lay envoys were generally not dukes or even counts of high rank.

Sometimes it happened that a choice was made of a person for a particular reason; if Otto I sent the monk John of Gorze to the caliph at Cordova, he did so because it would have been difficult to find an envoy in a nonmonastic milieu who would have accepted the dangers and lack of glory that such a mission involved; when he chose Liutprand, bishop of Cremona, for an embassy to the *basileus* Nicephorus Phocas in 968 he did so because of the knowledge of Greek of which Liutprand could boast, and because he had already fulfilled a mission in Constantinople. Similarly, the choice of the Bishop of Cambrai and the Abbott of Saint-Vanne of Verdun, whom the emperor Henry II in 1023 sent as his representatives to the King of France, Robert II, can doubtlessly be explained by the fact that they spoke French. Here is an example chosen from quite a different milieu and a different era: in order to negotiate a commercial treaty in 1157 with the Saracen "king" of Tunis, Pisa used a person of Saracen origin, to whom the Italian text of the treaty refers as Moimo, but whom the Arab text names, probably more precisely, as Abu Tamim Meimûn.

In Byzantium the embassies were composed of important persons belonging to the court, the central administration, the army, and the clergy; but here also it happened that specifically qualified individuals were called upon for this and that particular mission. It seems that the situation was not markedly different in the Islamic states.

Elsewhere we have stressed the extraordinary action taken by papal legates after the middle of the eleventh century. In the Middle Ages the intermingling of the ecclesiastical and the political was too complex for these legates to have always been charged with exclusively religious missions. Abroad they were, in the largest sense, the agents of papal policies. It is important to remember this.

During the period here discussed, it was not yet a general rule in the West for the heads of state to hand written documents over to their envoys; one might well state that the case was different in Byzantium. Even in the West, however, such documents were used more frequently, especially from the twelfth century on; and among them it is possible to distinguish rather clearly between credentials guaranteeing the recipient that he could place trust in what the envoy would tell him, and the "full powers," which testified that the bearer was qualified to negotiate and conclude matters. These full powers sometimes even included a promise of ratification. In some cases written instructions were given to the envoys; it is known that Otto I gave these to Liutprand, the bishop of Cremona, in 968 when he was charged with a mission to the *basileus* Nicephorus Phocas.

Nevertheless, more often oral instructions were given to the ambassadors in the era we are considering—except of course at Byzantium. It is probable that in certain states that had been under Byzantine influence, such as Venice, written instructions were used rather early: the oldest extant Venetian instructions (1197), are, indeed, in structure and in quality—notably in their precision—already quite highly developed.

It is not easy to determine who prepared the course of action of the envoys abroad. In Byzantium it can be claimed that it was, besides the immediate entourage of the emperor, the offices of the "logothete of the dromos," minister of posts, who at least had an important share of the foreign relations within his domain. In the West, where the constitution of a central administration was rather slow, the immediate entourage of the sovereign must have played the essential role, and it was inorganic and shifting. In the twelfth century, however, almost everywhere it can be observed that the chancellor played a particularly important role; and his offices issued written documents when necessary.

Except in special cases the envoys were accompanied by a fairly large suite and a great deal of baggage. This could be quite extensive if the embassy was guided by the desire to create an impression of power and riches. Generally care was taken that the personnel included people who could serve as guides or interpreters; in Byzantium, as was the case in the past, these were members of an official corps. During the famous mission that he accomplished in Cordova, accompanied only by one monk who served as a secretary, John of Gorze was flanked by a tradesman from Verdun—probably a slavedealer—who knew the Spanish roads and their conditions; the Mozarabian Bishop Recemond, envoy of the court of the Caliph to Otto I, while John of Gorze was retained at Cordova, received a similar companion for his return. It was a general and understandable custom. The sovereigns of Islamic countries followed the same practice as those of the western countries; the Jew Ibn Jaqûb, to whom we owe a description of northern Germany and the transelbe Slavic countries, was quite likely a slave merchant living in Andalusia who, in 965 or 973, accompanied a Cordovan embassy to Otto I.

The problem of subsistence and lodgings was to receive rather varied solutions. The Byzantine envoys were given funds or precious wares which they could sell; the foreign envoys within the entire imperial territory and in Constantinople were often maintained and lodged in public buildings and in every case at the expense of the state. The Russian princes of the eleventh and twelfth century were inspired by Byzantine practices; similar ones are found in the Islamic world. In the West hospitality in the Byzantine style would hardly have been possible. In the territory of the king or the prince whom they represented or to whom they went, the envoys could often requisition lodgings and food in the dwellings of the king's or the prince's subjects (*droit de gîte*); elsewhere they had to fall back on hospitality or pay for their lodging, which was less easy than for Byzantine envoys, owing to the very limited amount of available currency in the West; they, too, sometimes had goods to sell.

Baggage most often contained gifts for the sovereign and his entourage. These gifts continued to play a large role, in terms of marks of friendship and also as a means of obtaining the goodwill of the recipient. This is so true that a refusal to accept gifts constituted a grave offense, and the lack of an offer was an offense also. It was always fitting to give the envoys, when they departed on their return journey, presents for their master and for themselves. The accounts of embassy receptions frequently mention the generosity of these gifts.

The reception of the envoys was most often undertaken with considerable pomp. Allusion has already been made to the rigorous etiquette ruling these ceremonies in Byzantium, Baghdad, Cairo, Cordova, etc., and of the display often made on this occasion in the Christian or Moslem East, in the court that received them as well as by the envoys themselves. When a court where these customs prevailed received a monk, curious conflicts could occur: John of Gorze refused to bathe himself, to shave, and to put on appropriate dress as he was urged to do, when the Caliph of Cordova granted him an audience; he held fast, and he won his case. In the West etiquette was less rigorous, and the westerners were shocked by etiquette in Byzantium—to such a degree that during Alexios Comnenos' reception in 1097 of the Lotharingian crusaders, one of them deemed it right to install himself on the throne of the *basileus*, insisting that it was hardly fitting for only one man to be seated when so many valiant warriors remained standing. Sometimes one had to wait a long time before being received for an audience, but a refusal to grant audience was rare and was held to be a grave injury.

The personal immunity of the envoys was a generally accepted rule in the Moslem as well as in the western and eastern Christian worlds. It did not keep the envoys protected from all harm. Some of these difficulties were brought about by conflicts of precedence: in Byzantium the necessity of treating the Bulgars cautiously for a long time assured their envoys first rank after those of the caliph, whereas these came immediately after the highest civilian and military dignitaries—the patricians and the strategians—who were outranked only by the representatives of the Pope and of the patriarchs. In 968 the Italian bishop Liutprand, envoy of the western Emperor Otto I, formally objected—it is understandable—to being placed below a Bulgarian envoy at a banquet. He was not willing to accept any of the explanations offered him; in order to console him for this offense against his master, the *basileus* had to send a fat and deliciously stuffed kid from his own table. Later an attempt was made to isolate Liutprand and to discourage those who might have felt a desire to visit him. Lions from the imperial menagerie were placed in the house where he resided. He was detained in Constantinople for more than two months after the end of his mission: a less harsh fate than that of John of Gorze, who was confined in Cordova in an honorable captivity for three years before being admitted to see the Caliph. There are many more examples of the violation of immunity: envoys retained as hostages, as was an ambassador of Basil II to the Fatamite caliph at the end of the tenth century; or they were imprisoned, as were the envoys of Boleslav Chobry, duke of Poland, to Udalrich, duke of Bohemia, in 1014. Similar acts of violence seem to have been rarer during the twelfth century. However, the legates representing Pope Hadrian IV to Frederick Barbarossa at the Diet of Besançon in 1157 learned to their cost that missions abroad were still not without such perils.

When they had read and had translated into German a papal message that implied that the empire was a fief of the Holy See— at least it was so understood—the Count Palatine of Bavaria, Otto of Wittelsbach, unsheathed his sword. If the Emperor had not intervened, the legates, one of whom was the future Pope Alexander III, would have lost their lives. Barbarossa later had reason to regret his gesture. Immunities in the matter of tolls or customs—where customs existed—were not general. It was an express concession of the *basileus* that Liutprand invoked—in vain, however—when in Constantinople five pieces of purple silk that he had wanted to offer to his church were taken away from him before his departure.

Envoys could be absent abroad for a long time. Traveling was slow: in the middle of the tenth century, ten weeks from Cordova to Gorze, in Lorraine, seemed a normal time of travel. Poor connections and the lack of haste on the part of the responsible authorities could result in considerable delays: Liutprand took three months and one week in 968–969 to complete the journey from Constantinople to Ancona. Political factors on occasion caused delay. One can cite as an example the German embassy that left in 1027 for Constantinople and was refused passage by the King of Hungary: the envoys were forced to take a detour via Venice and to wait there for quite some time for transportation. Their absence lasted for fifteen months. It seems, however, that during the eleventh and twelfth centuries such prolonged absences became increasingly rare. Reports were certainly made by the envoys at the end of their mission and sometimes even during them: one often comes across allusions to these reports during a mission, presented in the form of letters. The final report was probably verbal in most cases, except in those states where the written word played an important and regular role in administration, as in the Byzantine Empire. In 969, Liutprand probably produced a written report on his mission of 968 and used it to compose the account of his mission, the picturesque *Relatio de*

Legatione Constantinopolitana, but this was a mission of particular importance, and Liutprand was a northern Italian, cultivated, belonging to a milieu and a country where the written word played a larger role than it did north of the Alps.

The embassies furnished valuable sources of information to the sovereign who sent them; they were, however, hardly the only sources: pilgrims and traders could also procure important information. There were states, such as the Byzantine Empire and the Moslem states, where these facts were carefully registered and kept in the archives used for foreign policy. The Emperor Constantine VII Porphyrogenetos (913–959) used them when he composed his treatise on the government of the empire (*De administrando imperio*) and on protocol (*De caeremoniis*). The judgments that the Caliph of Cordova gave John of Gorze in 966 on the structure and the very relative solidity of the German kingdom of Otto I reveal the accuracy of his information.

There is still a fact to which attention must be drawn when we discuss international negotiations in the Middle Ages, particularly from the twelfth century on: the importance taken on by mediation and the offer of good offices (it is useless to try to distinguish between them in this period). The mediator of mediators among Christian princes was the Pope. Alexander III intervened through the intermediary of his legates in the conflicts that were incessantly renewed between the King of France, Louis VII, and the King of England, Henry II—an action, moreover, in accord with his policy of tending to rely on the two western kingdoms in his conflict with Frederick Barbarossa. But other heads of state were frequently persuaded to attempt to stop or prevent conflicts: certain territorial princes of northern France—such as the Count of Flanders—and of Lotharingia in the second half of the twelfth century, almost made a specialty of offering their good offices. And here are some examples. In 1166, Philip of Alsace, count of Flanders, attempted to settle the question of the county of Mortain between his brother Matthew, count of Boulogne, and the King of

England, Henry II. In 1168 this same Philip of Alsace and Henry the Liberal, the Palatine count of Champagne, tried to re-establish peace between Henry II and Louis VII. In the preceding years the old Count of Flanders, Thierry of Alsace—who had in fact ceased to rule—Count Matthew of Boulogne, the counts of Guelders and of Clèves brought about the conclusion of the peace of Bruges between Philip of Alsace, count of Flanders, and Florent III, count of Holland. In 1177, Philip of Alsace negotiated the marriage of Alexios, son of Manuel Comnenos and Agnes, daughter of Louis VII. In 1182 the peace of La Grange-Saint-Arnoul between Philip of Alsace, count of Flanders, and the King of France, Philip Augustus, was concluded through the intervention of the kings of England, Henry II and his son Henry, of William of the White Hands, archbishop of Reims, of Thibaut IV, count of Blois, of his son Stephen, count of Sancerre, of Hugo III, duke of Burgundy, and of Baldwin V, count of Hainaut. In 1184, Philip of Alsace tried, morever, in vain to further the reconciliation of Frederick Barbarossa with Henry II by preparing a marriage between Richard, heir to the English throne, and a daughter of the Emperor and by trying to instigate the return to the Emperor's grace of Henry II's protégé, Henry the Lion.

Mediation was sometimes accompanied by pressure. An excellent example is furnished by the dispatch in 1181 of an embassy from Frederick Barbarossa to Philip Augustus who was at that moment at war with the Count of Flanders, Philip of Alsace—to bring him to make peace with his vassal, and threatening German military intervention if the King did not follow his suggestion.

Among the possible goals of negotiations we should point out the continuation and even the increase of those that were marked by a marriage uniting two dynasties. Several of these have been noted, and it may seem superfluous to cite other examples. It is, however, useful to note that the eastern schism did not hinder "political" marriages between Greeks and Latins. These were even numerous during the period of the Comnenos dynasty: Manuel I married Bertha of Sulzbach, sister-in-law of Conrad III, and later Mary, sister of Bohemund III, prince of Antioch; whereas the kings of Jerusalem, Baldwin III and Amaury I, like the Prince of Antioch, Bohemund III, married Byzantine princesses. Imperial policy in the Levant under John and Manuel Comnenos and the Byzantine-German entente before the accession of Barbarossa to the throne are reflected in these matrimonial alliances. One must be wary of exaggerations, however: politics does not explain everything, and the renown that her radiant beauty won for Mary of Antioch was most probably instrumental in the choice made by Manuel, who was an enlightened connoisseur throughout his life.

The matrimonial policy of a chief of state could, moreover, lead to nothing, and can be explained by intentions that were not realized. The marriages that Henry II made two of his daughters contract to the kings of Castile and Sicily, and the marriage he prepared for his son, the future John Lackland, with the daughter of the Count of Savoy, were connected apparently—like his designs on Toulouse and the alliance with Aragon—with a southern policy; but it scarcely made any progress.

Many treaties were concluded in the tenth, eleventh, and twelfth centuries. The written records established during this period served as proofs, whereas the agreements themselves were often made orally and included specific rites and in certain cases entailed, as we will see, homage. Even at the end of the period there was not a unique type. Treaties were written up in a diploma or a charter established by one of the parties; others were written up in two of these documents, each of which was written up in the name of one of the contracting parties and destined to be handed over to the co-contractant. One, however, comes across, notably in the twelfth century, instruments drafted in the names of different parties, which contained dispositions derived from a common accord and of which as many copies were made as there were participants. The external form of certain instruments may at first sight create confusion and conceal the real force of the act, notably for certain treaties Byzantium concluded with the Italian republics: the chrysobull—the imperial diploma sealed with gold —made a case for the demands introduced by the other party, and its terms contained the advantages granted by the emperor and the obligations imposed upon the applicants; the whole business took on the aspect of a concession, when in reality it was a synallagmatic contract in which the Italian republic in no way occupied an inferior position to the emperor.

The agreements concluded during the period under study were often affected by particular precautions. One of the most common was the oath pledged by the parties or their representatives. It must, however, be noted that the emperors and the kings often felt it repugnant to give an oath, and some of them refused, delegating to other persons the responsibility of doing so. In 1176, William II, king of Sicily, refused to confirm by oath an agreement relating to his future marriage with the daughter of Henry II: the kings of Sicily, he affirmed, do not swear; he contented himself with ratifying the oath his envoys had given in England. The following year Frederick Barbarossa would not himself confirm with an oath the peace of Venice, which he had concluded with the Pope: princes of the empire swore for him.

A type of personal insurance often practiced from the twelfth century on, was the institution of "pledges." As a rule they were "hostage-pledges," or guarantors, who were duty-bound to surrender themselves as prisoners if the head of state whose commitments they guaranteed did not fulfill his obligations. From the beginning of the century however, we come across "pledges" who were held for the payment of an indemnity and had to make themselves prisoners only if they did not pay that indemnity. This was the case in the treaty concluded at Dover in 1101 by Henry I, king of England, with Robert II, count of Flanders: the latter's twelve "hostage-pledges" (*obsides*) did not have to make themselves prisoners in the Tower of London if they each paid one hundred silver marks which they owed the King if the Count failed to fulfill his obligations. The obligations of the "pledges" of the King were parallel to those of the "pledges" of the Count.

The "pledges" (*obses, fideiussor*) were often important vassals, sometimes even high-ranking ecclesiastics. It is by virtue of the authority the lord exercised on them that he could force them to contract this obligation. On the occasion of the peace concluded in 1196, between Philip Augustus, king of France, and Richard Coeur de Lion, king of England, the latter went so far as to foresee the sanctions against those who would refuse to guarantee (*fideiubere*) the obligations of their masters. There have been agreements where in case of violation of his obligations by a lord, the homage and the fiefs of his guarantors had to be held from the other party. Such a situation was foreseen by the Count of Ponthieu, principal guarantor of the engagements Philip Augustus made in 1191 at Messina to Richard Coeur de Lion on the way to the Holy Land; if his master did not execute them, then at the request of the king of England, the Count was to hold from him all the fiefs he had held from the King of France. It is even more curious to see an obligation of this nature taken by a prince acting more like a plenipotentiary than a guarantor. Henry the Liberal, count of Champagne, negotiating with Frederick Barbarossa for King Louis VII, undertook to hold his French fiefs from the former if his master did not ratify and execute the engagement made in his name to end the papal schism in agreement with the Emperor. The meetings at Saint-Jean-de-Losne, where the affair was supposed to be settled, did not take place. As we know, in 1162 Henry mistakenly thought that the responsibility lay with the King of France, and that he himself should yield. However, his declaration was not put into effect.

Religious sanctions were also used in the twelfth century. In 1196, Philip Augustus forced Baldwin IX, count of Flanders, and Renaud of Dammartin, count of Boulogne—when they pledged him fealty and homage—to beg the archbishop and the bishop upon whom their counties were dependent to excommunicate them and to place their lands under an interdict if they failed in their obligations. This practice, as well as the guarantee imposed upon the principal vassals, was to be developed systematically in the thirteenth and fourteenth centuries by the kings of France.

Among the treaties concluded in this period particular attention must be paid to those that we may, with some temerity, call commercial treaties. The urban states of Italy are of particular importance, especially Venice. As for the continental side, the series of "pacts" concluded with the Italian kings since the eighth century continued almost without interruption. Most of the German kings who occupied the Italian throne concluded similar pacts with Venice, and the latter progressively increased her privileges: extension of the right of cutting wood (Otto I); the abolition of shipwreck rights and special protection for her markets (Otto II); authorization for Italians to trade freely with Venice, but no farther, and, as a consequence, Venetian monopoly in trade beyond the lagoon (the "pact" of Henry IV); a more explicit confirmation of this Venetian monopoly (Henry V); and finally in 1177, explicit acknowledgment by Frederick Barbarossa of the entry tax levied at Venice on Italian imports and an exemption from all dues for the Venetians, not only in Italy, but in the whole empire. Next to these commercial "treaties" that Venice concluded with the West, we must place the two "chryso-bulls" of 992 and 1082: these treaties established the legal management of Venetian trade in the Byzantine Empire. The first of these aimed at eliminating abuses by determining the rates, relatively low, of duties to be paid by the Venetian ships loaded with merchandise coming from or leaving Greece; by limiting to three days the delay that could be imposed on the departure of a Venetian ship anchored in a Byzantine port; and by submitting the Venetians to the exclusive judicial competence of the logothete of the dromos. The second treaty went much farther: as we know, it accorded to the Venetians absolute freedom of navigation and trade and freedom from all taxes and dues in the Byzantine Empire except, it seems, in the Black Sea. It is difficult to conceive of a more privileged arrangement. In 1111, Pisa was able to conclude a treaty with Byzantium assuring the import of precious metals free of all duty and a favorable tariff (4 per cent) on other articles; the same tariff was granted to Genoa in 1155.

Byzantium concluded commercial treaties with quite a few other peoples, notably with Moslem and Russian princes. The best-known date from the tenth century. The treaties with the Russians, with the great princes of Kiev, are usually dated 911 and 945, but these dates are not definite. They remained the judicial foundation for Russo-Byzantine commercial relations. The tone is quite different from the Venetian treaties: it concerns itself with more savage populations, with whom Byzantium had been at war, and who then were still pagans. If these treaties contained arrangements favoring navigation and trade, the latter was, however, subject to control, and measures of security were taken against possible attacks by the Russians, upon whom the treaty of 945 imposed passports issued by the Prince; articles regulated the repression of violence, the escape of slaves, etc. The danger of having Russians or Byzantines reduced to slavery is reflected in the arrangements whereby this practice is forbidden, and in the measures undertaken in both treaties to facilitate the buying back of prisoners.

Among the agreements made by Byzantium with the Moslem princes, that which came about in 969–970 between the Governor of Antioch, representing the empire, and the Prince of Aleppo is an excellent example; it undertook to bring about free traffic of Greek caravans for the city, to limit customs taxes, and to guarantee the security of persons, etc.

Commercial agreements were also concluded with the King of Jerusalem and with the autonomous Latin princes of Syria, by cities of Italy—Genoa, Pisa, and Venice—and Provence and

Languedoc, or of Catalonia—Marseille, Montpellier, Saint-Gilles, and Barcelona. Not all conferred the same rights on the beneficiaries, but they generally permitted the abolition of the shipwreck rights, and the withdrawing or the lessening of customs or other taxes on traffic and the sale of merchandise, or even taxes that concerned navigation. It dealt also frequently with measures preserving the goods of nationals who died in the country. It can be supposed that Venice, whose trade with Alexandria occupied so great a place in the economy of this republic, drew up "commercial treaties" with Egypt, but nothing of these remains.

Pisa, the site of the most important commercial activity in the Tyrrhenian Sea until the end of the twelfth century, drew up the oldest commercial treaties still extant with the Saracen states of Africa. The treaty drawn up in 1154 between Pisa and the Fatimite Caliph of Egypt guaranteed the protection of peaceful merchants and authorized the Pisans to set up a commercial settlement (*fondaco,* from the Arab *funduk*) at Alexandria and at Cairo. The treaty gave them facilities for importing certain goods, guaranteed them freedom of trade and the right to re-export goods that they imported and did not sell, while reserving the right of repurchase by local authorities. Also dispositions were laid down to protect the goods of dead Pisans. The commercial treaty concluded by Pisa with the "king of Tunis" in 1157 answered similar concerns; specifically it contained measures against the dangers of being carried off into slavery and others favoring the repurchase of slaves, with reciprocal clauses; the Pisans obtained some withdrawals and some lowering of the entry tax or the exit tax on certain goods. They were authorized to set up a warehouse within the city walls; its protection was guaranteed. The first treaties are cited and briefly analyzed as examples. They prevented neither mutual abuse nor wars nor revolutions, nor the interruptions of trade that these provoked, nor the violence committed in the midst of peace between Christians and Moslems or between Christians themselves, particularly armed

conflicts between Pisans and Genoans, or Pisan piracy in the
second half of the twelfth century. But after the wars and the
other periods of violence, new trade treaties were concluded. If
their terms differed sometimes from those of the earlier treaties,
their aim and certain of their dispositions remained the same.
Here once more the agreements that we have analyzed make a
base for further economic relations. Moreover, when violence
occurred, claims were sometimes followed up effectively. After a
Pisan ship had in 1168 seized a boat belonging to a Saracen
merchant of Gabes, the latter went to Pisa, furnished with a letter
from the "Rector" of the Christians in Tunis (without doubt
some Saracen official who had the job of controlling their activities), and obtained full satisfaction.

Genoa doubtless acted in the same way as Pisa, but there is less
information on this subject for the period. It is recorded that after
a war in the course of which a Genoese fleet ravaged Bougie
(1136), the town concluded a peace in 1138 with the Almoravide
sovereign of Africa, assuring him certain advantages and conferring benefits on the Provençal ports of Marseille, Fos, Hyères, and
Fréjus. At this time Genoa appeared to be the protectress of these
ports of Provence. Commercial navigation in Provençal waters, as
in those of Catalonia, was an activity of economic importance to
Genoa; one of the oldest "commercial treaties" that she signed
was an agreement in 1127 regulating Genoese navigation to and
from the Moslem ports of Spain in the waters subject to the
authority of the counts of Barcelona and of Provence.

A number of agreements drawn up in the period serving as the
frame of this chapter, took the form of vassalic or feudal-vassalic
agreements. From the twelfth century on, a particular form of this
last agreement was customary: a grant, in return for the swearing
of fealty and homage, of a money fief (French: *fief-rente* or *fief
de bourse*), that is, a fief consisting of a regular revenue. The aim
could be military: to ensure the services of an important prince or
lord who commanded knights; or political: to assure the support

or even the neutrality of a powerful prince or lord; or both military and political. One of the oldest examples is provided by the feudal-vassalic agreement drawn up, in the form of a treaty, at Dover in 1101 between Henry I, king of England, and Robert II, count of Flanders. The latter obtained a fief worth five hundred pounds, with the responsibility of providing the King with a contingent of as many as one thousand knights. The aim was to assure military support for the King against his brother, Robert Curt-hose, duke of Normandy; perhaps also to prevent the Count of Flanders, a great supporter of the house of Capet, from serving the King of France with more than twenty knights—his minimum feudal contingent—if the latter wished to support the Duke. Flemish military aid, however, was never required, but the fee was regularly paid. During the twelfth century English royalty used this money fief system abroad with the double plan that we have been indicating, and French royalty used this same plan from the reign of Louis VII on, particularly under Philip Augustus. The institution was to develop more extensively in the last years of the twelfth century and in the thirteenth century.

In the tenth, eleventh, and twelfth centuries feudal-vassalic relationships were used more than they were in the preceding period in order to make one political unit subordinate to another, or in order to cast similar relations in a legal form. We have come across enough cases in the course of our study where events have been treated chronologically, so that we can limit ourselves here to a few aspects of the history of these relations.

It is important to stress the fact that the formation of feudal-vassalic relations did not exclude recourse to other acts that created bonds of dependence or recognition of these bonds, such as accepting to pay a tribute or a quit-rent (they are the same thing). The Holy See used these two systems and others to serve in its policy which sought to subordinate to itself the greatest possible number of political units: Gregory VII's dispatch of a royal crown to the Croatian sovereign Zwonimir can be recalled.

Various systems were sometimes used in the same single case. In 1156 when Pope Hadrian IV had to resign himself to coming to terms with William I of Sicily, the "concordat" signed at Benevento laid down that the King would offer liege homage—which created the strictest dependence—to the Pope and would pay him an annual rent of six hundred scyphates for Apulia and Calabria and four hundred scyphates for the Abruzzi. The subordination of the King of Sicily remained, however, entirely theoretical. The case of Portugal is similar to that of Sicily: in 1143 King Alfonso Henriques, seeking the support of the papacy against the Castilian "emperor" Alfonso VII, admitted himself to be at the same time a vassal and a rent payer to the Holy See. The payment of a tribute or a rent was still common in the eleventh and twelfth centuries. Many examples are found in the various "fringes" of western Europe: just as much in Spain—where Moslem kings and princes had been tributaries of Christian heads of state before the Almoravide invasion—as on the eastern frontiers of Germany, where in 1041, Duke Bretislaw of Bohemia had to pay tribute to the King. In this last case, moreover, it accompanied homage and fealty. Perhaps the aim was to emphasize the dependency of a prince who had revolted and had just been subdued. Always on the "fringe" of the western world, Venice continued to pay tribute to the kings of Italy—that is, since Otto I (967), to the Emperor, king of Germany: fifty pounds of coined money and precious material (*pallium*), and since Henry V's reign, fifty pounds of pepper—a very revealing list of the needs of a continental court and of Venice's capacity to provide them. In that distant annex of the western world that the kingdom of Jerusalem and the great Syrian principalities made up, the practice of tribute is also encountered: it was paid by Saracen leaders who recognized the Frankish protectorate, and frequently consisted partly of cash and partly of goods, especially expensive oriental goods. As we have said with reference to the past centuries, tribute did not always imply among those who paid it any recognition of subordination; this certainly never existed among the Byzantine emperors, despite the fact that from 927 until 967 they paid a tribute to the Bulgars. However a regular payment of specie, in addition to the material burden, created at the least a sense of ill-feeling in the debtor, because of its possible interpretations. It is curious to note that in an epoch when the practice of fief rent was not yet extensively known in England, King Henry I refused, after his accession (1100), to pay rent to Robert II, count of Flanders —a rent that the counts had held in fief from the English crown since 1066— because he considered this annual payment a humiliating tribute. We know that Henry I modified his attitude in 1101!

Throughout the period under study, we have seen that the Byzantine Empire remained faithful to the tradition of surrounding itself with subordinate states. The aims pursued could be very diverse: political, economic, or military—guaranteeing, for example, in the eleventh century, the protection of frontiers for the princes of Lesser Armenia, and for those of Serbia, whose contingents had great importance in the eleventh and twelfth centuries. There was continued utilization of the old creative or recognitory methods, such as the concession of titles, palatine or others, or of rights, such as "the placing of the foot on the emperor's carpet," to which even emirs submitted. These various practices were combined.

The crusades, and the close contacts with the Latins that they entailed, had led the emperors of the Comnenian dynasty to introduce into their policies the use of vassalic relations that were not known at all in Byzantine law. This happened following the arrival of the crusaders at Constantinople in 1096 and 1097. In order to ensure their obedience and subordination to his imperial authority in the territories that they were to seize from the Turks—all lost fragments of the empire, which had never been renounced—Alexios Comnenos demanded that the Latin leaders give solemn pledges to him. Godfrey of Bouillon, duke of lower Lotharingia, who commanded a column of crusaders, finally accepted these demands: the *basileus*, in keeping with one of the usages current in Byzantium, adopted him as a son; and Godfrey, in keeping with western usages, became an imperial vassal giving fealty and homage. It seems that with the exception of the Count of Toulouse, all the leaders of the first crusade gave fealty and homage to the Emperor. In the eyes of Byzantium, subordination had been established; it is known that the crusaders had another opinion about it. However, the Comnenians succeeded in imposing their interpretation at least on the princes of Antioch: Bohemund I in 1108, Raymond of Poitiers in 1137, Renaud of Châtillon in 1159, and Bohemund III in 1165 had to recognize themselves as vassals of the empire. Two kings of Jerusalem, Baldwin III in 1158 and Amaury I in 1171, did as much. The adjective *lizios* was introduced into the Byzantine administrative code to designate liege vassals.

One must guard against considering as dependent on the Byzantine Empire states whose leaders became subject to Byzantine influence and recognized in the Emperor a certain pre-eminence, as was the case with the Russian princes, and particularly the most important among them—the great princes of Kiev in the tenth and eleventh centuries. Perhaps, moreover, the Emperor's interpretation was not the same as that of the Russian princes, and he considered them as dependents of his. It can be argued that the same situation existed for Venice, which was an allied power, but which Byzantium always considered as a dependent: from which stemmed the grant of a Byzantine title to the Doge and even, after the victory of 1082 over the Normans, of one of the highest titles, that of *protosebastos*.

During the tenth, eleventh, and twelfth centuries there were new developments in the notion of the frontier. If we consider western Europe, it seems that, on the whole, the often vague notion of frontier of the preceding period was still further accentuated. This was the case for the frontiers of states, properly speaking, and for the frontiers of principalities or of similar units within these states. The cause could have been the transformation of the physical milieu—for example, the disappearance or the breakup of a forest boundary because of land clearing; very often it was the result of the entangling of feudal-vassalic relations, especially as a result of the practice of multiple vassalic loyalties, which tended to become general in the eleventh century. The existence of approximate frontiers in an area did not exclude the existence of very clear boundaries elsewhere. It is thus that the line of the frontier between the duchy of Normandy and the Capetian "domain of the Crown" in France, which followed the river Epte, became faint and confused to the south of this river's junction with the Seine in the area of the Eure and the Avre. It seems that in this region the confusions that were mentioned above played a vigorous role. This imprecision contributed to the development of the notion of a frontier zone: the term "march" (*marca, marchia*), which was applied to the whole frontier and even to every border and came to mean, from the beginning of the eleventh and certainly from the twelfth century, more exactly the zones of the area where the forces of the two different political units both penetrated.

It is important to stress the existence of principalities whose leaders had authority over territories located within both states' frontiers, which were in fact international. The case of the Count of Flanders, a French prince, has been cited. In the eleventh century he acquired an important part of lower Lotharingia—and therefore part of Germany—imperial Flanders. But there are other cases: in the twelfth century the Count of Champagne had fiefs in upper Lotharingia; the Duke of Burgundy in the kingdom of Arles; the Count of Forez, prince of this kingdom, had some in France; in the second half of the eleventh century the counts of Toulouse and Barcelona argued over Provence, a part of the kingdom of Arles, and they shared it in 1125. Barcelona gained the county, and Toulouse a marquisate. Many other examples could be cited without difficulty. Similar situations permitted certain princes to defy their chief overlords on occasion; among these were Philip of Alsace, count of Flanders, who invoked the protection of Frederick Barbarossa against Philip Augustus, king of France, in 1181; and Hugh III, Duke of Burgundy, who did the same in 1183—both, incidentally, without success. The leaders of great states also took advantage of these situations. We know that Frederick Barbarossa used Henry the Liberal, count of Champagne, to pressure Louis VII, but in vain. On the other hand, the double vassality of the Count of Forez aided the reunion of that county with France; and the power acquired in Provence by the French dynasties made way for the incorporation of the greater part of the land into the Capetian kingdom, though only after a long period.

After the Turkish invasion the Byzantine Empire had, like the western states, entangled, imprecise, and contested frontiers, in Asia Minor as in other areas. But the phenomenon was much less widespread, as the feudal-vassalic factor was in no way involved. Not only was the Byzantine frontier frequently clearly drawn, but it even played an important role in the state. It constituted not only a military frontier, but also a zone or a line for which the safety of the state and concern for relations with foreign nations required police surveillance, both in Europe and in Asia. It also remained a fiscal frontier: the correct customs taxes were collected by different bureaus, at maritime frontiers, in the ports, and also on certain land frontiers. We have seen that exemptions or alleviations of these taxes were granted. The difference is clear in the West, where it is certainly difficult to make a distinction between customs taxes and the many taxes on the circulation of goods from various places to the interior of the territory. The situation in the West, moreover, allowed for exceptions: one of the most remarkable and one of the easiest to understand was that of Venice, where the *quadragesima*, levied on imports during the twelfth century, was an actual customs duty.

During the three centuries that serve as a chronological frame for this chapter, there is no doubt that war was often the most usual method of resolving conflicts among political units of some importance, duchies, territorial principalities, great overlordships and cities, as well as empires and kingdoms. There were other methods. Among those that involved some act of hostility, we should note political maneuvers that tended to provoke insurrections among the enemy. Byzantium often used this method, especially with the Normans in Sicily and southern Italy. There were also reprisals. These could take very varied forms; often they consisted of the arrest—sometimes accompanied by murder or other acts of violence—of subjects of the enemy and of the seizure or the confiscation of part or all of their goods. From the beginning of the twelfth century we find efforts made to avert reprisals and to facilitate the regulation of conflicts by negotiation or by other peaceful means. The development of trade at first favored the development of a system of reprisals. The leaders of states and city authorities had recourse to this procedure in cases of non-fulfillment of commercial obligations toward their subjects or toward those they administered, and in cases of hostile acts or misdemeanors toward them. The requirements of trade, however, which were gravely upset by reprisals, were largely instrumental in their elimination. The Italian cities, from the second half of the twelfth century, drew up agreements excluding reprisals among themselves. One of the oldest of these is a treaty drawn up in 1166 between Bologna and Modena. It was typical to see members of the Lombard League in 1168 also exclude reprisals at the same time that they guaranteed to each other no escalation of taxes on the circulation and sale of goods, by agreeing on tariffs to remain in force for thirty years. By the clauses of that type, recourse to reprisals was limited, but no one was ever able to exclude it fully.

One of the peaceful methods of settling conflicts—which became the most widespread in the twelfth century—was that of arbitration. Several factors contributed to it. At first the fact that in a great part of the West, because of the weakness of public power, many conflicts that today are seen as conflicts of private rights between physical or moral persons of a certain importance, were then settled, not by judicial decision, but by arrangements between the parties. In the eleventh and twelfth centuries these parties frequently appointed arbitrators to prevent similar occurrences.

There are examples of this for the whole of western Europe and notably for a number of principalities and great French seigneuries in the Burgundian and western regions. The absence of perfectly clear distinctions between public rights and a private right, according to the thinking of the times, explains the tendency to use the same methods for the regulation of conflicts between political units. It seems furthermore that the Church, whose efforts in favor of the Peace of God and the Truce of God, tended to eliminate private wars and to limit bellicose violence in general, favored an analogous design by the practice of arbitration. Eventually the towns worked for the same ends, as peace was favorable to trade.

There is no question of citing certain distinct principles of arbitration in the twelfth century: it is important only to indicate their foundations and how they were practiced. Many of them resulted from a compromise containing at least the nomination of an arbitrator or a panel of arbitrators, the definition of the litigation, the promise to submit to judgment, and sometimes other clauses, such as sanctions in case of nonfulfillment of this promise (frequently a heavy fine). As an example we can cite the arbitrational decision of Frederick Barbarossa given in 1165 in the case of Count Florent III of Holland and the Bishop of Utrecht; the Emperor laid down that the parties had put themselves in his hands (*in manu nostra compromiserunt*). Matters proceeded like-wise in the arbitration provided in 1177 by King Henry II of England in a dispute between the kings of Castile and Navarre on the basis of a compromise concluded in 1176. In other instances it was a prior agreement that contained an arbitration clause stipulating the arbitrators and the manner of appointing them. In the peace concluded by Louis VII and Henry II between Gisors and Trie in 1180, there is a similar clause granting competence to a panel of twelve arbitrators—six bishops and six laymen, half to be selected by each party. The Treaty of Montebello, concluded in 1175 between Frederick Barbarossa and the Lombard League, anticipated that suspended issues should be resolved by a panel of six arbitrators—three selected by each party; the consuls of Cremona were to intervene, if necessary, as supreme arbitrators.

The Italian cities, moreover, had frequently practiced arbitration, and they wrote it into the agreements which were drawn up among them. One of the earliest treaties of this order containing an arbitration clause was concluded in 1135 between Modena on the one hand and Bologna and the Abbey of Nonantula on the other: the decision was supposed to be taken by four arbitrators, two of whom were named by each of the parties. The fact that the common council of magistrates of the united cities in the Lombard League were to make a majority decision on differences among the members (1168), appears to us as an example rather of a federal judiciary than of a panel of arbitrators. However, we should have no illusions: most of the arbitration clauses did not prevent armed conflicts.

A part of this chapter dealing with the practice of international relations must, we believe, treat some of the principal problems that the joint habitation of different populations in the same "space" raise for the period under study; this examination must satisfy a particular concern for the question of structure and institutions.

One of these problems is that of the western colonies in the East and on the southern shore of the Mediterranean. Certain of them were established at an early date, especially those of Amalfi. At Constantinople and at Alexandria they go back perhaps to the tenth century. In any event, in the eleventh century merchants from Amalfi were established in these two great centers, and the members of one illustrious Amalfi family, the Pantaleone, played an important role. But it was a simple situation of fact at Alexandria, and we do not know of the statute that could have been peculiar to the colony of Amalfi merchants at Constantinople; it is known only that in 1082 it lost its autonomy and became subordinate to the Venetian colony.

This Venetian colony was still modest at the end of the tenth century. It grew in the eleventh century, and we know about the principal privileges that it obtained in 1082. At that time it already occupied a section of its own on the Golden Horn. We know its leaders from the middle of the twelfth century: two *legati* designated by Venice, assisted by judges (*iudex*): they exercised entire political, administrative, judicial, and financial authority, and they watched over the economic interests of the members of the colony. Pisa and Genoa obtained a site reserved for their colonies, in 1111 and in 1155 respectively; they also had their own magistrates. We know that at the end of the century there was a "viscount" (*vicecomes*) for the Pisan colony, who exercised an authority similar to that of the Venetian *legati* and was named by Pisa, and three "consuls" elected by the colony, after the fashion of the urban consuls of Italy. These colonies generally were on poor terms, and the Genoese colony suffered a great deal at the hands of the Venetians and Pisans. Contrary to the Italian, the Russian colony, as long as it lasted, was established outside the walls, at Saint-Mamas. The Byzantine government had, moreover, a "police force for foreigners" directed by the "superintendent for barbarians," and, in the eleventh century in particular, a "consul of Ishmaelites," charged with surveillance of the Moslems.

The cities of Italy and of the western Mediterranean, we know, had founded colonies in Syria and the Holy Land, which had had a mixed population since the time of the crusades. Their autonomous status had been determined by the "commercial treaties" discussed earlier. Genoa, Pisa, Venice, Amalfi, Marseille, Montpellier, Saint-Gilles, and Barcelona obtained, in various cities—notably in Acre, Tyre, and Tripoli—spacious sections including generally their own church, market, bathhouse, oven, entrepôts, and port. Extraterritoriality was widespread, and each colony had its own magistrates. Venice appointed her own consuls or viscounts as head of each colony, and at the end of the twelfth century a "bailie" (*baile*) who had authority over all the settlements and resided at Acre. Genoa and Pisa likewise had consuls or viscounts at the head of their various colonies; but in 1179, Pisa had a consul, residing in Acre, who was head of all the Pisan colonies in Syria; in 1192, Genoa did the same. In 1187, Marseille, Montpellier, Barcelona, and Saint-Gilles had consuls at Tyre and over them, a shared viscount. "Bailie," "consuls general," and "viscount" had analogous functions to those of the heads of the Italian colonies at Constantinople. They governed the homogeneous foreign enclaves which, while undertaking close relations with the other Latins of the Near East, did not assimilate with them and involved themselves exclusively with their own commercial interests and those of the mother country.

It is known that Genoa and Pisa had colonies in the various ports of Africa, but we have no knowledge of their status during this period. In 1164, Genoa had a secretary (*scriba*) in Bougie, who took care of Genoese commercial interests on the spot. Pisa obtained, by a commercial treaty, concluded with the Almohade caliph in 1166, the authority to create a *fondaco* in a place called Subilia which was perhaps situated in the territory of Bougie.

Whatever the importance of these Italian colonies in the country of Islam for trade in the Mediterranean basin, one has the impression that their existence was very precarious until the end of the twelfth century. We have much better knowledge of these colonies after the beginning of the thirteenth century.

The colonies in question existed like foreign bodies in a certain setting. At this point it is important to say a few words about the areas where numerous elements of various populations, differing in origin, language, and at times in religion and way of life, were brought to live together.

We can pass quickly over England. In the eleventh century the population included besides the English earlier and later Danish immigrants and Normans, but this last element was relatively few in number. Right after 1066 the population was very different: a mass of English peoples, dominated by a Norman monarchy, aristocracy, and High Church—that is to say, French. If a distinction between "English" and "French" was still made in the middle of the twelfth century, it disappeared before the beginning of the following century or lost all its importance: England was thereafter peopled by the English. The action of the same institutions and the play of economic, social, and moral forces had, in less than a century and a half, brought about the fusion of the two peoples, while the use of the French language may have been sustained at court and among the aristocracy.

In Spain we have to distinguish between two periods separated by the first half of the eleventh century. In the first period the leaders of Moslem Spain were generally tolerant toward their Christian subjects, the Mozarabs; the latter, while remaining remarkably faithful to their creed, showed an ability to adapt that often distressed foreign Christians, who were incapable of understanding the problems of their brothers living under the rule of the Crescent. On the other hand, Christians who were made prisoners during the war often were enslaved, unless an agreement could be made before their capture. In Christian Spain there was hardly any Moslem population apart from those enslaved, except perhaps for the crypto-Moslems. In the second period, which was marked by the great progress of the Christian reconquest, the situation progressively changed. The relations between Christians and Moslems became more humane: Saracen leaders became the protégés and the tributaries of the Christian chiefs of state; and in the second half of the century the Christian adventurer-warrior Rodrigo de Bivar served the Saracen King of Saragossa for several years and owed to him the name by which he became famous (*mio Cid*; in Arabic, "my lord") among his Moslem warriors. Slavery still existed here and there, but these slaves were principally prisoners taken during raids. The mass of the Moslem peoples from the reconquered territories and perhaps the influence of the Mozarab Christians from these territories and of those who emigrated from Moslem Spain, caused the Christians to give up the reducing to slavery of great numbers of Moslems and inspired them with some tolerance. In Castile the change was distinct from the reign of Alfonso VI (1072–1109); the Mudejar population— that is, Moslems under Christian authority—lived in very acceptable conditions, but they generally lived outside the walls of the towns. The Moorish concubines and even the Moorish wives were numerous in many different sections of Christian-Spanish society. Often, moreover, these "beautiful infidels" adopted the religion of their husband or lover: most notable was the case of the Moor Zaïda, stepdaughter of the Saracen King of Seville, widow of the Saracen prince of Cordova; by her Alfonso VI had his only son, who fell while fighting the Almoravides. In a large part of Christian Spain during the twelfth century four different elements of population were to be found: the people originating in former Christian Spain, the Mozarabs, the "Franks"—that is to say, the French—and the Mudejars. The fusion of the first two elements came about rapidly, though there was, in the time of Gregory VII and his successors, some difficulty in substituting the Roman for the Mozarab liturgy in the liberated countries; the French were absorbed before the end of the century; but the assimilation of the Mudejars was a longer task.

The Norman kingdom of Sicily likewise was a country of mixed population. The Normans themselves were not very numerous: a warrior aristocracy. In Apulia and Calabria the population was in part Hellenized and lived in conformity with Byzantine traditions; the north conserved the traditions of the Lombard principalities. In the maritime cities Latin and Byzantine traditions were mixed; Sicily included, besides its partly Hellenized autochthonous population, an important group of Arabs. From the second half of the twelfth century the Genoan colonies in the ports of Sicily became important and came to have their own consuls. The authority of the state, which combined, in the service of a monarchy with absolutist tendencies, Byzantine traditions in legislative and administrative matters with the feudal-vassalic institutions, was imposed equally on everybody but respected the traditions of the diverse groups; the kings used Latin, Greek, and Arabic in their decrees and charters. On the whole, great religious tolerance reigned; the Arab population maintained the freedom and practice of its religion, except in some rather rare cases when it had, for example, been put down by force—without capitulation—or when it had revolted.

As in Spain, the composite character of the population is reflected in art, where we once again find the influence of the various civilizations drawn upon by the subjects of the King of Sicily. In the composition of the population there are strong similarities between the kingdom of Sicily and the kingdom of Jerusalem and its great principalities. In the Holy Land and in Syria the population was even more mixed than in Sicily and southern Italy: Christians from the East—Greeks, Syrians, Armenians, even Arabs, most of whom belonged to the schismatic or heretical churches—the Greek, Jacobite, Nestorian, or Gregorian; Frankish or Italian Latins, all of whom were Catholics; Jews, Arabic and sometimes Turkish Moslems. Latins—knights, clerics, bourgeois, or farmers—made up a minority; it was thus even in Jerusalem, where after the massacres and the expulsions of 1099, the Holy City was repopulated, drawing in Greek or Syrian Christians from Transjordania. Among all these Christian elements of the population relations, and especially marriages, were frequent, but these relations were not always warm; conflicts of dogma or of politics were continuous and sometimes serious. With the Moslems from abroad—princes or merchants—and with those of the interior—especially the inhabitants of the countryside—there were also regular relations; and the Moslem influence made itself felt on the civilization of the Latin East, but the Islamic religion was not always or everywhere authorized, which is not to say that it was not practiced, although in secret, wherever there were Moslems.

Whether or not a population had a hybrid character, the presence of foreigners everywhere—"aliens" (*albanus*: Fr.: *aubain*)—raised a problem. It was solved in different manners in various countries and sometimes even, in the heart of the same country, in different principalities or lordships existing on its territory. In the countries that grew out of the breakup of the Frankish monarchy there was generally a tendency to consider that the foreigner owed the benefit of being protected by law to the favor of the king, of the prince, or of seignorial jurisdiction. From this comes the attribution to these authorities of a right to his inheritance. The concept of an alien could vary according to the country, the principalities, or the important seigneuries: there were those who were born outside the empire or the kingdom and those born outside the principality, and sometimes outside the seignorial jurisdiction. Likewise there were variations in the effective consequences of the prerogatives of the sovereign, the prince, or the lord; generally they were limited to gathering a part or a share of the inheritance: "the *ius albanagii* (Fr.: *droit d'aubaine*)." Often this right was limited in favor of "national" heirs. The towns tried, in the interest of their trade, to eliminate the *ius albanagii* and often succeeded in so doing. Similar usages are found—rules and limitations—in many countries totally foreign to the Frankish monarchy.

The regulations to which the Jews were submitted also varied greatly. But in the countries stemming from the dismemberment of the Frankish monarchy—and in many others—their status was generally based on a notion similar to the one at the base of the status of foreigners. In Germany the Jews depended upon the king; but this dependence could be delegated tacitly or expressly, and it was—mainly to the bishops of the imperial Church.

In France, this prerogative belonged, depending on the region, to the king, the prince, or the seignorial lord. Everywhere, as a result, taxes, sometimes very heavy ones, were levied on the patrimony of the Jews, on their living and on their dead. Their condition became much worse beginning with the last decade of the eleventh century; despite the protection of the bishops, the numerous and prosperous Jewish colonies of the Rhineland suffered cruelly from anti-Semitic excesses. These followed the departure of the people's crusade in 1096 and again the preaching of the second Crusade in 1146; the intervention of St. Bernard was necessary to put an end to the anti-Semitic cruelties of 1146.

Just as there were anti-Semitic outbursts, in certain regions, there were manifestations of xenophobia where the allogenic Christian elements were numerous, active, and influential. This was the case, for example, in Spain, where hostility to the French nobility became apparent in the second quarter of the twelfth century and provoked the elimination of this nobility, when it did not speed up its Hispanization. In the twelfth century England had given lively evidence of hostility against the Flemings who went about their business there; and following the accession of Henry II in 1154, popular opinion forced their expulsion.

It is true that among the Flemings in England there were not only merchants, but numerous mercenaries, knights and people of the most ordinary condition, who contributed to ravaging the country during the troubles of the reign of King Stephen. Foreign mercenaries were evidently a factor, and a scarcely sympathetic one, but a factor just the same in international relations. They were recruited in various countries, and the names they have been given at least indicate the regions that furnished the important contingents: men of Brabant, of Gascony, of Aragon, etc. They made up small troops, mainly of foot soldiers, bold, scarcely reliable, disposed to plunder, and cruel. The kings of France, the kings of England, and many princes used them in the twelfth century. These *cottereaux*, as they were often termed, were not the only mercenaries known in the period under study. We have seen the use that the Byzantine emperors made of Scandinavian and Russian warriors (Vikings or Varangians) in the tenth and especially in the eleventh centuries and, after 1066, of emigrant members of the English aristocracy, not to mention "Latin" knights. In the eleventh century in times of war, knights from all countries placed themselves in the service of heads of state or of princes: we know that the Norman kingdom of Sicily owed its first origins to Norman knights hired by Lombard princes.

In a survey of international relations there must be an indication of at least the principal routes that permitted communication by land across the great mountainous massifs—the Alps and the Pyrenees—separating Italy and Spain from the countries lying to their north. During the centuries treated in this chapter a few of these routes were regularly used by armies, merchants, and pilgrims, if we do not include local or interregional communications. As for the Alps, it was possible to follow them around toward the west and reach the lower Rhône by holding to the Ligurian and Provençal coasts. A single Alpine route crossing the western Alps was of major importance, that of Mont Cenis connecting the upper basin of the Po with the middle basin of the Rhône. In the Alps of the Valais, the Great Saint Bernard connected the upper basin of the Po to the upper basin of the Rhône; proceeding from the latter there was easy access to the passes of the Jura and to the upper basin of the Seine or to the Aar and the basin of the Rhine: the great Saint Bernard pass was, economically speaking, the most important of all these Alpine passes in the tenth, eleventh, and twelfth centuries.

At this time there were no passable routes through the center of the Alpine massif. It was farther to the east that the Septimer had to be sought, a heavily used route between the middle basin of the Po and the upper basin of the Rhine. Still farther east the Brenner pass allowed equally easy access from the lower basin of the Po and from the valley of the Adige to the middle reaches of the Inn and the basin of the Danube. The establishment of hospices on the Great Saint Bernard before 1086 by Saint Bernard of Menthon, archdeacon of Aosta, and on the Septimer toward the end of the same century, by Guy, bishop of Chur, bears witness to the frequent crossings of the range by means of these two passes.

The crossings from France to Spain could be made easily enough, on the Barcelona side, thanks to the depression neighboring the Mediterranean coast. Toward the west, two passes were heavily used for crossing the Pyrenees, the Somport and the Roncevalles pass. Finally, at the western extremity of the range, the peninsula could be reached by following the Atlantic coast.

The great interest of these three passes, from the point of view of the history of international relations, lies in their use by pilgrims. Pilgrimages brought, at the price of great fatigue and very real dangers, thousands of men both clerical and lay, from every walk of life, and even women into foreign countries. They came into contact with other milieus and other ways of thought and feeling. Certainly the preoccupations of these pilgrims were essentially religious, and only faith could give them the courage necessary to undertake these great adventures and to persevere in their undertaking; but they were unintentionally agents who transmitted numerous aspects of culture. There were many celebrated places of pilgrimage, but in the period we are treating three overshadowed all the others. Jerusalem, which has been sufficiently discussed with reference to the causes of the first crusade, and which thereafter enjoyed such a success that the maritime transportation of pilgrims was a great source of wealth to Genoa and to the ports of Provence and of Languedoc. Then Rome, so frequently, so intensely, and so regularly visited that this pilgrimage gave birth, in French, to a common name to designate those who accomplished it; this common name became a proper name: Romieu, Romier. So intense and so regular were these pilgrimages that in memory of them the equestrian statue of Marcus Aurelius opposite the Lateran—said to be of Constantine—was reproduced on the façades of many Romanesque churches in western France. Finally Santiago de Compostella, in Galicia, where from the tenth century pilgrims came from France to venerate the so-called relics of the eponymous saint. The number of pilgrims, mainly French, but also Spanish, German, Italian, and English, etc., increased considerably in the eleventh century, and the pilgrimage reached its apogee at the beginning of the twelfth century. Whereas the first pilgrims, coming overland, followed the difficult and dangerous roads of the Cantabrian coast, new routes were established from the first half of the eleventh century, which joined the outlets of the Somport and the Roncevalles pass at Burgos and at León and thus reached Compostella from the south: these were the so-called "French" routes (Span.: *camino frances*). At Antioch, at Jerusalem also, and elsewhere, hospices had been founded for pilgrims going to the Holy Places, since the tenth century among others by a certain Panteleon, for the use of his compatriots from Amalfi. Other hospices grew up on the roads to Rome, and this was the basic purpose of the one on the Great Saint Bernard. Many hospices were built on the roads leading to Compostella: that of Sainte Christine, at the Somport, dates from the second half of the eleventh century; at Roncevalles, an almshouse existed at the beginning of the twelfth century, and a hospice in the first half of

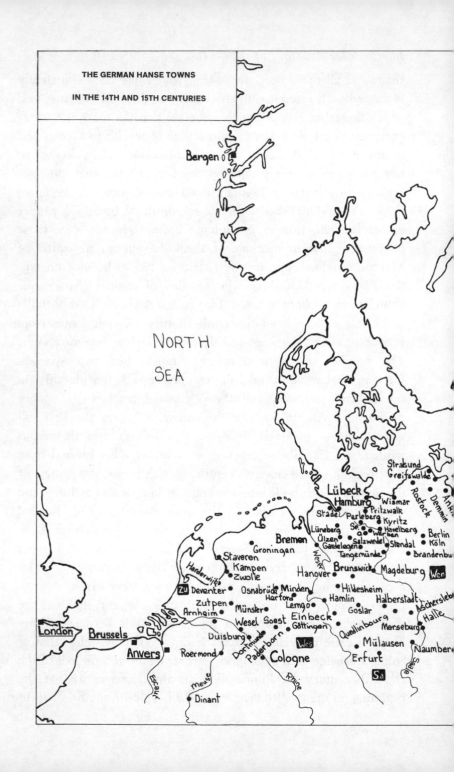

THE GERMAN HANSE TOWNS

IN THE 14TH AND 15TH CENTURIES

NORTH

SEA

Bergen

Stralsund
Greifswalde
Lübeck
Hamburg
Rostock
Demmin
Anklam
Stade
Wismar
Pritzwalk
Perleberg
Kyritz
Lüneberg
Se.
Havelberg
Berlin
Ülzen
Werben
Köln
Bremen
Salzwedel
Stendal
Groningen
Gardelegen
Brandenburg
Weser
Tangemünde
Staveren
Kampen
Hanover
Brunswick
Magdeburg
Wen
Harderwijk
Zwolle
Zu
Deventer
Osnabrück
Minden
Hildesheim
Zutpen
Harford
Hamlin
Halberstadt
Aschersleben
Arnheim
Münster
Lemgo
Goslar
Halle
Wesel
Soest
Einbeck
Quedlinburg
Merseburg
London
Duisburg
Göttingen
Brussels
Roermond
Mülausen
Naumber
Anvers
Dortmund
Wes
Erfurt
Paderborn
Cologne
Sa
Escaut
Meuse
Rhine
Dinant

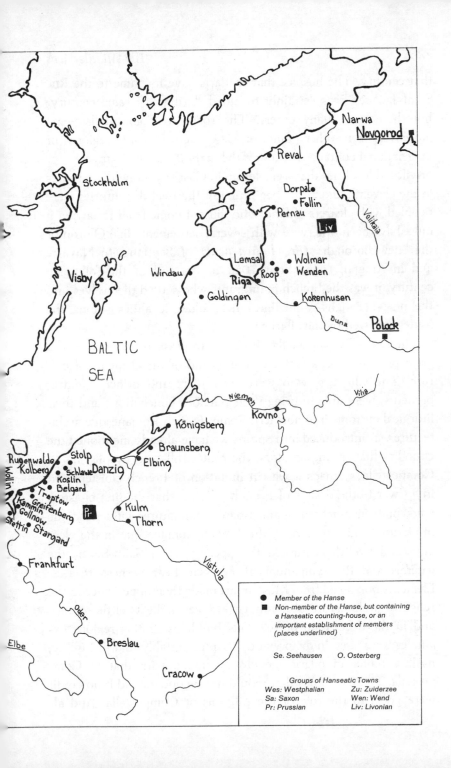

Narwa

Novgorod

Reval

Stockholm

Dorpat•
•Fellin
Pernau

Liv

Lemsal
•Wolmar
Roop Wenden

Windau

Riga

Visby

•Goldingen

Kokenhusen

Duna

Polock

BALTIC

SEA

Vilia

Niemen

Kovno

Königsberg

Braunsberg

Rugenwalde• Stolp
Kolberg• Schlawe Danzig
Koslin Elbing
Belgard
Treptow
Greifenberg
Kammin•
Gollnow
Stettin Stargard

Pr

•Kulm
•Thorn

•Frankfurt

Oder

Vistula

Elbe

•Breslau

Cracow•

● Member of the Hanse
■ Non-member of the Hanse, but containing
   a Hanseatic counting-house, or an
   important establishment of members
   (places underlined)

Se. Seehausen   O. Osterberg

Groups of Hanseatic Towns
Wes: Westphalian   Zu: Zuiderzee
Sa: Saxon   Wen: Wend
Pr: Prussian   Liv: Livonian

that century. The hospice that in Paris gave its name to the Rue Saint-Jacques, was certainly founded during this same century; but there were many others. The roads to Compostella were, moreover, from other points of view, factors in interregional or international contacts. Although the majority of the "sauvetés" or privileged localities that were set up in Gascony along these routes in the eleventh and at the beginning of the twelfth centuries were peopled with clearers of land who did not come from far away, it must have been otherwise with several settlements like Oloron or the "new borough" (Fr.: *bourg neuf*) of Bayonne. In Navarre and in Aragon, from about 1050 to the end of the following century, it was the French immigrants who settled themselves into the new boroughs—sometimes near older localities—along the routes followed by the pilgrims.

The case of Compostella allows us to grasp the influence of a great pilgrimage as a factor in the spread of the elements of culture. The Cluniacs, who were its leaders and principal entrepreneurs, were able to bring their religious conceptions and their liturgical customs into northern Spain. French Romanesque architecture was introduced into Spain: we have already mentioned the churches that sprang up along the routes followed by pilgrims to Compostella; perhaps it was in imitation of French cloisters and in answer to the desires of French pilgrims that the first cloisters were built in northern Spain. Spanish miniatures influenced the miniatures and sculpture of the French Romanesque in the eleventh and twelfth centuries: the apocalypse of Saint-Sever, the capitals and the tympanum of Moissac bear witness to this. Elements borrowed from Moslem art made their appearance in the religious architecture of southern France in the twelfth century and in the decoration of religious buildings of this region; examples were cited in the previous chapter, notably that of Le Puy, itself a center of pilgrimage closely linked with that of Compostella. These are facts that would not be understood if no credit were given to the role of the pilgrims of Compostella. And although we do not today accept that the *Song of Roland* (Fr.: *Chanson de Roland*) or the *Song of William* (Fr.: *Chanson de Guillaume*) was composed on the roads to Compostella, it is difficult not to link the pilgrimages both with the abundant French epic literature that evolved after the twelfth century from these two "great ancestors" and with the penetration of these celebrated French themes into Spanish historical or epic literature which began in the same period.

8

The Era of Theocracy and French Hegemony

THE HUNDRED YEARS that elapsed in western Europe between the decline of the twelfth century and the dawn of the fourteenth, saw further progress of the rise in population that had been characteristic of the two preceding centuries. It has been calculated that around 1300 there were 10,000,000 or 11,000,000 inhabitants within the actual boundaries of France and 3,500,000 in Great Britain. These figures are reasonably admissible. The effects of this demographic phenomenon, in so far as they matter in the study of international relations, have already been pointed out; during the thirteenth century they became increasingly important. The advance of western Europe toward the east became more marked; before the end of the century the ancient Slavic lands east of the Elbe were not only conquered—we shall come to this later—but were largely put under cultivation and Germanized as far as the river Oder. The greater extent of land under cultivation and the progress of Germanization in the countries of the middle Danube should also be mentioned here. Also it would be equally impossible not to mention the activity, parallel to the former, in the eastern part of Hungary, namely Transylvania, on the part of the Saxon colonies that were founded toward the middle of the twelfth century and were highly developed by the thirteenth. On account of the migration of peoples, the clearing or draining of new lands and the introduction of more intensive agricultural exploitation developed more than in the past. The migrations of the Flemings, of the people of Brabant, of the people of Holland, and of those of the Rhineland and of Westphalia beyond the Elbe are the best known and doubtless the most important. However there were many others. Today we would consider as "interregional" the migrations of the Bretons and the people of Limousin who cleared the left banks of the lower Creuse, and those of the Saintonge who populated the "Entre-Deux Mers" at the mouth of the Gironde. However, placed in thirteenth-century France, they warrant being cited in the same breath as the migrations of the Lotharingians and the Westphalians who moved toward the interior of Germany at that time. We should also mention that in Germany these migrations were often organized by genuine contractors, a situation not unknown in France.

No more than we did for the preceding centuries will we mention the changes that took place in agriculture and animal husbandry. We should, however, mention some of the effects these changes had on international relations and the action of these relations on certain aspects of the agrarian economy. They mostly consist of phenomena, whose first phases occurred in the twelfth century, but which expanded during the thirteenth: such as the development of viniculture and the production of wine in the Bordeaux and Saintonge regions as a result of the increased demand in England, the Low Countries and northern Germany; the intensification of sheep farming which reached its zenith in England during the thirteenth century, because the demand for English wool by the cloth industries of Flanders, Brabant, and Champagne, had grown, and because the cloth industries of Lombardy and Tuscany also made demands on it; and doubtless also the increased importance during this period of the cultivation of pastel in the region of Lauragais and Toulouse—a dye plant which could be exported to England via Bordeaux, a possession of the English sovereigns.

It is also important to note another consequence that the changes in agricultural economy had for international relations in the thirteenth century. To the detriment of direct exploitation and of revenues in kind, they increased the relative importance of revenues in coin acquired by the lords—revenues that for the most part were fixed. Furthermore, it appears certain that the value of money diminished during the twelfth and thirteenth centuries, with the result that these revenues progressively lessened. Corrective measures were doubtless introduced, even remedies for this state of affairs, notably leases for a term of years, either in return for a share of the harvest (fr. "bail à métayage") or for a fixed rent (Fr.: *bail à ferme*). But there is no doubt that the nobility, and in particular the middle and the lower aristocracy, were very hard hit. The result was that many members of this social milieu looked for other resources, not only by serving for pay in the armies of kings and important princes, but by going into the civil service which these princes were founding or developing, and by taking part in overseas enterprises: we are referring not only to those of the East, but also to conquest and colonization beyond the Elbe and to great expeditions, which will be mentioned later, such as the Albigensian crusade and the Angevin adventures in Italy.

In the field of international trade and of the industry that at least partially fed it, the thirteenth century saw the further development of the currents and tendencies that had taken shape during the preceding century. The trade linking northwestern Europe to the Mediterranean world henceforth had as its governing center the Champagne fairs, which virtually brought a halt to the direct transportation of merchandise by producers or by national intermediaries up to their destination. The products of the cloth industry of Flanders, Brabant and Hainaut and that of northern France and of Champagne, which at this time was undergoing a remarkable development, were exchanged at fairs for eastern and Mediterranean products brought by Italian merchants. The drawing power of the great merchant area of Champagne was, moreover, very strong. It even extended to Christian Spain, which exported leather known as "Cordovan" to the fair. It included England, which was able to sell part of her modest production of cloth there, and Western Germany, which sold its cloth and, apparently, bar silver. Although the fairs of Champagne were the main center for commerce between the North Sea and the Mediterranean, they were not the only ones: the Lendit fair at Saint-Denis and the Paris market played similar though smaller roles, particularly since the end of the century.

We must include the sale of English wool in the same current. The sale of this wool at English fairs, where Flemish and other merchants came to buy, became increasingly important; without excluding other wools—native, Spanish, or Scottish—it was English wool that Flemish cloth industry, the most important cloth industry in the weaving zone that extended from Chartres to Lotharingia, used more than any other for the manufacturing of their cloth: not only finished cloth, but also "raw" or "semi-finished" cloth, which was bought by Italians, and whose preparation, including principally dyeing, was done in Florence. In fact, at the southern end of the North Sea–Mediterranean axis, the weaving industry also became more so than in the past—though henceforth rather more in Tuscany than in Lombardy—an industry working principally for a foreign market: that of the Mediterranean and the East. Essentially a finishing industry, it also, however, became largely a producing industry, in Florence more than in any other place toward the end of the century. A condition for this new development lay in the importation of large quantities of English wool, in addition to the wool of Spain or of the Maghreb (from "Garbo."). Before this time, importation of this English wool had been undertaken only occasionally, through the intermediary of the merchants of Brabant or of Holland. But from the last years of the century on, the traffic became heavy and was handled directly from England.

The great merchant cities of Italy, Genoa, Pisa, and Venice further intensified their commercial relations with the Byzantine and the Moslem East, as with North Africa, during the thirteenth century. These relations fluctuated, and some of those fluctuations will be mentioned later. It is important to mention here the volume of traffic: it assured the products of European industry abundant markets; it provided Mediterranean, central, and western Europe with goods from the Near East, the Indies, and the Far East. It supplied the mordant needed by the cloth-making regions of Europe, by importing alum from the shores of the Aegean Sea and from the Black Sea or from North Africa; it furnished with corn from the Ukraine not only the Byzantine or the Latin Empire but also regions with poor soil bordering on the northern banks of the former *mare nostrum*. It gave Kuman, Tartar, Caucasian, Turkish or Russian slaves to the majority of the countries bordering on the Mediterranean, whether they were Christian or Moslem—the latter, however, more than the former. The settlements founded by Italian cities abroad gave a certain amount of stability to this ensemble of trade relations, despite piracy, wars, and political or religious conflicts. Those in the Holy Land and in Syria gradually disappeared because of the Moslem reconquest. On the other hand, those of the Mahgreb and Africa rather developed; after Genoa and Pisa, Venice and the kingdom of Sicily were to have their own there. In the East none were as important as those located at Constantinople; but since the second half of the century the Genoese settlement in Soldaia and then the Genoese colony of Caffa, both of them in the Crimea, were to play an important role. Barcelona was to be dragged in the wake of Genoa toward the East, but its relations with North Africa appear to have been self-engendered. The foreign trade of the merchant cities of Provence and Languedoc increased also. This is obvious as far as the traffic between Marseille and North Africa is concerned. Between 1194 and 1210, Marseille had in fact taken advantage of a series of disputes between Pisa and Genoa in order to free herself from the latter city and to conclude with it, in 1211, a treaty on the basis of equality and complete reciprocity.

The Italians, whose essential role we have already seen in the flow of trade linking northwestern Europe with the Mediterranean, were not only merchants and industrial contractors, but also bankers. It was in particular the transactions conducted at the fairs in Champagne that brought them to play this role, at least in international trade. During the twelfth century the merchants of Piacenza and during the thirteenth century those of Siena, Genoa, and Florence increasingly took charge of payments at the fairs, by way of compensation or otherwise. Grouped in companies throughout western Europe which conducted business in goods as well as dealing in money, these businessmen also undertook operations other than those we have just mentioned, such as draft payments and exchange and loan. These companies had their agents or their branch offices in Italy itself and in other countries. Toward the end of the century, one came across them in Paris, London, and Bruges, in Provence, Spain, and North Africa, in the Morea, at Rhodes, and at Cyprus. Kings, princes, nobles, the Church, and cities were their clients as well as traders. Owing to the importance and the volume of the business they conducted, the Italian bankers were much more important than local financiers, as for instance those of Arras in northern France.

During the thirteenth century, particularly its second half, and even more in the fourteenth, Italians other than the bankers, played a role in the trading of money in western Europe: namely, those peoples who were commonly called the Lombards, and who were in reality chiefly Piedmontese, chiefly from Asti and Chieri. One came across them throughout northern and eastern France, from Flanders to the duchy of Burgundy, in the Lotharingian principalities, in Lorraine, in the county of Burgundy, in Savoy, in villages, and in small towns as well as in large commercial centers. They made loans against pledged chattels; and since they undertook loans at interest forbidden by the Church without the precautionary measures taken by the bankers, they were the object of hatred on the part of their debtors and were mistrusted by the general public. The literature of the time abounds in cruel portraits of them. Their clientele ranged from princes to artisans, to farmers, and even to the working classes. They occasionally also traded in goods. Certain among them accumulated considerable fortunes. They were often given the name of "Cahorsins," probably because during the thirteenth century, this name, with its topographical significance, in England and soon elsewhere took on the pejorative sense of "foreign exploiter," as the people of Cahors had played a particularly active role in the commerce of this country and had aroused xenophobia among the English, as had the Flemings. One should also mention, as an important aspect of Italian activity in the field of international trade, the fact that in France and in England many members, former members, or agents of banking establishments or even "Lombards" went into the service of kings and princes as officers with financial duties—receivers, keepers of the purse, etc.—and as farmers of taxes or of other revenues.

This ensemble of international economic relations has as its core the northwestern flow from Europe to the Mediterranean, at the heart of which were the Champagne fairs. During the period we are discussing, it was no longer the only important trade route. The west-east flow—whose poles were England on the one side and Germany and the countries of central European countries on the other, and whose principal links were Bruges, the cities of Brabant, and the Rhineland cities—did nothing but increase in importance from the moment they began to develop in the twelfth century. Though they grew, diversified, and created new connections, they nevertheless conserved the traits by which we know them. Other flows were brought to full light at this time. Of the utmost importance was the flow that spread from Italy toward the countries of the North Sea, through central Switzerland and the Rhine Valley, with branches out toward the Parisian basin and toward Champagne through the Jura and Vosges passes. This was made possible by the opening of the Sankt-Gotthard road before 1230. The Atlantic should also be considered. Navigation by Genoese galleys to Flanders and to England is known to have taken place by 1277. That of the Majorcan galleys perhaps dates earlier, at least to England. But it was during the next century that land traffic through the Gotthard pass and that Italian or Catalonian shipping in the Atlantic took on the utmost importance; this will be examined when we treat the subject of international commerce during the fourteenth century. During the thirteenth century there was trade by sea between the Iberian peninsula and the coasts of the Channel and the North Sea. Not very much is known about this traffic, but it is thought to have transported iron and wool from Spain toward the north, and cloth from Flanders, from the north of France, and from Normandy toward the south. The Spanish ports along the Gulf of Gascony and those of Portugal on the one hand, and of Bruges and Rouen on the other, were the principal centers of departure and arrival. Also, another current can be discerned which used the Atlantic between England and the Saintonge—that is to say, the port of La Rochelle—and which, by way of Cahors, reached the Mediterranean at Montpellier, then on to Italy. English wool for Tuscany and Mediterranean goods for England must have been carried that way. Cahors benefited from this traffic in the same manner as she profited from the traffic between the Iberian peninsula and the fairs of Champagne, whence arose the role played by her merchants in outside markets, especially in England.

Maritime relations between Guyenne and Saintonge on the one hand, and between England and Flanders on the other, could only increase during the thirteenth century. They were fed through the importation to these two latter countries of wines from the southwest and of salt from the Bay of Bourgneuf. The north German towns—those of lower Saxony, and those colonized countries along the Baltic that were always more numerous and more prosperous—soon sent their ships to Bruges, where their merchants sold the products which they drained into the North Sea and Baltic basins. By the middle of the century the people of Hamburg and Lübeck had become not only great buyers of

Flemish cloth and, doubtless, purchasers of Mediterranean products from the fairs of Champagne, but also important buyers of
wine and salt, in the same way as they bought wool in England
used by the textile industry of northern Germany to produce
rather rough cloth. With the advent of these commercial activities
at Bruges and at London there appears the first outlines of an
organization, as yet tentative, among the German towns on the
North Sea and the Baltic and even among the Rhine-Westphalian
towns, for the defense of their interests: the future German
"Hanse."

During the thirteenth century the volume of international commercial transactions reached considerable proportions. The transactions required the circulation of an increased amount of currency, better controlled and of a finer alloy than the silver pieces
of mediocre quality that were issued in the West. Attempts were
made to satisfy this need in various ways. One way was the issue
of better silver currencies, such as the English penny of 1180, the
Venetian *grosso* or *matapan* of 1192, the French "gros tournois"
struck from 1266 on. Gold was used, the issuing of which began
in the West with the "augustales" of the Emperor Frederick II in
1231, with coins struck in Genoa in 1252, with the Florentine
"florin" of the same year, with the Saint Louis *écu* in 1266, and
the Venetian ducat in 1284. But the supply of money was still
short. In international commerce, compensatory payments, at
fairs or elsewhere, and the practice, spread by the Italians, of
transfers and papers of credit considerably cut back the drawing
on real currency.

We have seen that from the end of the twelfth century western
Christendom spread and intensified its trade relations; however,
the authority that it exercised over foreign territories was restricted. During the second half of this century the threat menac-
ing the Christian East increased. Turkish power in Iraq, with
Mosul as its center, was strengthened. Zenguî's son, Nûr-ad-Din,
gradually became master of the Syrian hinterlands and conquered

what remained of the principality of Edessa and part of that of Antioch. When Amaury I, king of Jerusalem, succeeded in 1167 in imposing his proctectorate upon Fatimite Egypt, the Sultan of Iraq exploited the Frankish mistakes and in the following year made himself master of this country. His governor in Cairo, Salah-al-Din Yussuf—the western "Saladin"—put an end to the Fatimite Caliphate in 1171 and re-established Islamic unity east of Tripolitania under the purely theoretical authority of the Abbasside Caliph of Baghdad. When Saladin succeeded Nûr-ad-Din in 1174, he was master of a Turkish empire that stretched from Cyrenaica to the southern and western reaches of Iraq. Christian Syria and the Holy Land were encircled. The task of the Turkish conquerors was made easier by divisions and blunders among the Latins—as well those who had settled in the country as those who took part in numerous western expeditions to the Holy Land—and the impossibility of achieving genuine cooperation with Byzantium, in spite of the recognized supremacy of Manuel Comnenos. The Turkish attacks began in 1177; they ended in 1187 with the conquest of Jerusalem, and in 1188 with the subduing of what remained of the kingdom. Only Antioch, Tripoli, and Tyre and their immediate environs remained unconquered. A crusade was organized—the third one according to the traditional numbering. The Emperor Frederick Barbarossa, conscious of his role as leader of Christendom, took part with a considerable army but was drowned in 1190 before reaching Syria. Philip Augustus, king of France, and Richard I Coeur de Lion, king of England, also set out; and fleets were equipped by the Italian republics and even by the three Scandinavian kingdoms. Acre, on the Palestinian coast, was besieged and taken in 1191. The following year the King of England reconquered the major part of the coastal area but did not succeed in taking Jerusalem. A treaty was concluded in 1192, with Saladin guaranteeing pilgrims free access to the Holy Places; but the Greek Church had succeeded the Latin Church in watching over and running the Christian churches. Cyprus, which

Richard had taken from the dissenting *basileus* Isaac Comnenos, became a Latin kingdom for Guy of Lusignan; the brother of the latter, Amaury II, also became King of Jerusalem in 1197. This kingdom—reduced to a narrow strip along the coast—maintained, both for the Christians and especially for the Italian merchant republics, control of the eastern Mediterranean and commercial entrepôts in the Near East, so vital for Italian trade. In the long run, this was doubtless the principal result of the third crusade.

The miserable defense of the Holy Land and of Syria against Saladin, the defeated attempts at reconquest by the crusaders, once again revealed the political and military incapacity that western knighthood displayed in the East—to say nothing of its moral deficiencies as demonstrated by the injustifiable cruelties on the part of the Christians. All these characteristics were manifested in, among others, Richard Coeur de Lion. On the contrary, Philip Augustus, king of France, possessed to the highest degree the military and political skills that the champions of Christianity who fought against Islam were lacking so cruelly.

After the accession of Philip Augustus to the throne in 1180, France played a major role in international politics. This was effected through the actions of the King at home, thanks principally to the talent that he shared with several of his successors for exploiting the possibilities that his prerogatives as a feudal lord or king gave him, and that until that time were often theoretical. To the detriment of the large principalities, he succeeded in extending the territories under the immediate control of the Crown. He was probably the first Capetian who consciously pursued this goal. In 1191 he managed to lay hands on the Vermandois, in the north of the kingdom, and on Artois, which was the southern part of the county of Flanders.

The intervention of royalty in Mediterranean France is, however, of much greater importance to the history of international relations. The region was in fact foreign to the Capetians and to northern France. Since the second half of the eleventh century not only the counties and seigneuries of Gascony, Toulouse, and Langedoc but also Provence were the cause of a struggle between the counts of Toulouse and the counts of Barcelona. The division of Provence into a "Barcelonian" county and a "Toulousian" marquisate in 1125 was only a truce, and the union of the Barcelonian county with the kingdom of Aragon in 1137 gave the conflict new scope. It even involved the King of England, Henry II, on the side of Aragon in 1158 and in 1181, and the King of France, Louis VII, on the side of the Toulousians in 1159. Frederick Barbarossa, suzerain of the county of Provence, and the Genoese fought against the King of Aragon when the latter, after having brought the territory to his crown (1166), refused homage to the Emperor in his capacity as King of Burgundy. And Pisa naturally fought against the Count of Toulouse.

It was a futile and endless struggle. It permitted neither of these houses to build the great state from the Ebro to the Alps that the King of Aragon, King Alfonso II, had almost created before he died in 1196. His death brought about the separation of the county of Provence, given to his younger son Alfonso, from the Spanish and Languedoc territories, which went to his eldest son, Peter II.

In spite of these struggles, in the "area" between the Ebro and the Alps the ruling classes—knights, clergy, and middle-class merchants—composed a fairly powerful homogeneous group, owing to their use of the *langue d'oc*, to a similar easy concept of life, to certain forms of art, to the direction of their interests, and to the frequency of relations of all sorts, peaceful or warlike. A religious war brought northern France into contact with this milieu, so different from hers. A doctrine of Manichaean origin, characterized by the belief in the dual divine principle of good and of evil and by its aversion to the sacraments, entered the south of France from Bulgaria via northern Italy and spread extensively among the population. Its followers called themselves

"Cathars"—that is to say, "pure"—though this term could be justified for only a very small number of "perfect ones," the only people to practice the extreme austerity preached to the members of the sect. They were also called "Albigensians," because there were many of them in Albi and in the countryside around the town. The pacific action of the clergy and rigorous local measures were unable to eliminate this danger to orthodox Catholicism. In 1208, Pope Innocent III announced a crusade against the heretics and their supposed protector, the Count of Toulouse, Raymond VI. Thousands of eager knights from northern France hurried south. The heretics defended themselves for some time, and during this defense against the northern barbarians the King of Aragon was allied with his hereditary enemy, the Count of Toulouse. Philip Augustus took no part in the crusade, but he allowed his vassals to participate. At one point he sent his son as delegate, and the latter, when he was King Louis VIII (1223–1226), took over command. The Crown was the chief political beneficiary of the crusade: Count Raymond VII had to surrender an important part of his territories to the King. The effect on the social order was even more profound: the settling in the south of France of numerous knights and clerics from the north and their suites. They took over lordships and ecclesiastical responsibilities, thus ruining a civilization that expressed itself through the *langue d'oc* poetry of the troubadours. They introduced into Languedoc and into the Toulouse area the language, the culture, and the outlook on life current in the north. In short, this was a real union with France of the country that extended from the eastern Pyrenees to the Rhône. The Ebro-Alpine "region" had lived out its time, and Aragon politics were to concern themselves with other horizons—Spanish and soon Italian.

Whereas Philip Augustus had managed to avoid personal engagement in the "Albigensian crusade"—as the conquest of the Languedoc and the Toulouse regions is called—he gave considerably of himself in the struggle against the Anglo-Angevin empire, the enemy that throughout his reign he strove to defeat. He roused his sons against Henry II; then, after the death of the old King in 1189, he fought against his son and successor, Richard I Coeur de Lion. When the latter died in 1199, he attacked the brother and successor to the dead King, John Lackland. In 1204 he had seized Normandy, Anjou and its dependencies, as well as the suzerainty of Brittany.

Since 1187 the conflict had taken on an international character following the alliance between the Emperor and the King of France against Henry II, brother-in-law of the rebel, the Guelph, Henry the Lion: the Franco-Ghibelline party (a corrupt nomenclature, stemming from Italy, of "Waiblingen," a castle of the Hohenstaufen in Swabia) against the Anglo-Guelph party.

After the death of Barbarossa, the struggle spread to the interior of Germany, where King Henry VI (1190–1197) was no longer in a position to contain the increasingly strong tendency of the princes toward autonomy and opposition to the central power; Henry the Lion back home lent assistance to the revolts. The adventures of the extraordinary character that Henry VI, the son of Barbarossa, revealed himself to be, involved him in this conflict.

Having become King of Sicily through his marriage with Constance, aunt and heiress of William II, he made efforts to consolidate his power in the island and in southern Italy by various means including the settling of German vassals there. He attempted to gain acceptance of a final union between the crown of Sicily and the imperial dignity and to make the latter hereditary. But he failed because of the hostility of the Pope, of the German princes, and of his Italian and Sicilian subjects. It appears that he hoped to conquer Constantinople, and he prepared a German crusade, some troops of which finally disembarked in the Holy Land without performing any useful task. In 1197 he himself was setting out for the East when he died, having succeeded in none of his enterprises and leaving his sovereign power in Italy and in Germany weaker than at his accession.

His death opened a new phase—and the most bitter—in the quarrel between the Anglo-Guelph and Franco-Ghibelline parties. The princes, now unchecked, elected two kings in Germany: Philip of Swabia, brother of Henry VI, and Otto IV, son of Henry the Lion. The struggle between the German princes, many of whom changed camps according to their interests, was combined with the wars conducted by their allies. Pope Innocent III (1198–1216) intervened in an attempt to gain from either the Hohenstaufens or the Guelphs the maximum concessions in favor of the Church in general, of the Holy See in particular. Philip of Swabia had just come to the fore when he was assassinated in 1208; Otto IV, who had just become master of the greater part of Germany, gave considerable support to John Lackland in his struggle against Philip Augustus. Even the Count of Flanders, Ferrand of Portugal, a French vassal who held his county from the King, took part in the Anglo-Guelph coalition under pressure from the Flemish cities, importers of English wool. However, Philip Augustus defeated them in 1214 at Bouvines. His victory was of the utmost importance: Germany was brought to her knees and once again became prey to divisive tendencies. England, successfully attacked in Poitou, retained only her possessions in southwestern France. Finally, the humiliating defeat of the Count of Flanders, the king's prisoner, constituted a warning to the other French territorial princes. The Anglo-Angevin empire had lived out its span; the French monarchy was hereafter the foremost political power in the West.

However, after the defeat suffered by Frederick Barbarossa in his efforts to give a certain reality to the imperial authority, and after the political weakening of Germany caused by this defeat, there was no longer any power that was able to exercise a hegemony or even to play a leading role in the life of western Europe. The papacy tried to seize this role from him during the first years of the thirteenth century.

Pope Innocent III, elected in 1198, was above all a priest who passionately desired the spreading of the faith, the restoration of peace and unity among the Christians. He thought that this ideal could be reached by the establishment of theocracy: that meant bringing under the authority of the head of the Church ecclesiastical and lay Christianity in all manifestations of its authority. He pursued or developed the work of his predecessors: the struggle against heresy, of which the Albigensian crusade was, from the point of view of international relations, the principal effort; regulations about papal jurisdiction and about the activities of the papal legates; the passing of a series of measures tending to render more efficacious the papal *plenitudo potestatis* at the Fourth Lateran Council. The international situation favored policies asserting papal supremacy over all states: the struggle between the Franco-Ghibelline and Anglo-Guelph parties, in fact, permitted him to excommunicate or to depose *ratione peccati* the kings whose policies displeased him. According to Innocent III, it was enough to term their governmental actions sinful for these kings to be brought into the jurisdiction of the sovereign pontiff.

One of the most effective means of ensuring a stable theocratic government in the West was to develop vassal relations between the kings and the Holy See. Innocent III made efforts to strengthen relations with former vassals, such as the kings of Portugal, Aragon, and Sicily. In this he succeeded. The results were of considerable importance in the case of Sicily when one realizes all the trouble that the "Sicilian" vassals had given to the predecessors of Innocent III and particularly the danger that the union of the crown of Sicily with the imperial crown would have presented to the Holy See if Henry VI had lived longer. The King was Frederick Roger, son of Henry VI and Constance of Sicily, and ward of Innocent. The latter thought him such a faithful vassal that he broke with the traditional Roman policy, at least for the time being, and allowed him to strive for the throne of Germany in 1212. When, after Bouvines, his protégé triumphed in

Germany and, under the name of Frederick II, was soon recognized by all as king, the Pope was looked upon by many as having in fact been the collator of the German crown.

Innocent III achieved a much greater success in England. John Lackland had for a long time quarreled with him, principally over the Archbishop of Canterbury, Stephen Langton, who had been consecrated by the Pope, but whom John refused to accept as primate of England. When Innocent III placed an interdict upon the kingdom, John Lackland seized the Church lands. The Pope excommunicated him, released his subjects of their duty of fealty, and invited Philip Augustus to seize the kingdom of England. But when in 1213 John Lackland transferred the ownership of England to the Roman Church, offering to take it back as a fief and to swear fealty and do homage to the Pope, the latter took his new vassal under his protection and forbade the King of France to invade the island. Every nation appeared in turn to become provinces of a vast empire, whose government would belong to the head of the Church.

The papacy was going to be able to support its action with an important force: that of the two first "mendicant orders" which were new expressions of spirituality and of aspirations toward religious perfection. They were "mendicants" because their members had to live from alms, as the convents of these orders were not allowed to own land. Both of them were born out of a reaction against the taste for luxury and for easy living which was gaining ground in many circles of society, and which, in the eyes of austere, peevish or critical people, corrupted the soul and inclined man toward immorality. The reaction was directed particularly against the members of the clergy whom the reformers thought susceptible to corruption. It is striking that it should manifest itself first in the Mediterranean countries where trade with the East accumulated the greatest wealth and gave the inhabitants the easiest access to the refined modes of existence known to the Byzantine and the Moslem worlds.

Innocent III, who was above all preoccupied with the struggle against heresy, played an active part in the decision that Saint Dominic, a Spanish canon, made in 1205 to devote himself to preaching *verbo et exemplo*—that is to say, to instructing through his theological knowledge and the example of his humility. Innocent encouraged the first group of "preaching friars" created by Saint Dominic in the diocese of Toulouse, where action against the Albigensian creed was particulary urgent. The "preaching friars," or "Dominicans," were not, however, consecrated as an order until 1216 by Pope Honorius III.

Innocent III also received and encouraged the son of a rich draper of Assisi, Saint Francis, who preached a life of total renunciation, humility, charity, absolute poverty, and blessed joy—conditions that he considered to be the true interpretation of the Gospels. His disciples, the "friars minor," were at first a simple fraternal and wandering community. It became an order in 1223, with a rule promulgated by Honorius III. After the death of Saint Francis in 1226, the members of the order became known as "Franciscans."

The birth and development of these orders constituted an essential factor in the history of international relations. They experienced, in fact, an extraordinary geographic diffusion. The "preachers" spread throughout France and into Spain, England, Germany, Italy, Poland, and Hungary; the "minors" throughout Italy and into France, Germany, England, Hungary, and Spain. It is not as easy to trace them as the Cistercians, for they did not erect one church of the same type in all of Latin Christendom. Large churches with two naves, particularly appropriate for preaching, were favored by the Dominicans in France; the Jacobin Church of Toulouse is the most famous example. And yet they did not remain faithful to this model in the following century. We must mention the traits particular to the action of the "mendicants" throughout the Christian world. They were, above all, the spiritual guides of urban populations, over whom they exercised a profound influence. They were also missionaries in lands beyond Christendom: we shall come back to this. The "preachers" played a decisive role in the "Inquisition"—that is to say, the institution charged with disclosing and pursuing heretics. They were also the great teachers of theology and philosophy; the "minors" took more time to establish themselves in the intellectual world but nevertheless managed to play an important role in the movement of ideas.

One of Innocent III's most constant concerns was the deliverance of the Holy Places. His efforts to reconcile the kings of France and England—which were quite useless, incidentally—had as its basic goal the possibility of their participation in a crusade. This came about, but without a single king in command. This crusade, like the first, was composed of princes and knights, particularly French, but also German and Italian. Venice had agreed to transport the army. She managed to turn the expedition to her own good: in 1202, the crusaders reconquered for Venice the settlement of Zara on the Dalmatian coast, which had been seized from her by the King of Hungary, Christian though he was! Then in 1203, instead of making their way to the Holy Land and seizing the tomb of Christ from the infidel, they attacked Constantinople. Venice aimed at consolidating its situation in the Byzantine empire, which had dangerously worsened. Genoese competition made her uneasy. But more particularly, she considered it necessary, as did other Latins, to assure herself of guarantees for her trade and for her colony at Constantinople, and to obtain compensation for the losses she had suffered on various occasions: notably in 1182 when, with the compliance of the pretender and future *basileus* Andronicos Comnenos, the mob in the capital had massacred all the Latins, whether merchants or mercenaries, whom they could lay their hands on, and had pillaged their homes and their entrepôts.

Furthermore, the empire was weakened. Manuel Comnenos' policy had demanded more from Byzantine resources than they had been able to give. The imbalance between resources and expenses upon them had even led the emperors to speed up the debasement of gold coinage, which had been going on since the middle of the eleventh century, but particularly so after the military disasters at the end of that century. The devaluation of the *nomisma*—the coin stamped with the imperial effigy which westerners called the "bezant" and the Greeks increasingly called the "hyperpuron," and which had been the most widely used currency of the major trades until the end of the twelfth century, brought a considerable loss of prestige. *Coups d'état* wrecked discipline in the army, brought about the succession of the Angeloi in the place of the Comnenoi in 1185, and weakened the power of the central authority. In the same year that the Hungarians conquered Dalmatia, Isaac Comnenos proclaimed himself independent in Cyprus, and William II, king of Sicily, ravaged Thessalonica and threatened Constantinople. Bulgars and Serbs regained their independence, and their princes, at the cost of a rather vague submission to the Roman Church, had themselves recognized as royalty by the Pope in 1204 and 1217, respectively. The Turks regained some land in Asia Minor. Furthermore, profound economic troubles had weakened the empire. The founding of the Latin states of Syria and Palestine, and particularly the Italian, Provençal, and Languedoc colonies in their ports, had turned away from Constantinople a considerable portion of the trade between Asia and Europe. In the empire itself exorbitant privileges had been conferred, for political reasons, on the Venetians, the Genoese, and the Pisans, that enabled them to handle the major share of business. Fiscal pressures prevented the development of a Byzantine capitalism that could have competed with the Italians, or that could have led the latter to create interests with it. The depreciation of the bezant, which we have already mentioned, played a part in this decline in trade. Art, virtually alone, upheld the prestige of Byzantium. It spread to Russia, Serbia, and Cyprus, and it is particularly striking to see the mortal enemies of Byzantium, the Norman kings of Sicily and the greatest of their servants, using Byzantine architectural and decorative themes in the construction and ornamentation of their palaces and churches. In the palatine chapel of Palermo, in the cathedral of Monreale, and at the Martorana, the art of the Comnenoi and the Angeloi can be seen in all its splendor.

As the Venetians expected, the resistance lacked vigor. Constantinople was taken in 1204, and the crusaders acted—in a schismatic but nonetheless Christian country!—with a savagery even greater than their predecessors in Jerusalem in 1099. The empire collapsed. The princes and knights of the fourth crusade were more mindful of serving Mammon than of serving God. The Count of Flanders and Hainaut became "Emperor of Romania," taking the name of Baldwin I. Out of conquered European territories the leaders carved themselves large principalities or seigneuries, subject to imperial suzerainty, but in fact independent. Religiously speaking, the "Romania" returned to the bosom of the Roman Church: the schism of 1054 had been ended. Innocent III was satisfied: if he blamed the excesses committed by the crusaders, he congratulated himself on the results obtained.

In the meantime the Bulgars, crossed with Vlachs, invaded the northern provinces and threatened the capital. Two Greek empires were set up in Asia. That of Nicaea was founded by Theodoros Lascaris I in 1208; he maintained himself in spite of the Latins and the Turks. In 1204, Alexios Comnenos I, grandson of Andronicos I, had founded another around Trebizond, on the Black Sea. A "despotat" was created by Michael Angelos I in Epirus. Thus the Byzantine tradition survived; a restoration was still possible. The Venetians were the great beneficiaries of the crusade. Masters of trade in the Empire of "Romania" (or Latin Empire as it is often called), holding strategic points in the islands and on the coast, and occupying Crete, they enjoyed a privileged position throughout the Orient, and they made their Genoese rivals feel it.

Innocent III died in 1216 without realizing his life's dream: the deliverance of the Holy Places. The great work whose foundations he had laid, the establishment of a theocracy in western Europe, was to be subjected to a fearful assault, actually by his former protégé, Frederick II. Crowned emperor in 1220, the grandson of Barbarossa was also to attempt to make of the empire a reality. But although he was just as concerned as his grandfather with the universal character of his imperial power, he made less of it before the western Christian world. Besides, his imperial policy differed in other respects from that of Barbarossa. According to the latter, the center of the empire was still Germany, and had he achieved his goals, western Europe would have been subjected to a superior German authority. But already Henry VI's imperial dream was based upon the Mediterranean, with Italy as its center. Frederick II's designs were also oriented toward the Mediterranean. This time the movement toward the south was realized. Frederick II foresaw in the immediate future the unification of Sicilian, pontifical, and royal Italy, governed by a cadre of regular officials dependent upon him, in the tradition of the Norman kingdom, only more strongly shaped. In order to attain this goal, he would, like his predecessors, set the cities and lords in Italy against each other. He would sacrifice to the ecclesiastical or lay princes the majority of the prerogatives the Crown still held in Germany. In war he would even have recourse to Moslem mercenaries, recruited among the Moslem populations that he had in large part deported from Sicily to Apulia—an extraordinary concept, which reveals a degree of indifference toward the Christian religion which was very exceptional for that time. Nonetheless during 1228 and 1229 he conducted a crusade in the Holy Land. He took the title of "King of Jerusalem" and obtained through negotiation the unhoped-for return of the Holy City to the Christians and at the same time various territories and advantages for the latter. But this was without any doubt part of his imperial policy in the Mediterranean.

Two popes, Gregory IX (1227-1241) and then Innocent IV (1243-1254), were faithful to Innocent III's theocratic ideal and resisted Frederick. The lords and the towns of Lombardy, Tuscany, and Liguria backed either the Pope or the Emperor, according to their interests; to be more precise, in the towns, the interests of a political faction or of a social group, that at the time was in power and were followed: nobles and great merchants who sometimes were one and the same; or *popolani*, that is to say, particularly the middle class of merchants and artisans. That was the time when in Italy the enemies of the Emperor were called "Guelphs"; his supporters were "Ghibellines." Pisa and Pavia alone were stanchly Ghibelline. With copious propaganda literature, Frederick was astute enough to represent his Italian subjects and particularly the Lombard League as rebellious subjects, which for a long time brought him support in England and even in France. In 1235 he attempted to ensure an English alliance through his marriage with the sister of Henry III; and if he was not successful, he at least had some sort of moral support from an England that had become very hostile toward Rome, as we shall later see. Nothing came of it, however. His policy caused anxiety. The number of his enemies grew in Italy; Venice even had supported them since 1238. The excommunications were not without effect; the deposition of the Emperor, which Innocent IV— obliged to seek refuge abroad—had pronounced in 1245 in a council convened at Lyon, had even deeper repercussions: it furnished a legal basis for the attitude of the rebels. Materially Frederick's forces had dwindled; but only his death in 1250 brought an end to the struggle.

The defeat of Frederick II ended the last serious attempt to build up in western Europe a lay authority superior to all others, based on considerable territorial power. Thirty years of effort had proved in vain. However, it was not only the imperial power that emerged shattered from the struggle. The papacy had used all its material and moral forces; furthermore—and we shall come back to this—it also was causing anxiety. It had had to flee both Rome and Italy. In the Church State and in its capital, pontifical power was held in check by the aristocratic families and the bourgeois or popular factions. The establishment of a theocracy in western Europe was excluded: from the point of view of our particular study, this was the most important result of the struggle between Frederick II and the Holy See.

During this struggle, the papacy and the Italian enemies of Frederick II had not hesitated to rouse the Emperor's enemies in Germany and to support antikings against him. One of his sons betrayed him. The passions aroused by the conflict, and the nearly complete autonomy acquired by the princes, explain the crisis, known as the "Great Interregnum," where central power almost entirely foundered in this country. After the deaths of the last great Hohenstaufen and of the antiking, William of Holland (1256), elected monarchs—among whom there was a Spaniard, Alfonso X, king of Castile, and an Englishman, Richard of Cornwall, second son of John Lackland—were stripped of all effective power. Germany as such ceased for some time to play a role in international politics. Furthermore, we should mention that it was Pisa that, acting on behalf of the people of the empire, offered—in the interest of its trade—the Crown to the Castilian. This was a further symptom of the decline of the imperial dignity and of the shifting of the principal seat of the empire from Germany toward Italy. Anarchy did not end until the election in 1273 of a Swabian lord, Rudolf of Hapsburg, Landgrave of Alsace. He and his two successors, Adolf of Nassau (1292) and Albert of Austria (1298)—the son of Rudolf—more or less completely abstained from intervening in Italy. The two kings of the house of Hapsburg attempted to restore the royal power in Germany so far as it was still possible; but in particular they tried to constitute a group of immediate territories: the beginning of a dynastic territorial policy. Rudolf seized Austria, Styria, and Carinthia from the King of Bohemia, whose royalty, after Barbarossa and Philip of Swabia, had been recognized by Frederick II. Albert tried to introduce a system of monarchical government in the southern territories of Swabia held by his house. But he failed before the opposition of the free peasants who inhabited the mountainous counties of Uri, Schwyz, and Unterwalden—counties that were newly important owing to the recent opening of the Sankt-Gotthard Alpine pass. He did not manage to unite these cantons to his other family lands. The federation, concluded by the cantons in 1291 with the aim of mutual assistance, can be taken as the birth of a new political unit—Switzerland.

If there is one area of the history of international relations where thirteenth-century Germany continued to be successful, it was in the expansion toward the east, in Slavic and even in Este countries. Conquest and colonization went hand in hand. The marquises of Brandenburg crossed the Oder toward the middle of the century. Farther north, the eastern part of Mecklenburg and Pomerania were conquered. And even more distantly, a military order formerly founded in the Holy Land, the order of the Teutonic Knights, conquered Prussia after 1226, supported by a crusade that the Pope had proclaimed in 1230, and that Germany and the neighboring countries supplied with troops. Another order, that of the Swordbearers (*Schwertbrüder*), followed a similar course in Livonia and in Estonia. The coast was occupied as far as the entrance to the Gulf of Finland. In all the colonized areas German towns were founded: Rostock, Greifswald, Danzig, Königsberg, and Riga are only the most famous among them. Furthermore, the German colonization was conducted very unevenly. If, toward 1300, we can assume that the colonization had been successfully accomplished west of the Oder, it was much slower, and in areas would remain very incomplete, beyond the river. Part of the regions colonized by the Germans had already been won over to Christianity by German or Polish missionaries. Others were pagan, and the conquest was accompanied by evangelization. In Prussia and beyond it was largely the work of the

Dominicans who received their orders from the Holy See. However, it is probable that the Teutonic knights and the crusaders massacred more Prussians than the missionaries gained through the Gospel. In Bohemia the German immigrants whom the King of this country had brought into the towns and mining districts, created German districts and population centers; but they did not Germanize the country.

The only power that could counterbalance the German influence in the Baltic was Denmark. But the positions that she had acquired along the southern coast, including Lübeck, were lost between 1225 and 1227, and the effective authority over Danish settlements built up in Estonia was reduced to but little. Reval became a German town. On the other hand, the Swedish political and religious penetration into Finland, begun during the twelfth century, developed considerably during the thirteenth and built up to a substantial colonization along the coasts, particularly around Abo. In order to stop Russian expansionist ambitions in this direction, the King of Sweden entrenched himself in Karelia at the end of the century. But it was not until 1323 that the attempts of the people of Novgorod to become masters of the region came to an end.

During the thirteenth century there were events of great importance that are not of direct interest to the study of international relations: we shall just mention them briefly. One of these is the long struggle in England, in which pitted against one another were, on the one hand, royalty which possessed a treasury and an administrative and judicial system that were more developed than in any other western nation, and on the other, the aristocracy, sometimes the clergy, and soon part of the population of towns. From this struggle stemmed the English Parliament. These events shall be treated here only insofar as they were immediately affected by international factors or exerted an immediate force on international relations. For example, one will note that the Anglo-

Guelph defeats of 1213 and 1214 were one of the factors that provoked the uprising of the barons against John Lackland in 1215—an uprising that forced the King to grant privileges to the rebels, the best known of which is Magna Charta. One notes also that John died in 1216 after revoking the Charter, as the barons had risen again and called the son of Philip Augustus to the throne. Once again the intervention of the Holy See saved the English monarchy: Honorious III protected young Henry III, vassal and ward of the Holy See, against the future Louis VIII who had landed in England. The French expedition resulted in failure in 1217. On the other hand, Louis VIII (1223–1226) was able, in 1224, to conquer Poitou and its dependencies, which, among other advantages, procured for him the port of La Rochelle on the Atlantic. Henry III made many an effort to reconquer the lost territories, but in vain. These inadequate expeditions, their expense, the costs the King incurred to support his brother Richard on the throne of Germany and to promote his son Edmund to the throne of Sicily (1254)—always without success—were among the causes of fresh conflicts between the Crown and the aristocracy. They therefore contributed to the weakening of the monarchy in England and to the emergence of institutions that limited its power.

France was the only nation that grew during the thirteenth century. This growth was manifested during the reign of Louis IX (1226–1270), whom the Catholic Church made a saint. It is evident that more than any other monarch at this time, he took care to govern his life by the teachings of the Church. And yet this concern did not prevent him from setting limits upon his duty to the Holy See when he thought that royal duties made it necessary. It was in this manner that he avoided compromising himself in the conflict between Frederick II and the papacy. It was only when the Emperor wanted to march on Lyon, where Innocent IV had sought refuge, that Louis IX made known his intention to defend the Pope in this eventuality (1247). And yet the Emperor

was in his right, as Lyon was situated in the kingdom of Burgundy or Arles, where the Emperor was king. It happened, moreover, that Saint Louis sacrificed the interest of his kingdom to his
religious ideals by undertaking two disastrous crusades: the first,
1248–1254, in which his army was wiped out in Egypt, and he
himself was taken prisoner; and the second, in 1270, also disastrous, which his brother, Charles of Anjou, succeeded in diverting
toward Tunis, where the King met his death. His highly Christian
concept of justice played a part in the fact that at the Treaty of
Paris in 1259, he not only relinquished Gascony to Henry III,
king of England, but also restored to him other territories that
were located farther north and had been lost by John Lackland or
by Henry III himself. This moderation had the advantage of
bringing back the King of England into a vassalic relation with
France through his title of Duke of Aquitaine—or of *Guyenne*, as
it was more often called.

The development of administrative and judicial institutions, of
a bureaucracy, and of the great body of central government in
royal France is not dealt with here at all: in sum, since Philip
Augustus a structure had developed that took its essential form
under Saint Louis. It is enough to recall the facts, because this is a
factor of some force for the French crown in international relations. However an important part of France was made into an
appanage granted to Alphonse of Poitiers, the King's brother:
Poitou and Auvergne and, following a marriage with the heiress
of the county of Toulouse, what remained of the latter. But the
greater part of these territories was returned to the Crown in
1271, and Alphonse had a foreign policy scarcely distinct from
that of his brother. The latter acquired exceptional prestige
through virtues pushed almost to bigotry. This prestige served the
establishment of French hegemony in western Europe during the
second and third quarters of the thirteenth century, as much as
did the material strength of the realm. French hegemony is clearly
shown in the importance of the conflicts that were submitted to

Saint Louis for arbitration. For example, that of 1264, between Henry III, King of England, and his barons; those of 1246 and 1256 between the houses of Dampierre and D'Avesnes, who were disputing not only for the county of Flanders, a French fief, but also the county of Hainaut, which was situated in the empire. In Europe of this period there was no power to be compared with that of France and its King.

This state of affairs is revealed in Italy. After the death of Frederick II the country was far from peaceful. His descendants maintained links with partisans; conflicts of ambition and of interest placed at loggerheads princely dynasties, noble houses, cities, and parties or social groups within them. The popes, deprived of protectors, were at the mercy of factions. It was essential that they should have, in the kingdom of Sicily, a trustworthy sovereign who could defend them. In order to root out the last of the Hohenstaufens—Manfred, Frederick II's bastard, and Conradin, the Emperor's grandson—the Pope looked to the King of England, Henry III, whose son, Edmund, could have received the crown; but all this came to nothing. Thanks to Louis IX and to two French popes, Urban IV and Clement IV, Charles of Anjou, the King's brother, won the infeudation of the kingdom of Sicily from the Holy See and undertook to support the papacy in Italy. This adventurer, who was endowed with both political and military talents, had married the heiress of the county of Provence and thus was preparing the reunion of this important part of the kingdom of Arles with France. He reached Italy in 1265 and progressively extended his power not only within the kingdom, but throughout the major part of the peninsula and even at Rome. Once Manfred was beaten and killed at Benevento (1266), and Conradin was wiped out at Tagliacozzo (1268) and executed at the victor's orders, all legitimate opposition was shattered. But Italy became ungovernable. Rivalries among cities the most important among which tried to build up territorial states, internal conflicts between the Guelphs and the Ghibellines, between nobility, bourgeois patriciates, the middle classes, the proletariat, the actions of princes and of seignorial families, and intrigues at the pontifical court. That proved more than Charles of Anjou could deal with. Moreover, a Ghibelline league, of which Genoa, Pavia, and even Milan became members, expelled him from northern Italy (1270–1277).

Despite these inextricable difficulties, however, like his predecessors, the Normans and particularly the Hohenstaufens, Charles was seduced by the mirage of Mediterranean imperialism. He occupied Corfu and tried, under the pretext of re-establishing the Latin empire of "Romania," to carve out possessions in the western part of the restored Byzantine Empire. In 1278 he acquired the Latin principality of Morea; he sent his fleet into Syrian waters, had Acre occupied by his troops in 1277, and had himself recognized as King of Jerusalem by what remained of the Latin East. After the death of his brother at Tunis (1270), he saved the situation, treated with the Caliph, and, faithful to the traditions of the Sicilian monarchy, demanded commercial advantages in North Africa for his kingdom—in exchange, of course, for reciprocity. The kingdom of Sicily was at this time on the way to becoming a center of great power in the Mediterranean, both politically and commercially. Moreover, it was the only part of Italy where Angevin authority had a base of any solidity. It was supported by a French nobility settled within the country by Charles chiefly on firm soil—this means southern continental Italy—and by French officials. It commanded financial resources furnished by a rigorous fiscal system. This was to last until the moment when in 1282 an uprising known to history as the "Sicilian Vespers" erupted at Palermo and resulted in the expulsion of Charles of Anjou and his partisans from Sicily. After about two centuries, a breach had occurred between Sicily and southern continental Italy. Only there did the Angevin kingdom hold out, with Naples as its capital. In Sicily, King Peter III of Aragon, who claimed the succession from Frederick II, in the name of his wife Constance, a daughter of Manfred—was recognized as king by the insurgents.

Aragon strengthened itself as the rival of the Angevins in the battle for hegemony in the western Mediterranean. We have to go back to the earlier situation in Spain to understand this great event, whose consequences were to develop over several centuries. Almohade strength and dissensions among the Christian states slowed the pace of the reconquest, as we saw, in the second half of the twelfth century. Navarre and León even made agreements with the Moslems, towards the end of the century against Castile. At the beginning of the thirteenth century the situation changed; revolts in North Africa diminished Almohade power. Jiménez de Rada, archbishop of Toledo and the driving force behind Castilian policy under Alfonso VIII, succeeded in bringing about the union of several Christian states and won an appeal for a crusade from Innocent III. In 1212, at Las Navas de Tolosa, south of the Sierra Morena, the coalition army of the kings of Castile, Navarre, and Aragon, supported by knights from the south of France, gained a decisive victory over the Almohade caliph. Castile could not make real progress with the reconquest, however, until her union with León (1230) removed the source of dynastic conflict. From that time on King Ferdinand III pushed on rapidly with the conquest of Andalusia: Cordova was occupied in 1236; Seville and Cadiz in 1248; and this same year saw the setting up of a Castilian protectorate over Murcia that allowed access to the Mediterranean.

The other kingdoms contributed unevenly to Christian reconquest. Portugal, which, like Castile, was supported by the military orders—those of Palmela and of Avis—continued to advance as far as the southern Algarves. Navarre, except for a part in the battle of Tolosa, played a minor role. The accession to the throne of Count Thibaut of Champagne in 1234 increasingly involved the kingdom in French affairs. On the other hand, since 1212, Aragon had continued to extend its domination at the expense of Islam. The death of King Peter II in 1213 during the Albigensian crusade marked the collapse of Aragon expansionist policies in the south of France; this phase of Aragon history was to be definitively terminated in 1258 at the treaty of Corbeil, by which King James I abandoned all his claims to the county of Toulouse and kept, out of all the former possessions of his house in Languedoc, only the lordship of Montpellier. Louis IX renounced his purely theoretical suzerainty over Roussillon and the county of Barcelona, distant inheritances of the Carolingian past. The efforts of Aragon and of Catalonia were directed toward the islands and the shores of the Mediterranean. The influence of the latter appears to have been decisive in this regard. The protection of Barcelonian maritime trade called for an operation against the Balearic islands. James I conquered them between 1229 and 1235. The kingdom of Valencia followed and was conquered in 1238. From this time on, Aragon was to become active in the farther reaches of the Mediterranean. The creation in 1276 of a "kingdom of Majorca"—which was made up of the Balearic Islands, Montpellier, and Roussillon—for a younger son of the royal house, doubtless constituted a weakness, which lasted until the end of its separate existence in 1344. But the essentials clearly remained in the hands of the King of Aragon, as his action in Sicily demonstrates. The mad "crusade" of Aragon was undertaken in 1285 by Philip III, king of France, at the instigation of Pope Martin IV and of Charles of Anjou, who wanted to take vengeance on his rival; it collapsed. It was a disaster for the French.

We have seen that the state of Moslem Spain favored the Christian reconquest. The first half of the thirteenth century saw the collapse of Almohade power in northern Africa, undermined by local rivalries and by the activity of the nomads of the southern Maghreb. Resistance in Spain was considerably weakened. Following Las Navas de Tolosa the Moslem empire had been broken up into several kingdoms. Toward the middle of the century only one was left, that of Granada. In Ifrikia and in the

Maghreb the continuing breakdown was completed in 1269. Three Berber kingdoms succeeded to the caliphate that had grouped together all of western Islam: to the east, that of the Hafsids, of Tunis, whose leader vainly took the title of caliph; in the center, that of Tlemcen; to the west, that of the Merinides of Fez. None of these caused any disturbance to Europe except through piratical activities, and apart from the western realm, they all traded with Europe.

Besides social, economic, and political aspects, which up until this point have been our particular concern, the history of international relations during the thirteenth century presents us with a purely intellectual aspect of monumental importance. This was the founding of universities. They were not all founded in the same manner. Bologna University, already famous during the twelfth century, represents a new stage in the development of law schools. In Paris the university grew out of schools of liberal arts and theology, whose importance has been pointed out since the time of Abelard. In Naples the university was founded by Frederick II in order to train a corps of civil servants. The fact that gave the institution its name, and that is its essential characteristic, was that the majority of the universities constituted collectivities of professors and students (*universitas magistrorum discipulorumque*), whose autonomy, in relation to episcopal power —and as necessary, against civil power—was defended by its privileges. The papacy protected these tendencies in the hope, which was often fraught with disappointment, of instituting organisms of higher learning under its direction; it even created universities like that of Toulouse, founded in 1229, to combat heresy. In essence the universities were international centers, and students came from all over the world: Manfred, Frederick II's bastard and king of Sicily, Rodrigo Jiménez de Rada, archbishop of Toledo and great architect of the *reconquista*, were students in Paris; famous examples could be cited ad infinitum. Equally, the professors sprang from the most diverse countries—we shall have occasion to return to this. The fact that from an early date the Dominicans furnished numerous persons to the teaching corps contributed strongly to its international character. The fame of the universities and the strength of their attraction often depended on a branch of teaching that was offered with particular success: the "arts"—that is, philosophy above all—at Paris and at Oxford; law at Bologna, at Padua, and at Orléans; medicine at Montpellier; theology at Paris—to cite a few of the great university centers of the period.

These universities were the core of one of the most important developments of intellectual life in the thirteenth century: the spread of Aristotelianism in the West. Despite the enforced austerity of the Almohade period, the Maghreb and Spain experienced a remarkable artistic development—which can still be seen in the gracious *Giralda* of Seville—and a remarkable increase in those intellectual activities that were not oriented toward theology. Among the number of intellectuals who brought fame to Islam during the twelfth century was Aristotle's most remarkable commentator, a medical doctor attached to the Caliph at Cordova, Ibn-Rushd (1126–1198), whom the West calls Averroës. Unknown or badly known works of Aristotle on physics, astronomy, metaphysics, and ethics were translated during the twelfth and thirteenth centuries in Italy and Spain into Latin, either from the Greek texts or from Arabic translations. Many other Greek, Arabic, and Jewish philosophical writings, and notably those of Averroës, were also translated under the auspices of the Hohenstaufens at Naples and of the Archbishop of Toledo, Jiménez de Rada. And if Aristotle, whose intellectual impact was immediate—through apparent contradictions with Christian dogma concerning problems as essential as the Creation and eternal life—was of concern to the authorities, his commentator, who was known in Paris after 1230, caused far more concern with the doctrine of the unity of the soul, which he thought he could draw from the work of Aristotle. Toward the middle and during the second half of the thirteenth century, two Dominicans who taught at the University of Paris—the German Albert von Bollstädt, better known as Albertus Magnus or Saint Albert the Great, and particularly the Italian, Saint Thomas Aquinas— devoted their activities to strengthen Christian thought by incorporating the Aristotelian doctrine with it but by eliminating that which in Aristotle's learning could be considered dangerous for the faith.

Christian Aristotelianism, or "Thomism," continued to flourish and spread after the death of Saint Thomas (1274). Nevertheless it suffered from the consequences of the condemnation pronounced in 1277 of integral Aristotelianism, influenced by Averroës and taught mainly in Paris by Siger of Brabant; its teaching was forbidden in Paris and in Oxford. Furthermore, Averroism survived and spread in Italy, where it had a brief brilliant success at Bologna and at Padua during the following century.

We have seen that this intellectual crisis affected religious life in a large part of western Europe. But during the thirteenth century there were religious crises as well. Some of them had to do with faith: we have mentioned Albigensianism and its repercussions in international relations. Another crisis—very serious owing to its consequences, and only in its early stage—had as its point of departure the financial policies of the Holy See. It consisted of drawing important resources from Christendom through the taxation of churches and the paying of ecclesiastical revenues to the Holy See, which claimed fees whenever livings were granted. The origins of these practices were ancient, but the papacy made increasing recourse to them as its needs mounted and as the resources drawn from its domains were reduced by its struggle against Frederick II. Innocent IV (1243–1254) was the chief architect of this system. This use of religion for political and financial ends provoked protest and resistance in several countries, principally in France. England, a vassal state of the Holy See, was extremely vehement. The submission of Henry III to the Pope was in fact instrumental in the rising of the barons and the defection of part of the clergy in 1258. In general we can say that throughout Christendom the pontifical financial policies became a cause of scandal for many souls.

In the West the thirteenth century witnessed three great downfalls: of theocracy, of empire, and, less explosively, of Angevin imperialism. On the other hand, it did see the growth and blossoming of France, both politically and intellectually. The same can be said in the artistic field. French Gothic architecture, which reached its zenith at Chartres between 1194 and 1220, and which prescribed the canon of its classicism in the parts of Amiens Cathedral that were built between 1220 and 1269, spread throughout Europe. Of course England superimposed her own characteristics; also the influence of romanesque traditions created a very particular form of Gothic architecture in Italy and throughout the south of France. Everywhere, however, French master builders and their disciples erected cathedrals modeled on those rising in northern and central France: until this very day Clermont, Limoges, and Narbonne, Assisi and Genoa, Cologne, Freiburg, Marburg, and Strasbourg, León, Burgos and Toledo, Upsala, and Nicosia evoke the prodigious flowering of the art of thirteenth-century France.

9

*The East in the Thirteenth
and at the Beginning of the Fourteenth Century*

A T THE DAWN of the thirteenth century western Christianity
had created the "Empire of Romania" in eastern Europe. The
second Emperor, Henry of Hainaut (1206–1216), brother of
Baldwin I, who died in captivity in Bulgaria, succeeded through
the force of his energy and his ability in holding together this
political unit and even in laying hold of an important bridgehead
in Asia. It was a very ephemeral success. The empire was nib-
bled away by quarrels among the western barons, between these
and the Greek population, and between the Latin high clergy—
the patriarch and the archbishops—and the lower Greek clergy,
whether the latter paid lip service to Latin doctrines, or whether
they refused to adhere to them, as did the immense majority of
the indigenous population. Another cause for weakness, at least
in the greater part of the empire, was the very small number of
Latin immigrants. The Greek "despot" who had maintained himself in Epirus, had had to recognize himself as a vassal of Henry I,
but one of his successors breached this allegiance, conquered
Thessalonica and its surrounding area in 1224, and proclaimed
himself emperor. The *basileus* of Nicaea seized from the Empire
its Asiatic possessions, several islands, and some territories in Europe; he put an end to the empire of Thessalonica, but was not
able to suppress the despotate in Epirus. The Greek and Bulgarian enterprises would have put an end to the existence of the
empire of Romania after the first half of the century, without
the action of two powers. Of these, one was Venice; the republic
saw one of the conditions for her prosperity in her privileged

position in the heart of the Latin empire, guaranteed by her mastery of the Bosphorus and the Dardanelles. The other power was the principality of Morea, or of Achaia, which belonged to the Villehardouin family, lords in Champagne, during the thirteenth century. They knew how to attract a relatively large number of French knights to the country, how to manage the religious feelings and material interests of the Greeks, and how to bring about a union between these two elements of the population, and thus to bring a solidity to this Latin settlement in the East that the empire of Romania had never known. The aid given by Venice and by the Villehardouin family prolonged the existence of the empire.

In Syria and in the Holy Land, Christian settlements lost ground. The political incompetence of the Latin aristocracy of the Levant, and the fierce egoism of the Italian merchant cities, which were primarily occupied with the immediate interests of their own businesses, weakened the resistance effort in what remained of this remnant of the kingdom of Jerusalem. This was evident in the struggles that broke out between the Hohenstaufen faction and the baronial party, led by members of the Ibelin family (1229–1243). The latter were victorious and completely devastated the central power in the kingdom, to the extent of leaving the throne vacant. It was also evident in the wars in which the counts of Antioch and of Tripoli—the two counties had been united since 1201—used up their forces to fight their own neighbors, the Christian kings of Lesser Armenia. It was evident still later during the wars between the Venetians and the Genoese settlements of Acre and their respective allies; the Pisans naturally fought on the side of the Venetians, and the Catalans on the side of the Genoese (1256–1258). Reinforcements sent from the West to the Holy Land in no way helped the situation. In any case they were too few to prevent the Turks—driven out of central Asia by the Mongols, and now in the service of the Sultan of Egypt—from seizing Jerusalem from the Christians in 1244—this time for good. After the disastrous outcome of his Egyptian expedition, Louis IX spent four years in Syria and in Palestine (1250–1254) and to some extent succeeded in putting the country into a state of defense.

It was the relative weakness of the Turkish enemy that maintained the Latin presence in the Levant for a longer time. There were also divisions among the Turks. Internal struggles had raged since the death of Saladin, and their military strength had also been reduced. The same weakness could be seen in Asia Minor among the Seljuk Turks and among other Turkish tribes, whose expansion scarcely affected the Greek states of Trebizond and of Nicaea. Moreover, they were soon threatened by a new and formidable force which had built up in central Asia—the Mongols. Since the beginning of the century the Mongol tribes that wandered to the east of Lake Baikal had been gathered together under an ambitious leader, Temujin, or Genghis Khan. By 1209 he was master of central Asia. Then, one by one, northern China or Cathay, Korea, Afghanistan, and Persia were conquered by the fierce horsemen of the Mongol khan or of his successors. These conquests came to an end in 1234; Genghis Khan had died in 1227. The surprising thing is that, unlike so many empires created by nomad leaders, that of Genghis Khan in no way broke up on his death. His successors divided the conquered territories among themselves, but one of them kept the greater part and maintained effective authority over his cosharers; this was the *khagan*, or "grand khan."

In 1237 the Mongols turned toward Europe, particularly toward Russia. This nation was in no position to repel such an assault. Moreover, already in 1223 a Mongol army had attacked Turkish tribes—the Quiptchacq, also called the Polovtzy or Kumans—who had settled in the steppes to the south of Russia proper; the Mongols had easily routed the forces which the Russian princes had sent to help their neighbors. Pushing as far as the Crimea, they now even sacked the Trebizond settlement of

Soldaia. Russia was divided. The south was made up of a federation of principalities: that of Kiev under a "grand prince" (*veliki
kniaz*) had a nominal preeminence over the others. Since the
twelfth century, the Russia of Kiev had declined: one of the main
reasons for this was the gradual ruin of its commerce, brought
about, as we know, by Kuman aggressions and by the change in
the Asia-Europe trade routes. In the northwest, Novgorod, while
keeping its princes, was in fact an independent republic, wealthy
through trade with the countries and towns bordering on the
Baltic. In the northeast, Suzdal and Vladimir were each the center
of principalities whose territories had been colonized and partly
cleared by colonists from the south. These leaders of the various
parts of Russia had practically no awareness of belonging to the
same political community and of being bound to one another
through the requirements of solidarity.

Farther west, Poland, which had ceased to be a kingdom
toward the end of the eleventh century, was also divided into
several rival and often hostile duchies under the generally ineffectual authority of a grand duke. The holder of this title was the
Duke of Cracow. Separated more and more from the Baltic by
German conquests and colonizations, Poland was threatened in
the east by the Lithuanians, who were still heathens and more or
less barbaric.

Although the kingdom of Bohemia, a persistently and strongly
autonomous part of the German realm, made up a relatively
stable unit, this was not the case with Hungary. This kingdom
had extended its territories to include Croatia and Dalmatia in the
twelfth century, and had forced Germany, Venice, and the Byzantine Empire to reckon with her. But at the same time she furthered
the development of a group of powerful landed lords among the
aristocracy who, at the beginning of the thirteenth century, were
to succeed in creating greater autonomy and increasingly to limit
royal prerogatives in favor of their own aims. Like Russia, like

Poland, Hungary was also in a state of extreme weakness toward the middle of the thirteenth century.

The attack was unleashed against Russia in 1237. Suzdal fell in 1238. Kiev was taken and sacked in 1240. In the following year Poland and Hungary were crushed. Germany in turn braced herself against the shock. Throughout Christendom there was a great fear of seeing an extension of the domination of the "Tatars" —as the Mongols were called, after the name of a Turkish tribe, living on the borders of Manchuria, which had been conquered by the Mongols. A crisis in the succession forced the Mongol leaders to return to Mongolia. The invaders withdrew toward the east, but part of their force, known as the "Golden Horde," settled in southeastern Russia; and all the Russian princes were reduced to the ranks of dependents. Only the republic of Novgorod escaped this fate. Mongol conquests began again in 1242, but this time in the southwest. In Asia Minor the *khagan* forced both the Sultan of Iconium and the Emperor of Trebizond to acknowledge themselves as vassals, and this same fealty was accepted by the Georgian princes and the King of Lesser Armenia. The Tatars then attacked the bulk of the Turkish lands beginning with Iraq. Baghdad was taken in 1258; and with the caliphate suppressed, eastern Islam found itself deprived of its religious leader: powerless though he might be, he was indispensable to spiritual and ecclesiastical life. In Syria the divided Turks were unable to offer resistance, and by 1260 they held only Egypt and its dependency, Palestine.

At this time the Mongol Empire comprised four parts: the great khanate of China and Mongolia; the khanate of central Asia or Tchaghataï; the khanate of Russia or of the "Golden Horde," also known as the Quiptchacq khanate; and the khanate of Persia or the "ilkhanate." The Grand Khan had a certain authority over the other khans, but it was not always effective, and there were sometimes conflicts between the Grand Khan and the khans, or among the khans themselves. In 1235 the Grand Khan had begun the conquest of southern China or Manzi, governed by the Sung dynasty. It was a country with a highly developed civilization and wealthy from intensive commerce with the East Indies and with India, to which it was bound by navigation routes. The reliable direction of the winds and the great skill of the builders of the huge Chinese junks, with both above- and below-deck storage, made such trade possible. The conquest of Manzi was only finished in 1279 by the Great Khan, Kublai. He succeeded in imposing his supremacy—purely theoretical—over the Burmese and Indochinese sovereigns, but he failed totally in his undertaking against Japan (Cipangu) and Java.

During its development Mongol power changed its character. At first purely destructive, putting an end, whenever possible, to urban and agricultural life and instituting nomadic livestock raising, it became increasingly transformed, especially in those of its territories that had old civilizations, such as the ilkhanate of Persia and the grand khanate, master of China. This transformation was at the root of the conflicts that occurred between a Grand Khan living in China—at Cambaluc, or Peiping —who was partially converted to the Chinese way of life, as was Kublai, and the khans of central Asia who to a great extent were still Mongol nomads. However, apart from intervals of armed conflict, the Grand Khans were able to impose a sufficient hold over the other khans to ensure internal peace. Although the core of Mongol military power always and everywhere was the wild and famous cavalry of the steppes, the administration of the whole empire of the Grand Khan was perfected, and the importance of its commercial relations became evident to the governing class: this demonstrates China's influence on her conquerors. A similar development occurred in the ilkhanate.

The Mongols, who worshiped a goddess of fecundity, were generally tolerant in religious matters except during periods of war. Some of their chiefs, such as the Grand Khan Kublai, seem to have shown sympathy for Buddhism and for Christianity. In

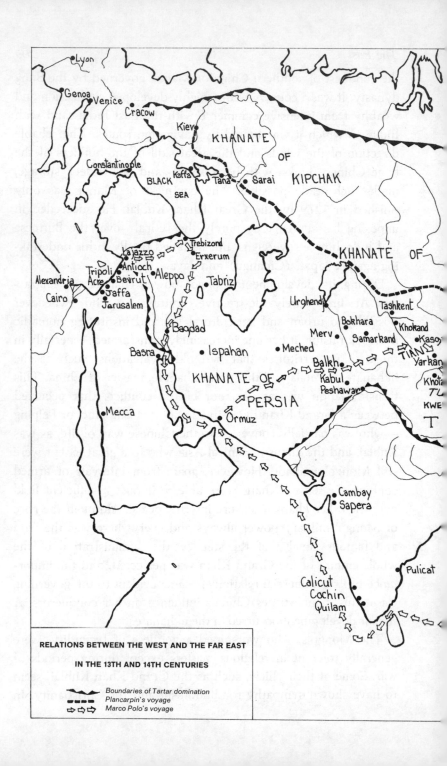

RELATIONS BETWEEN THE WEST AND THE FAR EAST

IN THE 13TH AND 14TH CENTURIES

〰〰〰 Boundaries of Tartar domination
‑ ‑ ‑ ‑ Plancarpin's voyage
⇨ ⇨ ⇨ Marco Polo's voyage

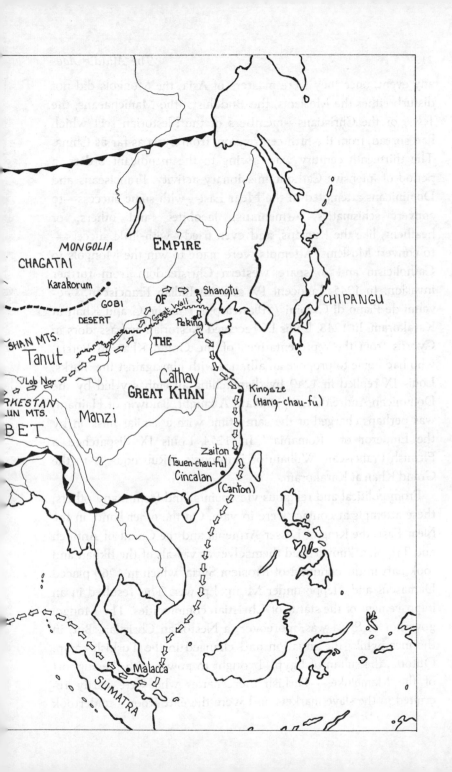

any event, once they were masters of Asia, the Mongols did not disturb either the Moslems, the Buddhists, the Manichaeans, the Jews, or the Christians—members of the Nestorian sect which had spread, from the fifth century on, from Syria as far as China. The thirteenth century was, owing to the mendicant orders, a period of intensive Catholic missionary activity. Franciscans and Dominicans attempted in the Near East—with some success—to convert schismatics, Armenians, Jacobites, and others, or heathens, like the Kumans, and even tried—with little success— to convert Moslems. Attempts were made to win the Mongols to Catholicism and to spare western Christendom from further invasion. In 1245, Innocent IV sent an Italian Franciscan, Giovanni de Piano di Carpini ("Plancarpin") to the Grand Khan at Karakoram. In 1248, Louis IX received Nestorian ambassadors in Cyprus from the representatives of the Grand Khan in Persia, who had come to propose an alliance with him against the Turks. Louis IX replied in 1249 by dispatching an embassy led by the Dominican André de Longjumeau. A knight, Baldwin of Hainaut, was perhaps charged at the same time with a similar mission by the Emperor of "Romania." In 1254 Louis IX dispatched a Flemish Franciscan, William of Rubrouck ("Rubruquis") to the Grand Khan at Karakoram.

From political and religious viewpoints, and from many others, these attempts at contact were in vain. On the other hand, in the Near East, the King of Lesser Armenia and the Count of Antioch and Tripoli acknowledged themselves as vassals of the Ilkhan and took part in the conquest of Moslem Syria, which in 1260 placed Damascus and Aleppo under Mongol power. This resulted in an improvement of the status of Christian communities. The Mongol governor of Syria was, moreover, a Nestorian Christian. But, in the meanwhile, the situation had changed in the Turkish camp. Qutouz, the sultan of Egypt, brought to power with the support of the Mamelukes—Turkish mercenaries who were partly recruited in the slave markets and were the élite troop—undertook the reconquest of Syria. The barons of the truncated kingdom of Jerusalem had no faith in the possibility of agreement with the Mongols, whose savagery they feared more than Moslem fanaticism. They took an attitude that differed from that of the King of Armenia and the Count of Antioch. By giving the Turks passage across their territory, they helped their operations against the Mongols. Before the end of 1260 the latter were vanquished and expelled from Syria, which thereafter was, as was Palestine, a dependency of Egypt. In the same year the commander of the Mamelukes, Baybars, eliminated Qutouz, proclaimed himself sultan, re-established an Abbasside caliphate, and thereafter ruled over all the Moslem Near East. The Latin territories found themselves encircled. From 1265 on they suffered attacks from Baybars, and half of them were overcome, notably Antioch in 1268. The anarchy and the chronic confusion in the heart of what still remained of Frankish possessions, the contest for the crown between the supporters of Henry II of Lusignan, king of Cyprus, and those of Charles of Anjou (who was recognized in 1277 at Acre), the intrigues among the military orders, and the insanities of an Italian peoples' crusade that landed in 1290, all eased the last phases of conquest for the successors of Baybars. The Mongol Khan of Persia sent embassies to the west to conclude alliances against the Turks, but these came to nothing. In 1289 war broke out again, and the Turks took Tripoli; in 1291 they took Acre; Tyre and other coastal settlements were evacuated that same year. This was the end of the kingdom of Jerusalem and of its vassal principalities. Only Cyprus, whose ruler bore the title of King of Jerusalem, continued to represent Latin Christianity in the eastern Mediterranean.

Thirty years earlier the weak empire of "Romania," the other eastern creation of Latin Europe, had collapsed: "almost a new France" (*quasi nova Francia*), to use the words of Pope Honorius III. The Emperor of Nicaea, Michael VIII Palaeologus retook Constantinople in 1261. The Christian East severed the bonds, weak as they were, that had linked it to Rome since 1205. In Morea, meanwhile, the Latins still held on and were to continue to do so for another two centuries. Because of their hatred for Venice, which controlled the international trade in the Latin Empire, the Genoese allied themselves with the Emperor of Nicaea against the former. Wherever possible, Genoa fought Venice and all her allies: hence the attack on Acre in 1267 while Baybars was conquering Syria. In the restored Byzantine Empire, Genoa benefited for the moment from an exceptionally privileged position. While opposing Venice, she continued to fight her other rival in Mediterranean commerce, Pisa. She succeeded in destroying the Pisan fleet and in crippling Pisa in 1284.

Italian merchants drew great profits from the unity that the Mongols established in Asia, and from the peace they enforced there. Peace and unity were relative, but nevertheless the situation was more favorable to international trade than the preceding one. It can be affirmed that Italian merchants made business journeys to Asia at the end of the thirteenth and at the beginning of the fourteenth century; but little is known about their activities. Nothing, or nearly nothing, is known of Genoese undertakings, which were certainly the most important. By chance, records of Venetian enterprises have come to light. Chief among them is the voyage of two merchants who were settled at Soldaia, on the Black Sea, at that time under Mongol protectorate. They left in about 1260 to sell jewels to the Golden Horde and finally turned up in China. These were the brothers Nicolo and Maffeo Polo. They went back to China in 1271 with Marco, Nicolo's son, and did not return until 1295. Marco Polo's account, entitled *Li Divisament du Monde* and written in French—which was common as a language of literature in Italy—has given us precise information concerning not only central Asia and China in that time, but also the routes used for trade relations with the Far East.

About 1266 the Genoese founded the colony of Caffa in the

Crimea, aimed at trade with Russia, central Asia, the Far East, and the northern coast of Asia Minor, on the one hand; and on the other, at trade with the Christian or Moslem countries of the Mediterranean. Caffa's maritime relations with the northern coast of Asia Minor, especially with Trebizond, were important, because this town was the terminus of one of the routes utilized for Indian goods on their way to the west—especially spices—and landed in the Persian Gulf at Ormuz. The other route led through Tabriz to the port of Aïas (the Lajazzo of the Italians), in Lesser Armenia, on the Gulf of Alexandretta. The Genoese also had a branch office there. There were routes by land or by sea from Caffa to Tana located at the mouth of the Don on the Sea of Azov. From the last quarter of the thirteenth century on, this port was used by Genoese merchants; and in the fourteenth century the Genoese and the Venetians had permanent settlements there. The land route for central Asia and for China started in Tana. Until the middle of the fourteenth century this route was an important commercial artery. The Florentine, Francesco Balducci Pegolotti, in his manual on international trade (*Practica della Mercatura*), written about 1340, describes the route and gives information for those who would use it on the way to or from Cathay. He cites as an example the typical charges on a return voyage with a cargo of silk to the value of £12,000. He considered the route entirely safe. It was certainly used around 1325 by some Venetians who stayed in the great city of Quinsay, today called Hangchow, in Manzi.

Like the traders, Catholic missionaries reached the Far East. The Franciscans followed the route just described. Others went down toward the Persian Gulf and used maritime routes with ports of call in the Indies. This was the case of Giovanni de Montecorvino, also a Franciscan, who in 1307 was the first Catholic Archbishop of Cambaluc. It was also the case of another Franciscan, Odoric de Pordenone, who left for China either in 1314 or in 1318. A papal legate, Giovanni de Marignolli, another

Franciscan, who stayed in China from 1342 to 1347, probably took the land route. In Manzi he visited the great port of Zayton (Tsinkiang), the seat of a recently created Catholic bishopric and of a Franciscan convent, near which was located a *fondaco* belonging to Italian merchants. He returned by the sea route and thus, like Montecorvino and Pordenone on their outward voyage, had the chance to make contact with Nestorian communities and with Catholic missions in India. These are only the most famous cases; there are many others.

Direct international relations between the West and Central Asia as well as Far Eastern Asia were more than once broken, notably by conflicts among Mongol leaders. It is characteristic of the situation existing at the end of the thirteenth and in the first half of the fourteenth century, that a connection was established between these conflicts and the rivalries among the western powers. The hostility between the Khan of Quiptchacq and the "Ilkhan" of Persia was combined with hostility between Venice, allied with the former, and Genoa, allied with the latter. It was a question for Venice of winning a position similar to that of Genoa in the Black Sea and, if possible, of excluding Genoa from that sea. War began in 1294 and ended with Genoese naval victory in the Adriatic at Curzola in 1298. These years of fighting did the greatest damage to trade with the East, but they were by no means the only setback.

Toward the middle of the fourteenth century, direct relations with central Asia and with China fell off and finally terminated. At this time the Mongol khanate of Persia broke up. The chiefs of its principal factions were fanatical Moslems, and it became difficult, if not impossible, for Christian travelers to cross the country. This last observation is true also of central Asia, especially from the time when in 1363 a Turkish emir, Timour (the Tamerlane of the West), made himself master of an empire in which the most fanatical and inflexible Moslem creed held sway. Finally the Mongol dynasty in China was overthrown by a national dynasty, that of the Ming, between 1368 and 1370, and this restoration led to a return to traditional xenophobia. The great development of international relations, from which western Europe had benefited, came to an end after less than a century. The consequences, especially the economic ones, of the cessation of direct relations with central Asia, India, and the Far East will be discussed later. One lasting benefit was gained: a better knowledge of the geography of Asia, especially of its coasts, which produced maps in the second half of the fourteenth century.

10

The Great Depression

THE ECONOMIC and social factors that, in the fourteenth century, acted on the nature and development of international relations, and that sometimes of themselves form aspects of these relations, should be studied chronologically, with occasionally references to the thirteenth and fifteenth centuries. One of these factors can be seen in the population graph. The growth of the European population which began in the eleventh century appears to have continued during the first years of the fourteenth. However the situation changed early in the West. Perhaps the incentive toward growth persisted in a certain number of towns for a considerable part of the century; but, on the whole, the population soon began to decline. Considerable losses were caused by famines and by epidemics, which in the fourteenth century were particularly harsh. The 1315–1317 famine, which devastated Europe north of the Alps and Pyrenees can be cited as an example: before the catastrophe the town of Ypres, an important center of the Flemish cloth trade, had a population of some 20,000 to 28,000; it lost a tenth of its population. These famines, creating a state of lowered resistance, contributed to the virulence and the diffusion of epidemics of which the most formidable was the Black Death, which raged from 1347 to 1351. Trade with the Far East brought the plague to Europe: the Mongols gave it to the Genoese at Caffa in the Crimea, a town they besieged, and a Genoese ship carried the germs to Italy. This country, Spain, France, Germany, Norway, and northern Russia were ravaged. A very few countries were spared: among them were the greater part of the Low Countries, eastern Franconia, Bohemia, and Silesia. In certain countries that were stricken especially harshly, such as England and France, the population fell to a considerable extent. But to appreciate the plague factor on the population graph, account must also be taken of a whole series of epidemics that broke out in the second half of the fourteenth or at the beginning of the fifteenth century, and that aggravated the effects of the Black Death. The population loss in England between 1348 and 1374 was 40 per cent—a fall from about 3,750,000 to about 2,250,000 inhabitants. A similar decline could also be claimed for important parts of France and Italy. In the first half of the fifteenth century the population decline seems to have continued in the most western parts of Europe north of the Alps. This phenomenon did not, however, occur everywhere; certain parts of southern, northeastern, and eastern Europe may not have been so gravely stricken.

The fourteenth century and an important part of the fifteenth were, at least for the most western areas of Europe, a period of economic depression. Neither all the details nor the exact nature of this depression nor even the periods of its onset and decline are known for certain. It appears that in certain areas, such as Flanders, it must have begun in or about 1280. In the second quarter of the fourteenth century agricultural prices collapsed in France and England, while the price of industrial materials was artificially maintained at a high level by the corporate managements, which, as we shall see, became a general practice. A deep malaise struck the people living on the land and diminished the buyers' market in industry and trade. The decrease of the population, partly as a result of the Black Death, cut back production. It also restricted the number of consumers—even in regions like Flanders and Brabant, which were the least severely affected. It brought distress to the cloth industry as the number of buyers dropped. Demographic factors contributed directly or indirectly to the contraction of the economy of western Europe. Other factors worked in the same way or delayed any improvement. The

Hundred Years War, the taxation and the monopolies it led to—
we will mention later that of English wool—and the monetary
reforms effected in order to increase state resources should be
mentioned here. A series of bankruptcies in the great Italian
banks—those of the Peruzzi and the Bardi of Florence in 1343
and 1346—contributed to the slump and created and supported a
credit crisis. Insufficient liquid funds in terms of their commitments placed these houses at the mercy of nonrepayment: in the
two cases cited here, the failure came about because the King of
England, to whom these houses had provided war funds, did not
pay his debts.

However, new commercial flows and the development or the
transformation of earlier flows came into being at the end of the
thirteenth century, during the fourteenth, and at the beginning of
the fifteenth century. The contributions of countries less heavily
stricken, or only later stricken, or not struck at all by the depression, played a role of some importance in this. Northern Germany
should be dealt with first. Her merchant towns—those of the
North Sea and of the Baltic—definitely attained their zenith
during the fourteenth century. Since the twelfth century their
sailors had been using the *kogge*, a type of sailing boat, carrying
deck cargo and having broad rounded sides; and after the thirteenth century they had also been using the "hulk," a larger ship
of similar structure. Long distance transportation became much
easier. The northern Germans were able to become the almost
exclusive suppliers of western Europe as far as some finished
agricultural products were concerned. Among these were beers of
high quality produced in northern Germany. They exported also
raw foodstuffs from Denmark, Sweden, Poland, Hungary,
and Russia, as well as from the colonized countries of the German
hinterland. As we will see, corn, produced in great quantities, was
important (it was mainly exported from Danzig). Also important
were wax and furs from Russia; iron and copper from Sweden,
whose foreign trade was in German hands (the population of the

town of Stockholm was more than half German in the thirteenth and fourteenth centuries); salted or dried fish, a staple food, which the Germans exported from Schonen on the southern point of the Scandinavian peninsula, or from Bergen on the western coast of Norway. These were not the only articles of trade, but they were the most important. Bruges and London were the main destinations of these goods. The return freight consisted of Mediterranean or Oriental luxury goods, Flemish or Brabant cloth, in smaller qualities English wool, cloth and tin, increasing amounts of wine and especially of salt from southwestern France; those were heavy materials which, if available, could relieve the shipmasters from using ballast as return freight. It happened that German sailors sought these last two items themselves on the French coast, and in the case of salt, in Portugal. Much of the trade between the eastern end of the North Sea and the Baltic was carried on via internal routes and waterways, which allowed for communication between Hamburg and Lübeck. But, during the fourteenth century, greater use was made of the sea routes that rounded Jutland by way of the Sound.

The weak bonds that linked the merchant associations of the German cities of the north and the northeast and the Rhine-Westphalian towns for the defense of their mutual interests in foreign countries were reinforced and extended in the fourteenth century. The general association, or "German Hanse," existed as an official and permanent institution from 1358. The Hanse used various means to achieve its aims, including war when these aims could be realized in no other way. It had had to fight against Waldemar V, King of Denmark, who had seized Visby, the great Hanseatic commercial entrepôt in the Baltic in 1361, and who had tried to prevent German navigation in the Sound. During a lengthy war the Hanse towns, led by Lübeck, emerged as victors: the peace of Stralsund (1370) gave them mastery of the Baltic and of the straits. This association of merchant towns, which was permanently in touch with the outside world through its branch

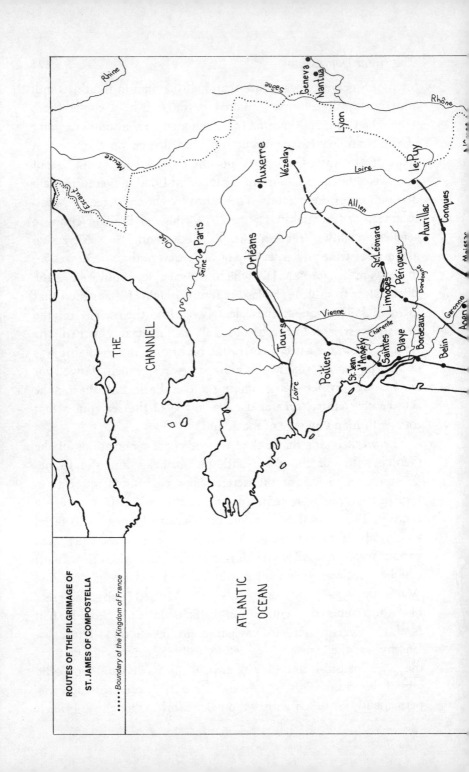

ROUTES OF THE PILGRIMAGE OF
ST. JAMES OF COMPOSTELLA

········ Boundary of the Kingdom of France

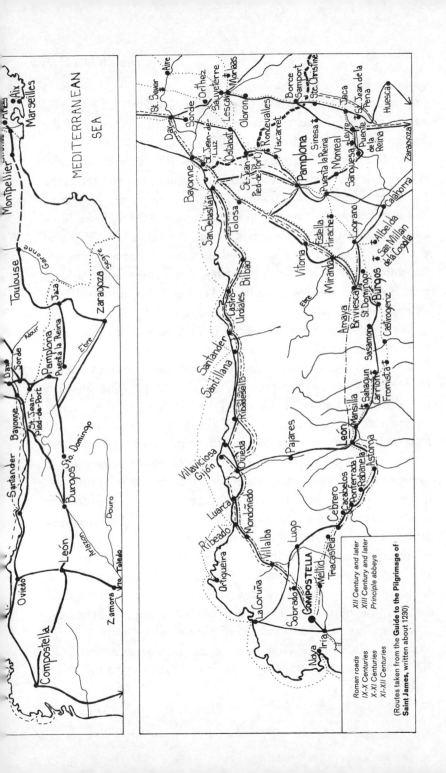

MEDITERRANEAN SEA

Marseilles
Aix
Arles
Montpellier
Toulouse
Zaragoza
Pamplona
Puenta la Reina
Bayonne
St. Jean-Pied-de-Port
Sto. Domingo
Burgos
Santander
León
Oviedo
Compostella
Zamora
Vta. Toledo

St. Sever
Aire
Orthez
Sauveterre
Dax
Sorde
St. Jean-de-Luz
Ostabal
Lescar
Oloron
Morlaas
Borce
Samport
Ste. Christine
Jaca
St. Jean de la Peña
Huesca
Roncevalles
Viscaret
Pamplona
Siresa
Leyre
Puente de la Reina
Sanguesa
Montreal
Zaraoza V
Bayonne
St. Jean-Ped-de-Port
Tolosa
San Sebastián
Puenta la Reina
Estella
Irache
Logroño
Albelda
San Millán de la Cogolla
Calahorra
Vitoria
Miranda
Ebre
Castro-Urdiales
Bilbao
Ribadesella
Santander
Santillana
Briviesca
St. Domingo
Amaya
Sasamon
Burgos
Castrogenz
Fromista
Carrión
Sahagún
Mansilla
León
Astorga
Pajares
Oviedo
Villaviciosa
Gijón
Luarca
Mondoñedo
Ribeado
Villalba
Orrigueira
La Coruña
Lugo
Triacastela
Mellid
Cebrero
Rabanal
Cacabelos
Ponferrada
Sobrado
COMPOSTELLA
Noya
Iria

Roman roads
IX–X Centuries
X–XI Centuries
XI–XII Centuries

XII Century and later
XIII Century and later
Principle abbeys

(Routes taken from the **Guide to the Pilgrimage of
Saint James**, written about 1230)

offices in London, Bruges, Bergen, Novgorod, and Pskov, gave a particular aura to the whole of northern Germany. The Scandinavian and Baltic countries were also under the influence of the league: it spread a spirit of enterprise and of liberty together with a certain cosmopolitan feeling throughout the area. Historically speaking, it was very peculiar, although it had been subject to the influence of other civilizations, especially those of the Rhineland and of Flanders. Its own character is conveyed through the brick architecture that was typical of the Hanse; a sense of volume and even of majesty in no way impeded a certain gracefulness nor decorative skills. Churches, town halls, town gates, and patrician mansions from Bremen to Lübeck, Danzig, Riga, or Reval bear witness to this.

The large volume of trade between the German Hanse and the countries bordering on the Baltic, the North Sea, and even the Channel and the Atlantic in the fourteenth century constituted a further development of a previous state of affairs. The situation was different in southern Germany and in the neighboring Danubian countries. Some aspects of their economic activity had their origins in an earlier period, but the importance taken by these countries in international trade was a new phenomenon in the fourteenth century; furthermore it was to increase during the fifteenth century. In the fourteenth century linen manufacture became a major export industry in Swabia and in the same region the cotton industry started its development.

Forming a contrast to the old mining regions whose deposits had been exhausted, southeastern Germany, Bohemia, and Poland seem to have undergone a development in their mining and metallurgical industries. This was most noticeable in Bohemian silver production. The southern German towns of Augsburg, Nürnberg, Regensburg, Ulm, and Vienna drew great profits from this industry in the fourteenth century. Their merchants, especially those of Nürnberg, were great exporters of the goods produced by these industries: to the west via Cologne and

London, or via the German and Rhone Valley fairs, which we will mention later; to the east as far as Russia; and to northern Germany or Scandinavia via Lübeck. In the Mediterranean region Venice, in keeping with her traditions, was a principal intermediary in the export of products from their "area" and of those of the Hanseatic "area." Venice in particular furnished the latter with Oriental products which they in turn redistributed.

We know how much the Italian towns, until the third quarter of the thirteenth century, benefited, in their trade with the Far East, from facilities furnished by Mongol domination in Asia. The collapse of Mongol power broke these relations toward the end of the century, and the advance of the Turks into Asia Minor made contacts with the east via Trebizond or Lesser Armenia very difficult, if not impossible. Nevertheless, the Genoese colonies in the Crimea, with Caffa as a center, had developed; at Tana the Venetian and Genoese trade settlements were now more important than in the past. These settlements at least allowed for an active trade with southern Russia, the Quiptchacq, and some parts of central Asia. Moreover, Venetian and Genoese possessions in the archipelago, Genoese settlements in Cyprus, the Venetian possession of the island of Crete, and the Venetian trade settlements in Mameluke Egypt enabled Italy to maintain trade relations with other parts of Asia. This was conditional on the employment of Turks, Turkish subjects or protégés as intermediaries. Trade settlements in North Africa—in the kingdoms of Tunis and particularly of Tlemcen, where the gold routes from the Sudan met—were also important to the foreign trade of Italian merchant cities during the fourteenth century. Many played major roles in international economic relations. Among them were Siena, although she was less prosperous than in the thirteenth century after the ruin of her principal banking family, the Buonsignori, and after the crushing defeat of her Ghibelline ally and her seaport, Pisa; Prato, an active center of the cloth industry; and Lucca, producer and exporter of silk. But none of them could be

compared to Venice or to Genoa, to Milan or to Florence, which
even became a maritime power with its annexation of Pisa in 1406
and its acquisition of Livorno in 1421.

   In the fourteenth century, and especially during the latter half,
Italian and particularly Genoese merchants showed an increased
interest in the western Mediterranean and particularly in the Iberian peninsula. Moreover, the western Mediterranean governed
access to the Atlantic, which had become a major communication
route to northwestern Europe. Genoese maritime relations—with
Bruges since at least 1277, and with England since 1278—became
firmly established. An important part of outgoing freight consisted of alum from Phocaea or the Trebizond region, intended
for the textile industry—just as English wool or Flemish or
Brabant cloth made up freight for the return journey. In the
fourteenth century Venice followed the Genoese example, and
from 1315 to 1317 her ships journeyed to Bruges or the Brabant
port of Antwerp, which had become the major transfer point of
trade between western Germany and England. Venetian ships
made frequent calls at Southampton. The Spanish, the Catalonians, especially the Majorcans and the Barcelonians, the Portuguese, and the Castilians used much the same routes. Journeys
were generally undertaken in convoys for protection against
piracy; and merchants in the ports of call and of arrival knew the
regular times of departure and the approximate duration of the
crossings. Galleys which were powered by both sail and oar, and
whose better construction allowed them to be used in the Atlantic,
in fact increased the regularity of navigation over those ships that
only used sail. Mediterranean merchants, moreover, like the Atlantic merchants or the North Sea merchants, sometimes used
sailing ships with built-out sides: their "carrack" was a close
relative, perhaps even an imitation of the *kogge*. While we are
discussing Atlantic trade in the fourteenth century, it is important
to point out that the English were in competition with the Bayon-
nese in the transportation of wines from the southwest and of

pastel from Lauragais and Toulouse to Bristol and Southampton, and that the traffic between England and the Iberian peninsula or between England and La Rochelle, where the inland route to the Mediterranean started, was important. We have already mentioned the Hanseatic *Baienflotten*.

The greatest change in the structure of international trade in the fourteenth century lay in these maritime links across the Atlantic, between the Mediterranean world and that of the North Sea. It was not the only major change. The cargo of a galley represented a very limited tonnage: six galleys only carried about as much merchandise as a train of fifty wagons. Land transportation was therefore still very important, probably more important than seaborne trade. The fairs of Champagne gradually broke up during the fourteenth century. But, with the opening of the Sankt-Gotthard Pass to trade, overland communications between Italy and northwestern Europe developed considerably: merchandise was shipped toward the Jura passes for entry into France; however, the greatest bulk was generally transported through the Rhine Valley north of the Alps as far as Cologne; or, leaving from Strasbourg, along the roads that led to Brabant and Flanders via Metz and Verdun, unless they went through Verdun and along the Meuse Valley. These routes were of course used in both senses. The Hundred Years War created insecurity in France, and its consequences caused traffic from the Low Countries to southern France and Spain to make use of these routes, at least north of Basel. Both the maritime and the overland axes converged upon Bruges and London, with Southampton as an outer harbor for the latter.

The world of the Mediterranean and the world of the North Sea and the Baltic met there. Part of the goods transported were destined for the Low Countries, for neighboring regions, or for England, but the remainder was exchanged between the two worlds that have just been mentioned. The vitality of the great markets in London and Bruges did not prevent the existence of other important commercial meeting places. The development of southern Germany, the proximity of Italy, the presence of the pontifical court in Avignon in the Rhône valley—a big center of consumption—the important role played by the ports of Marseille and Montpellier, especially in the first half of the century, all provide reasons for the activity at the southern and central German fairs (Frankfurt am Main, Zurzach, Friedberg) and in the Rhône basin (Chalon-sur-Saône and Geneva). Though secondary to Bruges, these fairs were nevertheless important to European commerce in the fourteenth century as well as—except for Chalon-sur-Saône—in the fifteenth. The great Parisian markets and the Lendit fair played similar roles, but in the course of two centuries the Hundred Years War limited their scope for long periods of time.

In spite of unfavorable demographic factors, wars, and political troubles of every sort, international trade underwent new developments in the fourteenth century, due in part to progress in commercial methods. This progress was particularly remarkable among the leaders of the great Italian mercantile houses, who operated both at home and abroad, using their own funds, or those of their clients, and, in the case of some, revenues that the Avignon papacy drained from all Europe and whose transfers they handled. If the great Florentine industrial, commercial, and banking groups—for they were still all of these—the great money handlers, and the great businessmen of Genoa, Lucca, Prato, Venice, and Pisa could spread their activities over such a considerable "area," it was mainly because of the increase of various forms of permanent representation abroad: branch offices, depots, factors, associates, etc. Much of this must have been based upon the creation of the letter of exchange, which probably dates from the end of the thirteenth century, and which appears to have occurred through the business conducted at the fairs of Champagne. This facilitated long distance payments and the exchanges they necessitated. Improvements in accounting should also be mentioned here. They were acquired in Italy. In the thirteenth century, progress was made in Siena, Genoa, Florence, and Venice: current accounts are known to have existed before the last quarter of the century, and they spread throughout Italy. Double-entry bookkeeping apparently was practiced in Genoa possibly by the thirteenth century, but certainly before 1340, and became part of Italian business during the fourteenth century. Efficiency in the conduct and control of businesses of the size of the great Italian enterprises, which were operated in every corner of Europe and even of Asia and Africa, depended in part on sound bookkeeping. The heads of great diversified enterprises had a more precise and a sounder knowledge of their situation because of progress in bookkeeping and in banking. Inadequate bookkeeping may have contributed to the bankruptcy of some great Sienese and Florentine companies, whose resounding failures have already been mentioned.

Other "companies" were saved by prudent management; it is not inconceivable that improvements in accounting played a part. The progress made in commercial methods, and its effect on international relations, was not limited to Italy. The phenomenon was manifesting itself elsewhere, though nowhere to the same extent. Hanseatic trade, for example—which was less diversified in terms of the activities of a single enterprise, less widespread geographically, and less remunerative owing to the nature of the goods traded—used much more rudimentary methods. Though papers of credit and foreign representatives were used, they were less organized and less stable. Hanseatic bookkeeping was geared to the needs of less complex enterprises: though well looked after, its use did not reach, during the second half of the fourteenth century in northern Germany, the level it had reached in Siena one hundred years previously.

One must realize that natural products still formed the bulk of the international commerce in the fourteenth century. Industrial products were not very numerous. Moreover, export industries

had been set back by the general depression in the West, by
unfavorable demographic factors, and by social troubles and
wars. The Flemish luxury cloth trade, which used English wool,
was one of those that had suffered most from these circumstances: the trade fell off in the fourteenth century and was ruined
in the fifteenth century. The cloth industry of Brabant slowly
supplanted it, extending its markets into France and southern
Germany, only to experience decline in the following century. The
Brabant trade also suffered from competition with the cloth
industries of Champagne and Normandy, and especially from
English cloth, which was on the way to becoming the chief
consumer of home-grown wool. Finally, the cloth industries of
Florence and Prato, which were growing rapidly beside the older
finishing industry, were to become powerful rivals of Flanders.
However, different types of cloth manufacture began to appear in
Flanders, also producing for export: the production of cheaper
articles made in the great towns, in part with Spanish wool; or the
production, in small towns and in the countryside, of a lower
grade of cloth for which poor grade wool was used, mainly from
Scotland and northern Germany. The Hanseatic and Italian
merchants were the great buyers of this cheap cloth. The former
resold it in the colonized lands, in Poland, in Sweden, and in
Russia; and the latter in the countries bordering the Mediterranean. The sale of the products of other textile industries in
addition to cloth making—cotton, canvas, and silk—increased in
the foreign markets, perhaps as a result of improvements in
clothing and in undergarments. Hainaut and the Walloon area of
Brabant became great producers of canvas. We have already
referred to the production of canvas and cottons in southern
Germany and of silk at Lucca. The finished silk that was woven
at Lucca and at Venice competed with silks from the Far East
and Byzantium, without being able either to match their quality
or to muster the power to eliminate them from the European
market.

Leather, principally from Spain, and paper from Spain, Italy, and the south of France can be cited among those nontextile industries whose products were widely distributed through international trade. One word should be said about the mining industries. Apart from rare exceptions, coal was used only in the regions or in the countries where it was mined. On the other hand, Bohemian silver, English tin, Polish copper, iron from Bohemia, Sweden, and Spain, and the objects manufactured with these three metals—sometimes a long distance from the mining site, such as brass objects in the Meuse Valley—played a role in international trade relations.

Events of the very greatest importance, which do not in themselves belong to a history of international relations, took place in the fourteenth century in the economic field and especially in the social structure. Such, for example, was the establishment of a corporate structure in a great part of Europe, and the repercussions of this phenomenon on the political life of the Continent. This fact should be noted here. As we have already pointed out, it had an effect on the general pattern and on certain important aspects of international trade; there will be an opportunity to mention its influence in the area of relations among states or other great political units. It consisted of a movement that attempted, and succeeded, to protect the interests of the small merchants, the artisans, and the workmen against the great merchants and entrepreneurs among the urban patriciate and, in the south, also among the nobility. The former, grouped into craft guilds, succeeded in imposing detailed regulations on production and distribution; their actions, in retrospect, heavily hampered the conduct of business and prevented improvements in production methods. This social and economic action went hand in hand with a political action that sought to bring the government of the towns partially or completely into the hands of the corporations and to assure them a voice in the government of the states and of the great principalities. This movement, aimed at the establishment of corporate organizations, was by no means under way everywhere at the same time. Its structure varied according to country and region, and it did not bring about similar results in all areas. The movement began in the second half of the thirteenth century, reached its zenith in the fourteenth, but continued to grow during the fifteenth. It could be said that almost everywhere it succeeded to a greater or a lesser degree in its social and economic claims, though less generally and less lastingly in its political claims.

Taken as a whole, fifteenth-century agricultural transformations were a continuation of those briefly dealt with in the preceding chapter, but they were complicated and worsened by well-known factors: generally unfavorable circumstances, population decline, wars, and agrarian revolts. The majority of these changes do not pertain to the history of international relations. Here we should stress the growth, in the fourteenth and especially the fifteenth centuries, of the wholesale production of cereals and, to a lesser extent, of cattle, in northeastern Europe. This occurred in the countries colonized by Germany, as well as in Bohemia, Poland, Denmark, and later in Russia. The rise in production was increasingly guaranteed by wholesale seignorial exploitation, which developed at the expense of landholdings occupied in return for rents, and which brought about the much stricter subjection of a peasantry bound to provide forced labor, even an extension of serfdom. It should be noted in passing that in the fourteenth and particularly the fifteenth centuries northeastern Europe became one of the great producers of corn for the countries of the northwest with their relatively high urban populations. The reduction of cultivated land in the northwest was possibly one of the factors that led to this situation. The fact is attested in England in the second half of the fourteenth century. It came about much more extensively in France at the same time, and more markedly in the first half of the fifteenth century, as a result of epidemics and of the Hundred Years War and its consequences. Another area in which changes in agrarian conditions are reflected in international relations was the continuation and intensification of an older phenomenon: the impoverishment, in western Europe, of the seigneurial milieu which consisted chiefly of people living on the income produced by landed property; monetary devaluation, wars, and the problems that followed them hastened this development. More so than in the past, the impoverishment of these groups led nobles to enter the service of kings or princes or to seek adventure abroad.

A second group of exceptions to the rule consists of situations where the action of great events having an international significance on agriculture and stock raising are reflected. It is important here to note the curtailment, which led up to a virtual collapse, of sheep raising on the great English estates in the second half of the fourteenth and in the fifteenth century. Production that henceforward was chiefly in the tenants' hands, as the major portion of the estates had been rented to them, diminished considerably in volume; by about one third in 1310–1311 and 1447–1448. There were various reasons for this decline: the fall in agricultural prices mentioned earlier, and crippling taxation and rigorous "controls" on the export of wool; these were results of royal policies at the onset of the Hundred Years War. There were always external factors, including decline in demand from the continental textile industry and, as we have mentioned, the abandonment of fine cloth in favor of silk among the aristocracy. Other factors could be cited to demonstrate the influence that great events of international importance had on agriculture in the fourteenth century. Among these was increased production of pastel, from Lauragais and Toulouse, required by the rapidly expanding English cloth industry; and also the increased production of wine in Bordelais and Saintonge, resulting from the heavy demand in England, the Low Countries, and the Hanseatic world. If we go on to other regions of France, it appears that in

Burgundy and in the Loire Valley wine production developed as a result of the establishment of the papal court at Avignon, where large quantities of wine were drunk.

The establishment of the papal court on the banks of the Rhône constitutes an event of great importance in the history of international relations. It was the indirect result of a quarrel between the Holy See and the French monarchy. Throughout the forty years between the death of Innocent IV (1254) and the accession of Boniface VIII (1294) the position of the popes weakened. The state of affairs in Italy and in the desperately disturbed city of Rome were largely responsible for this. Meanwhile the canonist who had just ascended the throne of Saint Peter intended to give reality once more to pontifical claims to supreme authority. In 1296 he addressed harsh strictures to the kings of England and France who were at war; he claimed his right to approve the validity of the election of a king of Germany who was a candidate for the imperial title; and he was even able to make one of them, Albert of Austria, swear fealty to him in 1303. France, now the principal power in the West, blocked these new hopes of establishing a theocratic regime. The French king, Philip the Fair (1285–1314) and his councilors, who were often "legists" influenced by the absolutist principles of later Roman law, considered monarchical power superior to any other. Royal sovereignty in France should not be subjected to any other power; there could be no question of pontifical supremacy. The conflict broke out over the authority of the King over the Church in France: there were questions of taxes and questions of jurisdiction. In answer to the very radical theocratic doctrine of the Pope, notably in the bull *Unam Sanctam*, published in 1302, the King took a positive stand in joint assemblies in 1302 and 1303, supported by the privileged members of the population—princes, nobles, clerics, and towns. They accused Boniface VIII of heresy and simony and called for his condemnation by a general council: now the religious aspect of the problem was hit. In 1303 an incident hastened the outcome: when a "legist," Guillaume de Nogaret, was sent to Anagni to deliver to the Pope orders to appear before a council, he was induced by the intervention of the Colonnas, a noble Roman family who opposed Boniface VIII, to arrest the latter. The detention was not lasting but the sovereign pontiff died the same year. Under Clement V, who was elected in 1305, it was readily apparent that the theocratic reaction had broken down and that the king of France was henceforth able to impose his will upon the Pope.

Terrified by the unrest in Italy, Clement dared not enter Rome; he became a wandering pope, at one point residing in France, and later in the kingdom of Arles. The extent of his submission to the King can be judged when the latter began to persecute the Templars, who, since the loss of the Holy Land, had become a wholly western order, rich in land and rich in money through the banking operations that they had taken up. Philip the Fair wanted their defeat, mainly in order to seize their wealth; and in 1307 he took legal steps against them in his kingdom, accusing them of heresy. The Pope, under pressure from Philip, pronounced the dissolution of the order in 1312.

The French ascendancy over the papacy appeared to be even stronger under John XXII (1316–1334), who was elected through the influence of the French cardinals and the "Limousins" (as the cardinals of the *langue d'oc* countries were called). Formerly bishop of Avignon, he made that city his seat. It was within the kingdom of Arles, but the vicinity of France—Villeneuve, on the other bank of the Rhône, was royal domain—gave the Capetian kings the means to control the papacy. In 1348, Clement VI (1342–1352), whose papal palace still provides a reminder of the generous patronage of Italian, French, and Provençal artists, even obtained the city area from Queen Joan of Naples, countess of Provence. Thereafter, the Pope occupied his own home in living by the Rhône, although this did not diminish the possibility of

French pressure. The fact that the popes resided at Avignon and scarcely moved was a change from the habits—voluntary or forced—of the papacy at Rome. This allowed the pontifical administration, which also henceforth ceased to wander, a greater stability and greater development. The ascendancy, above all the financial ascendancy, that the Holy See exercised over the Church became much more efficient; this was a factor of international importance, whose results we shall point out later. The voluntary residence of the popes at Avignon, which lasted until 1377, bears in history the Biblical name of "Babylonian captivity." It hardly enhanced the prestige of the Holy See.

The proximity of the pontifical residence and the close ties with the Holy See, which were facilitated by this proximity, on the contrary served the interests of the French monarchy. Furthermore the latter, on account of the development of its administrative and judiciary apparatus and, to a lesser degree, on account of the increase in its revenues and its military forces, disposed of "means of power" that were far more considerable than they had been in the second half of the thirteenth century. Among this series of events belonging chronologically to the reigns of Philip the Fair and his three sons who succeeded him to the throne until 1328, we shall mention only one in this account—the parliament. This former judicial department of the king's "court," which had become a very clearly defined body constituting the highest court of law in royal France, henceforth heard the appeals brought to it by the subjects of the territorial princes. This gave royalty a sure means of actual control of the several large autonomous territories that still existed, such as the county of Flanders, or the duchy of Guyenne, whose duke was the King of England.

The last direct descendants of the Capetians attempted to put an end to the autonomy of these territories. Nevertheless, despite several campaigns, Guyenne remained intimately linked to the crown of England. In Flanders, Philip the Fair supported the towns governed by a bourgeois patriciate, who were hostile to the

monarchical policy of their lords, against Count Guy of Dampierre: the King handled the situation so ably, using both judicial
power and military forces, that he was able to annex the county
"to the domain of the Crown" in 1300. But the middle and petite
bourgeoisie, the artisans, the workers in the textile industries, who
were hostile to the patriciate, rose up and, allied with the princes
of the ruling house, scored a decisive victory over the royal army
at Courtrai in 1302. The King managed, partially through an
alliance concluded with the Count of Hainaut, Holland, and
Zeeland, of the house of Avesnes, to regain the advantage and was
able to impose in 1305 stringent conditions of peace on Flanders;
the chief of these was the cession of the southern part of the
county (Lille and Douai). However royal France's expansionist
energies toward the north were broken for a long time. Although
the later Capetians often intervened in imperial lands—the kingdom of Germany and the kingdom of Arles that bordered their
frontiers, as much in the north as in the southeast, and although
they occupied some important positions under various claims,
they managed to extend the limits of the kingdom only in one
area: Lyon, which was annexed in 1312.

The foreign policy of the later Capetians even aimed at the
imperial dignity—although they never committed themselves
thoroughly. Philip the Fair played the boldest hand: in 1308,
upon the death of Albert of Austria, he attempted to get his
brother Charles of Valois elected King of the Romans, but
without success. A similar election might have been a solution
suggested for the imperial problem, which, by the end of the
thirteenth and during the fourteenth centuries, was the concern of
all men capable of political and legal thinking. The teaching of
Roman law and its increasing hold on the minds of men spread
the notion of the emperor as master of the world and, as a result,
of his having authority over kings. Obviously the King of France
and the King of England adamantly refused to admit subjection to
the Emperor in every respect. Most thirteenth- and fourteenth-

century jurists held no less strongly for the universality of imperial power. They insisted that the independence of kings, notably of the kings of France, existed only *de facto* and not *de jure*. The greatest of the Italian commentators, Bartole de Sassoferrato, still defended this point of view in the middle of the fourteenth century; though it was he who did draw up the doctrine of the sovereignty of kingdoms. However, since the thirteenth century, and perhaps even since the twelfth, a different legal doctrine came into existence in Italy, France, and England. This doctrine attributed to the kings of France, England, Castile, and Naples independence both *de facto* and *de jure* and recognized their rights—within their kingdoms—to powers which generally were considered as belonging to the emperor. The lawyers and civil servants in the service of Philip the Fair had incorporated this doctrine into their political program, affirming that the king of France was the "emperor in his kingdom." It is hardly surprising that Pope Clement V himself gave the support of the Holy See to the doctrine of the absolute independence of the French monarchy.

Furthermore, the kings of France took precautions in regard to Roman law against possible future imperial claims. Through an ordinance dated 1312, Philip the Fair confirmed that in parts of the kingdom—in the south where this law was in force—it was not so much Roman law, but customs conforming to Roman law. The teaching of Roman law was permitted in only a few universities, chiefly Orléans and Montpellier; at the request of King Philip Augustus it was forbidden in Paris in 1219 by Pope Honorius III. From the thirteenth and fourteenth centuries on, this did not, however, prevent private Roman law from becoming part of French law, principally in matters of contract. However, in the northern part of France, except for the law of contract, it never became a general complementary law which had to be enforced when customary law was silent or unclear. In England, directly or via canonical law, Roman law had a strong influence on legal thinking in the twelfth and thirteenth centuries, and even on legislation; but after the second half of the latter century, and even more during the fourteenth, the trend was checked owing to the fear that this law might be used in the service of absolutism: common law was essentially customary and national. If there was no "reception" of Roman law in the two great western kingdoms, it was because of the texts in Justinian's compilations which stressed the absolute and universal power of the emperor.

It is strange to have to say that imperial claims to universal power were more categorically asserted at times when its effective power had been reduced to virtually nothing. Upon the death of the King of the Romans, Albert of Austria, in 1308, the German princes, fearful of their autonomy, had no desire to elect a Hapsburg. Thus they had blocked attempts dating from Rudolf I's accession to the throne to rebuild in Germany a central power and a state worthy of the name under a dynasty that controlled very important territories. In fact, the new king who was elected, Henry VII, Count of Luxembourg, was a man of little substance, who took a course of action quite different from that of his predecessors. In 1310, he did indeed manage to seize on Bohemia and Moravia and to make a kingdom for his doltish adventurer son, John the Blind. Thus, to the benefit of his dynasty, he created a territorial power. However, this was of no use to the interests of the central power in Germany. On the contrary, elements of the Czech nobility, hostile to German influence, began to fashion the policies of the kingdom: Bohemia became an extraneous body in the heart of Germany. The accession of Henry VII also signaled a rupture with Hapsburg policies: the new King once again sought to realize the imperial dream and reached Italy in 1310; he managed to have himself crowned by cardinals in Rome. In the peninsula he had supporters who were anticipating peace throughout Christendom as a result of effective re-establishment of imperial power. The most eloquent and famous of these was Dante Alighieri, who had been expelled from Florence by the Guelphs. But Italy was a nest of vipers. Not only did the sympathies of the princes, lords, and cities, whether Guelph or Ghibelline, depend upon their personal and current interests, but a new phenomenon complicated the problem: this was the appearance of what might be termed the "tyranny" (*signoria*)—that is, the dictatorship of an urban lord who had managed to install himself as a result of struggles among parties, families, and social groups. Within a single city, families fought mercilessly for power: to cite one example, in Milan there were the Visconti, who were Ghibellines, and the della Torre, who were Guelphs. Henry VII immersed himself in these problems. Furthermore, the King of Naples, Robert of Anjou, opposed him. Using his imperial power Henry called upon the latter to appear before his court, and vainly had him condemned in his absence for the crime of *lèse-majesty!* He was marching against the "rebel" with the support of his ally, the Aragonian King of Sicily, when he died in 1313. The imperial "myth" was equally destructive to his successor: this time a Wittelsbach, Louis of Bavaria, who since 1323 also intervened in Italian affairs, and in 1328 had himself crowned emperor by a Ghibelline lord, Sciarra Colonna, military leader of a people in revolt against the absent Pope. The Roman people appeared as guardians and patrons of the imperial dignity —a direct blow against the Pope. The difficulties that beset Louis of Bavaria were even more serious than those that defeated his predecessor. Pope John XXII, himself possessed by the theocratic spirit, excommunicated and proclaimed the deposition of the Wittelsbach, because the latter did not accept that the validity of the royal German election depended upon pontifical approval. The excommunication and the declaration of deposition continued to be upheld by the successors of John XXII, notably by Clement VI. However, the struggle was endless, for despite the support of a majority of German princes who, at the Diet of Rense in 1338, sided with him against the aggressiveness of the Avignon papacy, Louis of Bavaria failed. Upon his death in 1347 imperial authority in Italy had not been re-established, and in

Germany it was weaker than at his accession. But the papacy consolidated its power neither in Italy nor in Germany, and had seen its moral authority dwindle. Increasing numbers of people, for political or religious reasons, considered that the papacy should no longer seek domination over the states, and saw in its attitude an overweening pride and greed.

This critical attitude toward pontifical authority took various forms, certain of which—chiefly among the groups of dissident Franciscans—gave birth to genuine sects which the Catholic Church considered heretical. But this attitude was shared by many Franciscans who had not separated from the order, who could not forget the poverty and humility of Jesus, and who struggled against the Holy See despite excommunication. In every country the doctrines taught to the court of Louis of Bavaria by Marsilius of Padua, a former professor at Oxford, gained ground. The doctrines affirmed that priestly labor should be exclusively spiritual; it should prepare the faithful for eternal life, while temporal life should be solely dependent upon public power. The lay concept of the State, formulated by avowed Christians, was making headway.

This phenomenon occurred throughout western Europe, even in France, despite the compliance of the court at Avignon and the Sacred College, with its ever growing proportion of French or "Limousin" cardinals, to the Capetian and Valois kings. This compliance did as much to discredit the pontifical authority as a new conflict which, in the second quarter of the century, pitted England and her allies against France. This conflict, with a few interruptions, was to last for a long time; it has been called the "Hundred Years War."

At the end of the thirteenth century and the beginning of the fourteenth, England underwent a relatively turbulent period. Although Edward I (1272–1307) had succeeded in retaining his duchy of Guyenne, in subjecting Wales, and in incorporating it into the kingdom, he failed in his efforts to make Scotland—however much it was Anglicized in terms of language, customs, and institutions—into a state that would be not only a legal vassal but also actually subordinate to England. The situation was worse under the incompetent Edward II (1307–1327); the King of Scotland, Robert Bruce, and his subjects routed the English army at Bannockburn in 1314, and Scotland remained independent. There is no need to go into the reaction that was aroused in England—among the aristocracy and the clergy, among the middle classes in a few important cities such as London or Bristol—by the efforts that the policies of the first two Edwards had required of the country, by England's final defeat, and by Edward II's arrogance. Nor do we need to go into the revolt that put an end to the reign and the life of Edward II, or into the new developments in the English Parliament, which was beginning to reflect national representation. In fact, on the outbreak of the Hundred Years War, royal power had been re-established by Edward III. He had improved the organization and the armaments of his army. He had a well-filled treasury thanks to royal control of the sale of English wool to the Continent by means of the staple.

France was ruled by Philip VI (1328–1350): a Valois, a Capetian of a minor branch. Although he succeeded in joining a fraction of the kingdom of Arles, the Dauphiné, to his kingdom, and in buying back Montpellier from the King of Majorca, he scarcely strengthened the "means of power" that the monarchy possessed for foreign endeavors. He pursued the traditional policies of his predecessors vis-à-vis England: by applying feudal law he attempted to seize the duchy of Guyenne from the Plantagenet king, and he allied himself with the Scots whom Edward II had in vain tried to conquer. This double threat incited the English sovereign to pursue claims to the crown of France through his mother, daughter of Philip the Fair, in 1337.

The war became a largely international conflict, as Edward III had succeeded in gathering together the King of the Romans and the majority of the princes of the lower Rhine and the Low Countries against Philip VI. Of some importance was a brief awakening of national pride that the Avignon papacy's opposition to Louis of Bavaria provoked among the German princes; but English gold was of much greater importance. Furthermore, the needs of the Flemish cloth trade—already under considerable strain—for English wool forced them to withdraw their allegiance, under the leadership of Ghent, from the count who had remained a loyal French vassal. The cloth towns formed a revolutionary government and after a period of neutrality allied themselves with Edward III, who at Ghent in 1340 took the title of king of France. However this coalition, whose members did not pursue the same goals, achieved nothing worthwhile. It was in the second phase of this war that Edward III's armies won decisive victories: Crécy (1346), Calais (1347), Poitiers (1356). That heroic idiot John II the Good (1350–1364) was captured by the victor in the latter battle.

This was the dawn of a crisis in which France almost succumbed to anarchy. The main reasons for this were defeat, the King's captivity, economic depression, the plague, the excesses of the mercenary bands, the increased demands of lords upon diminished revenues, and the behavior of opportunistic princes and merchants. Among these were the King of Navarre; Charles the Bad, great-grandson of Philip the Fair and undeclared claimant to the French throne; and Étienne Marcel, the "provost of the merchants" (Fr.: *prerôt des marchands*) of Paris.

Nothing positive issued from this crisis: neither from the attempt at government by the "estates," nor from a trial at government controlled by the cities and, above all, by the city of Paris, nor from the revolt of the peasants or *Jacquerie*. Certain of these efforts were linked to relations overseas: Charles the Bad maintained relations with the English, and Étienne Marcel with the Flemish cities. They came to nothing. For ten years France ceased to be an active agent in international relations, at least in the political domain, and was nothing more than a dormant state. The situation changed during the reign of Charles V (1364–1380) who as dauphin tried to govern the kingdom and in 1360 concluded a treaty at Brétigny with the English, giving them the southwest and a fraction of northwestern France. Peace was concluded in the same year at Calais. Owing to a reaction brought about by the chaotic situation, Charles managed to restore the functioning of the state, to silence the King of Navarre, to use in Spain the great mercenary bands who were given over to brigandage, and to place Henry of Trastamare, an ally of France, on the throne of Castile. When he felt himself sufficiently strong and following the custom of the Capetians, he found a legal pretext for confiscating the duchy of Guyenne.

The war began again in 1368 and the King regained everything he had ceded to the English, except Bordelais, part of Gascony, and Calais with its environs. He was less successful in the two great territorial principalities that still existed. Brittany, still very nationalistic, remained allied with England and with considerable success managed to resist an attempted reunion with the territories subject to direct royal control. As for Flanders, the King was irritated with the continued neutrality of Count Louis de Male; he tried to draw him into his camp and to prepare, for the future, a more intimate union of the county with the crown or with the dynasty. He had his brother, Philip the Bold, whom he had made Duke of Burgundy, marry the Count's daughter and heiress. He even went as far as to give the latter southern Flanders, which had once been ceded to Philip the Fair. The results of the operation, as we shall see, were not those foreseen by Charles V.

These conflicts that ravaged Europe hardly destroyed the idea of crusades. Numerous writers launched a flood of propaganda calling for crusades. But the circumstances were not favorable to any serious attempt to realize the idea. Christian expeditions did set out for the Moslem Near East—notably the one undertaken by the Lusignanian kings of Cyprus; and for some time yet knights were available and willing to participate. In 1365, King Peter I managed to take Alexandria, although he was unable to hold it. It was impossible to recruit crusaders after this disaster.

Eastern Christendom, be it Latin or Greek, entered a period of great hardship in the fourteenth century; under the dynasty of the Palaeologoi the history of the Byzantine Empire was one of a continued decline. Constantinople kept its importance as a market for eastern products, but the development already outlined rapidly progressed: trading profits went to the Italians, and even fiscal profits to a great extent bypassed the imperial treasury as a result of customs privileges granted to foreign powers. This catastrophe was reflected in the collapse of Byzantine gold coinage. Economic weakness was not the only factor that destroyed the empire's powers of resistance: dynastic and civil wars, social troubles at the end of the century, the weakness of the army and the navy, and violent reactions to the attempts—bound to fail—to re-establish union with Rome which were made by the emperors Michael VIII from 1262 to 1282, by Andronicus III in 1339, and by John V in 1369–1370. In addition, there were wars, sometimes bloody, between Genoa, whose colony was installed at Galata, and Venice who had been able to re-establish her own colony on the Golden Horn. When the *basileus* hired an army of foreign mercenaries, like the "Great Catalan Company," from 1302 to 1311, the latter oppressed the population, took every sort of adventurer into its service, and hindered the exercise of government. In 1333 and 1340 the empire conquered the despots of Epirus and of Thessaly, the last vestiges of what had been the empire of Thessalonica. The Bulgarians made some advances into the northern provinces. The Serbs appeared as a greater danger. They conquered Macedonia and Thrace; if their King Stephen Dushan, who had himself crowned emperor in 1346, had not suddenly died in 1355, he might have subjected the Byzantine Empire to his authority and built up a great Slav power in Christian Europe. The Byzantine emperors re-established their hold, in the fourteenth century and at the beginning of the fifteenth, over Morea, which previously had been part of their territory. Michael VIII Palaeologos forced William of Villehardouin to cede several areas to him, among them Mistra. During involved conflicts which lasted a century, Byzantium seized other small areas of her territory from the Angevin dynasty of Naples, which had at the end of the previous century succeeded to the possessions of the Villehardouin family. From 1381 on, Spanish mercenaries, the "Navarre Company," occupied the greater part of the territories not reconquered by Byzantium.

Apart from Morea, the Latins only held *membra disjecta*. The duchy of Athens and Thebes had been seized by the "Great Catalan Company" from "Frankish" barons in 1311. The company exercised power under the nominal suzerainty of the Aragonian kings of Sicily, later under that of the King of Aragon. But toward the end of the century this duchy passed into the hands of the Acciaiuoli, a Florentine banking family. The Venetians held some settlements in the Peloponnesus; they had occupied Euboea and held Crete and some islands in the archipelago. Their Genoese enemies had settled on other islands. Their situation in Cyprus had been strengthened: while they often had had to fight, usually against the Venetians, to maintain their economic leadership, they succeeded in imposing their protection over the kings of the island from 1383 on. It should be noted that in the fourteenth century Italy and Spain gradually occupied the position previously held by France in the Latin territories of the Near East.

A new group of Turkish tribes that had settled in Asia Minor during the thirteenth century were the main threat to the Byzantine Empire, to the Greek empire of Trebizond, and to the Latin Christian states. These were the Ottomans, named after the Emir Othman I, who had gathered them under his authority at the beginning of the fourteenth century. The Ottomans had conquered the greater part of the Byzantine territories in Asia Minor prior to 1350. Beginning in 1352 they crossed into Europe; Byzantine territories were soon conquered. Serbia, annihilated at Kossovo in 1389, was divided into tribute-paying principalities. At the end of the century Bulgaria and Wallachia suffered similar fates. King Sigismund of Hungary, seeing the Turk at his frontier, was able to rouse an expedition of western knights against the infidel; the incompetence of the leaders and the lack of discipline among the troops was worthy of the crusades. The battle of Nicopolis (1396) was a disaster for the Christian forces. In order to highlight his triumph, the victor, Emir Bajazet, obtained the right to bear the title of sultan from the Caliph, who was supported by the Mameluke Sultan of Cairo. The last Christian position in eastern Europe could be thought of as lost at this moment; and the *basileus*, Manuel II, took advantage of the victor's concern to strengthen his power base in Asia, and turned to the West for help between 1399 and 1403, but without success.

The constitution of the Turko-Mongol empire, whose base had been laid by Tamerlane, provided some respite for Byzantium. The conqueror overran not only central Asia but also part of India, Iran, Iraq, and Caucasian countries, southern Russia, and Syria. He then attacked the Ottomans and defeated Bajazet at Ankara in the heart of Asia Minor in 1402. When he died in 1405 during an expedition against China, his empire crumbled, as did almost all the "empires of the steppes."

If the history of international relations, even in the political sphere, is to be something more than a mere catalogue of facts, brief mention must be made of events of importance to the countries of the western Mediterranean. It is, nevertheless, difficult to discern the major trends. Bloody wars between states characterized Italy in the fourteenth century. In the term "states" we must include, in addition to the principalities, the urban republics and what have already been termed "tyrannies"—that is, the *signorie* of the della Scala at Verona, of the Visconti at Milan, of the Este at Ferrara, and the Malatesta at Rimini, to name a few of the better known. These wars generally had a twofold aim: to increase one's own territories while preventing others from increasing theirs. Until the middle of the century, these wars stemmed from Louis of Bavaria's undertakings and papal countermaneuvers. For this reason Milan, whose domination the Visconti had succeeded in extending over an important area of northern Italy, was attacked by the Pope and by towns threatened by the Milanese aims at hegemony. But when the danger of papal domination appeared and was part of the policy of the Pope's ally, John the Blind of Bohemia—who was engaged in setting up a great Italian state—a complete reversal came about. A new coalition crushed the allied forces in 1333, once more leaving the way clear for the Visconti. At Rome in 1347, Cola di Rienzi, a demagogue whose mind was possessed of mysticism and half-digested historical visions, imposed his dictatorship. Petrarch, with great lyrical imagination but with poor political sense, acclaimed this *coup d'état* as a glorious return to republican Rome, as the tyrant himself had claimed. This latter envisioned the unity of Italy under the authority of Rome. The harlequinade collapsed by the end of the year; Rienzi seized power again in 1354, but lost his life in the effort. Later the Pope intervened; his legate, Cardinal Albornoz, re-established legitimate authority at Rome and in the Church State from 1353 to 1363 and attempted, with some degree of success, to impose papal hegemony over Italy. However, because of the increasing burden of this hegemony, further compounded by the exactions of the papal agents, who were generally French, and because of the violence of the foreign or Italian papal mercenaries, the pontifical territories, the republics, and the "tyrannies" formed a league centered upon Milan and Florence. The Pope won a victory after a ferocious war lasting from 1375 to 1377; but his authority lacked a firm base. The

Angevin kingdom of Naples, governed from 1343 to 1381 by Queen Joan I, was greatly weakened by quarrels among various branches of the family and by complications produced by the four marriages of this queen of demanding temperament. Though Neapolitan interventions in external affairs were frequent, taken as a whole they present no more than a passing interest.

In Spain some facts of importance can be grasped in the wars between the kingdoms of Castile, Portugal, Aragon, Majorca, and Navarre and within these kingdoms, which at first glance seem as a whole to be highly complex and generally of only secondary interest. Navarre, united to the Crown of France through a marriage to Philip the Fair of the heiress of this kingdom and of the county of Champagne, took on new life with its own dynasty, that of Evreux, when the French crown passed to the Valois in 1328. We know that the essential concerns of the Evreux dynasty lay in France and only secondarily in Spain. The conflicts that Castile had suffered during the major part of the century, were additional to those of the Hundred Years War: France, as we have seen, and Aragon supported Henry of Trastamare, a bastard of Alfonso XI, against the legitimate king, Peter the Cruel, a barbarous monster. The latter naturally had the support of England and, for a period, of Navarre. The bastard defeated him in 1369. He was Henry II, founder of a dynasty that faithfully honored the French alliance. Moreover, he had to fight against King Ferdinand I of Portugal, who attempted to dethrone him for his own ends and, on this occasion allied himself with England. John I, king of Castile, attempted to annex Portugal on the death of Ferdinand, but he was prevented from doing so by an illegitimate brother of the dead king—John, the grand master of the Order of Avis. As victor, the latter reigned from 1385, maintaining the alliance with England, which was to last for several centuries. He founded a new dynasty, that of Avis, which we will refer to later. The increase of Aragonian power gave rise to another important event. From 1296 to 1409, Sicily had been a separate kingdom, ruled by a lateral branch of the dynasty; but on this last date the island itself once more became part of the central possessions of the Aragon dynasty. The kingdom of Majorca met the same fate in 1344. Finally the continuing conquest of Sardinia, at first from Pisa and then from Genoa—which was to last throughout the century—and the conquest of Corsica undertaken against Genoa, compensated for the loss of Montpellier, which, as we know, was sold to the King of France. If we include the theoretical but commercially profitable authority, at first of the Sicilian king and later of the King of Aragon himself, over the territories of the Near East that were occupied by the "Great Catalan Company," we can claim that that which once had been the small kingdom of the upper Ebro had become one of the major political and economic powers in the Mediterranean world.

Obviously Spain, weakened by the Black Death and torn by wars among Christians, could not advance with the *reconquista* during the fourteenth century. On the other hand, civil wars within the Nasrid kingdom of Granada, and wars between the kingdoms of the Maghreb or the African hinterlands—made mere wishful thinking any Islamic plan of attack. The only events that amounted to a threat occurred toward the middle of the century; they met opposition in Alfonso XI of Castile. Although the Tunisian pirates were often a hindrance to navigation, they did not prevent the Spanish or the Italians from trading with northern Africa.

After this attempt to outline international relations in southern Europe, we can once more turn to central Europe and the northwest. First of all, Germany and its role in the second half of the century must be considered. The election of Charles IV, son of John the Blind, by Louis of Bavaria's enemies in 1346 reinstalled the Luxembourg dynasty on the throne. The new King was supported by the Pope, but he in no way conceded that the latter had the right of approving the election. Outside Germany, however, he was powerless. He had himself crowned at Rome in 1355 by a cardinal whom the Pope had delegated for this purpose. But in Italy he showed his total lack of power. His coronation at Arles in 1365 did not prevent France from steadily absorbing what had been the kingdom of Burgundy: all he was able to achieve here was to separate the county of Savoy and attach it directly to Germany. Even in this country he did little enough to maintain what still remained of royal authority, despite the support he could have found in the leagues of towns that had been drawn up to protect their members from the takeover policies of the princes. Moreover, his "Golden Bull" of 1356, governing the royal election, favored the leaders among the princes; it reaffirmed the practice that had developed of restricting the election to a college of seven electors: the archbishops of Cologne, Mainz, and Trier, the King of Bohemia, the Marquis of Brandenburg, the Duke of Saxe-Wittenberg, and the Count-Palatine of the Rhine. No place was given to papal approval. It is important to note that during his reign the changes that had been under way for more than a century, were further emphasized: Germany increasingly took on the character of a federation of states.

Charles chiefly thought as a prince; his most reasoned effort was concerned with the increase of the power of his own house of Luxembourg: he added Silesia and Brandenburg and territories bordering on the River Main to Bohemia. On behalf of his brother Wenceslas, he prepared in the Low Countries a personal union of Brabant and Limbourg with the county of Luxembourg, which he had promoted to a duchy. Any clear-cut concern to use this territorial power for the development of royal authority in Germany or for strengthening this country is hard to discern in his policies.

Events important to the history of international relations occurred in both northern and southern Germany. In the south this revolved around the formation of Switzerland, in which two great factors were of much importance. One was the victorious resistance in 1291 of the confederated cantons to the new Hapsburg efforts to impose over them authority similar to that imposed over other Hapsburg territories: the victory of Morgarten in 1315 over Duke Leopold of Austria was the decisive factor. The other factor was to a great extent the result of the first. Other territories and towns joined the initial union: Lucerne (1332), Zurich (1351), Bern (1353), etc. This free confederation of rural cantons and towns, an autonomous unit—Switzerland—in the heart of the German kingdom shattered every effort made by the Hapsburgs and their allies to defeat it in the course of that century. It had the great advantage over the German urban leagues of including also peasant and Alpine stock.

The important factor in northern Germany was an increased slackening and finally the halting of German colonization. The demographic factors that concerned the western countries, and that have been already mentioned, stemmed the flow of immigrants. The Teutonic Knights (who had absorbed the Sword-bearers) had always found crusaders throughout European knighthood to aid them in Prussia and in the most northern regions that bordered the Baltic. But the German groups who settled in the conquered lands had become less and less numerous, and although during this period it had been possible to partly Germanize Prussia, it had not been possible to expel the Lithuanians from the coast. On the other hand, even after the peace of Stralsund, the Hanseatic League had met with many difficulties as a result of wars between Denmark, since 1380 united with Norway, and Sweden, which was governed by the house of Mecklenburg, and as a result of a disturbing increase in piracy, first in the Baltic and then later in the North Sea. The Teutonic Knights and Hamburg had to organize great maritime expeditions to end the excesses of the fearsome *Vitalienbrüder*. The union of the three Scandinavian states under the King of Denmark and Norway, concluded at Kalmar in 1397, brought a more peaceful state of affairs in the north and served the interests of German maritime trade.

Meanwhile, in northeastern and eastern Europe non-German political forces became increasingly important in the second half of the fourteenth century. Of the greatest threat to German penetration was Lithuania, which was still heathen, but which now reached as far as the Ukraine as a result of conquests undertaken by its great prince. The Great Prince Ladislas Jagellon, who had become a Catholic, was elected king of Poland in 1386 by the nobles of that country. A great Slav state was in the process of formation. Furthermore, within Poland itself, where royalty had been restored in 1320, German influence, mainly supported by immigrant colonies settled in towns like Cracow, was in decline. The Hanse had many conflicts between 1368 and 1392 with the Russian republic of Novgorod, the seat of one of the chief Hanse offices. Farther east the territory of the great princes of Moscow had been increasing since the thirteenth century. In 1380 one of them had succeeded in throwing off his subjugation to the Golden Horde, but two years later he had to once more recognize himself as a tributary. He was no longer dangerous either to Novgorod or to the Hanse. In contrast, in Hungary, the Anjou-Naples dynasty, which succeeded to the throne in 1308, introduced Italian and French influences at the expense of German ones.

Among the "intangible factors"—that is, among those dealing with currents of thought and of attitude that affected international relations during the second half of the fourteenth century—we should mention one that dominated the thinking of the period, and that had material effects of the greatest importance. We have already referred to the vehement reactions aroused by the papacy's active role in international affairs—especially by its efforts to establish a hegemony over all Italy. Although the Holy See had previously been able to claim, with a certain amount of right, that it defended some principle of spiritual superiority, especially against the German sovereigns, it became very clear in the course of this century that these claims had no foundation. The Pope framed his policies as an Italian sovereign might have done, and used the weapons placed at his disposal as a result of his power as leader of the universal Church. It has also been said that Christians from every nation reproached the Holy See for its greed as well as for its domineering outlook. Actually, the Avignon papacy, with its highly developed and long-term bureaucracy, had monstrously extended its fiscal grasp: the "reservation" of an increasing number of benefices—that is, of ecclesiastical positions that produced revenue—granted only for a fee; various charges levied upon the holders of ecclesiastical positions; "tenths" or taxes on the clergy, shared or not with the sovereigns; "taxes" owed by vassal or tributary states; etc. Discontent grew among many members of the clergy and among the faithful. Other matters that caused indignation were the distribution of benefices among the relatives of the Pope—nepotism—and to clients of the cardinals; the accumulation of benefices in the hands of members of the sacred college, or of people close to the Pope; and the use, especially by Clement VI, of large amounts of the money furnished by an overtaxed Christendom, for luxury expenses. The most vehement protests rose from the most pious breasts. These were accompanied by the desire to see the papacy return to Rome, provided abuses were excised, and the Church was reformed "both in its leader and in its members." Urban V returned to Rome in 1367 but feeling by no means secure on Italian soil, he returned to Avignon in 1370, where he died some months later. Only after victories by the papal troops over his enemies—that is, over Florence and the allies of the republic—and after the suppression of a violent revolt in the Church States, did Gregory XI return to the Eternal City in 1377. The objurgations of Petrarch and of the great mystics, Saint Bridget of Sweden and Saint Catherine of Siena, appeared to have borne fruit. This was an illusion.

11

*The Decline of the Middle Ages
and the Dawn of the Modern Era*

𝔍 N THE ACCOUNT of economic factors pertaining to a history of international relations in the fourteenth century, we have, as was necessary, broadly touched upon the following century. From now on we must discuss those facts that specifically concern the fifteenth century.

In order to understand the general course of international relations during this century, it would be important to determine exactly the point when we can acknowledge a rise in the population graph, and the point when the economic situation became more promising. It is impossible to give any answer to this first question that would be valid throughout western Europe. Factors such as famine and plague continued to have their effects, and without doubt we must attribute to them the continuing decline that we believe we can discern in England and in the Low Countries. It is generally acknowledged, though without clear proof, that in France there was an improvement toward the end of the century. At the most it can be held as certain that the end of the devastation brought about by the Hundred Years War, and that the general efforts in rural reconstruction undertaken by the landed lords, created circumstances in the second half of the century that were more favorable for a population increase. There are reasons for believing that a similar increase occurred in northern and central Italy. As for the general picture, it seems that the latter improved in several European regions toward the end of the century: France, England, and northern and central Italy. We do not deny the hypothetical nature of this account, which is based upon facts that are difficult to interpret and have been little studied.

What we can term the Hanseatic flow remained important in the fifteenth century in international trade. We have mentioned the development of the *Baienfahrt* (travel of Hanseatic fleets to and from the Baie de Bourgneuf in the southeast of Brittany, in order to buy salt) during this period; and it was also at this time that the export of wheat toward the west, through Danzig and other Baltic ports, reached its highest levels. But other factors acted adversely: competition from English and Dutch shipping, which was now increasing; maritime wars and the reprisals brought about by this competition; opposing interests among the groups of towns within the Hanse; the wars between Denmark and Sweden and their respective allies, brought on by the collapse of the union of Kalmar—a result of the Swedish uprising of 1434—wars in which the Hanseatic towns did not always find themselves on the same side; struggles with the Teutonic Knights; greater difficulties in trading in the territories that the latter lost after the defeat at Tannenberg and the treaties of Thorn. However, the defeat and the submission of the republic of Novgorod in 1471 by Ivan III, the great prince of Moscow, was the most damaging blow to Hanseatic trade: for the Hanseatic warehouses, the principal center of trade with Russia, found life difficult under the harsh Muscovite domination. Moreover, the warehouses were closed down in 1478, when Ivan III deported to Muscovy the greater part of Novgorod's population. The decline of the Hanse and of its trade had begun.

The various trade routes between northwestern and southern Europe had been maintained: they were always either the sea or the land routes that we have mentioned. This in no way discounts the possibility of a change in the previous state of affairs. It seems that maritime trade between the Iberian peninsula and Bruges had increased considerably without replacing overland trade, and that increased quantities of Spanish goods, especially wool, were imported at Bruges. It also appears that cargoes leaving Bruges were composed of an important volume of the products of the "new" cloth industry, which has already been mentioned. This manufacturing had grown considerably in Flanders, also in Brabant and in Holland. Similar changes in the cloth industry took place in other countries and perhaps should be discussed together with the growing market for Spanish wool and the greater importation of Scottish wool into the Continent. In Italian trade we also come across the products of the "new" cloth industry, and they were often re-exported from Italy to the East. In addition to these, we should also mention the tapestries of Flanders, Artois, and Brabant, whose style was such that they were much in demand abroad. Cloth and especially wool were sent from England to the south. Among the most important products exported from Italy to the north were precious materials, especially Luccan and Venetian silk, alum which was then being mined in Italy—particularly at Tolfa in the Church State—and cotton, and paper. Until the eighties, Bruges remained a major market, where these products— together with many others—were traded and distributed throughout the region and also in the basins of the Channel, the North Sea, and the Baltic.

The transportation of goods in maritime commerce between northwestern and southern Europe was undertaken in the fifteenth century by the same people who handled it in the fourteenth: the Genoese, the Venetians, the Catalans, the Portuguese, the northern Spanish, and the Biscayans. To these we must, however, add the Bretons, who had played a minor role previously, but who will become important; and also the Normans, whom we will mention further. It is especially important to mention the convoys of galleys that Florence sent to England and Bruges after the conquest of Pisa in 1406, which had given her direct access to the sea. If we now move from maritime commerce to overland trade and especially to trade between eastern France, southern Germany, the Rhône Valley lands, and northern Italy, we must draw attention to the activities at the fairs already mentioned and to the development of these at Lyon in the second half of the fifteenth century. The aim of the French monarchy, which supported the fairs at Lyon, was to ruin those of Geneva and to take over their clientele. Owing to the pressure politics practiced by the King of France, these aims were largely realized.

Far from being hindered in this last phase of the Hundred Years War, "transversal" maritime trade in the Atlantic and in the Channel benefited in general, especially between France and western England. Guyenne remained under the authority of the King of England, and Normandy was subject to him. The export of Bordeaux wine to England profited but, after the French reconquest of 1453, required some time to recover its former volume. English wool, the raw material of the Norman textile industry, fed the trade of the English and Norman ports during part of the fifteenth century; but other cross-Channel trade goods were more important and remained so for longer. Burgundy wines exported through Rouen, fish exported from Dieppe, Spanish iron or cork, and Portuguese fruit imported via Harfleur should be mentioned here. This Norman maritime trade continued after the French reconquest. England, moreover, was not its only market: the Low Countries also offered outlets or markets for Norman cloth and wines carried in Norman ships. The Hundred Years War had aided the development of the English navy, which played a continuously increasing role in maritime transportation. Together with the Hanseatic traders, who exported English wool and English cloth to northern Germany and to the Baltic countries, together with the Italians and the Catalonians who handled this trade for southern Europe, the English themselves shipped wool intended for the Low Countries and for the neighboring regions. Its sale was still organized by a monopoly entrusted to a privileged organization—the company of the staple, based at Calais since 1363.

The growing importance of the English cloth industry, however, increased cloth export in terms of volume during the fifteenth century. New taxes on exported wool in the second half of the century and the prohibition on the import of foreign cloth were major contributory factors in this situation. This prohibition even gave rise to a new flow in international trade: its center was the Brabant port of Antwerp. The latter's role in trade between western Germany and England during the first half of the fourteenth century was of concern to Bruges, who saw Antwerp as a rival. Due to a dynastic war, Count Louis de Male and the Flemish towns captured Antwerp in 1356; it was annexed to the county and harassed. But Antwerp was restored to Brabant by Count John the Fearless of the house of Burgundy at the beginning of the fifteenth century, and was then able to receive English cloth, especially that exported by the London "merchant-adventurers." This cloth was often transported in a semifinished state and was finished at Antwerp. Imported either finished or to be finished locally, this cloth was offered for sale at the fairs at Antwerp or at the small neighboring town of Bergen-op-Zoom. The merchants of Cologne and other Germans of the Rhine-Westphalian region traveled there to buy and redistribute it in central and southern Germany, which was at that time in the first full flood of expansion. Soon the merchants of these regions themselves appeared on the banks of the Scheldt. An important international market was born—out of new developments which we will further discuss later. Among the old commercial flows that changed profoundly in the fifteenth century, special attention should be paid to the trade between Italy, on the one hand, and the Levant and the Black Sea, on the other. These changes had decisive and lasting effects on international trade. Turkish conquests will be treated where they belong, but some mention must be made of the fact that they progressively eliminated the majority of Genoese and Florentine settlements in eastern Europe and in Asia and also, though to a lesser extent, those of Venice. Because of its continued presence in Crete and the establishment of a protectorate over the island of Cyprus in the second half of the century, Venice, with some degree of ease, maintained her contacts with the Moslem Near East, especially with Syria and Egypt. She was able to continue to play an active role in the importation of oriental products to Europe, especially spices. This role grew in importance as the xenophobic Moslem domination of central Asia and of Persia pushed the export of Asiatic goods intended for the West almost entirely toward the Indian Ocean routes. The caravan routes that formed a continuation of the sea routes, began at the Syrian ports and at Alexandria, where the authorities allowed Venetian *fondachi* to be set up. But, with the exception of Venice, Turkish control over Asiatic trade was absolute; Genoa and Florence were virtually excluded. There is no doubt that as a result the Italians, during the fifteenth century and especially in its second half, lost their leading position in international commerce.

The Italian merchants sought to find other sources of wealth to replace those that had been partially or completely curtailed. North Africa furnished them. We know that Genoa had always maintained important commercial relations with this continent. As a result of armed conflicts with the kingdom of Tunis, at the end of the fourteenth century the republic had been forced to close its African settlements for some time. But the efforts of individuals appear to have been more important than in the past. These efforts even spread into the western Maghreb where, during the fifteenth century, Genoese merchants and financiers were to be found at Fez, on the Atlantic coast, and even up to the Atlas Mountains. The Venetians also increased their relations with North Africa, especially with Tunis and Oran. There they could acquire the Sudanese gold required to pay for the fraction of their purchases in their Levant settlements that was not covered by the sale of timber or of German or Hungarian metals. Meanwhile, the Iberian peninsula was for Genoa, and to a lesser extent for Florence, the great region where their merchants undertook their most profitable trading. This was a development of an earlier state of affairs: more than once we have mentioned commercial bonds between western Italy, on the one hand, and Spain and Portugal, on the other. Since the twelfth century Genoa had occupied a major position in the export of the oil produced by these countries. The Genoese shared to a great extent in Spanish and Portuguese expansion into Africa and into the Atlantic islands. This expansion had begun with the Portuguese conquest of Ceuta on the coast of the western Maghreb in 1415; in the course of the century this conquest was followed by a series of military settlements on the Maghreb, the Mediterranean, and finally Atlantic coasts. Trade with the interior through the intermediary of these *presidios* was largely in the hands of the Genoese and especially of those Genoese who had settled in Spain. Between 1325 and 1339, Malocello, a Genoese in Portuguese service, had discovered the Canaries off the cost of Africa. Expeditions to this archipelago were undertaken in the fourteenth century by the Portuguese, the Aragonians, and the Castilians, with the aid of Italian navigational technicians. In 1403, Castile established her authority over these islands. The data shown on fourteenth-century maps—commonly but improperly called "portolanos"—lead us to believe that at the same time Italian or Catalan navigators had explored the coasts of more distant archipelagoes, including the Azores.

The Portuguese considerably extended the area of European expansion in the Atlantic up to the end of the century. They were not alone in possessing the technical means that allowed them to sail farther out into the ocean than had been done hitherto. Since the fourteenth century Mediterranean ships had been using hinged stern rudders, which had already been widely used in the Baltic and North Seas during the thirteenth century. The "caravelle," a three-master with even sides and large sails, which was armed with a fairly effective artillery, was in use in Castile and in Aragon as well as in Portugal. The compass with a magnetic needle—used by the Vikings—fixed on a pivot and combined with a compass card was known in the fourteenth century. But Portuguese expeditions had an additional advantage: their technical preparation, which was due to the initiative of one of the sons of King John I, the "infant" Henry, known as the Navigator (1394–1460), who surrounded himself with pilots, mathematicians, and cartographers in order to study the possibilities of new maritime expeditions. The Portuguese occupied Madeira in 1425, the Azores in 1427; they rounded Cape Bojador in 1434 and Cape Verde in 1445; they discovered the Cape Verde Islands from 1456 onward and reached the Ivory Coast in 1470. The Portuguese had both military and religious motives in attacking the coast of the Maghreb: namely, to fight Islam, to spread the Christian faith, and to occupy pirate strongholds. Similar aims guided the first oceanic expeditions. This does not imply that they had few economic concerns, and if they did lack them at first, they soon acquired them. In any event, the economic effects of these discoveries were not long in making themselves felt. The Portuguese and the Italians, particularly the Genoese, who had settled in the peninsula, immediately organized trade with territories conquered or known. A trade in black slaves arose, replacing the slave trade from the hinterlands of the Black Sea. Lisbon became a great market. The spice trade flourished—mainly in *malaguette*, or "false pepper," from the coast of Guinea. Soon enough, in competition with Venetian sugar producers of Cyprus, the Portuguese introduced the cultivation of Sicilian sugar cane to Madeira. In the second half of the century molasses was sold at Lisbon, Bruges and Antwerp. Apparently the Portuguese benefited, in these commercial undertakings which they established in the middle of their colonial settlements, not only from the help of numerous Italians, but from the experience the latter had acquired in their Levantine colonies.

The Portuguese trade in colonial goods contributed to the development of Antwerp. From the end of the fourteenth century ships set out for the northwestern part of the Continent, unloading their cargoes and taking on return freight in the Zeeland port of Middelburg, close to the estuary of the western Scheldt, rather than at Bruges or in one of its approach ports. This trade continued during the fifteenth century. Sometimes shipping was diverted, and from Middelburg goods were transported to Bruges or Antwerp. When the Portuguese had more colonial goods to sell, they sent them to Bruges. But the continued presence at Antwerp of merchants from western Germany and soon from southern Germany—now developing rapidly—induced the Portuguese to prefer this latter port where they found an abundant demand for their own goods. Furthermore, these Germans were the producers or sellers of cotton goods and copper goods, which were in great demand among the African populations. The attractive theory has been offered that in order to settle their liabilities, the Portuguese made payments in Sudanese gold earned by their sales of cheap goods in Africa. Be that as it may, these contacts among the Portuguese, the west Germans, and the south Germans made Antwerp, after the second half of the fifteenth century, an exceedingly important international market. By the end of the century its importance grew even more through the appearance there of the great south German merchant bankers; chief among them were the Fuggers of Augsburg, whose wealth came from silver mines in the Tyrol. They involved themselves in the trade in colonial goods. Bruges, on the other hand, fell into a decline: her prosperity, linked to that of the Italian trade with the Levant and to that of the Hanse, suffered from their decline; by the end of the century she was a second-class city whose only important market was Spanish wool.

Perhaps the drainage of Sudanese gold by the Portuguese explains the lack of means of payment complained of in the end of the first half of the fifteenth century. Among the attempts to remedy their situation, recourse was had to the striking of new and pure silver coins, notably in Germany (the *Joachimstaler-groschen*, or taler) : this was made possible by an improvement in the mining of this precious metal in Bohemia and southern Germany.

The role of the great Italian banks in international trade became still more important. They involved themselves in diversified enterprises, combining the trade in goods and sometimes industry with banking operations. As in the past, we find such houses in all the important Italian centers: at Genoa, at Lucca, at Venice, and at Florence. Furthermore, they maintained their particular character in these various cities. The Florentine houses require special attention because of their extensive operations. Resounding failures in the middle of the fourteenth century caused the companies that were not involved in the collapse, and the newer firms, to be more prudent. Among certain of them, however, this caution did not exclude an aggressive business policy. Such was the case with a new firm that was both banker, merchant, and industrialist—that of the Medici. The members of this family had established branches in Rome, Venice, Milan, Pisa, Genoa (later replaced by Lyon), Bruges, London, and Avignon. But usually they were separate companies, controlled and directed by the mother house—a system that offset the risks. Certain of these branches specialized: thus the house of Bruges, without excluding other banking and commercial activities, attached particular importance to the trade in Tolfa alum, extracted in the Church States. The Medicis, who until 1471 benefited from pontifical patronage, were doubtless the greatest international businessmen of their time. However, they failed before the end of the century. They had linked their fate with the house of Burgundy, and they were seriously affected by the defeats of Charles the Bold. As we shall see, they were to become leaders of the Florentine state. Furthermore, in Italy itself after the seventies, they were the victims of their foreign and Florentine enemies, which by 1474 included the papacy. Theirs was a particularly striking example of the direct effect of international politics on the fate of a great international commercial and banking enterprise.

The great Italian commercial and banking houses had their imitators, mostly in southern Germany. The most famous was founded at the end of the fourteenth century at Ravensburg near Constance by Joseph Hompys (*die grosse Ravensburger Gesellschaft*) : it placed factors in Italy, Spain, France, Avignon, Hungary, Bruges, and Antwerp, to say nothing of many German cities. It was not the only one to prosper in the sixteenth century. In France, even by the end of the Hundred Years War, houses of that kind played less important roles. However there were several great businessmen involved in multiple activities, such as Jacques Coeur who, during the reign of Charles VII, accumulated lucrative public posts and the farming of taxes, along with the exploitation of mines, trade in silk, spices, and slaves, and maritime transport in the Mediterranean.

We must mention also the provision for regular meetings of merchants of various countries and native merchants in specified places in certain towns to discuss business. This fact should be stressed because in many towns, principally German towns, foreign merchants were rigorously subjected to "the law of the guests" (*Gästerecht*) and as a result were authorized to treat only with local merchants and only in certain kinds of business: trading between "guests," that is, between strangers, was on the whole forbidden. Meetings of this type regularly took place in Venice, but foreign participation was strictly limited. However, at Bruges during the fifteenth century these meetings brought together chiefly Italians, but also Spaniards, Portuguese, Englishmen, Scotsmen, Germans, French, and the people of Bruges. The latter were sometimes merchants but, more often than not, brokers, and as such they played an important role in the transactions: sometimes they acted as general agents of foreign merchants in Bruges. These meetings were all the more important, as Bruges at the time was not only a great market for goods, but a very important financial market, and the buying and selling of bills of exchange was widely practiced. The merchants gathered

in a square called the "Bourse" (*beurs* in Dutch), named after a
hostelry that belonged to the Uter Beurse family; thus the gather-
ings themselves took the name of "bourse" (*bursa, beurs*): the
name has remained the same in French, Dutch, Italian, and
German.

The growing complexity of economic factors should not obscure other aspects of fifteenth-century international relations.
Schism was the most serious crisis to affect relations in the religious world. In 1378 a majority of the cardinals, who considered
residence at Rome uncomfortable and continually menaced by
popular uprisings, declared null the papal election of that year
and deposed Pope Urban VI, who was entirely unwilling to leave
the Eternal City. They elected as pope Cardinal Robert of
Geneva, with the name of Clement VII, and obtained support for
him from the King of France. Clement returned to Avignon and
settled there. Christendom was split into two camps: "Urbanists,"
that is the majority of Italians, Germans, Scandinavians, English,
Portuguese, and Flemings; and "Clementists," that is, the majority
of the French, apart from those of the county of Flanders, the
Castilians, the Aragonians, the Navarrese, the Savoyards, the
Neapolitans, and the Scottish. The religious scandal, and the an-
guish caused by this war between the two alleged leaders of
the Church, created considerable support for movements hostile to
the absolute power of the papacy. These movements explain the
audacity shown by the cardinals in 1378; but these same movements, now fed by indignation and by deep concern arising in the
breasts of the faithful in every land, produced the opinion that a
general council should be called to reform the Church. On more
than one occasion in the fourteenth century it had been claimed
that a general council was qualified to pass judgment on the pope.
Both Philip the Fair and Louis of Bavaria had proclaimed this;
but they were kings, and the calling of a council to meet would
have served their policies. Since the schism, it was theologians and

moralists who made claims for conciliar authority over the Holy See. The masters of the University of Paris, who enjoyed great prestige among their colleagues—the old universities of which the more important have been cited, and also the newer ones, growing up in the fourteenth and fifteenth centuries, such as Prague, Pavia, Cologne, Louvain, and Glasgow, to name a few of the better known—played a major role in this movement. Pierre d'Ailly and Jean de Gerson were among the spokesmen who reached the largest audiences. The first efforts only complicated the issues. The Council of Pisa (1409) deposed Gregory XII, the Roman pope living at Rimini under the protection of the Malatesta family, and Benedict XIII, the Avignon pope, who resided at Perpignan under the protection of the King of Aragon. The council then elected Alexander V. Since both the deposed popes refused to accept deposition, there were now three popes in the place of two.

A resurgence of imperial ideology facilitated a final decision. Sigismund, of the house of Luxembourg, king of the Romans, was persuaded that the role of protector of the Church and architect of peace among Christians belonged to him; he forced Pope John XXIII, a former *condottiere* and successor to Alexander V, to call a new council. Sigismund had a powerful influence over the council when it met at Constance from 1414 to 1418. The deposition of all three popes and the election of Martin V in 1417 as the new pope put an end to the "Great Western Schism." On the other hand, "the reform of the Church in her leadership and in her members," the need for which this painful crisis had revealed, could not be achieved either at Constance or at Basel, where a new council sat from 1431 to 1449. At the closing of the latter, the Church fathers once again proclaimed the superior authority of the council. But their failure was very obvious, and the papacy, under Nicholas V, had re-established its full authority over the Church. Hopes for reform remained only stronger and more widespread.

In the same period other religious crises had shaken Christendom and had demonstrated the deep discontent over matters of dogma, ceremony, and piety. During the last quarter of the fourteenth century John Wycliffe, an Oxford theologian, preached against papal power, the episcopal hierarchy, transubstantiation, confessions, indulgences, clerical wealth, and the lack of spiritual energy in the members of the clergy. He offered the faithful an English translation of the Bible as the only true spiritual nourishment. The effects of this on the faithful was as far-reaching as was the hostility against the Avignon papacy and its taxation, which had been particularly heavy in England. Possibly the economic depression that the country was suffering at the time, contributed to the success of the movement. The persecution of the "Lollards"—as Wycliffe's disciples were called after his death in 1384—was violent but did not eradicate a spiritual attitude to which were linked certain aspects of the English Reformation of the sixteenth century.

It is very indicative, both of the religious feeling of the period and of the extent of relations between countries, that "Wycliffism" had repercussions in Bohemia. Under the direct influence of the English reformer, a Czech theologian, Jan Hus, founded a religious movement that had the same goals as Wycliffe's. There was an essential difference between the two: although Hus demanded communion under both species, he accepted transubstantiation. This was not the first time that such doctrines had been expressed in Bohemia, but Hus's preaching met with immense success. Although he had been given a royal safe-conduct, he was called before the Council of Constance and there condemned to death; he was burned at the stake in 1415. But "Hussitism" did not die out. On the contrary, it not only grew but developed into a revolution with nationalist tendencies directed against all things German: the King and his agents, the colonists of the mining districts, the German bourgeoisie in the cities, and the Silesian Germans. It was only much later, in 1434, after ferocious wars, that Hussitism and Czech nationalism were eradicated. But in order to achieve this, the Emperor and the Council of Basel in 1433 had to grant political and religious concessions to win over the moderate elements. Among these were taxes and communion under both species. Final agreement was reached in 1436.

At this time, war had broken out again between France and England. Both countries had undergone formidable internal crises. In England there were social troubles under Richard II (1377–1399); the latter's deposition by his cousin Henry IV (1399–1413), head of the house of Lancaster; uprisings among the great aristocratic families; and struggles waged by Parliament against absolutism during both these reigns. In foreign affairs, even if we omit the Hundred Years War, Richard led two futile expeditions against Ireland to restore effective English authority, which had been neglected owing to its engagements in France. During both reigns there were revolts in Wales that required military intervention, and ceaseless conflicts with Scotland, allied to France, which involved fighting on the Border and even the threat of a French fleet in 1385, though this came to nothing. Nevertheless, despite everything, Henry IV succeeded in restoring order in his kingdom; and when he died, Henry V (1413–1422) was able to resume the war against France.

The French situation was more than desperate. Since the accession of Charles VI (1380–1422) the internal situation had rapidly deteriorated, especially as a result of exploitation of the country by the King's uncles. In 1381 and 1382 social troubles had broken out in Paris, Rouen, and Amiens, among other towns, and in the farmlands of Languedoc. There were even signs of solidarity between some of these movements and the great revolt of the working people in the Flemish towns, led by the weavers of Ghent in 1380. The latter were supported by large sections of the urban populations of Brabant, of the district of Liège, and of other areas. Probably the depression and its effect on the living standards of the working population lay at the root of most of these uprisings. Only after the King had crushed the Flemish rebels at Westrozebeke in 1382—at the request of his uncle, the Duke of Burgundy, Philip the Bold, a son-in-law of the Count of Flanders—was he able to crush completely rebellion in the French towns and countryside. The situation worsened considerably when the King went mad in 1392. When the "princes of the blood" seized power, they began a complete dismemberment of the kingdom: each of the princes governed his own territories as a separate state. The quarrel that set Louis of Orléans, the King's brother, and his first cousin John the Fearless, duke of Burgundy, against each other, became a regular war after the assassination of the former in 1407. The country was torn apart by two factions: the Armagnacs (the Count of Armagnac was the father-in-law of Charles of Orléans, son of Louis) and the Burgundians.

The war between France and England had been somewhat sporadically pursued during the last years of Charles V and during the reign of Charles VI. Furthermore it was interrupted by truces. Fighting continued on occasion despite these truces, notably for Guyenne at the beginning of the fifteenth century. These conflicts were linked with the struggles of the Armagnacs and the Burgundians. But the war was not officially resumed until 1415. For France it was catastrophic: in the same year she suffered military disaster at Agincourt and the progressive occupation of the whole northern sector of the country. The mad King was in the hands of the English at Paris. When the Duke of Burgundy was assassinated in 1419, his son and successor, Philip the Good, accused the dauphin of having been the instigator of the crime and openly allied himself with the English. In 1420 he brought about the Treaty of Troyes, whereby Charles VI made Henry V his successor and entrusted him with the government of the kingdom. Several years later Charles VII (1422–1461) was a refugee at Bourges, controlling little north of the Loire and struggling vainly against the armies of Henry VI (1422–1471); there was then good reason to believe that the crowns of France and England were about to be reunited under an English sovereign. After the intervention in 1429 of a young visionary girl, Joan of Arc, events took a very different turn: supported by the enthusiasm of the soldiers and the people who believed in her providential mission, she won a series of military actions for the French troops. This was the beginning of a reconquest that was to last for a long time: that of Normandy was only achieved in 1450; that of Guyenne in 1453.

From the point of view of international relations, the Hundred Years War clearly has a twofold importance. The French victory prevented the dynastic union of the two kingdoms; that is, it prevented England, at this time a less attractive throne for her highly Frenchified kings, from becoming a dependency of France. But as far as we can see, the main effect of the Hundred Years War was the development of a national awareness in these two countries or, more precisely, the spreading of this awareness through many walks of life—an awareness that before this time was restricted to a very small number of individuals. The fact that at the same time the English language, though profoundly influenced by French, gradually replaced Anglicized French as the language of administration, of justice, and of the aristocracy in England contributed to the same result. It is hardly necessary to stress the importance of this development.

For England the second half of the fifteenth century was a period of relative decline, at least in the political arena. She, in turn, experienced a civil war—an effect in many respects of defeats suffered during the last phase of the Hundred Years War. We need not discuss this in a history of international relations. It is enough to state that it was a conflict between the house of Lancaster and another branch of the Plantagenet family, that of York. The "Wars of the Roses"—so named after the heraldic flowers that figure upon the arms of the two houses—began in 1455 and was interrupted on several occasions. It did not come to an end until 1485 with the victory and accession to the throne of a member of a third house, who was descended from the Lancastrians through the female line—Henry Tudor, the future King Henry VII. Beginning with his reign, the course of English history took a different turn; the era of continental adventures was over.

The Hundred Years War led to the birth of a new political unit, which was called upon to play a major role in international politics: the state of Burgundy. This was the work of Duke Philip the Good (1419–1467), who succeeded in joining most of the Low Country principalities to the duchy and the county of Burgundy, to Flanders and to Artois, which he inherited from his father: in short the major part of what is now Belgium, Netherland, Luxembourg and an important fraction of northern France. The English alliance and the peace of Arras, which he concluded with Charles VII in 1435, in fact made him independent of the Crown. In the case of the majority of the territories that stood under the higher authority of Germany, he managed to break the resistance of the German sovereigns, Wenceslas, king of the Romans, and finally the Emperor Sigismund. They were both hostile to Burgundian policy: not only because Burgundy scorned the futile pretensions that the empire still pursued in regard to its purely theoretical authority over the western territories, but more particularly because as members of the Luxembourg dynasty they themselves aspired to its further aggrandizement in the Low Countries. Charles the Bold (1467–1477) sought to exceed his father's successes and to join his possessions in the Low Countries ("pays de par-deçà") with the duchy and the county of Burgundy ("pays de par-delà"); to subjugate Lorraine and Alsace, and to obtain a royal crown from the Emperor for the great state that he dreamed of building. A passionate and audacious person, incapable of adapting his aims to his means, he failed completely. The King of France, Louis XI, succeeded in involving him with the Swiss, who inflicted resounding defeats upon him. Charles died fighting the Duke of Lorraine. The political edifice constructed by the dukes did not, however, founder entirely in 1477, despite the efforts of Louis XI, who seized Artois and the two Burgundies. A united existence under one single dynasty had created a basis for cohesion in the Low Countries. Marie of Burgundy, daughter of Charles the Bold, and her husband, Archduke Maximilian, a Hapsburg and son of the Emperor Frederick III, found support among their subjects. The "Burgundian state" survived. But although Artois and the Franche-Comté were restored to the Burgundian state in 1493 by Charles VIII, son of Louis XI, this state no longer included the duchy of Burgundy proper or the protectorate over the episcopal principality of Liège.

The struggle against Charles the Bold was virtually a necessity for Louis XI (1461–1483). The great reconstruction effort that had to be achieved in France after the Hundred Years War—the renewed cultivation of abandoned land, the re-establishment of interrupted commercial relations—was the work of individuals. However, in the area of politics, the task belonged to royalty. It took the form primarily of a struggle against the fragmentation of the country by the princes of the blood who, since the reign of Charles VI, tended to conduct themselves as sovereigns within their own appanages. Under Louis XI the holders of these appanages, the Duke of Brittany and other great lords, found a leader in Charles the Bold. As Count of Charolais in the reign of his father and then as leader of the state of Burgundy, he fought a ferocious war against the King. This struggle even affected the Wars of the Roses: the King supported the Lancastrians; and the Duke, the Yorkists; and vice versa. Charles was beaten, as were the other princes. Only the Duke of Brittany maintained his autonomy and in fact his independence. The danger of seeing France revert to the political condition of the twelfth century—a condition like that to which Germany had been reduced—was a distinct possibility. Louis XI forestalled this event. He even extended the frontiers of the kingdom: Provence, the last southern vestige of the kingdom of Arles, was annexed when the appanage of the house of Anjou once again came under the immediate authority of the Crown; Cerdagne and Roussillon were taken from Aragon; but Navarre passed from the French sphere of influence into that of Aragon.

Sigismund of Luxembourg, who was elected king of the Romans in 1410 and crowned emperor at Rome in 1433, has been mentioned more than once. His two predecessors—his brother Wenceslas (1378–1400), a political jumping-jack and a drunkard, and Robert of Bavaria—were politically powerless. Sigismund, as aware of the interests of his house as any territorial prince, was conscious of his imperial duties. This is seen with regard to the schism, Church reform, and even the lands comprising the "state of Burgundy." But this awareness also manifested itself in other ways: for instance, his interventions, though vain, to end the Hundred Years War. The universalist conception of empire, which had never corresponded to any material reality, continued to be argued in doctrinal works. The lawyers who sat in the supreme tribunal of the empire (Reichskammergericht), and who paved the way there for the "Reception" of Roman law as a general supplementary legal code for all of Germany, considered this universalism fundamental to their ideology. This doctrine, and at the same time the affirmation of the role reserved to Germany as the material support of the empire, found a particularly vigorous interpreter in Cardinal Nicholas of Cues.

Sigismund was the last German sovereign who tried to mold these concepts into reality. His pretensions were ludicrous. Not only was he totally restricted by the Hussite war, but he was unable to impose peace among the princes and the urban leagues of southwestern and western Germany, whose struggles are important in the history of international relations. For although Germany, or the empire with whom she became increasingly closely identified, remained a political unit, at the same time the principalities and even the urban leagues and the cities that had obtained the privilege of being subject only to the Empire

—the imperial cities—conducted themselves more and more as real states. Two of those principalities belonging to "colonial" Germany, should be specifically mentioned here because of the roles they were called upon to play later: the marquisate of Brandenburg, and Austria. It is enough to point out that in 1415–1417 Sigismund gave the former as a fief to Frederick of Hohenzollern, the burgrave of Nürnberg. For a long time Austria was divided between two branches of the Hapsburg family, and the latter spent their energy unsuccessfully attempting to conquer the Swiss, whose confederation had continued to grow. The situation did not noticeably improve when in 1438 and 1440, respectively, Albert II and Frederick III, both Hapsburgs, became "kings of the Romans." The situation changed only toward the end of the reign of Frederick who, in 1452, was the last emperor to have himself crowned at Rome. His son Maximilian, elected king of the Romans in 1486, restored the unity of Austria, elevated it to an archduchy, and grouped around it other territories, such as the Tyrol. Thus he gained a solid territorial basis for his house.

In the fifteenth century there was a marked decline in German influence in eastern and northeastern Europe. Hungary, acquired by Sigismund in 1388, and Bohemia escaped the rule of German dynasties when Albert II, the son-in-law and heir of his predecessor, died. These two kingdoms were thereafter ruled by various national or Polish sovereigns. At the end of the century, moreover, a son of the Polish king occupied the thrones of both Bohemia and Hungary. In the north the decline of German power was even greater. We have already mentioned the decline of the Hanse, which was obvious in the area of politics as well as in economic wealth. Nevertheless it remained a power to be reckoned with. However, the Teutonic Knights had been severely tried. Defeated by the Poles and the Lithuanians at Tannenberg in 1410, the order was forced to sign a very unfavorable peace at Thorn in 1411. Moreover, wars continued. These wars had a much greater importance for Poland—now united by dynasty with Lithuania—as the Turkish advance was cutting her off from the Black Sea. Expansion toward the Baltic was now essential. In 1466 the Teutonic Knights were forced to conclude a second peace at Thorn and had finally to abandon western Prussia, which was systematically "Polanized." The order had to accept Polish suzerainty over eastern Prussia. The northern territories—Kurland, Livonia, Estonia—were thereafter completely isolated, with all the dangers that this situation implied.

The great Poland of the Jagellon dynasty, together with Hungary, formed a rampart for Christian Europe against the Turkish threat. This threat became progressively more real during the century. In the first quarter of the century Ottoman pressure did not make itself too heavily felt. The Byzantine Empire even succeeded in once more bringing the Latin part of Morea under its authority. Here a Genoese, Centurione Zaccaria, had succeeded the Navarrese rulers. Byzantine Morea, and its capital of Mistra, was an extremely lively center of culture at the end of the fourteenth century and at the beginning of the fifteenth; and its flowering belongs to the history of international relations. Its philosophical movement strongly influenced the renaissance of Italian neoplatonism, and its painting has left a deep imprint on the religious art of the Christian population of eastern Europe.

The Turkish advance, however, began again in 1421. In her effort to resist, Byzantium had to resort to diplomatic overtures and feeble military forces. The idea of the crusade was by no means dead, and concrete plans were still being worked out in the fifteenth century: the most energetic were those of Philip the Good, duke of Burgundy, but they never materialized. Had expeditions actually set out, they might have acted as a diversion and assisted the defense of Christendom. Emperor John VIII (1425–1448) came to the West to seek assistance. None was granted him. The Greek schism was an obstacle, and although in 1439 unity was re-established at the Council of Ferrara-Florence, the decision was ineffectual: the Christian East chose to remain Christian in her own manner, and the Christian West refused to yield. Only the kings of Hungary took military action, but they were defeated by the Turks at Varna in 1444 and at Kossovo in 1448. Constantinople, beseiged by Sultan Mahomet II, fell during the night of May 28-29, 1453. Constantine XI, the last Roman emperor, fell fighting to the end. In the following years the other Christian territories of the Near East—Greek or Latin—were conquered one by one: Byzantine Morea, and the Florentine duchy of Athens, much of the archipelago, the Greek empire of Trebizond, and the Italian settlements on the Black Sea fell at the same time as their Tatar neighbors. In 1480 the Christians still held Crete and Cyprus, the islands to the west of Greece, some enclaves on the Peloponnesian coast belonging to Venice, the Genoese island of Chios, and Rhodes, held by the Hospitalers.

Those continental Christian populations that had been nurtured upon the finest flowers of Byzantine civilization, also suffered from the Turkish conquest, accompanied as it was by a resurgence of Moslem fanaticism: what remained of autonomous Serbia was completely conquered by the Sultan, and Albania suffered the same fate. More successful in the defense of their autonomy were Moldavia and Wallachia, which lay between the Balkans and the Carpathians, and whose population was descended from the Roman colonists of Dacia and recently leavened by Slavs and Bulgarians. Russia was beyond the grasp of the Turks. During the second half of the century Ivan III, great prince of Moscow, succeeded in conquering a series of Russian principalities, including, as we know, the republic of Novgorod. He shattered the last remnants of his subordination to the Tatars. In some respects he presented himself as the heir to the Byzantine Empire, and his marriage in 1472 to a niece of the last emperor strengthened this illusion.

Turkish power, dominating the greater part of the Near East and firmly rooted in the European continent, created serious political problems. They would have been even more serious had not Mamaluke Egypt still escaped Ottoman rule, and had not the Moslem states of Ifrikia and of the Maghreb not been paralyzed by wars and civil conflicts. This state of affairs made somewhat easier the Portuguese conquests we have already discussed. It also facilitated the last phase of the Spanish *reconquista.* This Christian counteroffensive did not, however, take place until the end of the century: international conflicts and interior struggles had burdened the Christian kingdoms of the peninsula. Aragon was the greatest political and economic power in the western Mediterranean in the fifteenth century. King Alfonso V even succeeded in 1442 in ousting a French prince of the blood, René of Anjou, count of Provence and duke of Lorraine, who claimed the crown of Naples, and he joined this kingdom to his other states. After his death, however, Aragon was threatened by a terrible revolt in Catalonia which lasted from 1461 to 1472, and which allowed the King of France to nibble at the monarchy's pyrenean possessions. King John II finally re-established royal authority. Castile had long been prey to dissension or revolt among aristocratic groups, and the intrigues of Aragon, Portugal, and France destroyed royal authority; this authority was re-established only after 1469, when Isabella, the last heiress to the house of Trastamare, married Ferdinand, heir to Aragon. They were joint monarchs of Castile in 1474, and Ferdinand became king of Aragon in 1479. This personal union of the two great Iberian kingdoms allowed the war against Islam to be resumed again. It was undertaken in 1485, and in 1491 with the fall of Granada the Christian reconquest, which had been going on since the ninth century, was finally accomplished. The spirit of the reconquest was to remain and to produce a markedly national flavor in Spanish relations with the exterior.

We have been able to discern certain general patterns in Spanish affairs during this period. We cannot do the same within the range of this book for Italy, so complex was her situation—

even more so than in the previous century. We must confine ourselves to a brief outline. The peninsula was prey to constant struggles, but the outcome altered nothing. Every state sought to extend its territorial power, sought alliances to this end, hired mercenaries, a *condottiere*, a prince, or an adventurer. If a state gained victories that could assure it of predominance, another state would undertake to form a league against it; and war once more broke out. Foreign powers participated. The interference of the "king of the Romans" or of the emperor became sporadic; on occasion it consisted of support given this or that Italian potentate, or of titles granted one, such as that of duke obtained from Wenceslas in 1395 by the lord of Milan, John Galeas Visconti. Altogether, little enough was accomplished. A more active role was played by the French—especially by the princes of the blood, Orléans and Anjou—and by the dukes of Burgundy than by the King. We have mentioned the King of Aragon's activities in Italy. As for purely Italian powers, the Pope deserves to be discussed first, be he the "Roman pope" during the schism or the "universal" pope thereafter. In terms of political activity, papal undertakings were more than ever essentially Italian and aimed at hegemony. It appears that the Holy See's main preoccupation was to guarantee itself an extensive and firm territorial base for its ecclesiastical sovereignty. It is hardly worth referring back to Naples or to a confused period of struggles between pretenders that began in 1382 with the death of Joan I and did not end before the Aragonian victory.

If we exclude the principalities and secondary lordships, whose role in the leagues was hardly negligible, we should still discuss the three Italian states of Venice, Milan, and Florence. In the fifteenth century Venice extended its domination over the eastern part of northern Italy, including Verona and Padua. Probably Venice found in this *terra firma* the resources necessary to defend its positions that were being threatened in the Levant and in the Adriatic. Milan was her main rival, for between the Lombard

territories where the dukes exercised their authority and the
Venetian *terra firma*, there were some contested territories, as
there were others farther south, fought over by Milan and Florence or by Milan and the Pope. Moreover, in 1450 the duchy of
Milan came into the hands of a *condottiere*, Francesco Sforza,
who succeeded in 1463 in laying hands on Genoa, which since
1396 had known only brief periods of independence between
periods of submission to France or to the Visconti. Florence,
which had for a long period kept its character of an urban
republic, became in its turn, in fact, a seigneurie. It was governed
from 1434 to 1494 by the Medici, powerful businessmen although they did not assume princely titles. These great international capitalists, who were also great friends of free thought and
great patrons of the arts, had long pursued a peaceful policy,
based on good relations with the pope, with France, and with the
Sforza. However, during the second half of the century they, too,
were drawn into the conflicts that ravaged Italy. Their fall no
longer pertains to the subject of this book.

Any history of international relations at the end of the Middle
Ages has to discuss certain intellectual and spiritual trends, especially humanism. This latter relates to older tendencies, which
underwent a remarkable development in Italy during the second
half of the fourteenth century and in the fifteenth century. Above
all, humanism must be seen as an attitude of mind, seeking to
offer man every spiritual, intellectual, moral, and physical possibility. Knowledge of the classical past was the means recommended to achieve this successfully: it allowed man to model his
soul and his character on those of the men and citizens of the
ancient world, who were taken as the most perfect examples of
man aware of his grandeur. This was an attitude that at the same
time induced a deeper study of ancient texts and a major revision
of current philosophical tenets. These spiritual, intellectual, and
moral attitudes spread from Italy to other western lands and

contributed to the founding of other centers of humanistic thought. French or German humanism of the second half of the fifteenth century—that of Lefèvre d'Étaples, of Wimpfeling, or of Reuchlin—could not have been conceived without the philological criticism of Lorenzo Valla, or the neoplatonic constructions of Marsilio Ficino, or the cabalistic speculations of Pico della Mirandola.

We will not discuss the Renaissance here—the transposition of humanist thought into the plastic arts. It is in the sixteenth century that the Renaissance was an essential element in international relations. On the other hand, it seems essential to say a few words about the effect humanism had on religious life and on the Church. The fifteenth century humanists had all been Christians and had often been willing to serve the Christian faith. But their attacks upon the routine forms of theological or philosophical instruction, their conflicts with certain ecclesiastical authorities or certain groups in the Church hierarchy, above all with the regular clergy, contributed to the decline of the authority of the Church and of those who spoke in her name. In every country the effect of humanism was linked with the manifestation of an increasingly critical spirit in matters pertaining to the papacy and its institutions. Papal policy in Italy, the reorganization of papal financial policies, the increasingly frequent use of the sale of indulgences, favoritism in the granting of benefices, and the pope's claim to supremacy within the Church after the great councils had affirmed their own superiority—all scandalized many people. Criticism of the papacy and the renewed signs of the desire for reform of the Church recognized no frontiers. These criticisms took various forms in various countries: "Wycliffist" or "Hussite" traditions in England and in Bohemia; the desire of French theologians and lawyers to have the liberties of the French Church respected; an anti-Roman sentiment among many of the German humanists. But essentially it was a state of mind widespread in western Europe, especially among cultivated people.

It spread more rapidly after the discovery of a simple mechanical printing process: printing on paper by means of movable metal type. It appeared toward the middle of the century in Avignon, at Mainz, at Bruges, and at Haarlem. A Bible, with forty-two lines to the page, printed in 1450 or thereabouts by Johann Gutenberg at Mainz, began production. We cannot claim that the first printing done elsewhere was independent of that of Gutenberg; in any event, once the process was general knowledge, movements among printers from place to place were constant; and these movements increased the use of printing. To cite a single example, Caxton learned at Bruges the printing techniques that he introduced to England. There is no doubt that acquisition of the means to broadcast thought in a practically limitless manner constitutes one of the most important facts in the history of international relations at the end of the Middle Ages.

12

The Practice of International Relations
in the Last Three Centuries of the Middle Ages

BUILDING UP AN ACCOUNT of the technique of international relations during the thirteenth, fourteenth, and fifteenth centuries is an arduous task. The major difficulty to be overcome is probably the abundance of primary sources. This is the result of both the intensity of these relations—henceforth far greater—and their increasing complexity. This in itself is an aspect of the story we are trying to tell: it is perhaps its essential characteristic. The same could be said of all the aspects of international life, but it is particularly justifiable in respect to negotiations. During the last centuries of the Middle Ages negotiations were constantly in progress; doubtless in certain parts of western Europe and in Italy negotiations played a more important role than did war— and God knows wars in Italy were common enough!

As in the preceding centuries, the later Middle Ages saw direct negotiations between heads of states. We cannot, of course, list even the most important. They were particularly numerous between the kings of England and the kings of France from the Treaty of Paris, concluded in 1259, to the beginnings of the Hundred Years War: feudal-vassal relations between the two sovereigns, and the enormous number of problems that they raised, were at the same time both the object and the cause of these negotiations. Meetings took place between sovereigns even during the war, such as the meeting at Ardres in 1396 between Charles VI and Richard II, where they tried to put an end to the hostilities by marrying the King of England to the daughter of the King of France.

Certain German sovereigns also practiced personal negotiations. It was on the initiative of Louis of Bavaria that the meeting at Koblenz took place with Edward III in 1338; this was the point of departure of the first phase—the international phase—of the Hundred Years War. The Luxembourgs were about to undertake journeys to meet the warring sovereigns and to attempt to re-establish peace among Christians. With these goals in mind, Charles IV undertook a solemn visit to Charles V, king of France, in 1378, and Sigismund visited the King of England, Henry V, in 1416. Neither of them was a match for his host; they were forced into an *entente cordiale* which lacked every efficiency. At least Sigismund received English support for the solution of the Great Schism. During meetings of this sort personages of lesser rank also negotiated. Even the leading role was played by someone other than the sovereign: such was the case at the meeting at Ardres when on the French side, the Duke of Burgundy, Philip the Bold, conducted negotiations with Richard II. Philip was a re-markable negotiator: he demonstrated this during numerous meet-ings with Joan, duchess of Brabant; it was he who was able to bring her officially to designate, in 1396, the second son of the duke, Antony, as heir, thus preparing the union of Brabant with the other "Burgundian" territories.

Meetings between sovereigns were frequently preceded by dis-cussions between lesser persons. Philip the Fair thought it incon-venient to proceed in any other manner. The ceremonial sur-rounding these meetings—descriptions of which still charm the readers of Froissart—often had their own significance. Charles V, during his visit in Paris, offered the Emperor Charles IV a power-ful black charger while he himself mounted a white steed: he did this because the king of France in no way appeared to recognize imperial authority, one of whose symbols was a white mount. The meeting place for such interviews varied considerably. Among other examples, the fact that the *basileus* ever more frequently did not refuse private negotiations unless they took place in his capital, was a sign of the decline of the Byzantine Empire: the humiliating requests made personally by John V in Hungary and Italy between 1366 and 1371, those of John VIII in Italy from 1437 to 1439 bear eloquent witness to this new state of affairs. Although rare in the West, it happened that meetings took place in the marches, such as that between Philip the Fair and the King of the Romans, Albert of Austria, in 1299, and that between the French town of Vaucouleurs and the German town of Toul. On occasion, for reasons of prestige and security, the meetings took place on the middle of a bridge: the most famous examples are the conversations between the dauphin Charles (the future Charles VII) and the Duke of Burgundy, John the Fearless, on the bridge of Montereau on the Yonne in 1419; and those between Louis XI and the King of England, Edward IV, on the bridge of Picquigny on the Somme in 1475. The murder of John the Fearless by the dauphin's men demonstrates that direct negotiations were not without an element of danger for the parties present. When Louis XI was made prisoner by Charles the Bold in 1468 during the meeting at Péronne, and when he saw himself obliged to participate in the suppression of the Liège revolt provoked by his own emissaries, his thoughts must have run along these lines. In any event, Philippe de Comines reflected on his master's downfall when he labeled such meetings "grand follie."

The sovereigns also used correspondence in their relations with foreign governments. Letters and other documents were borne to their destination by messengers—"horse riders" (Fr.: *chevaucheurs*). It happened however that they were entrusted to envoys of higher rank, with or without instructions to comment upon them. This was sometimes the case with a declaration of war: in 1337, Edward III instructed the Bishop of Lincoln, who was accompanied by the earls of Northampton and Suffolk and a large entourage, to deliver to Philip VI the letters of defiance that began the Hundred Years War. On other occasions writings intimating the state of the war to an enemy or transmitting verbal communications on this subject were made by heralds-at-arms.

The use of correspondence in the conduct of foreign affairs appears to have risen in importance during the last centuries of the Middle Ages. One can cite as an example the 252 letters sent by Richard II or in his name to foreign courts between 1377 and 1399. There were doubtless many more. It is true that this series of letters came from England—that is to say from a country where central power had more frequent recourse to the written word than any other country north of the Alps.

Nevertheless, throughout this period, as during preceding centuries, foreign relations were more often than not conducted by envoys. Furthermore, these latter and the frequency of their missions abroad increased in number. The figure of 125 people whom the King of England, Edward III, charged with such missions between 1327 and 1339, is a typical example, even if one considers that these years either immediately preceded the Hundred Years War or belonged to its first phase. These envoys were still recruited from very different milieus. At Byzantium they were the highest government officials and courtiers, high-ranking clerics, and often, since the fourteenth century, learned men who were skilled by their profession at haranguing the other party. In the West they were members of the great and lesser aristocracy, bishops, and, much more than in the past (we will come back to this), civil servants having had, when possible, a legal training. But other people were also charged with negotiating abroad: during the fourteenth century Venice, on more than one occasion, dispatched captains of her galleys on missions to the King of England. Sometimes the sovereigns even called upon very lowly people who had their confidence: the King of the Romans, Charles IV, sent two of his jesters to Strasbourg, a free city within the empire; and in 1477 Louis XI sent Olivier LeDaim, a Flemish *petit bourgeois* whom he had made his barber, to the Low Countries. One should not forget that the wives of sovereigns were occasionally given diplomatic missions: well known are those that Lucrezia, wife of Piero de' Medici, "lord" of Florence, and of

Beatrice d'Este, wife of Lodovico the Moor, duke of Milan, respectively, accomplished in 1467 to the Pope and in 1493 to the Most Serene Republic of Venice. As in the past, certain personalities were chosen for specific missions for their particular abilities. This was a widespread practice and was also common in the Byzantine Empire and in the Moslem or Mongol states. When the Ilkhan of Persia, Arghun, tried unsuccessfully to mount a combined Mongol and Latin offensive against the Mamelukes, he sent embassies to the Pope, Philip the Fair, and Edward I and gave the command of these missions to Christians: in 1287 to the Nestorian priest, Rabban Çauma; in 1289 to the Genoese merchant established in Persia, Buscarel de Gisolf. The same type of preoccupation inspired the western sovereigns who in certain cases gave diplomatic missions to foreigners: more than once Italian businessmen were found in the service of the kings of France or England, or of the dukes of Burgundy, when a mission abroad was a financial one. Musciato Guidi (whom the French called Mouche), a Florentine in the service of Philip the Fair; Antonio di Passano, a Genoese, and Andrea Portinari, a Florentine, in the service of Edward III; and Dino and Giovanni Rapondi, Luccans in the service of Philip the Bold and John the Fearless are among the examples that it is fruitless to multiply.

We come across an increasing tendency toward specialization of the personnel in foreign service: but this was only a tendency, and there was as yet no indication of the founding of a cadre or a diplomatic corps. The phenomenon occurred in England particularly since the reign of Edward I, when the same people were sent abroad as envoys or as members of an ambassadorial entourage. This was true, from this reign on, of high-ranking clerics and royal officials, such as Walter Langton, bishop of Coventry and Litchfield and Master of the Wardrobe; of a great lord such as Hugh Despenser; or of a jurist like Francesco Accorso, son of the famous glossator. This Italian appears even to have been chiefly employed on missions to the peninsula, particularly to Rome.

Specialization in the objectives of negotiations increased in the fourteenth and fifteenth centuries: it can be observed during the reign of Edward III; high-ranking members of the clergy or the aristocracy, such as Henry Burghersh, bishop of Lincoln, William of Clinton, count of Huntington, Yves of Clinton, or a cleric like John of Thrandeston were men responsible for the Low Countries and western Germany. These few examples chosen from among many others suffice to give a distinct idea of the development of a practice that became widespread. Nevertheless, it is important to stress that this practice was also introduced into other countries in the fourteenth century, and was widespread by the fifteenth. Master Ulric of Augsburg, a cleric in the service of Louis of Bavaria and a specialist in the affairs of France and Avignon, and Nicholas Creyselmeister, a specialist in the affairs of the kingdom of Arles under Sigismund, can be cited as examples for the imperial court. Robert Dangeul, a ducal secretary, and Jean de Poucques, châtelain of Lille, and Nicholas Chavre, a Brabantine official in the service of Philip the Bold, count of Flanders and duke of Burgundy, were specialized agents of the latter for missions pertaining to Brabant and the lands between the Meuse and the Rhine. Again, many more examples could have been cited.

Embassies with large entourages remained very much in favor during the three centuries under discussion. One should stress the frequent presence of specialists among their members, "clerks of the chancery," preferably lawyers. This was the same throughout Europe. But, once more, it seems that England most often organized these well-balanced embassies: a great lord involved in the affairs of state, endowed with personal and social prestige; a bishop, who was or had been a high-ranking royal official; a few people of more modest background, with experience in commerce—for example, a leading English or Italian merchant; and one or two "clerks of the chancery." This is a simple outline of a type that had many variations.

The hierarchy among those sent abroad and their respective titles remained vague. The Latin term most generally used was *legatus*; *Nuntius* was the equivalent for a long time, but in the fifteenth century, there was a tendency to use it rather for envoys with a message to deliver, a communication to make, than for those charged with negotiation. From the thirteenth century on, the Italians, particularly the Venetians and the Pisans, more often than not employed the term *ambasciator*. The name became widespread in the following centuries. *Orator* should be considered a synonym. Sometimes the title of *procurator* was added to others; we shall soon be discussing such agents.

Only the Holy See, at least at the beginning of the fifteenth century, applied certain rules to these matters. However, it has been stated that since the pontificate of Innocent III, the permanent granting of the rank of legate (*legatus*) to individuals in the ecclesiastical hierarchy became very rare. The exceptions were a few metropolitans, who were granted the rank of legate because of their Church; from the beginning of the second half of the thirteenth century, these were known as *legati nati*, such as the Archbishop of Canterbury. They rarely played a major role in the conduct of international relations. The "legates" that we meet during the pontificate of Innocent III and his successors were generally *legati de latere* (sometimes *a* or *e latere*), a rank that was increasingly reserved for cardinals. Although there were some exceptions, this was general in the fourteenth and especially in the fifteenth centuries. These legates, representing the Pope himself, were charged with especially solemn or important missions of a religious, political, or financial nature and held wide powers in matters of jurisdiction and in the granting of benefices. We also find papal envoys who were called simply *legati*—sometimes they were called, at least nonofficially, *legati missi*—of episcopal or of archepiscopal rank, and whose powers were less extensive than those of the *legati de latere*. By the fifteenth century there were fewer of them, and they disappeared after 1460 or so.

On the other hand, those pontifical agents called *nuncius* took on increasing importance. We meet them frequently since the thirteenth century, and they multiplied during the following centuries. Their missions were very varied. The "nuncios," (called "messagés" in French during the fourteenth century) who should receive some attention here, were charged with missions to sovereigns and especially with negotiations. Their rank and authority was subordinate to that of legates. As a rule they had no jurisdictional power, and they could not grant benefices. Their title was *nuncius et orator Sedis Apostolicae*, the second noun emphasized the essentially political character of their missions. Among them we find archbishops and bishops and also clerics of less exalted rank, who were often attached to the pontifical bureaucracy. In the fifteenth century they were frequently given the powers of a legate *de latere* (*nuncius et orator Sedis Apostolicae cum potestate legati de latere*), which did not, however, give them equal rank to the latter. Sometimes they were granted other powers, particularly financial ones. It could be said that around 1460 they had in fact replaced legates other than those *de latere*. The Holy See made clear distinctions among the agents accredited to its court from the fifteenth century on. It recognized in an ambassador or an "orator" the role of personal representative of his lord: the latter spoke through the mouth of his envoy, while other agents spoke in the name of their lord. Only sovereign states were allowed to be represented by an ambassador at Rome; nonsovereign princes, towns, and urban leagues were denied this privilege, with the exception of "the seven German Electors."

Originally *procuratores* were very different from envoys charged with a political mission. They were often clerics and nearly always jurists (*legum professores*) or officials—sometimes they were all of these at the same time—charged with representing a party at a trial: in short, they were attorneys (Fr.: *procureurs*). Since the thirteenth century some of them handled the affairs of foreign powers at the Holy See: the kings of England, France, and Aragon maintained such men, as did princes like the counts of Flanders or associations like the Teutonic Knights. The multiple problems of application and the innumerable difficulties raised by or drawn up in the Treaty of Paris of 1259 led the King of England to appoint often *procuratores* to represent him at the Parliament of Paris until the eve of the Hundred Years War. However, *procuratores* were used on many other missions. Many negotiations presented simultaneously both legal and political aspects; thus the *procurator* more often than not became a diplomat of inferior rank in the fourteenth and fifteenth century, with the task of handling questions that did not require the dispatch of an ambassador. He spoke in the name of his master, but this latter was not present in the person of his *procurator*. At Rome in the fifteenth century the distinction between *procurator* and ambassador was even more clearly defined than elsewhere. On Easter Sunday in 1422 at Saint Peter's, during the Pope's mass, the Castilian ambassador and the Bishop of Chichester, the envoy of the King of England, exchanged blows over a matter of precedence. Pope Martin V ruled in favor of the Castilian diplomat because the latter was an *orator*, while Henry V's representative was, according to the Pope, only a *procurator*, and "that there was a world of difference between the function of an ambassador and that of a *procurator!*" The nature of the business that these procurers conducted often caused them to extend their visits or to make frequent journeys to the same place; should the occasion arise, this placed them in a position to furnish ambassadors with valuable information.

Among these negotiations we should make special mention of those involving a conference of some sort. By this we mean assemblies composed of representatives of two or more powers, brought together for the purpose of discussing common interests. During the centuries we are studying, these conferences can be divided into two categories, although it is not always easy to distinguish between them. Some were convened to resolve conflicts between agents of a power or private persons, and some aimed at putting an end to genuine international conflicts. We shall discuss the meetings of the first group later.

The Hundred Years War provided occasions for meetings of the second category. Some of these are famous. The Anglo-French conference at Avignon between October and December of 1344, summoned by Pope Clement VI, came to nothing. Anglo-French conferences took place at Calais and at Bruges between 1372 and 1377 through the initiative of Pope Gregory XI, who was represented by his nuncios. They were made possible by the good offices of the Count of Flanders, Louis de Male. The goal of the conferences—to put an end to the Hundred Years War—was not achieved, but they enabled truces to be set up. The Arras conference—an international congress which was attended by French, English, and Burgundians, and also a papal representative, envoys from the Council of Basel, from the Emperor, from the Spanish sovereigns, and from the King of Poland, etc.—lasted from August to September of 1435. Although peace was not concluded between France and England, it was between Charles VII and the Duke of Burgundy, Philip the Good. Sometimes meetings were arranged through negotiations which could last a long time; such was the case at Nevers and at Arras in 1435. At the meetings themselves the delegations were generally numerous and counted among their members a few chief councilors or officials of the sovereigns. Chancellor Nicolas Rolin was the most important Burgundian negotiator at the Congress of Arras. Much political maneuvering took place backstage. Similar conferences could have the most diverse aims: such was the case of an Anglo-papal conference that met in 1374 to solve a conflict over the taxes the Holy See was claiming on the English clergy. Wycliffe was a member of the English delegation. This conference also sat at

Bruges, a favorite location during the fourteenth century for those who had international agreements to negotiate.

The fifteenth century saw a transformation of great importance in the practice of international relations: the appearance of permanent diplomatic missions abroad. We must beware of confusion and not include among the members of permanent missions the numerous envoys whose stay at a foreign court or republic had lasted a long time. This often happened during the fifteenth century owing to the increasing complexity of international relations, principally in Italy. One of the best examples of this is the long mission of Comines to Venice between 1494 and 1495, whose length can be explained by the task he had been charged with by the King of France: to urge the Most Serene Republic to abandon its adherence to the league that had been formed against his lord. The first permanent envoys abroad were exchanged between Italian states after the middle of the fifteenth century. Francesco Sforza appears to have instituted such representation. He accredited Nicodemus of Pontremoli as his permanent representative in Florence in 1446—before he had made himself master of Milan. Nicodemus was still retained, after the great *condottiere* his lord had been, became a duke of Milan. In 1450 there was a permanent Florentine ambassador to Milan for the first time. In 1455 the Duke of Milan was represented in a permanent manner in Naples, and the King of Naples was likewise represented at Milan in 1466. Permanent representation of Milan at Venice probably dates back to 1458, and that of Venice to the Duke of Milan to 1457, but there is no positive evidence of the first until 1494. As for the permanent representation of Venice at Naples, it seems to have been initiated in 1457.

During a meeting in 1464 between Louis XI and the nonpermanent Milanese ambassador, Alberigo Malleta, the former considered permanent diplomatic missions as usual practice in Italy, but exclusively Italian. He himself would not allow any to be sent to him as accredited agents. In 1465 he made an exception to this rule in favor of J. P. Panigarola, Francesco Sforza's ambassador, but this was because in the midst of struggles with the princes grouped against him in the League of the Public Good, the Duke of Milan was his only ally. To the north of the Alps, permanent representatives were looked upon with suspicion. We do not come across them until the end of the century. Although Venice appears to have sent a permanent representative to the Duke of Burgundy in 1471, it was not until 1495 that she sent one to the Emperor and another to the Spanish sovereigns. She perhaps sent one to the King of England in 1496, but there is nothing to lead us to believe that one was sent to the King of France before 1500. Not until 1490 did Milan have a permanent ambassador to England, and not before 1494 can one recognize a permanent character in the Milanese embassy to the Emperor Maximilian. As for Spain, it is generally considered that the mission of the ambassador, Lorenzo Suarez de Figuerola, of the "Catholic Kings"—that is to say, of Ferdinand and Isabella of Aragon-Castile—to the republic of Venice, became permanent between 1494 and 1498. It appears that the same can be said for the ambassador of these sovereigns to the English court, Roderigo Gondesalvi de Puebla—namely before 1500. It is believed that at this time, the Scottish court expressed the desire of receiving a permanent Spanish ambassador.

The situation at Rome presents rather special characteristics. Certain Italian heads of state—the Duke of Milan, the Venetian republic—probably sent permanent envoys from 1458 on. In the meantime the Pope expressed little interest in permanent missions, and it was only toward the end of the century that England, France, and Spain were able to dispatch them. England's permanent mission seems to have arisen out of the institution of the *procurator*. We know that John Shirwood, archdeacon of Windsor, *procurator* at Rome and the future bishop of Durham, was on several occasions accredited as *orator*—that is, as ambassador—from 1478 on, and that he managed to have conferred upon himself the privileges attached to this rank after the expiration of his missions. It appears that after 1490 his successor as permanent *procurator* and *orator*, was a Luccan, born at Bruges, former papal tax collector in England and future bishop of Worcester, Giovanni Gigli. Henceforth this was a permanent appointment. Although prior to the fifteenth century permanent envoys were attached to the Pope, the latter did not send any abroad: his "legates" (*legatus*) and his "nuncios" (*nuntius*) had only temporary tasks or missions to fulfill. The fact that on occasion a nuncio resided for a long time in the same place is explained by the nature of the business that he might have to attend to. An excellent example is furnished by Luke of Tolentis, bishop of Sebenico and nuncio to the dukes of Burgundy from 1462 to 1465, from 1466 to 1474, and from 1476 to 1484. Despite the length of his missions, this prelate was never accredited, save in regard to negotiations pertaining to specific and "complicated" business arrangements, as recorded in his safe-conduct of 1476. The nature of his mission—privileges to grant in the importation of "papal" alum to the Low Countries; the preparation of a crusade against the Turks: the levying of papal revenues—justified his remaining an envoy of the Holy See for so long a time. We must also briefly mention certain clerics charged with levying papal revenues, the "collectors" (*nuntius et fructuum, iurium et proventuum Camerae Apostolicae debitorum et debendorum collector et receptor generalis*), an institution furthered by the Avignon papacy during the fourteenth century. These functions were often performed by the same persons for a long period of time. They could also be combined with a diplomatic mission, by a *nuntius et orator*—a situation that often arose during the fifteenth century.

The Byzantine Empire appears to have had permanent ambassadors only during the very last period of its existence. The *basileus* Manuel II (1391–1425) sent an ambassador to reside permanently at the court of the Ottoman sultan, Mahomet I (1413–1421). His task, if one is to believe contemporary witnesses, was to keep the court at Constantinople informed of the plans and activities of its redoubtable neighbor. Moreover, even in the West, a permanent ambassador was primarily a collector of information and only secondly a negotiator. His presence did not prevent the dispatch of extraordinary ambassadors on temporary missions to the court where he resided; and the latter handled questions of great importance. Permanent ambassadors did not enjoy the same consideration as these extraordinary envoys. According to some, they were similar to those settled foreign merchants whom Florence, Venice, and other states used to obtain information and to communicate with the governments of the countries where they were settled. They had few people in their service and appear to have been poorly paid. They were frequently undignified in their mode of living. For instance, Giovanni Gigli, the second permanent ambassador from England to the Holy See, borrowed tapestries from the English hospital of Saint Thomas at Rome to decorate his apartment, and never returned them. The conduct of Doctor Puebla, the first permanent ambassador of the "Catholic Kings" to England, was even more questionable: he begged for assistance from the English sovereign, lived in a house of ill-repute, and used his diplomatic immunity to cover his activities as a procurer.

Whether they were permanent or not, ambassadors were furnished with documents. This was not a new custom, but by the end of the Middle Ages it became a regular practice. A considerable number of these documents have survived from the thirteenth, fourteenth, and fifteenth centuries. Contemporary authors who wrote about international relations stress the importance of these letters. In the second half of the thirteenth century Guillaume Durand, the famous French commentator, wrote that the powers of an envoy were dependent on the importance of the letters he could produce, and that these letters ought to indicate the principal purpose of his mission. Among these "documents," the credentials, which we have met in previous centuries, were of prime importance. These documents tended to become uniform in the various western countries. Their essential content was the invitation made by one chief of state to another to add credence to the verbal declarations of his envoys. The credentials furnished by Edward II in 1309 to his ambassadors to Clement V stated that in listening to his envoys, the Pope would be hearing the King of England's own voice. The French term *lettres de créance* occurs after the beginning of the thirteenth century: Villehardouin reported that in 1201 the leaders of the fourth crusade sent envoys, bearers of *lettres por seignor* to the Doge of Venice, and that *les lettres erent de creance*. Envoys responsible for concluding agreements were generally furnished with letters containing the clause of "full powers" (in Latin documents, *plena et libera potestas, mandatum, procuratio*). The "full powers" sometimes contained promises of ratification. When it was a question of *procuratores* who were responsible for dealing with a matter that was more legal than political, or who represented their lord before a court— for example, the King of England before the Parliament of Paris— the document that conferred powers was sometimes drawn up like powers of attorney. Generally envoys received a safe-conduct that had to be obtained from the heads of states to whom they were accredited, and whose lands they would cross; the failure to have a safe-conduct exposed them to serious annoyances. The importance of similar documents was very great in times of hostilities. Froissart stresses the fact that after the delivery of Edward III's "defiance" to Philip VI, which, on November 1, 1337, began the Hundred Years War, the King of France had sent to Henry Burghersh, bishop of Lincoln, "a valid safe-conduct for him and all those with him, under which safe-conduct he passed through the kingdom of France without danger and returned to England." And finally envoys could receive written instructions. Although not yet universal, this practice spread more and more in the

thirteenth, fourteenth, and fifteenth centuries. General and extremely extensive instructions are extant from this last century
and offer us an insight into a whole aspect of politics. In the same
period, and in order to allow ambassadors personally to disclose
their instructions, or through fear of seeing these instructions
become known by agents of the other party, secret orders, different from those in the official documents, began to be issued. The
use of "ciphers" tended to avoid the danger just mentioned, and
at the end of the Middle Ages the Venetians were considered the
virtuosi of diplomatic cryptography.

The delivery of presents by envoys to the sovereigns to whom
they were accredited continued to be practiced and, as in previous
periods, led to an exchange of courtesies. These gifts were of the
greatest variety. The ambassador of Edward I of England to the
Ilkhan of Persia between 1292 and 1293 brought the latter two
gerfalcons jessed in silver, and brought back for his master a
leopard that had to be fed with live sheep en route! But during the
last part of the Middle Ages envoys were often responsible for
giving gifts other than "gifts of honor" to the heads of state and
the other important people of his entourage: sums of money,
money fiefs, pensions—in reality attempts at bribery. Gifts given
to ambassadors could have similar goals. Thus, measures were
taken in different states to submit them to authorization or to
forbid them. Venice stopped the practice early—in 1236 and
1268—laying down rigorous instructions in the matter.

Envoys sent abroad received remuneration and allowances in
order to cover their expenses. The amount of these is so variable
that there is little value in citing any figures. It depended upon the
rank of the ambassador, the duration and nature of his mission,
and also on the generosity of the sovereign and of the state of the
latter's finances. More than once envoys did not succeed in being
paid the promised amounts. There was one western state in the
Middle Ages where a mission abroad was for its subjects an obligation sanctioned by financial penalties: this was Venice. The

first law in this regard dates from 1272, and a series of others were formulated in the thirteenth, fourteenth, and fifteenth centuries. The task was even more burdensome in that mistrust was considered a virtue at Venice, and a priori the state suspected its overseas representatives: after 1268, it imposed a personal oath upon them and subjected them to persistent harassment.

Not only was the personal immunity of envoys widely accepted, but it was also stated as a law, specifically by Pope Gregory X when he wrote to Charles of Anjou: "The law of nations demand that envoys of any nation whatever enjoy security even among their enemies" (*ius gentium exigit ut legati cuiuslibet gentis securitate gaudeant, etiam apud hostes*). Guillaume Durand expressed the same idea when he stated that the case of an ambassador was a sacred one. Moreover, the principle was accepted throughout Christendom and to a certain extent in the Moslem states. We know of grave penalties imposed upon those guilty of violence against ambassadors. In 1340, for example, persons close to the Curia who had seized an English ambassador to the Pope from Avignon, were condemned to death and executed. Commercial treaties and plans for these treaties concluded or negotiated by the German towns with the prince of Smolensk in 1229 and 1250 and with the prince and the republic of Novgorod in 1189 and in 1268–1269, doubled the scale of penalties for murder when the victim was the envoy of one of the parties. These two examples from very different circumstances have been chosen on purpose; it would not be difficult to cite more, nor to cite cases of violated diplomatic immunity other than the incident at Avignon in 1340. One of the most patent was the arrest of two Florentine ambassadors to King Charles VI of France in 1406 on the orders of the King's uncles, the dukes of Orléans and of Burgundy. The detention of these unfortunate ambassadors lasted until 1408. The authorities of a state to which the foreign ambassador had been accredited, could, through suspicion or for other reasons, make his life difficult, by lengthy delay before authorizing him to enter the country, without going so far as to violate his usual privileges. Thus in 1479 the Milanese ambassadors at the court of Louis XI complained of lack of courtesy, of irritating surveillance measures, of systematic calumny against them, and of the royal entourage's efforts to avoid them.

The ever more rigorous etiquette governing the royal courts, the observation of the proper privileges of ambassadors, and questions of precedence, particularly from the fifteenth century on, caused friction and sometimes even conflict. They poisoned the lives of sovereigns and of their councilors and gave rise to painful and sometimes violent incidents in the lives of the ambassadors themselves. We cited a Roman example earlier, but the pontifical court had no monopoly on these diplomatic dramas. At the court of Maximilian, King of the Romans, in 1497, the Florentine envoy did not wish to cede his place to that of the Venetian envoy, and the latter threw his colleague into a pile of refuse, accompanying his act with appropriate gestures.

It was usual for envoys abroad to send their lords written reports on the progress of their missions. We know that the Byzantine Empire required this from a very early date. Despite their increasing frequency in the West, we cannot be sure that written reports were furnished in every western state, for every mission, and by every envoy. England was one of the countries where the dispatch of reports during missions or at their conclusion was most generally practiced. It is true that often the final written report did not treat the core of the matter, which was reserved for an oral report, *"relatio,"* to the king and eventually to his council. In Italy written reports were frequently used and were standard practice at Venice. From 1268 on, a written summary at the close of a mission was required of the ambassadors, and a detailed report was made orally before the doge and the senate. For a long time written reports had been sent during a mission. As a consequence, rules were made to establish these two kinds of report. The oldest extant report made in the course of a mission (*dispaccio*) and the oldest extant report at the close of a mission (*relazione*) date from 1379–1380 and from 1492, respectively. They certainly existed before these dates. Ciphers were used for reports during a mission in the fifteenth century at Venice.

During the last centuries of the Middle Ages—no more at Byzantium than in the western states—there was no administrative organization to direct foreign affairs and plan the conduct of missions abroad. This task devolved upon various organizations and various people. It could be said that in the sovereign's "council" most of the decisions concerning important missions were reached. This was the case in France, England, and the Burgundian state under its last two dukes. Certain personages— for example, the chancellor, who was a member of the council— could play a major role in its deliberations. The secretaries attached to the council could be brought to play an important role in the preparation of the agenda and in all the administrative activity this involved. This explains the fact that in England the chancery clerks who normally discharged these functions were often sent abroad on missions because of their knowledge of matters of state. In this country, where the over-all system of public institutions was more organized than in others, the administration of foreign relations was more or less specialized. From the fourteenth century on, this administration was largely reserved for the Keeper of the Privy Seal. A specialized service, however, had existed from 1304 to 1339; it was responsible for assembling the necessary documents and for providing all pertinent advice for those charged with negotiations with France concerning the immensely complex feudal-vassal-relations between the Plantagenets and the Capetians. This was organized by an official with the suitable title of *custos processuum*, "Keeper of processes." At Venice also, foreign affairs came within the competence of a specific organization. The Senate deliberated such matters; but from the fourteenth century on, they were examined by the permanent college of "Sages" (*Savi*).

Negotiations could lead to international agreements. The latter were often realized through marriages. What has been said of political marriages and of the politics of marriage during earlier centuries is valid for the later Middle Ages. Matrimonial agreements sometimes constituted real treaties, made effective by sureties, which usually accompanied them. Because of its great importance, we shall cite one example from among many others: that of the double marriage of John the Fearless, eldest son of Philip the Bold, duke of Burgundy, and heir to Brabant and to Limburg, to Marguerite of Bavaria, daughter of the Count of Hainaut, of Holland, and of Zeeland; and the marriage of William of Bavaria to Marguerite of Burgundy, concluded at Cambrai in 1385. It was the basis of the formation of the Burgundian state. The towns and the nobles of Hainaut, of Holland, and of Zeeland were called upon to give their consent to the agreements concluded on this occasion.

The agreements to which certain negotiations led were often of only temporary importance: here we mention truces made in the course of international conflicts. There were many of them in the periods under consideration. Most wars were stayed by similar interruptions in the fighting. The Hundred Years War is a typical example.

As for agreements designed to have lasting effects—that is, treaties—it is important to indicate that there were, as a rule, as many copies of the same text as there were contracting parties. The instruments more and more took on the character of an act, designed to serve as proof of a synallagmatic contract. Sometimes this went together with unilaterally complementary documents. The Treaty of Paris, concluded between Louis IX and Henry III in 1259, of which there were two identical copies of the same text drawn up for the two contracting parties, anticipated the renunciation by the King of England of all claims on Normandy, and the accession of Richard of Cornwall, king of the Romans, heir presumptive to the English throne. These legal acts were the reason for separate instruments, drawn up in the names of the parties concerned. There were even occasions when the unilateral and bilateral complementary documents were so numerous and so important that they had to be considered as instruments drawn up on the occasion of the conclusion of the agreement and as part of the text of the treaty itself. For example, this is the case of the treaty concluded in 1328 that brought about the peace of Northampton between England and Scotland. Its text includes not only the instrument containing the principal agreements undertaken by the two parties, but also a second instrument concerning the payment of an indemnity by Robert Bruce, king of Scotland, if he did not marry his son David to Joan, the sister of Edward III, king of England. There were also two notarized acts concerning the agreement made by Robert Bruce to pay an indemnity of £20,000 to Edward III, and finally a letter patent of Robert Bruce's dealing with an annual income assigned by him to his future daughter-in-law. The drawing up of a single instrument in several copies, accompanied or not by other documents, has nevertheless never been a rule without exceptions: treaties have been concluded in the form of parallel instruments based upon the old custom. As in the past, there even existed treaties disguised as purely unilateral acts, as if they were concessions made by a sovereign authority. As an example we can cite the constitutions of Frederick II made on behalf of the lay and ecclesiastical princes of Germany, true agreements made in 1220 and in 1232. The first of these constitutions, moreover, was quickly named "alliance (*confoederatio*) with the ecclesiastical princes."

The sureties with which certain treaties had been effected remained the same, on the whole, as they had been in the twelfth century. Such was the oath taken by both parties, with the reservation that not only the emperor but also kings could have others swear for them, but they made an undertaking to God through their intermediaries: their representatives swore *in animam imperatoris, in animam regis*. It is also noteworthy that following the conclusion of treaties between the German towns and the Russian states of Novgorod, Smolensk, etc., the oath was accompanied by the kissing of the Cross. However, it is not certain whether the *Kreuzküssung* was really a surety affecting the agreement or an important formality at its conclusion. We also meet ecclesiastical sanctions (excommunication and interdict), and the provision of guarantors. A guarantee was frequently required from the emperors and from the Kings of the Romans: written engagements taken by the great princes, particularly by the Electors. These acts were called *Willebriefe*. One type of surety spread widely from the thirteenth century on: engagements taken under oath by the principal vassals and by the towns belonging to one of the parties. This system was frequently used by the kings of France. A clause of this type is found in the treaties of Melun (1226) and of Paris (1227), settling relations between Flanders and France, on the occasion of the release of Count Ferrand, a prisoner since Bouvines. The kings had these oaths renewed and recorded upon the accession of a new monarch in France or in Flanders. Philip the Fair himself made the towns swear an oath before the signing of the Treaty of Athis-sur-Orge, which in 1305 ended the war between France and Flanders. Then, on account of clauses in the treaty, new oaths were imposed on the Count, the nobles, the town administrators (Fr.: *échevins*), and all Flemings over fourteen years of age. It happened that a fraction of the country was given as a guarantee when a treaty included an undertaking to pay a sum of money: such dispositions were part of the treaties cited here. This type of guarantee was frequently used in the most diverse ways. It was often a means for preparing for territorial expansion.

Among the treaties concluded in the last three centuries of the Middle Ages, we should once more make special mention of what we have already called trade treaties. A number of Christian Mediterranean states drew these up with Moslem states. Pisa, Genoa, Venice, and Florence signed such treaties with the kings of

Tunis and of Bougie in particular. The kings of Sicily—counts of Provence—the kings of Aragon, and the kings of Majorca did the same. But in the fourteenth century the King of Majorca drew up treaties with the King of Tlemcen. These agreements were not very different from those of the twelfth century. Basically they assured the nationals of the Christian state of their own settlement (*funduk,* in Italian, *fondaco*) usually including a church, a cemetery, a bath, and a bakehouse; of guarantees for their persons and for their goods, and of privileges in legal affairs, in navigation, in circulation, and in taxation, etc. They also included engagements taken by the Christian settlers, notably for the outlawing and the repression of piracy.

We should further examine those treaties that were concluded by German, Baltic, and North Sea towns. First, the agreements drawn up with the heads of state of northwestern Europe: agreements with England, beginning with the grant Lübeck obtained from Henry III in 1237, of exemption from tolls and other taxes for the "community of German merchants living on the island of Gotland"—that is, the Germans involved in trade in the eastern basin of the Baltic; agreements with the Count of Holland and the Bishop of Utrecht guaranteeing, from 1243 to 1244 on, fixed assessments for Hamburg and Lübeck shipping on the inland waterways to Flanders. The first agreements with the Countess of Flanders in 1252 and 1253 led to a grant "to all the merchants of the empire"—that is, the "Gotland group"—represented by Hamburg and Lübeck, of a reduced scale of tolls at Bruges and in its approach port of Damme, and of a list of the rights of German merchants in Flanders. Then a second group of treaties guaranteed regular and secure commerce to the countries east of the Baltic. Here also initiative came from Lübeck. Treaties were undertaken with Hamburg from 1241 on, seeking security in communications; and from 1259, treaties with the "Wend" towns —that is, the German towns located along the coast of the Slav countries in the process of Germanization and especially Rostock and Wismar. The essential aim was the same, and thus we have the important clauses concerned with piracy and with brigandage. And lastly we have the treaty of 1280 for the protection of trade with Russia, drawn up by Lübeck together with Visby and joined by Riga in 1282 and by Reval in 1283. We are limited to discussing the prototypes; but each of these series of treaties continued to operate, with changes and with adaptations to new conditions, throughout the last three centuries of the Middle Ages.

This is equally true of a third group of treaties: those having as their aim the protection of German-Russian trade within Russia: be it at Novgorod and at Pskov, be it at Polock, Vitebsk, or Smolensk. As for the Germans—and curiously this contracting party went under the name of "all those of the Latin tongue"— the first of these treaties was drawn up, on the one hand, in the name of the German and "Gothic"—that is, Swedish—communities of Gotland and the city of Lübeck and, on the other, in the name of these same communities and of the towns of Riga, Lübeck, Bremen, Soest, Münster, and Groningen. Later, in regard to Novgorod, the principal role belonged to Lübeck and the Hanse in the fourteenth century and to the German towns of Livonia in the fifteenth century. In regard to Smolensk, the principal role belonged to Riga. The Russian contracting parties were the Prince and the republic of Novgorod, or the princes of Smolensk, Vitebsk, and Polock, and after the fourteenth century, the great prince of Lithuania, who had imposed his authority on their territories. The treaties with Novgorod date from 1189, with a plan for an agreement that was never signed, but that nevertheless appears to have been the source of customary law, and with a treaty concluded in 1259. In the case of Smolensk, the first treaty was drawn up in 1229. In this period two sets of rules became and remained the principal concerns: liberty and security of navigation on the River Neva, Lake Ladoga, the Wolchow, or the Dvina; the protection of land traffic and the protection of the persons and goods of the merchants and the settlements the treaties allowed them to create. These agreements implied a reciprocity of rights and of obligations. German-Russian trade treaties were extremely numerous because of the frequent breaches caused by acts of violence on the part of the Russians, by conflicts between the Swordbearers or the Teutonic Knights, and their Slav or Scandinavian neighbors; and because of the retaliatory measures taken by German towns against the Russians. Such was the commercial interest of both parties that despite everything, attempts were made to place relations on a solid basis.

Other agreements worthy of mention in a history of international relations concern banishments and political refugees. These agreements figured in many treaties of general importance, in the form of clauses forbidding the residence in either country of those who had been banished or had fled from the other, and on occasion even requiring their delivery. Agreements were especially drawn up for this very purpose. This was particularly the case among the towns of Flanders, Brabant, Liège, and Italy—that is, in places where political, social, and interfamily hatred raged spasmodically.

The traditional means of building, consolidating, or keeping up relations of subordination between political units remained the same in the thirteenth, fourteenth, and fifteenth centuries. Under Innocent III the Holy See increased the number of vassal states that paid it tribute in recognition of its overlordship. We have seen the circumstances under which England joined a group to which Hungary, Sicily, Aragon, and Portugal already belonged. From these bonds of vassaldom the Holy See gained the arms required in the conflicts in which it became involved: for example, we could cite Pope Clement V, who in 1313 threatened the Emperor Henry VII with excommunication if he dared invade the kingdom of Naples, a fief of the Church. Western heads of state used feudal-vassal relations in their various forms for similar ends. The kings of England increased the grants of "money fiefs" to the princes and lords of the Low Countries, western Germany, and the kingdom of Arles, especially at the time of the struggles between Edward I and Philip the Fair and at the beginning of the Hundred Years War. The kings of France also used feudal-vassalic relations in the thirteenth and fourteenth centuries to extend their power both in the southwest, in the interior of their kingdom, at the expense of the Plantagenets, or in the northeast and the east beyond their frontiers at the expense of the empire. They made special use in these plans of such institutions as double vassality and wardships. "Money fiefs" also secured them military services; nonfeudal rents and pensions, however, had progressively displaced the latter during the fourteenth century and supplanted them in the fifteenth. Another feudal institution was the pledged real estate (Fr.: *engagère*), with fealty owed to the creditor. Louis de Male, count of Flanders, and his son-in-law and successor, Philip the Bold, made particular use of it in the extension of their territorial authority between the Meuse and the Rhine during the second half of the fourteenth century. The phenomenon, moreover, had a general importance and could be illustrated by cases from other parts of Europe, such as Italy, where vassalic relations had been created among princes, lords, and cities in the period that forms the basis of this study.

We should note that subordinate relations that can be likened to those created by homage and fealty existed between the leaders of Christian states and the leaders of Moslem states in Spain. In 1246 the King of Granada became the vassal of Ferdinand III, king of Castile, and undertook to pay him tribute. These relations were interrupted by wars in the following centuries, but they were renewed several times during the fourteenth and the fifteenth centuries. At the other end of Europe in the last quarter of the fourteenth century, the last Byzantine *basileis*, John V, Manuel II, and John VIII, had to accept a similar subordination in their relations with the Ottoman sultans and pay them tribute.

The treatment of frontier problems did not change greatly in the course of the later Middle Ages. In the thirteenth and fourteenth centuries, in the frontiers of Byzantine or Frankish Europe or Asia Minor, it appears that we have to accept a greater fluidity and a greater degree of confusion than in the past. The cause must be sought in political fragmentation; in the extension of feudal-vassal relations that were characteristic of the Empire of Romania; and after the restoration of 1261, in the overlapping of the Byzantine and Frankish territories; and finally in the Turkish conquests. In many countries located in western Europe, frontier areas called "marches" still existed. Their legal standing was to become more precise in the last centuries of the Middle Ages: we will return to this later with regard to the conflicts that they sustained or provoked. The frontiers of some great states or territorial complexes, such as those of the Plantagenets in France, at the same time became more confusing than in the past: partly as a result of vague treaties, such as that of Paris in 1259, and the systematic development of double vassality, wardship, and other feudal or administrative institutions by the kings of France and their officials. In the period from 1355 to 1356 one could, by examining the question from various points of view, have given contradictory answers to matters concerning the Franco-German frontier in the Barrois, Lorraine, and in the Franche-Comté. A concern for giving precise boundaries to a territory was not necessarily incompatible with such a state of affairs. Agreements to fix certain land frontiers were not rare. One of the oldest was the Treaty of the Goulet in 1200 dividing the Evrecin between royal France and Normandy. We even have the actual record of the hearing that dealt with the boundaries. French doctrinal and political works from the end of the thirteenth and at the beginning of the fourteenth centuries reveal attitudes that were to influence events. There was a tendency to consider the four rivers—Scheldt, Meuse, Saône, and Rhône—as the boundaries of France; and it was argued that imperial territories within these boundaries had been usurped. But annexations beyond these limits were justified by other historical considerations. Lyon was a notable case.

Maritime frontiers presented problems in the later Middle Ages. In the Mediterranean, Venice claimed jurisdiction over the whole Adriatic, and Genoa over the whole "Ligurian" sea, an area less easy to define. However, at least in theory, the doctrine of the greatest of the Italian commentators, Bartole de Sassoferrato was accepted in Italy: the state bordering the sea had authority over this "neighboring" sea, and this neighborhood was compared to two days' sailing—that is, about 100 Roman miles or approximately 150 kilometers. In the Atlantic, the Channel, and the North Sea the great seaside nations claimed jurisdiction over the seas that washed their shores but did not agree upon precise limits. This was the case of both France and England, who claimed sovereignty over the Channel and all the waters from Brittany to the Pyrenees—a source of insoluble conflicts. On the other hand, in Flanders, Zeeland, and Holland the sea was considered free; but in the interest of trade and of the security of navigation, from the fourteenth century on, Flanders proclaimed that a coastal strip, called the *stroom* (Fr.: *estrum*), was subject solely to Flemish jurisdiction. In 1392, to satisfy the Hanse, Flanders had to acknowledge its responsibility for any acts of violence that were committed there. Shortly afterward it undertook a similar agreement with Scotland. France recognized the "Flemish *stroom*" in 1370, and England in 1403. Holland—which had proclaimed the Zuyderzee to be a Dutch *stroom* in 1394— and Zeeland recognized the Flemish *stroom* in 1414. In the fifteenth century the width of the *stroom* was estimated as a "view": that is, the distance from which it was possible to see the coast and its buildings; this might be three German "leagues" or about 21 kilometers. In the Baltic similar rules appear to have existed at Lübeck from the middle of the thirteenth century, for a roadstead *lato sensu*, which was then called "the little sea" (*breve mare*). The term *stroom* is also found in the fifteenth century. Thus developed the concept of territorial waters.

The question of customs at frontiers should also be mentioned. It seems that the idea of customs law, which evolved centuries ago in the Byzantine and Moslem worlds, in Venice, and shortly thereafter throughout the Mediterranean world, took root in Europe north of the Alps at the beginning of the thirteenth century—in the sense that in ports and at certain frontier passages the tolls ceased to be a simple exaction as it still was in many places: it is thought that about sixty tolls burdened navigation on the Rhine. England, royal France, Flanders, and the Burgundian state, to cite a few examples, had a varied policy in customs matters and especially in tariffs, discounts, and exemptions. The subject, which has been little studied, remains largely obscure.

Frontier adjustments were often the result of war. The latter, as we have stated, remained the means par excellence of settling conflicts between states. But, as in the past, there were other means of settlement. We will limit ourselves to citing, owing to their curiosity, the propositions offered to avoid armed conflict between two countries by setting to battle in a closed field the kings, each assisted by a hundred knights. Similar encounters were to take place in 1283 at Bordeaux, before Edward I, between Peter III of Aragon and Charles of Anjou, and in 1340, beneath the walls of Tournai, between Edward III and Philip VI. These projects were never realized, however.

On the other hand, we must recognize the great and increasing importance of reprisals. As a means of procedure against enemies, against the compatriots of a guilty party, or against a contumacious debtor, reprisals had as their basis the notion of solidarity among the subjects of a particular king. They normally led to counterreprisals. They burdened a very great number of individuals when they consisted of the seizure or the confiscation of the goods of enemy subjects, which was sometimes accompanied by their arrest and of harassment of navigation or of the land trade of their compatriots. The Anglo-French conflicts furnish many examples of this. Reprisals of this type could assume major proportions. After the Treaty of Montreuil-sur-Mer (1274), which finished the first phase of an Anglo-Flemish war caused by the greed and vanity of the Countess of Flanders, an accounting was made of the goods seized by the two sides. English goods seized in Flanders amounted to £10,627, 10s. 2½d., while Flemish goods seized in England amounted to £5,871 13s. 2½d.—amounts that were considerable for the period. In another type of reprisal a public authority moved, at the demand of a creditor, against the subject of a sovereign who refused to pay a debt. These creditors were often Italian financiers. One example would be: Robert of Béthune, count of Flanders, had borrowed 12,000 Paris pounds at short term from three Florentine merchants; in 1309, when the debt had not been repaid, Gérard Alloudier, one of the creditors, had the guards of the fairs of Champagne seize the goods of the men of Ypres that were on display at the fair. The town of Ypres retaliated by seizing all credits held by the Florentine houses (Bardi, Peruzzi, Cerchi, della Spina, and Portinari) on the men of Ypres. The fair guards threatened Ypres with "exclusion from the fair"— that is, a prohibition on trading at the fairs; the King of France and the Parliament of Paris had to intervene to put an end to the conflict.

Finally, reprisals could be taken by individuals, because of acts of ill-will, violence, theft, or nonpayment of debts. In the thirteenth, fourteenth, and fifteenth centuries men who had suffered wrongs of this type and had not been able to obtain reparation or satisfaction could ask the authorities of their own country for the right to take reprisals against the compatriots of the author of the wrongdoing or the recalcitrant debtor. At the beginning of the thirteenth century in Italy and in Aragon, letters authorizing reprisals were issued in this case; in the fourteenth century they were also issued in France, England, and elsewhere. These documents were called "letters of marque" (marca), almost certainly because many reprisals stemmed from acts of violence committed by the inhabitants of the "marches" (*marca*) between two territories. It is worthwhile to quote a typical case of reprisal that arose from a private matter. Turks had been victims of the brigandage of inhabitants of the Genoese colony of Caffa. A Genoese merchant who was not connected with these outbreaks, left Caffa and traveled through Gallipoli. The Turks, by way of reprisal, stopped him and stripped him of his merchandise—to wit, twelve slaves, six men and six women, together worth 500 florins. When the merchant reached Genoa in 1449, he sought to be indemnified from the colony's funds that were banked in the city, or to receive a grant of a right of reprisal against the Turks or the Saracens.

The results of reprisals were so formidable for business that many commercial towns were driven to have them limited or suppressed: this is true of the Italian towns and also of those of the Low Countries. It suffices to cite the series of privileges, the oldest of which dates back to 1232, granted to the Flemish merchants in England; those granting these same privileges since 1261 to the Brabant merchants; those, dating from 1268, that favored the Flemish merchants as much as the English merchants in Hamburg; without mentioning those that the King of France had conceded to the men of Ypres in 1193. The essential disposition was always the same: the beneficiaries could be held responsible only for those debts where they were the principal debtor or guarantor. These privileges were often transgressed; even an individual safe-conduct did not always protect its bearer from reprisal.

When it was a question of violence committed "on the march" by individuals or public officers, and followed or not followed by reprisals, in accordance with the law of the "march," reprisals could be stopped or delayed by the intervention of the march laws. These laws existed in the marches of England and Scotland, of Guyenne and Périgord, of Gascony and Castile, of

Brittany and Anjou, of Namur—as much toward Hainaut as toward the Liège country—and many others. Furthermore, these laws varied from country to country in their composition, scope, and effectiveness. Concerning questions of conflicts that came about "on the march," at sea or elsewhere, between subjects and officials of the kings of France and the kings of England during the first forty years of the fourteenth century, more than one attempt was made to stop or to prevent reprisals by submitting them to bipartite conferences, which we have already mentioned. The "trials" of Montreuil in 1306, of Périgueux in 1311, and of Agen, in 1332–1333 are examples. Attempts were also made to resolve the difficulties entailed in the vassality of the King of England to the King of France. All these conferences came to no avail.

One must also mention, among the means used to solve the conflicts, the prohibition of trade. This was an instrument that the Hanse used several times and often with success. The Hanseatic *Handelssperre* was accompanied by a withdrawal of the German merchants toward other ports. Bruges was the victim of a similar economic boycott in 1280, 1307, 1358, 1388, and finally in 1451. On the first two occasions the Germans moved to Aardenburg in Flanders, on the third and fourth times to Dordrecht in Holland, and on the fifth to Utrecht. But Bruges and the Hanseatic cities had such a great need of each other that after a while an accord was agreed upon.

During the period that we are studying, good offices and mediation—it is still impossible to distinguish between them—contributed greatly to settling conflicts. Numerous truces, peace treaties, and various accords were facilitated or made possible by interventions of this kind. The same goes for the whole of western and even for eastern Christendom and to a certain extent for the Moslem world. Emperors, kings, princes, and prominent members of the clergy, such as archbishops and bishops, abbotts and abbesses, were among the mediators. Certain of them chose to specialize, thus enhancing their power and their prestige or their alliances. Such was William I, count of Hainaut and count of Holland and Zeeland under the name of William III, father-in-law of Edward III, and leader of the English party in the Low Countries at the outbreak of the Hundred Years War. He managed numerous accords between warring princes and lords from the North Sea to the Rhine. On the other hand, his efforts to reconcile his son-in-law, Louis of Bavaria, with the Pope in 1330 failed; when he set out on this course, Pope John XXII had ordered bridges to be demolished in order to prevent him from reaching Avignon. The greatest mediator of international conflicts was the papacy. During the fourteenth century it extended itself in preventing, then in halting, the conflicts between France and England or between England and Scotland, in the hope of orienting the kings toward a crusade. These efforts were not entirely in vain: during the Hundred Years War, the Treaty of Brétigny in 1360 and the conferences of Calais and Bruges between 1372 and 1377 were due to the initiative of Innocent VI and Gregory XI. Needless to say, when popes, emperors, kings, and princes acted as mediators, they had recourse to the intervention or the assistance of envoys, ecclesiastic or lay.

Sometimes the same persons agreed to act as mediator and as arbitrator: a double role, as the two tasks were quite different. Guillaume Durand mentions that the *arbiter* settles a conflict according to the law, while the *amicabilis compositor* arranges an accord, a transaction, without being held to the rules of law. Imprecision in terminology, so frequent in the Middle Ages, explains why a third term, *arbitrator*, was generally understood in the sense of "friendly compounder," especially by Guillaume Durand, though sometimes as arbiter. Arbitration, already widely used in the twelfth century, was even more common in the thirteenth, fourteenth, and fifteenth centuries. The legal basis remained unchanged. Arbitrators came from the same circles as mediators, and the same parties used arbitration or mediation:

emperors, kings, princes, towns, and sovereign orders. The Pope, himself, as leader of the Church, in 1435 submitted for arbitration a conflict between Florence, Venice, and himself on the one part, and the Duke of Milan on the other. The arbiters were two cardinals and the Marquis of Este. It was the personal authority of kings that made them particularly sought after as arbiters: we have already mentioned the arbitrations of Saint Louis. A great deal of litigation was submitted not to a single arbiter but to a panel of arbiters, sometimes composed of many members. A good example is furnished in a territorial conflict between the Duchess of Brabant and the Duke of Gelder. It should have been settled in 1389 by a panel made up of the archbishop of Cologne, the duke of Lorraine, and the lords of Coucy and of La Trémoille. Since the duke defaulted, a new compromise was arranged designating a panel of twelve arbiters, mainly neighboring lords or vassals of the parties involved. The latter accepted the verdict, which was given in 1390. At times the arbitration of the Pope was sought or accepted; but from the end of the thirteenth century, the parties, anxious to preserve their sovereignty, specified that the sovereign pontiff act only in the capacity of a private person; the compromise of 1298 concluded between Philip the Fair and Edward I named Boniface VIII as arbiter *tamquam in privatam personam et dominum Benedictum Cayatanum*. Moreover, the position taken by the popes in international conflicts during the pontificate of Boniface VIII and during the "Babylonian captivity" diminished their authority as arbiters. In conflicts among numerous parties, it happened that in addition to the principal judgment (*sententia, laus, laudum, dictum*) the arbiters handed down judgments valid only for certain of the parties. Philip VI, king of France, did this, for example, in 1334 when he arbitrated an armed conflict between John III, duke of Brabant, and a group of Lotharingian princes.

The compromissary clause we have already seen in twelfth-century treaties, especially in Italy, became more and more common in the centuries that followed. Italy remained the country where it was the most widely used: the towns and the *signorie*, which had often taken over from urban governments, used it a great deal. The institution had also developed north of the Alps, and towns contributed to its diffusion. Since the thirteenth century the constitutions of the German urban leagues—notably those of 1254 and 1265—contained a compromissary clause. This double influence seems to explain the success of the institution, from the thirteenth century on, in regions that make up present-day Switzerland, as well as their appearance in the first pact of the original three cantons (1291) and in a series of other agreements connected with the growth of the confederation. These historical milieus are cited purely as examples, for the compromissary clause was met with throughout Europe beginning in the thirteenth century, and increasingly in the fourteenth century, even in agreements concerning truces. One of the most remarkable examples of a compromissary clause of the most general type was introduced in the treaty of alliance (in 1339) between Flanders and Brabant, as the result of the influence of the towns and with the purpose of favoring commerce: any conflicts whatsoever that might arise between princes or between their subjects fell within the competence of a mixed panel of arbiters. Together with these compromissary clauses figuring in international agreements, there were treaties of arbitration, but these were much fewer in number. As one of the most remarkable cases, we could cite the Italian treaty of 1272 between Verona and Mantua. But agreements of this kind are met in all other milieus, such as the treaty of arbitration drawn up between the Prince-Bishop of Liège and the Count of Namur in 1342. The compromissary clause or the treaty of arbitration could name a final chief arbiter. For example, the treaty of 1343 between the kings of Denmark and Sweden named the Archbishop of Lund as chief arbiter if the mixed panel of twenty-four arbiters were unable to reach agreement. The first Treaty of Thorn of 1411 between the King of Poland and the

Teutonic Knights named the Pope as chief arbiter in the event that a mixed panel of twelve arbiters were unable to settle the conflict. Although numerous compromissary clauses remained dead letters, although arbitral decisions were not carried out or were violated, and although their existence prevented neither wars, nor reprisals, nor *Handelssperren*, they nevertheless allowed for the peaceful settlement of numerous conflicts in the later Middle Ages.

In the thirteenth, fourteenth, and fifteenth centuries the problems that arose from the cohabitation of different populations in the same "area" appeared under aspects that sometimes conformed with those known in the twelfth century and sometimes were very different. We learn this from a study of western merchant colonies in the Near East and on the northern coasts of Africa. There is nothing of importance to stress concerning the eastern colonies in Syria or in the Holy Land, unless it be their disappearance before the end of the thirteenth century. As for the Italian colonies at Constantinople, the new facts are that Venice, after having had a *podestà* as leader of its colony within the Empire of Romania, employed an ambassador (*bailo*) with these duties after the Byzantine restoration. This person sometimes played a very important role in the political and trade relations between the mother country and Byzantium. We should point out that the Genoese colony of Caffa in the Crimea was organized on the model of Genoa itself in the thirteenth century, with two councils, one great and one small, where the Genoese, the only citizens (*cives*), were in the majority, but where foreign Christians—Russians, Greeks, and Armenians—known as "bourgeois" (*burgenses*), were represented. A Genoese magistrate, the consul, governed the colony. From the beginning of the first half of the fourteenth century, a special organization in the administration of the mother country, the *officium Gazariae* (office of the country of the Khazars), controlled the administration of the colony. As for the Italian, Provençal—that is, Marseillaises—or Spanish colonies in North Africa, we need only add one essential fact to what has been said of their beginnings in the twelfth century or of trade treaties concluded with the kings of Tunis, of Bougie, or of Tlemcen in the later Middle Ages: where there was a colony, and as a result a *funduk*, there was at its head one or more consuls, named in principle by the national authorities. The consul was the judge and administrator of his fellow nationals: he checked the regularity and the smooth running of trade; he represented Genoa, Pisa, Venice, Florence, Sicily, Provence, Aragon, or Majorca, to the king or to the Saracen governor. The southern merchant colonies in northwestern Europe had a different organization: Italians, Spanish, and Portuguese did not settle themselves within a closed quarter, or *fondaco*, but formed communities. In royal France, in the thirteenth century and the first half of the fourteenth, Italian immigration had been favored. The community had a captain general at its head, and its members benefited from a privileged personal status. Many of them were assimilated and founded families in France. This situation was rarer in England and in the principalities of the Low Countries, especially in Flanders. There the status of Italians was different. At Bruges, for example, Venice, Lucca, and Genoa had their organized communities called "nations" from the fourteenth century on. Florence and Milan followed in the fifteenth century. As in the Mediterranean regions, the consuls at their head exercised civil and commercial jurisdiction over their nationals and represented them before regional and local authorities. Each of the nations located its consulate in a private mansion.

German merchant colonies also had their own organization. Most often the northern German merchants founded a strictly disciplined community and lived in a vast closed building, a Germanic *fondaco*. That of Novgorod (the *Skt. Petershof*) was registered from 1259; in the fourteenth century it constituted a fortified quarter with its own church, which also served as a "communal house" and an entrepôt. The German group in Bergen, registered in the fourteenth century near the harbor (*Tyskebriggen*, or the "German landing"), was made up of groups of houses; it was closed but not fortified. It had its own church. These groups did not let in German women. In London the complex of buildings consisting of the Guildhall (*Gildehalla*) of Cologne dating back to the twelfth century, a series of houses, and the steelyard (Germ.: *Stalhof*)—the place where one spread out the merchandise for sale—and all situated near London Bridge, gradually spread during the fourteenth and fifteenth centuries into a kind of Hanseatic settlement. Those merchants were far more active in the life of the city and of the country where they were than their associates in Russia and in Norway. At Bruges there was no regulation; the German merchants settled where they wished to stay. And in 1478 the Hanse merchants who were called *Oosterlingen* at Bruges, built a sumptuous house, which played a role similar to that of the mansions occupied by the Italian consulates. On the other hand, at Venice, the *fondaco dei Tedeschi*, a vast building registered in the thirteenth century, which increased in importance in the fourteenth and fifteenth centuries, served as an obligatory residence for the merchants of the cities that supported it. First they came from the south and the center of Germany and later from a few towns in the north. All these communities had their leaders and their regulations. From the thirteenth century at Novgorod these regulations were a veritable law, known as the *shra*.

In Spain the problem of the cohabitation of mixed populations that were essentially different, continued to arise owing to the importance of the Mudejar element—that is, the Moslem element—in the Christian kingdoms. The bitter struggles during the period of the Almohades, the action of the Holy See and of the Dominicans helped to reduce the interpenetration of the Christian and Moslem worlds and to diminish the social and material standard of living among the Mudejars. The latter nevertheless preserved their essential rights and were protected by legislative and administrative measures from arbitrariness and violence. Such at least was the situation in Castile and in Aragon until the period of the "Catholic Kings," when it was seriously worsened. The situation of the Mudejars was much less favorable in Portugal and in Majorca, and many of them were reduced to slavery.

For our subject Sicily is of little importance during this period. The Hellenestic characteristics of a part of its population faded and disappeared. During the beginning of the reign of Frederick II, Arabs or Berber Moslems were persecuted, decimated, reduced to slavery, and ceased to be of any importance as an entity in themselves. Those who were established in the southern portion of the peninsula as a colony of mercenaries were not numerous enough to constitute a distinct element within the population. On the island and on the mainland the survivors were Christianized and assimilated into the existing milieus.

As for Greece, the fourth crusade and the Turkish conquest, the mixed nature of its population, and the relations among diverse elements of the population that lived there in common, have been sufficiently discussed above.

Apart from the territories with mixed populations, the problem of foreigners who had not formed separate colonies, continued to rise everywhere. The development that took shape in the twelfth century and that tended to make the position of "aliens" more favorable, was generally followed. However, there were regressions also. Sometimes public power, moved by financial interests, took measures against such groups of foreigners and proceeded to expulsions and confiscations. Various measures of this type were taken, for example, in the thirteenth and fourteenth centuries by the French crown against the unpopular Lombard moneylenders. In addition there were tides of xenophobia, especially in England: Flemish, Brabant, Italian, and German merchants suffered several times in the thirteenth, fourteenth, and fifteenth centuries. The condition of the Jews generally worsened, especially from the fourteenth century on: blind crowd hatreds and the greed of certain princes jointly held them responsible for public calamities, such as the Black Death, or imputed invented sacrileges to them. In every country there were frequent expulsions followed by returns authorized through payments, confiscations, and heavy taxes. The condition of the Jews was most favorable in the Christian kingdoms of Spain. It should be noted that in Avignon the popes gave the Jews effective protection against waves of anti-Semitism.

Certain aspects of military life in this period take on importance with regard to international relations. We should mention first the mercenary troops. They were important in the eleventh and twelfth centuries and more so in the centuries that followed. We have referred to the armies of Catalan and Navarrese mercenaries in the Byzantine Empire and in "Frankish" Greece. The "Great Companies," which were active in France during the Hundred Years War—more as troops of brigands than as part of an army—were largely made up of Bretons, Béarnese, English, and Germans. There were many Germans also, and likewise Hungarians, Bretons, and English in the bands of Italian *condottieri* during the fourteenth century; but in the fifteenth the Italian element dominated. In the fifteenth century there were a number of Scots and Spaniards in the service of the kings of France. All in all, whatever their rank or birth, these mercenaries were, from the fourteenth century on, members of an international troop of bandits.

A different aspect of the military factor in international relations is provided by the warlike ventures that involved the wellborn of every nation. In the fourteenth century nothing was more famous than the Prussian "crusade" in which, in addition to the Germans, knights from a great variety of countries participated, especially English, Gascon, Portuguese, Low Country, and Scandinavian. These military undertakings brought knights from a good part of Europe into contact with one another. It is curious to state that the Moslem sovereigns of Tunis, Tlemcen, and Morocco enrolled knights of Christian Europe in their armies—especially the Aragonese, who were numerous enough to be permanently commanded by an "alcaide" named by the king of Aragon. There were also French, English, and Germans. The same international importance cannot be recognized in these ventures in Barbary as in those in Prussia.

In the first third of the thirteenth century new routes across the great mountainous massifs separating southern Europe from the countries farther north were opened to traffic. These were the Sempione Pass and principally the Sankt-Gotthard Pass in the central Alps. The latter's importance has been pointed out, and we return to it only to stress one fact about it. Use of the Sankt-Gotthard Pass was made possible because a stone bridge was successfully built across the gorge where the Reuss flowed. Technical progress made possible this great event in the history of communication routes and all its economic and political results.

Finally, a few words should be said about the most important pilgrimages. Those previously mentioned still continued, even though Jerusalem was at times very difficult to reach. The series of extraordinary pilgrimages to Rome which brought plenary indulgences on the occasion of a jubilee or a holy year, was initiated by the pilgrimage of 1300, to which Boniface VIII invited Christendom. In 1350, from Avignon, Clement VI proclaimed a new holy year, and thereafter there were others at still closer intervals. They drew crowds of believers from every country to the Eternal City. Pilgrimages to Rome undertaken in these circumstances occupy a place in the history of international relations to which no other can lay claim.

13

Conclusion

℘HE AUTHOR hesitates to append a conclusion to this sketch of international relations in the Middle Ages. Not only is the subject so complex, but it is so lacking in unity.

We have to bear in mind that very different economic worlds have been related to each other. Certainly we could illuminate Christianity's conquests either in its Greek or in its Roman form and stress the generality of the same practices, the same kinds of piety, the same types of religious sensibility. Certainly we could call to mind the spread of so-called heretical doctrines or hostile attitudes to papal absolutism—above all, in the last centuries of the Middle Ages. Doubtless we could stress the spread of certain philosophical systems and more strongly emphasize that of certain art forms. All this is known. What then is the point in repeating it?

Perhaps an aspect of the history of international relations in the Middle Ages justifies the effort of extracting some general trends from the facts: the attempts to bring some degree of order into the chaos that the barbarian invasions and the collapse of the Roman Empire created in western Europe.

The first of these attempts that should be cited is an effort at restoration: the sixth-century *reconquista* of Justinian, the legitimate emperor living in the East. He tried to reincorporate the lost western empire and to rebuild from this empire the core of an ordered life that was always, according to him, the *Orbis Romanus*. The effort was not successful.

Nevertheless the idea of empire survived in the West. But it was the Church that became its guardian, especially the papacy under

Gregory the Great at the end of the sixth and at the beginning of the seventh century. The empire no longer corresponded to historical reality; in the thinking of the ecclesiastics it was confused with the Christian world; the emperor, the successor of Constantine and of Theodosius, had as his essential task the defense and promotion of the Church and the faith and the prevention or the limitation of strife among Christians.

Meanwhile there had developed a political power strong enough to make itself felt over almost all continental Christian Europe and to maintain a minimum of peace and order there. This was the Frankish monarchy of the Carolingians. Charlemagne, in having himself crowned emperor at Rome on December 25, 800, effected the synthesis of two forces: on the one hand, the imperial institution, invested with the mission of bringing order and peace; and on the other, a state of adequate strength.

It required less than fifty years for the Carolingian state to crumble and for the beginning of the breakup of the vast territories where the first emperors had tried to fulfill their task. Chaos speedily returned to western Europe.

The imperial idea, however had not entirely perished. In 962 it was once more incorporated into a political power: into the state that had most successfully resisted disorder, the Germany of Otto I. Events analogous to those of 800 followed. But although educated men, capable of thinking in general terms, still believed in the universal character of the empire, this latter was in fact limited to Germany, to Italy, and after 1034, to the kingdom of Burgundy. Between the tenth and the eleventh centuries certain emperors did exercise a hegemony beyond their own frontiers, particularly in countries recently won over to Christianity: Denmark, Sweden, Poland, and Hungary. But it was ephemeral and had little effect. The empire was only very ineffectually a core of order and of peace in the western world.

Another institution tried to play this role: the papacy. Its plans were of a spiritual order. But it implied the exercise by the pope of a discretionary power that emperors and kings had to obey, even in temporal matters. At the end of the eleventh century the Pope succeeded in mobilizing western knighthood under his leadership for the first crusade: he contributed, thus, to the awareness in the West of belonging to an ecumenical Christianity led by the Holy See. But in their efforts to realize their aspirations to supreme authority, the popes naturally clashed with the German sovereigns, who were invested with the imperial dignity. The struggle that began in the eleventh century was to last until the middle of the thirteenth.

In the second half of the twelfth century the points of view became more clearly delineated. Emperor Frederick Barbarossa, aided and inspired by the renaissance of Roman law, dreamed, in addition to victory over the Pope, of the effective re-establishment of imperial power over the whole of the West. The popes, relying on fast-developing canon law, fought for the establishment of a theocratic regime in which all states would be governed according to papal instructions. For some years Pope Innocent III did direct the destiny of the West; it could be claimed that he governed, from his lofty position, an important part of Europe. In its turn this theocracy also collapsed in the wars between the popes and the Emperor. By the time this conflict ended toward the middle of the thirteenth century, the empire was shattered, and Germany, which furnished it with the most direct means of power, was in the midst of total breakup; but weakened, undermined, and exposed to ever more hostilities, the papacy could no longer play its role as the power directing the West.

The France of Saint Louis took up the mission of providing order and peace, which was no longer discharged by the two institutions to which it belonged by right. France did not act through any claim: it exercised hegemony. Favorable circumstances, considerable material strength, and the sanctity of the King made this possible. The French hegemony was so well founded that the papacy, in making a new effort at the end of the thirteenth century to erect a theocratic government over Christianity, came into conflict with Philip the Fair and suffered a total defeat. Soon the popes, settled at Avignon, became the protégés of France and remained so for a long period.

The Hundred Years War ended French hegemony. Thereafter there was no institution that could order the life of western Europe to any great degree. The last sixty years of the fourteenth century and the whole of the fifteenth century were a new period of unbridled international anarchy. The Great Schism, tearing the Church apart, brought disorder to its zenith. These overwhelming ills most clearly showed the need for some order-giving element and certainly added to the concept of empire. The desire to see a power act that could prevent violence among Christians, lead a victorious war against Islam, and bring the Church back to unity and purity showed itself more strongly than ever during these two centuries. Dante, at the beginning of the fourteenth century, made himself the herald of the imperial ideal. For almost two hundred years theologians, jurists, and political thinkers defended and built up this same ideal. The German sovereigns—the emperors— used their power to try to make it a reality: Henry VII and Louis of Bavaria in the fourteenth century, Sigismund in the fifteenth. But these were vain, laughable efforts. Empire was a religion in which only its priests believed.

There was still another attempt to introduce a regulating and pacifying element into the life of the Christian West. It stemmed from the Church: not from the divided and discredited papacy, but from bishops, from members of the regular and secular clergy, and from the ecclesiastics teaching in the universities. It was they who provoked the calling of the great councils of the fifteenth century—of Pisa, Constance, Basel, and Ferrara; it was they who sat at these sessions and fought for the doctrine of supremacy of councils over popes. These "fathers" sought the re-establishment of unity in the Church, the reform of the Church "in its leadership and in its members," and also peace and harmony among Christians. Only the first aim was attained—at least within the Roman Church—but other aims failed completely largely because the opposition among the states from which the "fathers" came was too great.

Antagonism, division, partitioning, and unceasing wars between political units were characteristic of the close of the Middle Ages. The author of this book believes that this state of affairs can be contrasted only in terms of intensity with what had existed during the previous centuries. Nothing is more lamentable than the history of the attempts made during those centuries to provide western Europe with some permanent factor of peace and order. It is the history of a succession of defeats.

Bibliography

I   *Histoire générale*, by G. Glotz. Paris. One volume dealing with Roman history and eleven volumes dealing with the Middle Ages will be referred to in their appropriate chapters.

II   *Peuples et Civilisations*, edited by L. Halphen and P. Sagnac. Paris. Three volumes, will be referred to in their appropriate chapters. A general history.

III   *Clio: Introduction aux Études historiques*, edited by J. Calmette. Paris. Contains 2 volumes by J. Calmette on the Middle Ages: *Le Monde Féodal*, 3rd edition, published in collaboration with C. Higounet, 1951; and *L'Élaboration du Monde moderne*, 3rd edition, 1949.

IV   *Nouvelle Clio. L'histoire et ses problèmes*, edited by R. Boutruche and P. Lemerle. Paris. Containing L. Musset, *Les invasions. Les vagues germaniques*, 1965 and *Les invasions. Le second assaut contre l'Europe Chrétienne*, 1965; L. Génicot, *Le XIIIe siècle européen*, 1968; J. Heers, *L'Occident aux XIVe & XVe siècles. Aspects économiques et sociaux*, 2nd edition, 1966.

V   *Histoire de l'Église*, edited by A. Fliche and Msgr. V. Martin. Paris. Twelve volumes concerning the Middle Ages will be referred to in their appropriate chapters.

VI   *The Cambridge Economic History*, formerly edited by Sir John Clapham and Eileen Power, and currently edited by M. M. Postan and H. J. Habakkuk, 2nd edition. Volume I, *The Agrarian Life of the Middle Ages* (edited by M. M. Postan); Volume II, *Trade and Industry in the Middle Ages* (edited by M. M. Postan and E. E. Rich); Volume III, *Economic Organization and Policies in the Middle Ages* (edited by the same and E. Miller). Cambridge, 1966, 1952, 1963.

VII   *Allgemeine Wirtschaftsgeschichte des Mittelalters u. der Neuzeit*, I, by J. Kulischer. Munich and Berlin, 1928.

VIII   *Handbuch der deutschen Geschichte*, edited by A. O. Mayer.

Potsdam. Volume I, finished in 1940, concerns the Middle Ages and
is the work of F. Metz, H. Steinacker, F. Steinbach, E. Caspar,
E. Maschke, and H. Heimpel. A new edition has been in preparation since 1954 at Constance, edited by L. Just.

IX   *Handbuch de deutschen Geschichte*, edited by B. Gebhardt, 8th
     edition. The Middle Ages are treated in Volume I edited by H.
     Grundmann, the contributors being F. Baethgen, K. Bosl, M.-L. Bulst-
     Thiele, F. Ernst, K. Jordan, H. Löwe, E. Wahle. Stuttgart, 1954.

X   *History of England. G. M. Trevelyan*, 3rd edition. London, 1945.

XI   *Histoire de France pour tous les Français*. Paris, Volume I, which
     appeared in 1950, includes a treatment of the Middle Ages by
     E. Perroy.

XII *The Cambridge History of Poland: From the origins to Sobieski*,
     edited by W. F. Reddaway, J. H. Penson, O. Halecki, and D. Dy-
     boski. Cambridge, 1950.

XIII *Histoire générale des civilisations*, edited by M. Crouzet. Volume
     III, *Le Moyen Age*, by E. Perroy, in collaboration with J. Auboyer,
     C. Cahen, G. Duby, and M. Mollat. Paris, 1955.

XIV *Handbuch der Kirchengeschichte*, edited by H. Jedin. Freiburg i.
     Breisgau; One volume concerning the late Roman history and two
     volumes concerning the Middle Ages will be referred to in their ap-
     propriate chapters.

In the bibliographies for each chapter the reader will, when necessary,
be referred to the collections and works of this general bibliography by
the initials "GB" followed by the Roman numeral of the title in question.
When it is a question of a work that is part of the collection described
under (I) above, the numeral will be followed by "R" (Roman history)
or "MA" (Middle Ages).

In the following bibliography a work is described fully only at the
first citation. In later citations of a particular work, the name of the
author is given along with the Arabic number of the chapter giving the
full citation.

1 *The Breakdown of Roman Unity*

P. BATIFFOL. *Saint Grégoire le Grand*. Paris, 1928.

O. BERTOLINI. *Roma di fronte a Bisanzio e ai Langobardi*. Bologna, 1941.

———. *J Germani. Migrazioni e Regni nell'Occidente già Romano*. Milan, 1965.

L. BRÉHIER. *Le Monde Byzantin*. I. *Vie et mort de Byzance*. II. *Les institutions de l'Empire byzantin*. III. *La Civilisation byzantine*. Paris, 1947–1950. 3 vols. (*L'Évolution de l'humanité*, edited by H. BERR).

L. BRÉHIER and R. AIGRAIN. *Grégoire le Grand, les États barbares et la Conquête arabe*. Paris, 1938 (GB V, 5).

A. CARTELLIERI. *Weltgeschichte als Machtgeschichte. Die Zeit der Reichsgründungen*. Munich, 1927.

E. CASPAR. *Geschichte des Papsttums*, I. Tübingen, 1930.

R. G. COLLINGWOOD and J. N. L. MYRES. *Roman Britain and the English Settlements*. 2nd edition. Oxford, 1937. In the *Oxford History of England*, I.

C. COURTOIS. *Les Vandales et l'Afrique*. Paris, 1955.

M. DEANESLY. *A History of Early Medieval Europe*. London, 1956.

P. DE LABRIOLLE, G. BARDY, L. BRÉHIER, G. DE PLINVAL. *De la mort de Théodose à l'Élection de Grégoire le Grand*. Paris, 1939 (GB V, 4).

C. DIEHL and G. MARÇAIS. *Le Monde oriental de 395 à 1081*. Paris, 1936 (GB I, MA 3).

W. ENSSLIN. *Theoderich der Grosse*. Munich, 1947.

E. F. GAUTIER. *Le Passé de l'Afrique du nord, Les Siècles obscurs*. Paris, 1937.

A. GRABAR. *L'âge d'or de Justinien*. Paris, 1966.

L. HALPHEN. *Les Barbares*. 5th edition. Paris, 1948 (GB II, 5).

L. M. HARTMANN. *Geschichte Jtaliens im Mittelalter*, I. 2nd edition, II, 1–2. Gotha, 1923, 1900, 1903.

C. A. JULIEN. *Histoire de l'Afrique du Nord, des origines à la conquête arabe*. 2nd edition, by C. COURTOIS, Paris, 1951.

R. LATOUCHE. *Les Grandes Jnvasions et la Crise de l'Occident au Vᵉ siècle*. Paris, 1946.

————. *Les Origines de l'économie occidentale.* Paris, 1956 (*L'Évolution de l'humanité*, edited by H. BERR).

A. R. LEWIS. *Naval Power and Trade in the Mediterranean. A.D. 500–1100.* Princeton, 1951.

F. LOT. *La Fin du monde antique et le début du Moyen Age.* 2nd edition. Paris, 1951. (*L'Évolution de l'humanité.* Edited by H. BERR; English translation: *The End of the Ancient World and the Beginning of the Middle Ages.* London, 1931).

————. *Les Invasions germaniques.* 3rd edition, Paris, 1945.

————. *Les Invasions barbares.* Paris, 1937, 2 vols.

F. LOT, C. PFISTER, F. L. GANSHOF. *Les Destinées de l'Empire en Occident de 395 à 888,* 2nd edition. Paris, 1940–1941 (GBI, MA, 1).

G. LUZZATTO. *Storia economica d'Italia,* I. Rome, 1949.

R. MENÉNDEZ-PIDAL. *Historia de España,* III. *España Visigoda* (collaborators as follows: M. TORRES, R. PRIETO BANCES, M. LOPEZ SERRANO, DOM. J. PEREZ DE URBEL, E. CAMPO CAZORLA, J. FERNANDIS). Madrid, 1940.

G. OSTROGORSKY. *Geschichte des byzantinischen Staates.* 3rd edition. Munich, 1963.

A. PIGANIOL. *L'Empire Chrétien.* Paris, 1947 (GBI, R4, 2).

H. PIRENNE. *Mahomet et Charlemagne.* Brussels, 1937; English translation: *Mahomet and Charlemagne,* 2nd edition, London, 1957.

P. RICHÉ. *Éducation et culture dans l'Occident barbare.* Paris, 1962.

B. RUBIN. *Das Zeitalter Justinians.* I, Berlin, 1959.

L. SCHMIDT. *Geschichte der deutschen Stämme,* I. Die Ostgermanen, 2nd edition. Munich, 1934. II. *Die Westgermanen,* 2nd edition, in collaboration with H. ZEISS, I, 2, I ibid., 1938–1940; 1st edition, 2. Berlin, 1918.

E. SESTAN. *Stato e nazione nell' Alto Medioevo.* Naples, 1952.

E. STEIN. *Geschichte des spätrömischen Reiches,* I. Vienna, 1928.

————. *Histoire du Bas-Empire,* II. *De la disparition de l'empire d'occident à la mort de Justinien.* Paris, 1949.

F. STEINBACH. *Das Frankenreich* (GB VIII, 1, 2nd ed.), 1957.

F. M. STENTON. *Anglo-Saxon England.* 2nd edition. Oxford, 1950. (*Oxford History of England,* II.)

D. TALBOT RICE. *The Art of Byzantium.* London, 1959.

G. TESSIER. *Le baptème de Clovis.* Paris, 1964.

A. VAN DE VIJVER. *Clovis et la politique méditerranéenne,* in *Études d'histoire dédiées à la mémoire de Henri Pirenne par ses anciens élèves.* Brussels, 1937.

H. VON SCHUBERT. *Geschichte der christlichen Kirche im Frühmittelalter.* Tübingen, 1921.

C. VERLINDEN. *L'Esclavage dans le monde médiéval.* I. Bruges, 1955.

J. M. WALLACE-HADRILL. *The Barbarian West.* 2nd edition. London, 1957.

2   *The Carolingian Epoch*

H. AHRWEILER. *Byzance et la mer.* Paris, 1966.

E. AMANN. *L'Époque carolingienne.* Paris, 1937 (GB V, 6).

H. ARBMAN. *Schweden und das karolingische Reich.* Stockholm, 1937.

H. G. BECK, E. EWIG, J. A. JUNGMANN, F. KEMPF. *Vom kirchlichen Frühmittelalter zur gregorianischen Reform.* Freiburg i. Br., 1966 (GB XIV, 3, 1).

O. BERTOLINI. *Roma.* Chap. 1.

L. BRÉHIER. *Monde byzantin.* Chap. 1.

W. BRAUNFELS. *Die Welt der Karolinger und ihre Kunst.* Munich, 1968.

P. BREZZI. *Roma e l'Impero medioevale.* Bologna, 1947.

D. BULLOUGH. *The Age of Charlemagne.* London, 1965.

J. CALMETTE. *L'Effondrement d'un Empire et la Naissance d'une Europe.* Paris, 1942.

A. CARTELLIERI. Chap. 1.

E. CASPAR. *Geschichte des Papsttums,* II. Tübingen, 1933.

————. *Das Papsttum unter fränkischer Herrschaft.* 2nd edition. Darmstadt. 1956.

C. DAWSON. *The Making of Europe: An Introduction to the History of European Unity.* London, 1932.

M. DEANESLY. Chap. 1.

J. DE GHELLINCK, S.J. *Littérature latine au Moyen Age.* Paris, 1939. 2 vols.

C. DIEHL and G. MARÇAIS. Chap. 1.

F. DÖLGER. *Byzanz u. die europaïsche Staatenwelt.* Ettal, 1953.

——. *Byzantinische Diplomatik.* Ettal, 1956.

A. DOPSCH. *Die Wirtschaftsentwicklung der Karolingerzeit.* 3rd edition. Darmstadt, 1962.

L. DUCHESNE. *Les Premiers Temps de l'État pontifical.* 3rd edition. Paris, 1911.

F. DVORNIK. *Les Slaves, Byzance et Rome au IXe siècle.* Paris, 1926.

——. *Le Schisme de Photius. Histoire et Légende.* Paris, 1950.

R. FOLZ. *Le couronnement impérial de Charlemagne.* Paris, 1964.

F. L. GANSHOF. *Qu'est-ce que la Féodalité?* 4th edition. Brussels, 1968. (English translation: *Feudalism,* 3rd edition, London and New York, 1964.)

J. GAY. *L'Italie méridionale et l'empire byzantin.* Paris, 1904.

H. GRÉGOIRE. *L'Origine et le Nom des Croates et des Serbes,* in *Byzantion,* XVII, 1944–1945.

L. HALPHEN. *Les Barbares.* Chap. 1.

——. *Charlemagne et L'Empire carolingien.* 2nd edition. Paris, 1949. (*L'Evolution de l'Humanité,* edited by H. BERR.)

L. M. Hartmann. *Gesch. Italiens.* Chap. 1. Vols. II, III, 1–2, 1908–1911.

A. HAUCK. *Kirchengeschichte Deutschlands,* II. 3rd and 4th editions. Leipzig, 1912.

Karl der Grosse (Collective work edited by W. BRAUNFELS, P. E. SCHRAMM, etc.), I (History), II (Letters), III (Art), IV (Posthumous fame), Düsseldorf, 1965–1967.

R. LATOUCHE. *Origines.* Chap. 1.

W. LEVISON. *England and the Continent in the eighth century.* Oxford, 1946.

A. LEWIS. Chap. 1.

M. LOMBARD. *L'or musulman du VIIe and IXe siècle,* in *Annales,* 1947.

F. LOT. *Les Invasions barbares.* Chap. 1.

F. LOT, C. PFISTER, F. L. GANSHOF (in collaboration with H.-X. AR-QUILLIÈRE, M. AUBERT, R. P. G. THÉRY, F. VERCAUTEREN). Chap. 1.

G. LUZZATTO. Chap. 1.

H. MITTEIS. *Lehnrecht und Staatsgewalt.* Weimar, 1933.

L. Musset. *Les Peuples scandinaves au Moyen Âge*. Paris, 1951.

——. GB IV.

G. Ostrogorsky. Chap. 1.

H. Pirenne. Chap 1.

F. Rörig. *Magdeburgs Entstehung u. die ältere Handelsgeschichte*, in *Miscellanea Academica Berolinensia*, II, 1, 1950.

E. Sabbe. *Les Relations économiques entre l'Angleterre et le Continent au haut Moyen Âge*, in *Le Moyen Âge*, 1950.

T. Schieffer. *Winfrid-Bonifatius und die christliche Grundlegung Europas*. Freiburg i. Br., 1954.

Dom P. Schmitz, O.S.B. *Histoire de l'Ordre de Saint Benoît*, I and II. 2nd edition. Maredsous, 1948.

E. Sestan. Chap. 1.

F. Steinbach. Chap. 1.

F. M. Stenton. Chap 1.

D. Talbot Rice. Chap. 1.

W. Ullmann. *The Growth of Papal Government in the Middle Ages*. London, 1955.

A. A. Vasiliev. *Histoire de l'Empire byzantin* (translated from Russian by P. Brodin and A. Bourguina). Paris, 1932. 2 vols. (English translation: *History of the Byzantine Empire*, 2nd edition, Madison, 1952.)

C. Verlinden. Chap. 1.

G. Vernadsky. *Ancient Russia*. New Haven, 1949. (In *History of Russia*, by G. Vernadsky and M. Karpovich, I.)

W. Vogel. *Die Normannen und das fränkische Reich*. Heidelberg, 1906.

H. von Schubert. Chap. 1.

J. M. Wallace-Hadrill. Chap. 1.

3   *The Practice of International Relations in the Early Middle Ages*

S. Bakhrouchine and E. Kosminski. *La Diplomatie du Moyen Age*, in *Histoire de la Diplomatie*, edited by W. Potiemkine (translated from Russian by X. Pamphilova and M. Eristov), I. Paris, 1946.

B. BLUMENKRANZ. *Juifs et Chrétiens dans le monde occidental*, 430–1096. Paris, 1960.

G. B. BOGNETTI. *Note per la storia del passaporto e dell' salvo condotto*. Pavia, 1933.

L. BRÉHIER. *Le Monde byzantin*, *II*. *Les Institutions de l'Empire byzantin*. Paris, 1949. Chap. 1.

J. CALMETTE. *La Diplomatie carolingienne du traité de Verdun à la mort de Charles le Chauve*. Paris, 1901.

P. CLASSEN. *Karl der Grosse, das Papsttum und Byzanz*, in *Karl der Grosse*, I. Chap. 2.

M. DEFOURNEAUX. *Charlemagne et la Monarchie asturienne*, in *Mélanges d'histoire du Moyen Âge dédiés à la mémoire de L. Halphen*. Paris, 1951.

F. DÖLGER. *Byzanz*. Chap. 2.

————. *Diplomatik*. Chap. 2.

P. DUPARC. *Les Cluses et la Frontière des Alpes*, in *Bibliothèque de l'École des Chartes*, CIX. 1951.

E. EWIG. *Die fränkischen Teilungen u. Teilreiche* (511–613) : Akad. d. Wissensch. u. Literatur zu Mainz, Abhamdl. d. Geistes-u. Sozialwissensch. Kl., 1952.

————. *Die fränkischen Teilreiche im 7. jahrhundert* 613–714. Trierer Zeitschrift, 1954.

A. FANTA. *Die Verträge der Kaiser mit Venedig*. Mitteilungen des Instituts für Oesterreichische Geschichtsforschung, I. Ergänzungsband, 1885.

F. L. GANSHOF. *L'Étranger dans la monarchie franque*, in *L'Étranger*, II (Recueils de la Société Jean Bodin, X. 1958).

————. *Merowingisches Gesandtschaftswesen*, in *Aus Geschichte und Landeskunde . . . F. Steinbach gewidmet*, Bonn, 1960.

————. *Les traités des rois mérovingiens*, Tijdschrift voor rechtsgeschiedenis, *Revue d'histoire du droit*, XXXII, 1964.

————. *Les relations extérieures de la monarchie franque sous les premiers souverains carolingiens*, Annali di storia del diritto, V–VI, 1961–1962.

————. *A propos du tonlieu sous les Mérovingiens*, in *Studi in onore di A. Fanfani*, II, Milan, 1962.

————. *A propos du tonlieu à l'époque carolingienne*, in *La città nell'alto Medioevo*, Spoleto, 1959.

————. *The treaties of the Carolingians*, in *Medieval and Renaissance Studies*, III. Chapel Hill, 1968.

W. HEYD. *Histoire du Commerce du Levant au Moyen Âge* (translated from German by FURCY RENAUD). Paris, 1885, 2 vols.

E. JORANSON. *Danegeld in France*. Rock Island, 1924.

H. KRETSCHMAYR. *Geschichte von Venedig*, I. Gotha, 1905.

A. LOEHREN. *Beiträge zur Geschichte des Gesandtschaftlichen Verkehrs im Mittelalter*, I. *Die Zeit vom vierten bis zum Ende des neunten Jahrhunderts*. Heidelberg, 1884.

V. MENZEL. *Deutsches Gesandtschaftswesen im Mittelalter*. Hanover, 1892.

B. PARADISI. *L' "amicitia" internazionale nell'Alto Medio Evo*, in *Scritti in onore di Contardo Ferrini*. Milan, 1947.

————. *Storia del diritto internazionale nel Medio Evo*, I. Milan, 1940.

4   *The West:*
from the Breakup of the Carolingian Empire
to the First Triumph of the Papacy

E. AMANN and A. DUMAS. *L'Église au Pouvoir des Laïques*. Paris, 1939 (GB V, 7).

H. G. BECK, etc. Chap. II.

A. BECKER. *Studien zum Investiturproblem in Frankreich*. Saarbrücken, 1955.

M. BLOCH. *La Société féodale*. Paris, 1939–1940. 2 vols. (*Évolution de l'Humanité*, edited by H. BERR).

M. BOULET. *Le Commerce médiéval européen* (*Histoire du Commerce*, edited by J. LACOUR-GAYET, II. Paris, 1950).

L. BRÉHIER. *Le Monde byzantin*, III. *La Civilisation byzantine*. Paris, 1950. Chap.1.

P. BREZZI. Chap. 2.

Z. N. BROOKE. *Lay Investiture and Its Relation to the Conflict of the Empire and Papacy.* London, 1939. (Proceedings of the British Academy, XXV).

A. CARTELLIERI. *Die Weltstellung des deutschen Reiches.* Munich, 1932.

———. *Der Aufstieg des Papsttums im Rahmen der Weltgeschichte.* Munich, 1936.

F. CHALANDON. *Histoire de la Domination normande en Italie et en Sicile.* Paris, 1907. 2 vols.

P. DAVID. *The Church in Poland, from its Origins to 1250* (in GB XII).

J. DHONDT. *Études sur la Naissance des Principautés territoriales en France.* Bruges, 1948.

E. ENNEN. *Frühgeschichte der mittelalterlichen Stadt.* Bonn, 1953.

G. FASOLI. *Le incursioni ungare in Europa nel secolo X.* Florence, 1945.

R. FAWTIER. *Les Capétiens et la France.* Paris, 1942.

A. FLICHE. *La Réforme grégorienne et la Reconquête chrétienne.* Paris, 1940 (GB V, 8).

R. FOLZ. *La naissance du Saint-Empire.* Paris, 1967.

———. *L'idée d'empire en Occident du Ve au XIV siècle.* Paris, 1953.

F. L. GANSHOF. Chap. 2.

J. GAY. Chap. II.

L. GÉNICOT. *Les Lignes de Faîte du Moyen Âge.* 3rd edition. Tournai, 1961.

L. HALPHEN. *Les Barbares.* Chap. 1.

———. *L'essor de l'Europe.* 3rd edition. Paris, 1948 (GB II, 6).

———. *La conquête de la Mediterranée par Européens au XIe et au XIIe siècle,* in *Mélanges d'Histoire offerts à Henri Pirenne,* 1. Brussels, 1926.

K. HAMPE. *Das Hochmittelalter.* 4th edition. Münster, 1953.

———. *Deutsche Kaisergeschichte in der Zeit der Salier und Staufer.* 7th edition by F. BAETHGEN, Leipzig, 1937.

L. M. HARTMANN: *Gesch. Italiens.* Chap. 1. Vol. III, 2; Vol. IV, 1. 1911–1915.

A. HAUCK. Chap. 2. Vol. III. 3rd and 4th editions. 1904.

W. HEYD. Chap. 3.

R. HOLTZMANN. *Geschichte der Sächsischen Kaiserzeit.* Munich, 1941.

———. *Der Weltherrschaftsgedanke des mittelalterlichen Kaisertums und die Souveränität der Europäischen Staaten,* in *Historische Zeitschrift,* CLIX, 1939.

H. JANKUHN. *Haithabu.* 3rd edition. Neumünster, 1956.

F. KEMPF. *Die Kirche im Zeitalter der gregorianischen Reform* (GB XIV, 3, 1).

S. KETRZYNSKI. *Introduction of Christianity and Early History of Poland* (in GB XII).

W. KIENAST. *Deutschland und Frankreich in der Kaiserzeit.* Leipzig, 1943.

H. KRETSCHMAYR. Chap. 3.

R. LATOUCHE. *Origines.* Chap. 1.

J. F. LEMARIGNIER. *Le gouvernement royal aux premiers temps capétiens.* Paris, 1965.

E. LIPSON. *The Economic History of England,* I. 10th edition. London, 1949.

M. LOMBARD. Chap. 2.

F. LOT and R. FAWTIER. *Histoire des institutions françaises au moyen âge,* I (14 chapters on the principalities by 14 contributors), II (royal institutions by the editors), III (institutions of the Church by three contributors).

G. LUZATTO. Chap. 1.

T. MAYER. *Fürsten und Staat.* Weimar, 1950.

H. MITTEIS. Chap. 2.

———. *Der Staat des hohen Mittelalters.* 4th edition. Weimar, 1953.

L. MUSSET. Chap. 2.

W. OHNSORGE. *Abendland und Byzanz.* Darmstadt, 1958.

H. PIERENNE. *Histoire économique et sociale du Moyen Âge,* 3rd edition revised by H. VAN WERVEKE. Paris, 1969.

———. *Les Villes du Moyen Âge.* Brussels, 1927.

H. PLANITZ. *Die deutsche Stadt im Mittelalter.* Cologne, 1954.

A. L. POOLE. *From Domesday Book to Magna Carta.* Oxford, 1951 (*Oxford History of England,* III).

Y. RENOUARD. *Les Hommes d'affaires italiens du Moyen Âge,* 2nd edition. Paris, 1968.

H. G. RICHARDSON and G. O. SAYLES. *The Governance of Medieval England from the Conquest to Magna Carta.* Edinburgh, 1963.

F. RÖRIG. Chap. 2.

L. SANTIFALLER. *Zur Geschichte des ottonisch-Salischen Reichshirchensystems.* 2nd edition, Vienna, 1964.

A. SCHAUBE. *Handelsgeschichte der Romanischen Völker des Mittelmeergebiets bis zum Ende der Kreuzzüge.* Munich, 1906.

DOM. P. SCHMITZ. Chap. 2.

P. E. SCHRAMM. *Kaiser, Rom, und Renovatio.* Leipzig, 1929, 2 vols.

————. *Herrschaftszeichen und Staatssymbolik* (with 9 contributors), Stuttgart, 3 vols, 1954–1956.

A. SCHULTE. *Geschichte des mittelalterlichen Handels und Verkehrs zwischen Westdeutschland und Italien.* Leipzig, 1900, 2 vols.

R. W. SOUTHERN. *The Making of the Middle Ages.* London, 1953.

E. E. STENGEL. *Kaisertitel und Souveränitätsidee,* in *Deutsches Archiv fur Geschichte des Mittelalters,* III. 1939.

F. M. STENTON. Chap. 1.

Studien zu den Anfängen des europäischen Städtewesens (16 chapters by 16 contributors) edited by T. MAYER, Lindau, 1958.

G. TELLENBACH. *Die Entstehung des deutschen Reiches.* Munich, 1940.

————. *Libertas.* Stuttgart, 1936.

————. *Vom Zusammenleben abendländischer Völker im Mittelalter,* frqm *Festschrift für G. Ritter.* Tübingen, 1950.

W. ULLMANN. Chap. 2.

C. VERLINDEN. Chap. 1.

Z. WOJCIECHOWSKI. *L'État polonais au Moyen Âge.* Paris, 1949.

5   *The Byzantine World and the Islamic World*

H. AHRWEILER. Chap. II.

L. BRÉHIER. Chap. 1.

C. CAHEN. *La Syrie du nord à l'époque des Croisades et la Principauté d'Antioche.* Paris, 1940.

F. CHALANDON. *Essai sur le règne d'Alexis I Comnène.* Paris, 1900.

P. DAVID. *Études historiques sur la Galice et le Portugal.* Lisbon and Paris, 1947.

M. DEFOURNEAUX. *Les Français en Espagne aux XIe et XIIe siècles.* Paris, 1949.

L. G. DE VALDEAVELLANO. *Historia de España,* I. 2nd edition. Madrid, 1955, 2 vols.

C. DIEHL. *Manuel d'Art byzantin.* 2nd edition. Paris, 1925–1926, 2 vols.

C. DIEHL and G. MARÇAIS. Chap. 1.

C. DIEHL, L. OECONOMOS, R. GUILLAND, R. GROUSSET. *L'Europe orientale de 1081 à 1453.* Paris, 1945 (GB I, MA 9, 1).

F. DÖLGER. *Byzanz.* Chap. 2.

———. *Diplomatik.* Chap. 2.

C. ERDMANN. *Die Entstehung des Kreuzzugsgedankens.* Stuttgart, 1935.

A. FLICHE. Chap. 4.

———. *Urbain II et la Croisade,* in *Revue d'Histoire de l'Eglise de France,* XIV, 1927.

F. L. GANSHOF. *Robert le Frison et Alexis Comnène,* Byzantion, XXXI, 1961.

J. GAY. Chap. 2.

S. D. GOITEIN. *From the Mediterranean to India,* in *Speculum,* 1954.

P. GRIERSON. *The Debasement of the Bezant in the Eleventh Century.* Byzantinische Zeitschrift, 1954.

R. GROUSSET. *Histoire des Croisades et du Royaume franc de Jérusalem.* Paris, 1934–1936, 3 vols.

———. *Histoire de l'Arménie des origines à 1071.* Paris, 1947.

———. *L'Empire du Levant.* Paris, 1946.

———. *L'Empire des Steppes.* 2nd edition. Paris, 1941.

P. GUINARD. *La Péninsule ibérique, la Reconquête chrétienne de la dislocation du Califat de Cordoue à la mort de saint Ferdinand,* in C. PETIT-DUTAILLIS and P. GUINARD, *L'essor des Etats d'Occident.* 2nd edition. Paris, 1944 (GB I, MA 4, 2).

A History of the Crusades (a collective work), I, edited by MARSHALL W. BALDWIN, Philadelphia, 1958.

J. L. LA MONTE. *Feudal Monarchy in the Latin Kingdom of Jerusalem.* Cambridge (Mass.), 1932.

P. LEMERLE. *Le style byzantin.* Paris, 1943.

E. LÉVI-PROVENÇAL. *L'Espagne musulmane au Xᵉ siècle*. Paris, 1932.
———. *Histoire de l'Espagne musulmane*. 2nd edition. Paris, 1950–1953, 3 vols.

M. LOMBARD. Chap. 2.
———. *Arsenaux et bois de marine dans la Méditerranée musulmane*, in Travaux du deuxième colloque d'histoire maritime, Paris, 1959.

R. S. LOPEZ. *Silk Industry in the Byzantine Empire*. in Speculum, XX, 1945.
———. *The Dollar of the Middle Ages*, in Journal of Economic History, 1951.

F. LOT. *Invasions Barbares*. Chap. 1.

G. MARÇAIS. *La Berbérie musulmane et l'Orient au Moyen Âge*. Paris, 1946.
———. *Manuel d'art musulman*. Paris, 1926–1927, 2 vols.
———. *L'art de l'Islam*, Paris, 1946.

R. MENENDEZ-PIDAL. *La España del Cid*. Madrid, 1929, 2 vols.

G. OSTROGORSKY. Chap. 1.
———. *Quelques problèmes d'histoire de la paysannerie byzantine*. Brussels, 1956.

J. PRAWER. *Colonization Activities in the Latin Kingdom of Jérusalem*, in Revue belge de Philologie et d'Histoire, XXIX, 1951.
———. *Les premiers temps de la féodalité dans le royaume latin de Jérusalem*, Tijdschrift voor Rechtsgeschiedenis. Revue d'histoire du droit, XXII, 1954.
———. *Histoire du Royaume latin de Jérusalem*, I. Paris, 1969.

J. RICHARD. *Le Comté de Tripoli sous la dynastie toulousaine*. Paris, 1945.
———. *Le royaume latin de Jérusalem*. Paris, 1953.

P. ROUSSET. *Les Origines et les Caractères de la Première Croisade*. Neuchâtel, 1945.

S. RUNCIMAN. *A History of the Crusades*. I. *The First Crusade*. Cambridge, 1951.

C. SANCHEZ ALBORNOZ. *L'Espagne et l'Islam*, in Revue Historique, CLXIX, 1932.
———. *España. Un enigma historico*. Buenos Aires, 1957, 2 vols.

————. *Despoblacion y repoblacion del Valle del Duero.* Buenos Aires, 1966.

R. W. SOUTHERN. Chap. 4.

D. TALBOT RICE. Chap. 1.

H. TERRASSE. *Jslam d'Espagne.* Paris, 1958.

————. *Conséquences d'une invasion berbère: Le rôle des Almoravides dans l'histoire de l'Occident,* in *Mélanges L. Halphen.* Paris, 1951.

F. THIRIET. *La Romanie vénitieme au moyen âge.* Paris, 1959.

A. A. VASILIEV. Chap. 2.

C. VERLINDEN. Chap. 1.

G. VERNADSKY. *Kievan Russia.* 1948 (Chap. 2, Vol. II).

M. VILLEY. *La Croisade. Essai sur la formation d'une théorie juridique.* Paris, 1942.

A. WAAS. *Geschichte der Kreuzzüge.* Freiburg i. Br., 1956, 2 vols.

G. WIET. *L'Éypte arabe, de la Conquête arabe à la Conquéte ottomane,* in *Histoire de la nation egyptienne,* edited by G. HANOTAUX, 4. Paris, 1937.

6   *West and East*

H. AHRWEILER. Chap. 2.

H. APPELT. *Die Kaiseridee Friedrich Barbarossas.* Vienna, 1967. (Akad. d. Wiss.).

M. AUBERT. *Les plus anciennes croisées d'ogives,* in *Bulletin monumental,* 1934.

E. BACH. *La Cité de Gênes au XJJ siècle.* Copenhagen, 1955.

R. H. BAUTIER. *Les foires de Champagne,* in *La Foire* (Recueils de la Société JEAN BODIN, V, 1953).

M. BLOCH. Chap. 4.

A. BORST. *Das Rittertum im Hochmittelalter.* Saeculum, X, 1959.

A. BRUCE BOSWELL. *Twelfth Century: From Growth to Division* (in GB XII).

M. BOULET. Chap. 4.

J. BOUSSARD. Le gouvernement d'Henri II Plantagenet. Paris, 1956.

L. BRÉHIER. Chap. I.

P. BREZZI. Chap. 2.

C. BROOKE. The Twelfth Century Renaissance. London, 1969.

Z. N. BROOKE. The English Church and Papacy from the Conquest to the Reign of John. Cambridge, 1931.

E. H. BYRNE. Genoese Shipping in the Twelfth and Thirteenth Centuries. Cambridge (Mass.), 1930.

C. CAHEN. Chap. 5.

A. CARTELLIERI. Der Vorrang des Papsttums zur Zeit der ersten Kreuzzüge. Munich, 1941.

E. CASPAR. Roger II und die Gründung der normannisch-sicilischen Monarchie. Innsbruck, 1904.

F. CHALANDON. Chap. 4.

————. Les Comnène. Jean II et Manuel Comnène. Paris, 1918.

G. CONSTABLE. A Note on the Route of the Anglo-Flemish Crusaders of 1147, Speculum, 28, 1953.

J. CRAEYBECKX. Un grand commerce d'importation. Les vins de France aux anciens Pays-Bas. Paris, 1958.

P. DAVID. Chap. 5.

M. DEFOURNEAUX. Chap. 5.

J. DE GHELLINCK. Chap. 2.

————. L'Essor de la Littérature latine au XIIe siècle. Louvain, 1946, 2 vols.

C. DEREINE. Chanoines, in Dictionnaire d'Histoire et de Géographie ecclésiastiques, organized by CARDINAL BAUDRILLART, edited by A. DE MEYER and E. VAN CAUWENBERGH, XII, Paris, 1951.

L. G. DE VALDEAVELLANO. Chap. 5.

C. DIEHL. Art byzantin. Chap. 5.

C. DIEHL, L. OECONOMOS, R. GUILLAND, R. GROUSSET. Chap. 5.

F. M. A. DIMIER. Recueil de plans d'églises cisterciennes. Paris, 1949, 2 vols.

R. DION. Histoire de la vigne et du vin en France des origines au XIXe siècle. Paris, 1959.

P. DOLLINGER. La Hanse. Paris, 1964.

A. DUPONT. *Les Relations commerciales entre les Cités maritimes de Languedoc et les Cités méditerranéennes d'Espagne et d'Italie du Xe au XIIe siècles.* Nîmes, 1942.

H. P. EYDOUX. *L'architecture des églises cisterciennes d'Allemagne.* Paris, 1952.

R. FAWTIER. Chap. 4.

A. FLICHE. *Réforme grégorienne et Reconquête chrétienne.* Chap. 4.

———. *Du Premier Concile du Latran à l'avènement d'Innocent III.* Paris, 1944–53. (GB V, 9).

H. FOCILLON. *Art d'Occident.* 2nd edition. Paris, 1947.

R. FOLZ. *Idée d'empire.* Chap. 4.

A. FOREST, F. VAN STEENBERGHEN, and M. DE GANDILLAC. *Le Mouvement doctrinal du XIe au XIVe siècle* (GB V, 13).

L. GÉNICOT. Chap. 4.

L. K. GOETZ. *Deutsch-Russische Handelsgeschichte des Mittelalters.* Lübeck, 1922.

R. GROUSSET. *Histoire des Croisades.* Chap. 5.

L. HALPHEN. *Essor de l'Europe.* Chap. 4.

K. HAMPE. *Hochmittelalter.* Chap. 4.

———. *D. Kaisergesch.* Chap. 4.

———. *Der Zug nach dem Osten.* 3rd edition. Leipzig, 1935.

C. H. HASKINS. *The Renaissance of the Twelfth Century.* Cambridge, (Mass.), 1927.

A. HAUCK. *Kirchengesch. Deutschl.* Chap. 2. Vol. IV. 3rd and 4th editions, 1913.

W. HEYD. Chap. 3.

C. HIGOUNET. *Mouvements de population dans le midi et la France du XIe and XVe siècles,* Annales, 1953.

A History of the Crusades, I. Chap. 5.

R. HOLTZMANN. *Weltherrschaftsgedanke.* Chap. 4.

A. O. JOHNSEN. *Les relations intellectuelles entre la France et la Norvège, 1150–1214,* in *Le Moyen Âge,* LVII, 1951.

E. JORDAN. *L'Allemagne et l'Italie aux XIIe et XIIIe siècles.* Paris, 1939 (GB I, MA 4, 2).

W. KIENAST. Chap. 4.

P. KOSCHAKER. *Europa u. das römische Recht.* 2nd edition. Munich, 1953.

R. KÖTZSCHKE and W. EBERT. Geschichte der ostdeutschen Kolonisation. Leipzig, 1937.

H. KRETSCHMAYR. Chap. 3.

J. L. LA MONTE. Chap. 5.

G. LE BRAS, C. LEFEBVRE, J. RAMBAUD. L'âge classique, 1140–1378. Paris, 1965 (Histoire du droit & des institutions de l'Eglise en Occident, VII).

P. LEMERLE. Chap. 5.

E. LÉVI-PROVENÇAL. Histoire de l'Espagne musulmane. Chap. 5.

E. LIPSON. Chap. 4.

M. LOMBARD. Chaps. 2 and 5.

R. S. LOPEZ. Studi sull'economia genovese nel Mediaevo. Turin, 1936.

F. LOT and R. FAWTIER. Chap. 4.

G. LUZZATTO. Chap. 1.

J. B. MAHN. L'Ordre cistercien et son gouvernement des origines au milieu du XIIIe siècle. 2nd edition, Paris, 1951.

G. MARÇAIS. Berbérie. Chap. 5.

P. MARIOTTE. Le comté de Bourgogne sous les Hohenstaufen, 1156–1208. Paris, 1963.

T. MAYER. Chap. 4.

H. MITTEIS. Der Staat d. h. Mittelalt., Chap. 4.

L. MUSSET. Chap. 2.

W. OHNSORGE. Chap. 4.

G. OSTROGORSKY. Chap. 1.

M. PACAUT. Louis VII et son royaume. Paris, 1964.

———. Frédéric Barberousse. Paris, 1967.

S. PAINTER. French Chivalry. Baltimore, 1940.

R. PERNOUD. Le Moyen Âge jusqu'en 1291, in Histoire du Commerce de Marseille, edited by G. RAMBERT. Paris, 1949.

C. PETIT-DUTAILLIS and P. GUINARD. Chap. 5 (under GUINARD).

H. PIRENNE. Un Grand Commerce d'exportation au Moyen Âge: Les Vins de France, in Annales d'Histoire économique et sociale, V. 1933. Reproduced in Histoire économique de l'Occident médieval, Paris, 1951.

H. PIRENNE and H. VAN WERVEKE. Histoire économique et Sociale. Chap. 4.

A. L. POOLE. Chap. 4.

E. POWER. *The Wool Trade in English Medieval History*. Oxford, 1941.

J. PRAWER. *Royaume de Jérusalem*. Chap. 5.

Y. RENOUARD. Chap. 4.

J. RICHARD. *Royaume*. Chap. 5.

H. G. RICHARDSON and G. O. SAYLES. Chap. 4.

F. RÖRIG. *Die Europäische Stadt*, in *Propyläen Weltgeschichte*, edited by W. GOETZ, IV. Berlin, 1932 (re-edited separately: Göttingen, 1955).

———. *Hansische Beiträge zur deutschen Wirtschaftsgeschichte*. Breslau, 1928.

P. ROUSSET. Chap. 5.

S. RUNCIMAN. Chap. 5. Vol. II. *The Kingdom of Jerusalem*, 1952.

C. SANCHEZ ALBORNOZ. *España*. Chap. 5.

A. SCHULTE. Chap. 4.

F. J. SCHMALE. *Studien zum Schisma des Jahres 1130*. Cologne, 1961.

P. SCHMITZ. Chap. 2. Vols. III–VI. 1948–1949.

P. E. SCHRAMM. *Herrschaftszeichen*. Chap. 4.

A. SCHULTE. Chap. 4.

R. W. SOUTHERN. Chap. 4.

D. TALBOT RICE. Chap. 1.

G. TELLENBACH. *Zusammenleben*. Chap. 4.

H. TERRASSE. Chap. 5.

F. THIRIET. Chap. 5.

W. ULLMANN. Chap. 2.

H. VAN WERVEKE. *Bruges et Anvers*. Brussels, 1944.

A. A. VASILIEV. Chap. 2.

C. VERLINDEN. Chap. 1.

A. WAAS. Chap. 5.

G. WIET. Chap. 5.

H. WOLTER and H. G. BECK. *Das Hochmittelalter* (GB, XIV, 3, 2), 1968.

7   The Practice of International Relations in the Tenth,
                  Eleventh, and Twelfth Centuries

L. G. ARIAS. Una embajada cristiana a un soberan Musulman hace mil
    años, Cuadernos de historia diplomática, I, 1954.
J. BACHMANN. Die päpstlichen Legaten in Deutschland und Skandinavien,
    1125–1159. Berlin, 1913.
S. BAKHROUCHINE and E. KOSMJNSKI. Chap. 3.
L. BITTNER. Die Lehre von den völkerrechtlichen Vertragsurkunden.
    Stuttgart, 1924.
BLUMENKRANZ. Chap. 3.
G. B. BOGNETTI. Chap. 3.
M. BOULET-SAUTEL. L'aubain dans la France contumière au moyen âge,
    in L'étranger, II. Chap. 3.
J. BOUSSARD. Les mercenaires au XIIᵉ siècle. Bibliothèque de l'école des
    Chartes, 1945–1946.
L. BRÉHIER. Monde byzantin. II and III. Chap. 1.
F. CHALANDON. Chap. 4.
P. DAVID. Chap. 5.
M. DEFOURNEAUX. Chap. 5.
A. DEL VECCHIO and E. CASANOVA. Le rappresaglie nei comuni medi-
    evali. Florence, 1894.
L., COMTE DE MAS LATRIE. Traités de Paix et de commerce et documents
    divers concernant les relations des chrétiens avec les Arabes de
    l'Afrique septentrionale au Moyen Âge. Paris, 1866. Supplément,
    1872.
M. DE TAUBE. Les origines de l'Arbitrage international. Antiquité et
    Moyen Âge, in Recueil des Cours de l'Académie de Droit interna-
    tional, XLII, 1932.
R. DION. Les frontières de la France. Paris, 1947.
F. DÖLGER. Byzanz. Chap. 2.
———. Diplomatik. Chap. 2.
G. DUNKEN. Die politische Wirksamkeit der päpstlichen Legaten in der
    Zeit des Kampfes zwischen Kaisertum u. Papsttum in Oberitalien
    unter Friedrich J. Berlin, 1931.

A. FANTA. Chap. 3.

A. FLICHE. *Le rôle international de la papauté,* in *Bulletin du comité international des sciences historiques,* I, 5, 1928.

S. FREY. *Das öffentlichrechtliche Schiedsgericht in Oberitalien im XII. und XIII. Jahrhundert,* 1928.

I. FRIEDLÄNDER. *Die päpstlichen Legaten in Deutschland und Italien am Ende des 12. Jahrhunderts.* Berlin, 1928.

F. L. GANSHOF. *Recherches sur le lien juridique qui unissait les chefs de la Première Croisade à l'empereur byzantin,* in Mélanges offerts à P. E. MARTIN. Genève, 1961.

A. GRABOÏS. *De la trève de Dieu à la paix du Roi,* in Mélanges offerts à René Crozet. Poitiers, 1966.

H. GRUNDMANN. *Rotten u. Brabanzonen, Deutsches Archiv f. Gesch. d. Mittelalters,* V, 1942.

W. HEYD. Chap. 3.

C. HIGOUNET. *Les Chemins de Saint-Jacques et les sauvetés de Gascogne,* in *Annales du Midi,* LXIII, 1951.

H. HOFFMANN. *Gottesfriede und Treuga Dei.* Stuttgart, 1964.

G. JACOB. *Arabische Berichte von Gesandten an Germanische Fürstenhofe.* Leipzig, 1927.

W. JANSSEN. *Die päpstlichen Legaten in Frankreich vom Schisma Anaklets II bis zum Tode Coelestins III. 1130–1198.* Cologne, 1960.

W. KIENAST. Chap. 4.

————. *Die deutschen Fürsten im dienste der Westmächte bis zum Tode Philipps des Schönen von Frankreich.* Utrecht, 1924–1931. 2 vols.

————. *Zur Geschichte des Cid,* in *Deutsches Archiv für Geschichte des Mittelalters,* III, 1939.

G. KISCH. *The Jews in Medieval Germany.* Chicago, 1949.

H. KRETSCHMAYR. Chap. 3.

E. LAMBERT. *La Cathédrale de Saint-Jacques de Compostelle et l'école des grandes églises romanes des routes de pèlerinage,* in *Etudes Médiévales* by this scholar, I. Paris, 1956.

————. *Le Livre de Saint-Jacques et les routes de Pélerinages à Compostelle,* in *Revue géographique des Pyrénées et du Sud-Ouest,* XIV, 1943; *Etudes,* I.

———. *Ordres et Confréries dans l'Histoire du Pèlerinage de Compostelle*, in *Annales du Midi*, LV, 1943; and *Etudes*, I.

———. *Les Routes dans les Pyrénées Atlantiques*, in *Primer Congresso internacional del Pireneo*, Saragossa, 1951; and *Etudes*, I.

J. F. LEMARIGNIER. *Recherches sur l'Hommage en Marche et les frontières féodales*. Lille, 1945.

E. LEVI-PROVENÇAL. *Esp. mus. au Xe siècle*, Chap. 5.

M. LINTZEL. *Studien über Liudprand von Cremona*. Berlin, 1933.

R. S. LOPEZ. *Storia delle Colonie genovesi nel mediterraneo*. Bologna, 1938.

F. LOT. *L'Art militaire et les armées au Moyen Âge*. Paris, 1946. 2 vols.

B. D. LYON. *From Fief to indenture*. Cambridge (Mass.), 1957.

E. MÂLE. *L'Art religieux du XIIe siècle en France*. 5th edition. Paris, 1947.

R. MENENDEZ-PIDAL. Chap. 5.

V. MENZEL. Chap. 3.

H. MITTEIS. *Politische Verträge im Mittelalter in Zeitschrift der Savigny Stiftung für Rechtsgeschichte. Germanistiche Abteilung*, 1950, and in *Die Rechtsidee in der Geschichte*. Weimar, 1957, by this scholar.

W. OHNSORGE. *Päpstliche und gegenpäpstliche Legaten in Deutschland und Skandinavien, 1159–1181*. Berlin, 1929.

R. OURSEL. *Les pélerins du moyen âge*. Paris, 1963.

B. PARADISI. *Storia*. Chap. 3.

J. PRAWER. Chap. 5.

———. *Dai "fœdera iniqua" alle "crisobulle" bizantine*. Rome, 1954.

———. *The Settlement of the Latins in Jerusalem*. Speculum, XXVII, 1952.

———. *Royaume*. Chap. 5.

J. RICHARD. *Le "conduit" des routes et la fixation des limites entre mouvances féodales*, Annales de Bourgogne, XXIV, 1952.

S. RUNCIMAN. Chap. 5.

C. SANCHEZ ALBORNOZ. *Espagne*. Chap. 5.

T. SCHIEFFER. *Die päpstlichen Legaten in Frankreich vom Vertrage von Meersen (870) bis zum Schisma von 1180*. Berlin, 1935.

A. SCHULTE. Chap. 4.

M. SZANIECKI. *Essai sur les Fiefs-rentes.* Paris, 1946.

M. SZEFTEL. *La condition légale des étrangers dans la Russie novgorodo-kievienne,* in *L'étranger,* II; Chap. 3 (under GANSHOF).

L. VASQUEZ DE PARGA, J. M. LA CARRÁ, and J. URIA RIU. *Las Peregrinaciones a Santiago de Compostella.* Madrid, 1948–1949. 3 vols.

L. VERCAUTEREN-DE SMET. *Étude sur les rapports politiques de l'Angleterre et de la Flandre sous le règne du comté Robert II,* in *Études d'histoire dédiées à la mémoire de Henri Pirenne par ses anciens élèves.* Brussels, 1937.

C. VERLINDEN. Chap. 1.

J. VIELLIARD. *Le guide du pélerin de Saint-Jacques de Compostelle,* 3rd edition. Macon, 1953.

8   *The Era of Theocracy and French Hegemony*

H. AMMANN. *Deutschland u. die Tuchindustrie Nordwest-Europas im Mittelalter, Hansische Geschichtsblätter.* 1954.

E. BARATIER. *De 1291 à 1423* in *Histoire du Commerce de Marseille,* edited by G. RAMBERT, II. Paris, 1951.

R. H. BAUTIER. Chap. 6.

A. BON. *Le Péloponnèse byzantin jusqu'en 1204.* Paris, 1951.

A. BORST. *Die Katharer.* Stuttgart, 1953.

M. BOULET. Chap. 4.

J. BOUSSARD. *Henri II.* Chap. 6.

L. BRÉHIER. Chap. 1.

P. BREZZI. Chap. 2.

Z. N. BROOKE. Chap. 6.

R. BRUNSCHVIG. *La Berbérie orientale sous les Hafsides,* I. Paris, 1940.

L. BUISSON. *König Ludwig IX, der Heilige und das Recht.* Freiburg i. Br., 1954.

E. H. BYRNE. Chap. 6.

C. CAHEN. Chap. 5.

A. CARTELLIERI. *Philip JJ, August, König von Frankreich*. Leipzig, 1899–1922. 4 vols. (Vol. IV in two parts).

C. CIPOLLA, J. DHONDT, M. M. POSTAN, and P. WOLFF. *Démographie. Moyen Âge*, in *JXe Congrès International des sciences historiques. Rapports*. Paris, 1950.

J. CRAEYBECKX. Chap. 6.

P. DAVID. Chap. 4.

R. DAVIDSOHN. *Geschichte von Florenz*. Leipzig, 1896–1927. 4 vols. (two vols. in several parts).

J. DE STURLER. *Les relations politiques et les échanges commerciaux entre le duché de Brabant et l'Angleterre au Moyen Âge*. Paris, 1936.

L. G. DE VALDEAVELLANO. Chap. 5.

C. DIEHL. *Art Byzantin*. Chap. 5.

C. DIEHL, L. OECONOMOS, R. GUILLAND, and R. GROUSSET. Chap. 5.

R. DION. Chap. 6.

R. DOEHAERD. *Les Relations commerciales entre Gênes, la Belgique et l'Outremont*. Brussels, 1941. 3 vols.

P. DOLLINGER. Chap. 6.

C. E. DUFOURCE. *L'Espagne catalane et le Maghreb aux XJJJe et XJVe siècles*. Paris, 1966.

R. FAWTIER. Chap. 4.

———. *L'Europe occidentale de 1270 à 1328*. Paris, 1940 (GBI, MA 6, 1).

A. FLICHE, C. THOUZELLIER, and Y. AZAÏS. *La chrétienté romaine*. Paris, 1950. (GBV, 10).

H. FOCILLON. Chap. 6.

R. FOLZ. *Jdée d'empire*. Chap. 4.

A. FOREST, F. VAN STEENBERGHEN, and M. DE GANDILLAC. Chap. 6.

L. GÉNICOT. Chap. 4.

———. *XJJJe siècle*. (GB IV).

L. K. GOETZ. Chap. 6.

R. GROUSSET. *Histoire des Croisades*, Chap. 5.

L. HALPHEN. *Essor de l'Europe*. Chap. 4.

K. HAMPE. *Hochmittelalter*, Chap. 4.

——. *Kaisergesch.* Chap. 4.

——. *Zug nach d. Osten.* Chap. 6.

C. H. HASKINS. *The Rise of the Universities.* New York, 1923.

A. HAUCK. *Kirchengesch. Deutschl.* Chap. 2, Vol. IV; V, 1. Leipzig, 1911.

C. HIGOUNET. *Un Grand Chapître de l'histoire du XIIIe siècle: La rivalité des maisons de Toulouse et de Barcelone pour la prépondérance méridionale,* in *Mélanges d'histoire du Moyen Âge dédiés à la mémoire de Louis Halphen.* Paris, 1951.

G. HILL. *History of Cyprus,* I, II. Cambridge, 1940–1948.

History of the Crusades, J. Chap. 5; II, edited by R. L. WOLFF, 1962.

E. JORDAN. Chap. 6.

——. *Les Origines de la domination angevines en Italie.* Paris, 1909.

F. KEMPF. *Papsttum u. Kaisertum bei Innozenz III.* Rome, 1954.

W. KIENAST. Chap. 4.

H. KRETCHMAYR. *Gesch. v. Venedig,* II. Gotha, 1920.

C. V. LANGLOIS. *Saint Louis, Philippe le Bel, les derniers Capétiens directs.* Paris, 1902. (*Histoire de France,* III, 2, edited by E. LAVISSE.)

H. LAURENT. *Un Grand Commerce d'exportation au Moyen Âge. La draperie des Pays-Bas en France et dans les pays méditerranéens.* Paris, 1935.

E. LIPSON. Chap. 4.

R. S. LOPEZ. *La prima crisi della banca di Genova.* Milan, 1956.

——. *Majorcans and Genoese on the North Sea route in the 13th Century,* in *Revue Belge de Philologie et d'histoire,* XXIX, 1951.

F. LOT and R. FAWTIER. Chap. 4.

G. LUZZATTO. Chap. 1.

E. MÂLE. *L'Art Religieux du XIIIe siècle en France.* 4th edition. Paris, 1919.

G. MARÇAIS. Chap. 5.

T. MAYER. Chap. 4.

H. MITTEIS. *Staat,* Chap. 4.

L. MUSSET. Chap. 2.

G. Ostrogorsky. Chap. 1.

R. Pernoud. Chap. 6.

C. Petit-Dutaillis and P. Guinard. Chap. 5. (Under P. Guinard.)

H. Pirenne. Histoire de Belgique, I. 5th edition. Brussels, 1929.

H. Pirenne and H. Van Werveke. Histoire économique et sociale. Chap. 4.

A. L. Poole. Chap. 4.

E. Power. Chap. 6.

F. M. Powicke. Stephen Langton. Oxford, 1928.

———. The Loss of Normandy. Manchester, 1913.

———. King Henry III and the Lord Edward. Oxford, 1947.

W. Reese. Die Niederlande und das deutsche Reich, I. Berlin, 1941.

Y. Renouard. Chap. 4.

———. Les Voies de communication entre pays de la Méditerranée et pays de l'Atlantique au Moyen Âge, in Mélanges d'histoire du Moyen Âge dédiés à la mémoire de L. Halphen. Paris, 1951.

J. Richard. Chap. 5.

F. Rörig. Hansische Beiträge. Chap. 6.

———. Stadt. Chap. 6.

S. Runciman. Chap. 5. Vol. III. The kingdom of Acre, 1954.

C. Sanchez Albornoz. España. Chap. 5.

A. Sapori. Studi di Storia economica medievale. 2nd edition. Florence, 1947.

A. Schaube. Chap. 4.

P. E. Schramm. Der König von Frankreich. Weimar, 1939. 2 vols.

P. E. Schramm. Herrschaftszeichen. Chap. 4.

A. Schulte. Chap. 4.

J. R. Strayer. Laïcisation of French and English Society in the 13th Century, in Speculum, XV, 1940.

D. Talbot Rice. Chap. 1.

F. Thiriet. Chap. 5.

H. Tillmann. Papst Innocenz III. Bonn, 1954

F. van Steenberghen. Aristote en occident. Louvain, 1946.

H. van Werveke. Essor et déclin de la Flandre, in Studi in onore di Gino Luzzatto, I. Milan, 1950.

———. Introduction historique (sur la draperie médiévale), in G. de

POERCK, *La Draperie médiévale en Flandre et en Artois. Techniques et Terminologie*, I. Bruges, 1951.

F. VERCAUTEREN. *Documents pour servir à l'histoire des financiers Lombards en Belgique*, in Bulletin de l'Institut historique belge de Rome, XXVI, 1950–1951.

C. VERLINDEN. *The Rise of Spanish Trade in the Middle Ages*, in Economic History Review, X, 1940.

A. WAAS. Chap. 5.

P. WOLFF. *Le Problème des Cahorsins*, in Annales du Midi, LXII, 1950.

R. L. WOLFF. *The Second Bulgarian Empire*, in Speculum, XXIV, 1949.

H. WOLTER and H. G. BECK. Chap. 6.

9   *The East in the Thirteenth and at the Beginning of the Fourteenth Century*

R. BACCHELLI, A. MONTEVERDI, R. S. LOPEZ, Y. RENOUARD, and O. DEMUS. *La civiltà veneziana del secolo di Marco Polo.* Florence, 1955.

A. BON. *Recherches sur la principauté d'Achaïe*, in Études médiévales offertes à A. Fliche. Montpellier, 1952.

G. BRATIANO. *Recherches sur le commerce genois dans la Mer Noire au XIIIe siècle.* Paris, 1920.

L. BRÉHIER. Chap. 1.

———. *Les missions franciscaines au Moyen Âge*, in Saint François d'Assise. Paris, 1927.

A. BRUCE BOSWELL. *Territorial Division and Mongol Invasions* (GB XII).

C. CAHEN. Chap. 5.

C. DIEHL, L. OECONOMOS, R. GUILLAND, and R. GROUSSET. Chap. 5.

F. DÖLGER. *Byzanz.* Chap. 2.

———. *Diplomatik.* Chap. 2.

H. FRANKE. *Europa in der Ostasiatischen Geschichtschreibung des 13. u. 14. Jahrhunderts*, in Saeculum, II, 1951.

R. Grousset. Histoire des Croisades. Chap. 5.

――――. Empire des Steppes. Chap. 5.

――――. Empire du Levant. Chap. 5.

R. Grousset, J. Auboyer, and J. Buhot. L'Asie orientale des origines au XVe siècle (GB I, MA 10, 1). Paris, 1941.

L. Halphen. Essor de l'Europe. Chap. 4.

W. Heyd. Chap. 3.

G. Hill. Chap. 8.

H. Kretschmayr. Chap. 8.

J. L. La Monte. Chap. 5.

M. Lombard. Caffa et la fin de la route mongole, in Annales, 1950.

J. Longnon. L'Empire latin de Constantinople et la Principauté de Morée. Paris 1949.

R. S. Lopez. Studi. Chap. 6.

――――. European Merchants in the Medieval Indies, in Journal of Economic History, III, 1943.

A. C. Moule. Christians in China. London, 1930.

G. Ostrogorsky. Chap. 1.

P. Pelliot. Les Mongols et la Papauté, in Revue de l'Orient Chrétien, XXIII, XXIV, XXVIII. 1922–1923, 1924, 1931–1932.

E. Power. The Opening of the Land Routes to Cathay, in A. P. Newton, Travel and Travellers of the Middle Ages. London, 1926.

J. Richard. Royaume. Chap. 5.

――――. La Papauté et les missions catholiques en Orient au Moyen Age, in Mélanges d'archéologie et d'histoire, LVIII, 1941–1946.

F. Reisch. Wilhelm von Rubruck, Reise zu den Mongolen. Leipzig, 1934.

A. A. Vasiliev. Chap. 2.

C. Verlinden. La Colonie vénitienne de Tana, centre de la traite des esclaves au XIVe et au début du XV siècle, in Studi in onore di Gino Luzzatto, II. Milan, 1950.

――――. Esclavage et ethnographie sur les bords de la Mer Noire, in Miscellanea in honorem L. van der Essen. Brussels, 1947.

――――. Traite des esclaves et traitants italiens à Constantinople, in Le Moyen Âge, 1963 (vol. published on the occasion of the jubilee).

C. Vernadsky. Chap. 5.

A. WAAS. Chap V.

M. WALRAET. *Sur les traces de Marco Polo.* Brussels, 1948.

Z. WOJCIECHOWSKI. Chap. 4.

R. L. WOLFF. *The Second Bulgarian Empire.* Speculum, XXIV, 1939.

SIR HENRY YULE. *The Book of Ser Marco Polo.* 3rd edition, by H. CORDIER, London, 1903, 2 vols. and *Addenda*, 1920.

10 *The Great Depression*

H. AMMANN. *Tuchindustrie.* Chap. 8.

———. *Die deutschen u. schweizerischen Messen im Mittelalter,* in *La Foire.* Chap. 6.

———. *Die Zurzacher Messen im Mittelalter.* Aarau, 1923.

———. *Neue Beiträge zur Geschichte der Zurzacher Messen.* Aarau, 1929.

———. *Nachträge zur Geschichte der Zurzacher Messen im Mittelalter,* in *Argovia,* XLVIII, 1936.

———. *Die friedberger Messen,* in *Rheinische Vierteljahrsblätter,* XV–XVI, 1950–1951.

———. *Die Anfänge der Leinenindustrie des Bodenseegebietes und der Ostschweiz,* in *Zeitschrift für schweizerische Geschichte,* XXIII, 1943.

H. AUBIN. *The Lands East of the Elbe and German Colonization East-wards,* in *Cambridge Economic History,* I (GB VI).

F. BAETHGEN. *Europa im Spätmittelalter.* Berlin, 1951.

E. BARATIER. Chap. 8.

F. BASTIAN. *Das Rutingerbuch, 1383–1407, und verwandtes Material zum Regensburger süd-ostdeutschen Handel und Münzwesen,* I. Regensburg, 1944.

F. BOCK. *Nationalstaatliche Regungen in Italien bei den Guelfisch-Ghibellinischen Auseinandersetzungen von Innocenz III bis Johann XXII,* in *Quellen und Forschungen,* XXXIII, 1944.

A. BON. Chap. 9.

F. BOREL. *Les Foires de Genève au XVe siècle*. Geneva, 1899.

M. BOULET. Chap. 4.

R. BOUTRUCHE. *La Crise d'une Société. Seigneurs et Paysans du Bordelais pendant la Guerre de Cent Ans*. Paris, 1947.

L. BRÉHIER. Chap. 1.

F. CALASSO. *Le glossatori et la sovranità*. 2nd edition. Milan, 1951.

E. M. CARUS-WILSON. *La Guède française en Angleterre*, in *Revue du Nord*, 1953.

————. *Medieval Merchant Venturers*. London, 1954.

C. CIPOLLA, J. DHONDT, M. M. POSTAN, and P. WOLFF. Chap. 8.

E. COORNAERT. *Draperies rurales, Draperies urbaines. L'Évolution de l'industrie flamande au Moyen Âge et au XVIe siècle*, in *Revue belge de philologie et d'histoire*, XXVIII, 1950.

A. COVILLE. *Les premiers Valois et la Guerre de Cent Ans*, in *Histoire de France*, edited by E. LAVISSE, IV. Paris, 1902.

————. *De 1328 à 1380*. Paris, 1941 (GB I, MA 6, 2).

J. CRAEYBECKX. Chap. 6.

G. DE LAGARDE. *La Naissance de l'Esprit laïque au déclin du Moyen Âge*. Saint-Paul-Trois-Châteaux, 1934–1946. 6 vols.

E. DÉPREZ. *Les préliminaires de la Guerre de Cent Ans*. Paris, 1902.

R. DE ROOVER. *La Formation et l'Expansion de la Comptabilité à partie double*, in *Annales d'histoire économique et sociale*, 1937.

————. *L'évolution de la lettre de change*. Paris, 1953.

J. DE STURLER. Chap. 8.

L. G. DE VALDEAVELLANO. Chap. 5.

C. DIEHL, L. OECONOMOS, R. GUILLAND, and R. GROUSSET. Chap. 5.

R. DION. Chap. 6.

R. DOEHAERD. Chap. 8.

P. DOLLINGER. Chap. 6.

R. FAWTIER. *Europe Occidentale*. Chap. 8.

K. A. FINK and E. ISERLOH. *Das Spätmittelalter* (GB XIV, 3, 2,), 1968.

R. FOLZ. *Idée d'empire*. Chap. 4.

L. K. GOETZ. Chap. 6.

R. GROUSSET. *Empire du Levant*. Chap. 5.

————. *Empire des Steppes*. Chap. 5.

B. HAGEDORN. *Die Entwicklung der wichtigsten Schiffstypen bis ins 19.*
   Jahrhundert. Leipzig, 1914.

O. HALECKI. *Casimir the Great. From the union with Hungary to the*
   union with Lithuania (in GB XII).

A. HAUCK. *Kircheng. Deutschl.* Vol. V, 1, Chap. 2, 1911.

H. HEIMPEL. *Deutschland im späteren Mittelalter,* in *Handb. d. deut-*
   schen Gesch., edited by A. O. MEYER (GB VIII).

P. HEINSIUS. *Das Schiff der Hansichen Frühzeit.* Weimar, 1956.

G. HILL. Chap. 8.

History of the Crusades, II. Chap. 8.

M. Z. JEDLICKI. *German Settlement in Poland* (in GB X).

E. JORDAN. *Dante et la théorie romaine de l'Empire,* in *Revue historique*
   de droit français et étranger, XLV–XLVI, 1921–1922.

N. IORGA. *Geschichte des Osmanischen Reiches.* I. Gotha, 1908.

W. KIENAST. *Die Anfänge des europäischen Staatensystems im späteren*
   Mittelalter, in *Historische Zeitschrift,* CLIII, 1936.

P. KOSCHAKER. Chap. 6.

R. KÖTZSCHKE and W. EBERT. Chap. 6.

H. KRETSCHMAYR. Chap. 8.

G. LADNER. *Das heilige Reich des mittelalterlichen Westens,* in *Die Welt*
   als Geschichte, XI, 1951.

H. LAURENT. Chap. 8.

M. P. LESNIKOV. *Beiträge zur Baltisch-Niederländischen Handelsges-*
   chichte, in Wissenschaftliche Zeitschrift der Karl Marx Universität,
   1957–1958.

S. LIPSON. Chap. 4.

J. LONGNON. Chap. 9.

R. S. LOPEZ. Chaps. 5, 7, and 8.

H. S. LUCAS. *The Low Countries and the Hundred Years' War.* Ann
   Arbor, 1929.

G. LUZZATTO. Chap. 1.

C. M. McILWAIN. *The Growth of Political Thought in the West.* New
   York, 1932.

————. *The English Common Law, Barrier against Absolutism,* in
   American Historical Review, 1943–1944.

M. MALOWIST. *Histoire sociale. Époque Contemporaine* (misleading title: it consists of Poland and neighboring countries on the Baltic from the fourteenth to the sixteenth centuries), in *IXe Congrès international des sciences historiques. Rapports.* Paris, 1950.

G. MARÇAIS. Chap. 5.

F. MELIS. *Storia de la ragioneria.* Bologna, 1950.

———. *Ancora sulle origini della partita doppia.* Bolletino Ligustico, 1954.

———. *Aspetti della vita economica medievale. Studi nell'Archivo Datini di Prato,* I, Siena, 1962.

S. MOCHI ONORI. *Fonti canonistische dell'Idea moderna dello Stato.* Milan, 1951.

G. MOLLAT. *Les Papes d'Avignon.* 9th edition. Paris, 1949.

L. MUSSET. Chap. 2.

N. NABHOLZ (for the Middle Ages), L. VON MURALT, R. FELEN, and E. DÜRR. *Geschichte der Schweiz,* I. Zurich, 1932.

J. U. NEF. *Mining and Metallurgy in Medieval Civilization,* in the *Cambridge Economic History,* II (GB VI).

G. OSTROGORSKY. Chap. 1.

K. PAGEL. *Die Hanse.* Berlin, 1942.

E. PERROY. *Aux Origines d'une économie contractée. Les Crises du XIVe siècle,* in *Annales,* 1949.

———. *La Guerre de Cent Ans.* Paris, 1945. (Revised English edition: *The Hundred Years War,* Oxford, 1951.)

G. PEYRONNET. *Les Relations politiques entre la France et l'Italie principalement au XIVe siècle et dans la première moitié du XVe siècle,* in *Le Moyen Âge,* LX, LVI, 1949–1950.

H. PIRENNE. *Histoire de Belgique.* Chap. 8. Vol. I. 5th edition, Vol. II, 3rd edition, 1932.

H. PIRENNE, A. RENAUDET, E. PERROY, M. HANDELSMAN, and L. HALPHEN. *La Fin du Moyen Âge.* Paris, 1931. 2 vols. (GB II, 7).

H. PIRENNE and H. VAN WERVEKE. *Mouvement économique et social.* Chap. 4.

C. W. PREVITÉ-ORTON. *Marsilius of Padua,* in *Proceedings of the British Academy,* XXI, 1935.

F. Quicke. *Les Pays-Bas à la veille de l'unification bourguignonne.* Brussels, 1948.

H. Reincke. *Bevölkerungsprobleme der Hansestädte,* in *Hansische Geschichtsblätter,* LXX, 1951.

Y. Renouard. Chap. 4.

———. *Conséquences et Interêt démographiques de la Peste noire de 1348,* in *Population,* 1948.

———. *Les Relations des papes d'Avignon et des compagnies commercantes et bancaires de 1316 à 1378.* Paris, 1941.

F. Rörig. *Mittelalterliche Weltwirtschaft.* Jena, 1933.

———. *Wesen und Leistung der deutschen hanse,* in *Propyläen Weltgeschichte,* additional volume: *Die Nordische Welt,* Berlin, 1937.

———. *Stadt.* Chap. 6.

———. *Das Meer u. das europäische Mittelalter,* in *Zeitschrift des Vereins für Hamburgische Geschichte,* 1951.

A. A. Ruddock. *Italian Merchants and Shipping in Southampton.* Oxford, 1951.

I. Saltmarsh. *Plague and Economic Decline in England in the Later Middle Ages,* in the *Cambridge Historical Journal,* VII, 1941.

C. Sanchez Albornoz. *España.* Chap. 5.

A. Sapori. *La crisi delle compagnie mercantili dei Bardi e dei Peruzzi.* Florence, 1926.

———. *Le Marchand Italien au Moyen Âge.* Paris, 1952.

F. Schneider. *Kaiser Heinrich VII.* Greiz, 1924–1928.

A. Schulte. Chap. 4.

Kenneth M. Setton. *Catalan Domination of Athens, 1311–1388.* Cambridge (Mass.), 1948.

E. E. Stengel *Avignon u. Rhens.* Weimar, 1930.

K. Tyminiecki. *Reunion of the Kingdom* (in GB XII).

W. Ullmann. *Medieval Papalism.* London, 1949.

———. *The Development of the Medieval Idea of Sovereignty,* in *English Historical Review,* LXIV, 1949.

J. A. van Houtte. *Bruges et Anvers, marchés nationaux ou internationaux du XIVe siècle au XVIe siècle,* in *Revue du Nord,* XXXIV, 1952.

H. VAN WERVEKE. Chap. 6.

―――. *De zwarte dood in de Zuidelijke Nederlanden*, in *Mededelingen van de Koninklijke Vlaamse Academie voor Wetenschappen van België*. 1950 (with summaries in French).

F. VERCAUTEREN. *Note sur les rapports de Marino Sanudo avec le Hainaut, le Brabant et la Flandre*, in *Bulletin de l'institut historique belge à Rome*, 1953.

C. VERLINDEN. *La grande peste de 1348 en Espagne*, in *Revue belge de philologie et d'histoire*, XVII, 1938.

P. VINOGRADOFF. *Roman Law in Medieval Europe*. 2nd edition by F. DE ZULUETA. Oxford, 1929.

Z. WOJCIECHOWSKI. Chap. 4.

P. WOLFF. *Un Chemin de Flandre*, in *Le Moyen Âge*, 1946.

―――. *Le Moyen Âge*, in *Histoire générale du travail*, Paris, 1960.

G. ZELLER. *Les Rois de France, candidats à l'Empire*, in *Revue historique*, CLXXIII, 1934.

11 *The Decline of the Middle Ages and the Dawn of the Modern Era*

H. AMMANN. *Messen*. Chap. 10.

F. BAETHGEN. Chap. 10.

J. N. L. BAKER. *History of Geographical Discovery and Exploration*, Rev. ed. London, 1953.

J. BARTIER. *Charles le Téméraire*. Brussels, 1944.

M. BLOCH. *Les caractères originaux de l'histoire rurale français*. 2nd edition. Paris, 1952.

P. BONENFANT. *Philippe le Bon*. 3rd edition, Brussels, 1955.

―――. *Du meurtre de Montereau au traité de Troyes*. Brussels, 1958.

F. BOREL. Chap. 10.

A. BRUCE BOSWELL. *Jagielo's Successors* (in GB XII).

M. BOULET. Chap. 4.

F. BRAUDEL. *La Méditerranée et le monde meditérranéen au temps de Philippe II*, 2nd edition. Paris, 1967.

L. BRÉHIER. Chap. 1.

J. CALMETTE and E. DÉPREZ. *La France et l'Angleterre en conflit.* Paris, 1937. (GB I, MA 7, 1).

————. *Les Premières grandes puissances.* Paris, 1939 (GB I, MA 7, 2).

J. CALMETTE and G. PÉRINELLE. *Louis XI et l'Angleterre.* Paris, 1930.

E. M. CARUS WILSON. Chap. 10.

C. CIPOLLA, J. DHONDT, M. M. POSTAN, and P. WOLFF. Chap. 8.

H. COING. *Römisches Recht in Deutschland.* Milan, 1964 (Ius Romanum Medii Aevi, V, c).

E. DELARUELLE, E. R. LABANDE, and P. OURLIAC. *L'Eglise au temps du Grand Schisme et de la crise conciliaire.* Paris, 1962 (GB V, 14).

H. DE MAN. *Jacques Coeur.* Berne, 1950.

R. DE ROOVER. *The Rise and Decline of the Medici Bank.* 2nd edition. Cambridge (Mass.), 1963.

————. *Money, Banking and Credit in Mediaeval Bruges.* Cambridge (Mass.), 1948.

L. G. DE VALDEAVELLANO. Chap. 5.

C. DIEHL, L. OECONOMOS, R. GUILLAND, and R. GROUSSET. Chap. 5.

S. D'IRSAY. *Histoire des Universités françaises et étrangères,* I. Paris, 1933.

R. DOEHAERD and C. KERREMANS. *Les Relations commerciales entre Gênes, la Belgique et l'Outremont, 1400–1440.* Brussels, 1952.

P. DOLLINGER. Chap. 6.

K. A. FINK, E. ISERLOH, J. GLAZIK, and H. G. BECK. *Das Spätmittelalter.* Chap. 10.

J. GILL *The Council of Florence.* Cambridge, 1959.

L. K. GOETZ. Chap. 6.

A. GRUNZWEIG. *Correspondance de la Filiale brugeoise des Medici.* Brussels, 1931.

B. HAGEDORN. Chap. 10.

O. HALECKI. *Problems of the New Monarchy, 1434–1436* (in GB XII).

A. HAUCK. *Kirchengesch. Deutschl.* Chap. 2. Vol. V, 2, 1920.

J. HEERS. *Gênes au XVe siècle.* Paris, 1961.

H. HEIMPEL. Chap. 10.

P. Heinsius. Chap. 10.

W. Heyd. Chap. 3.

G. Hill. Chap. 8. Vols. II, III, 1948.

N. Iorga. Chap. 10. Vols. I, II, 1909.

V. Kliutchevsky. *Geschichte Russlands,* I. II. Stuttgart, 1925.

P. Koschaker. Chap. 6.

H. Krause. *Kaiserrecht u. Rezeption.* Heidelberg, 1952.

H. Kretschmayr. Chap. 8.

La Roérie. *Les transformations du gouvernail, Annales d'histoire économique et sociale,* 1935.

H. Laurent and F. Quicke. *Les Origines de l'État bourguignon. L'accession de la maison de Bourgogne aux duchés de Brabant et de Limbourg.* Brussels, 1939.

Lefebvre des Noëttes. *De la Marine antique à la Marine moderne. La Révolution du Gouvernail.* Paris, 1935.

E. Lipson. Chap. 4.

J. Longnon. Chap. 9.

J. Loserth. *Hus und Wyclif.* 2nd edition. Munich, 1925.

C. H. McIlwain. Chap. 10.

V. Magalhaes Godinho. O *"Mediterraneo" Saariano et las caravanas de ouro,* in *Revista de Historia* (Sao Paulo), 1955–1956.

————. *Les Grandes Découvertes,* in *Bulletin des études portugaises,* 1953.

J. Maréchal. *Bruges, centre du commerce de l'argent aux derniers siècles du Moyen Âge,* in *Revue de la Banque,* 1950.

C. Marinesco. *Philippe le Bon, duc de Bourgogne et la Croisade,* I, in *Actes du VIe Congrès international des Études byzantines,* Paris, 1948 (appeared in 1951); II, in *Bulletin des Études portugaises,* Coimbra, 1949.

————. *L'Ile de Rhodes au XVe siècle,* in *Miscellanea Giovanni Mercati, V, Città del Vaticano,* 1946.

M. Martens. *Les Maisons de Medici et de Bourgogne au XVe siècle* in *Le Moyen Âge,* LVI, 1950.

L. Mirot. *La Politique française en Italie de 1380 à 1422.* Paris, 1934.

M. Mollat. *Le Commerce maritime Normand à la fin du Moyen Âge.* Paris, 1952.

K. E. MURAWSKI. *Zwischen Jannenberg und Jhorn*. Göttingen, 1953.

L. MUSSET. Chap. 2.

G. OSTROGORSKY. Chap 1.

K. PAGEL. Chap. 10.

F. PAPÉE. *Imperial Expansion 1466–1506* (in GB, XII).

E. PERROY. *Guerre de Cent Ans*. Chap. 10.

———. *L'Angleterre et le Grand Schisme d'Occident. Étude sur la politique religieuse de l'Angleterre sous Richard II*. Paris, 1933.

———. *Feudalism or Principalities in Fifteenth Century France*, in *Bulletin of the Institute of Historical Research*, XX, 1945.

G. PEYRONNET. Chap. 10.

H. PIRENNE. *Histoire de Belgique*. Chap. 10. Vols. II, III. 3rd. edition, 1923.

H. PIRENNE and H. VAN WERVEKE. *Histoire économique et sociale*. Chap. 4.

E. POWER. *Wool Trade*. Chap. 6.

E. PRESTAGE. *The Portuguese Pioneers*. London, 1933.

F. REYNAUD. *De 1423 à 1480*, in *Histoire du commerce de Marseille*, II. Chap. 8.

A. RENAUDET. *Autour d'une définition de l'Humanisme*, in *Bibliothèque d'Humanisme et Renaissance*, VI, 1945.

Y. RENOUARD. Chap. 4.

R. RICARD. *Contribution à l'Étude du Commerce génois au Maroc durant la période portugaise*, in *Annales de l'Institut d'Études orientales de l'Université d'Alger*, III, 1937.

D. TALBOT RICE. Chap. 1.

F. RÖRIG. *Wesen u. Leistung d. deutschen Hanse*. Chap. 10.

C. SANCHEZ ALBORNOZ. *España*. Chap. 5.

L. SCHICK. *Jacob Fugger*. Paris, 1957.

A. SCHULTE. *Geschichte der grossen Ravensburger Handelsgesellschaft*. Stuttgart, 1923. 3 vols.

M. R. THIELEMANS. *Bourgogne et Angleterre*. Brussels, 1966.

H. TOUCHARD. *Le commerce maritime breton à la fin du moyen âge*. Paris, 1967.

W. ULLMANN. *Med. Pap.* Chap. 10.

———. *The Origins of the Great Schism*. London, 1948.

NOËL VALOIS. *La France et le Grand Schisme d'Occident.* Paris, 1896–1902. 4 vols.

————. *La crise religieuse du XVe siècle. Le Pape et le Concile.* Paris, 1909. 2 vols.

H. VAN DER WEE. *The Growth of the Antwerp Market and the European Economy.* The Hague, 1963. 3 vols.

J. A. VAN HOUTTE. *La genèse du grand marché international d'Anvers à la fin du Moyen Âge,* in *Revue belge de philologie et d'histoire,* XIX, 1940.

————. *Bruges et Anvers.* Chap. 10.

H. VAN WERVEKE. *Bruges et Anvers.* Chap. 6.

C. VERLINDEN. *Deux Aspects de l'expansion commerciale portugaise au Moyen Âge,* in *Revista portugesa de Historia,* IV, 1951.

————. *Influenza italiana nella colonisazione Iberica,* in *Nuova Rivista Storica,* XXXVI, 1952.

————. *À propos de la politique économique des ducs de Bourgogne à l'égard de l'Espagne,* in *Hispania,* XLI, 1952.

————. *Vasco da Gama in het licht van zijn Portugese en Arabische voorgangers,* Mededelingen van de Koninklijke Vlaamse Academie voor Wetenschappen van België, 1957.

————. *Les origines de la civilisation atlantique.* Neuchâtel and Paris, 1966.

O. VON LIPPMANN. *Geschichte der Magnetnadel bis zur Erfindung des Kompasses.* Berlin, 1932.

H. B. WORKMAN. *John Wyclif.* Oxford, 1926. 2 vols.

12   *The Practice of International Relations in the Last Three Centuries of the Middle Ages*

S. BAKHROUCHINE and KOSMINSKI. Chap. 3.

J. BALON. *L'Organisation judiciaire des marches féodales,* in *Annales de la sociéte archéologique de Namur,* XLVI, 1951.

B. BEHRENS. *Origins of the Office of English Resident Ambassador at Rome*, in *English Historical Review*, XLIX, 1934.

————. *Treaties on the Ambassador written in the XVth and early XVIth Century*, in *English Historical Review*, LI, 1936.

L. BITTNER. Chap. 7.

G. B. BOGNETTI. Chap. 3.

A. BOSSUAT. *A. de la taverne, Journal de la paix d'Arras, 1435*. Arras, 1936.

L. BRÉHIER. *Monde byzantin*, II, and III. Chap. 1.

G. I. CASSANDRO. *Le Rappresaglie e il Fallimento a Venezia nei secoli XIII–XVI*. Turin, 1938.

P. CHAPLAIS. *Réglement des conflits internationaux franco-anglais au XIVᵉ siècle*, in *Le Moyen Âge*, LVII, 1951.

————. *Some Documents regarding the Fulfillment and Interpretation of the Treaty of Bretigny*, in *Camden Miscellany*, XIX, 1952.

————. *Treaty Rolls preserved in the Public Record Office*, I. 1234–1325. London, 1955.

G. P. CUTTINO. *English Diplomatic Administration, 1259–1939*. Oxford, 1940.

————. *The Process of Agen*, in *Speculum*, XIX, 1944.

A. DEGERT. *Louis XI et ses ambassadeurs*, in *Revue Historique*, CLIX, 1927.

A. DEL VECCHIO and E. CASANOVA. Chap. 7.

L., COMTE DE MAS LATRIE. *Traités*. Chap 7.

R., DE MAS LATRIE. *Du Droit de Marque ou Droit de Représailles au Moyen Âge*. 2nd edition. Paris, 1875.

E. DÉPREZ. *La Conférence d'Avignon (1334)*, in *Essays in Medieval History presented to T. F. Tout*. Manchester, 1925.

M. DE TAUBE. Chap. 7.

L. G. DE VALDEAVELLANO. Chap. 5.

R. DION. Chap. 7.

F. DÖLGER. *Diplomatik*. Chap. 2.

F. ERNST. *Ueber Gesandtschaftswesen und Diplomatie an der Wende vom Mittelalter zur Neuzeit*, in *Archiv. f. Kulturgeschichte*, XXXIII, 1950.

A. FLICHE. *Rôle international de la Papauté*. Chap. 7.

S. Frey. Chap. 7.

W. Friccius. Der Wirtschaftskrieg als Mittel hansischer Politik, in
    Hansische Geschichtsblätter, 1932–1933.

T. W. Fulton. The Sovereignty of the Sea. Edinburgh and London,
    1911.

J. Gilissen. Les Légistes en Flandre aux XIIe et XIVe siècles, in Bulletin
    de la Commission des anciennes lois et ordonnances de la Belgique,
    XV, 3, 1939.

C. Gilliard. Problèmes d'histoire routière. L'Ouverture du Gothard, in
    Annales d'histoire économique et sociale, 1929.

L. K. Goetz. Chap. 6.

——. Deutsch-Russische Handelsverträge des Mittelalters, I. Hamburg,
    1916.

W. Heyd. Chap. 3.

P. Kallmerten. Lübische Bündispolitik von der Schlacht bei Bornhöved
    bis zur dänischen Invasion unter Erich Menved, 1227–1307. Kiel,
    1932.

G. Kisch. Chap. 7.

O. Krauske. Die Entwicklung der ständigen Diplomatie vom 15.
    Jahrhundert bis zu den Beschlüssen von 1815 u. 1818. Leipzig, 1885.

H. Kretschmayr. Chap. 8.

H. Laurent and F. Quicke. Chap. 11.

G. E. Lesage. La Titulature des envoyés pontificaux sous Pie II, in École
    française de Rome, Mélanges d'archéologie et d'histoire, LVIII,
    1941–1946.

F. Lot. Chap. 7.

B. D. Lyon. Chap. 7.

J. Maréchal. Chap. 11.

B. Mendel and F. Quicke. Les Relations politiques entre l'empereur et
    le roi de France de 1355 à 1356, in Revue belge de philologie et
    d'histoire, VIII, 1929.

V. Menzel. Chap. 3.

E. M. Meyers. Des graven stroom, in Mededelingen der koninklijke
    Academie van Wetenschappen, Amsterdam, Afdeling Letteren,
    1940.

L. Mirot. Un Conflit diplomatique au XVe siècle. L'arrestation des am-

bassadeurs florentins en France, in *Bibliothèque de l'École de Chartes*, XCV, 1934.

L. MIROT and E. DÉPREZ. *Les Ambassades anglaises pendant la guerre de Cent Ans*, in *Bibliothèque de l'École des Chartes*, LIX, LX, LXI, 1898–1900.

H. MITTEIS. Chap. 7.

E. NIJS. *Les Origines du Droit international*. Brussels, 1894.

————. *Les Commencements de la diplomatie et le droit d'ambassades jusqu'à Grotius*, in *Revue de Droit international et de Législation comparée*, XV–XVI, 1883–1884.

R. OURSEL. Chap. 7.

J. PAQUET. *Les Missions dans les Pays-Bas de Luc de Tolentis, évêque de Sebenico*, in *Bulletin de l'Institut historique belge de Rome*, XXV, 1949.

E. PERROY. *Louis de Mâle et les négotiations de paix anglo-françaises*, in *Revue belge de philologie et d'histoire*, XXVII, 1949.

————. *The Diplomatic Correspondance of Richard II*. London, 1933. *Camden, third series*, No. XLVIII.

————. *The Anglo-French Negotiations at Bruges, 1374–1377*, in *Camden Miscellany*, XIX, London, 1952.

A. PIEPER. *Zur Entstehungsgeschichte der ständigen Nuntiaturen*. Fribourg en-Brisgau, 1894.

H. PIRENNE. *Un Conflit entre le magistrat yprois et les gardes des foires de Champagne en 1309–1310, avec le texte de la seule charte sauvée de l'incendie des archives d'Ypres*, in *Bulletin de la Commission Royale d'Histoire*, LXXXVI, 1922.

D. E. QUELLER. *The Office of the Ambassador in the Middle Ages*. Princeton, 1967.

————. *Early Venetian Legislation on Ambassadors*. Geneva, 1966.

A. RAESTAD. *La Mer territoriale. Études historiques et juridiques*. Paris, 1913.

J. RICHARD. *Conduit*. Chap. 7.

F. RÖRIG. *Zur Rechtsgeschichte der Territorialgewässer. Reede, Strom und Küstengewässer*, Berlin, 1949, in *Abhandlungen der deutschen Akademie der Wissenschaften zu Berlin, Philosophisch-historische Klasse*, 1948, 2.

K. RUES. *Die Rechtliche Stellung der päpstlichen Legaten bis Bonifaz VIII.* Paderborn, 1912.

C. SANCHEZ ALBORNOZ. *España.* Chap. 5.

A. SCHAUBE. *Zur Entstehungsgeschichte der ständigen Gesandtschaften,* in *Mitteilungen des Instituts für Oesterreichische Geschichtsforschung,* X, 1889.

A. SCHULTE. Chap. 4.

M. SCZANIECKI. Chap. 7.

E. L. G. STONES. *An addition to the Rotuli Scotiae,* in the *Scottish Historical Review,* XXIX, 1951.

———. *The Treaty of Northampton,* History, 1953.

M. SZEFTEL. Chap. 7.

G. M. THOMAS. *Die ältesten Verordnungen der Venezianer für auswärtige Angelegenheiten,* Munich, 1875, in *Abhandlungen der Philosophisch-Philologischen Classe der königlichen bayerischen Akademie der Wissenschaften,* XIII.

P. C. TIMBAL. *Les lettres de marque dans le droit de la France médiévale,* in *L'étranger* II. Chap. 3.

E. USTERI. *Das öffentlichrechtliche Schiedsgericht in der Schweizerischen Eidgenossenschaft des XIII.–XV. Jahrhunderts.* Zurich, 1926.

J. A. VAN HOUTTE. *Les Courtiers au Moyen Âge,* in *Revue Historique de droit français et étranger,* 1936.

F. VERCAUTEREN. *Henri de Jodoigne, légiste, clerc et conseiller des princes,* in *Bulletin de l'Institut historique belge de Rome,* XXVII, 1952.

A. VON REUMONT. *Italienische Diplomatie u. diplomatische Verhältnisse.* Berlin, 1853.

A. WYNEN. *Die päpstliche Diplomatie.* Freiburg im Breisgau, 1922.

Index